CHARLOTTE BRONTË AT THE ANTHROPOCENE

SUNY SERIES, STUDIES IN THE LONG NINETEENTH CENTURY
Pamela K. Gilbert, editor

Charlotte Brontë
AT THE ANTHROPOCENE

Shawna Ross

Cover image: Amanda White, *Over the Moors*. Reproduced with permission by Amanda White. ©2017 Amanda White.

Published by State University of New York Press, Albany

© 2020 Shawna Ross

All rights reserved

No part of this book may be used or reproduced in any manner whatsoever without written permission. No part of this book may be stored in a retrieval system or transmitted in any form or by any means including electronic, electrostatic, magnetic tape, mechanical, photocopying, recording, or otherwise without the prior permission in writing of the publisher.

For information, contact State University of New York Press, Albany, NY
www.sunypress.edu

LIBRARY OF CONGRESS CATALOGING-IN-PUBLICATION DATA

Names: Ross, Shawna, author.
Title: Charlotte Brontë at the Anthropocene / Shawna Ross.
Description: Albany : State University of New York Press, 2020.
　| Series: Suny series, studies in the long nineteenth century |
　Includes bibliographical references and index.
Identifiers: LCCN 2019044606 | ISBN 9781438479873 (hardcover) |
　ISBN 9781438479880 (ebook) | ISBN 9781438479866 (pbk)
Subjects: LCSH: Brontë, Charlotte, 1816-1855—Criticism and inter-
　pretation. | Human ecology in literature. | Nature in literature.
Classification: LCC PR4169 .R67 2020 | DDC 823/.8—dc23
LC record available at https://lccn.loc.gov/2019044606

10 9 8 7 6 5 4 3 2 1

CONTENTS

	Acknowledgments	vii
	Introduction Anthropocene Fictions at the Scale of a Lifetime	1
ONE	**Bog Burst at the Dawn of the Anthropocene** Observing the Moors under Crisis	37
TWO	**Three Days on the Moors with Jane Eyre** Defining *Anthropos*	91
THREE	***Shirley*'s Tale of Valley, Factory, and Lioness** Gathering Multispecies Romances of Ecological Degradation	161
FOUR	**Provisional Survivors in Postnatural *Villette*** Learning to Love the Storm	221
	Conclusion Climates for Mourning, Editing, and Scholarship	279
	Notes	301
	Works Cited	303
	Index	317

ACKNOWLEDGMENTS

Thanks are due in many quarters, not the least of which is my home department of English at Texas A&M, which has provided a wonderful professional home for me. I am especially thankful that my office next-door neighbor, Britt Mize, is always so generous when time-sensitive advice is needed.

SUNY has also provided a lovely intellectual home. I am grateful for the enthusiasm of my editors, Rebecca Colesworthy and Amanda Lanne-Camilli, and the book's reviewers, Deborah Denenholz-Morse and Roger Whitson, who provided invaluable feedback.

Three very good friends have kept up my spirits throughout the entire process of writing and revising: James Gifford, Jonathan Martin, and Amber Pouliot. There are not enough emoji in the world.

This book is dedicated to Andrew. You are the only one who, as Deleuze would say, knows both books—the one written in ink and the one written in blood.

Parts of the conclusion have been previously published as "The Last Bluebell: Anthropocenic Mourning in the Brontës' Flower Imagery," in *Victorians: A Journal of Culture and Literature* 134 (Winter 2018): 218–33. Reprinted with permission from Ohio State University Press.

Introduction

ANTHROPOCENE FICTIONS
AT THE SCALE OF A LIFETIME

Kneeling before a pear tree, Lucy Snowe, the reserved and melancholic first-person narrator of Charlotte Brontë's final novel, *Villette* (1853), bids farewell to an impossible romance. Resigned that her love for the merry and charismatic Dr. John will remain unrequited, Lucy buries the evidence that conspired to convince her otherwise: letters he wrote in a friendly (and professional) bid to soothe her long-overwrought nerves. Having "wrapped them in oiled silk, bound them with twine," and secured her precious clutch of missives inside an airtight container sourced from "a sort of broker's shop; an ancient place, full of ancient things," she retreats to a garden in the grounds of the school at which she is employed (328). Within this garden, she stages the burial and memorial ceremonies she needs to reconcile herself to loss:

> Methusaleh, the pear-tree, stood at the further end of this walk, near my seat: he rose up, dim and gray, above the lower shrubs round him. Now Methusaleh, though so very old, was of sound timber still; only there was a hole, or rather a deep hollow, near his root. I knew there was such a hollow, hidden partly by ivy and creepers growing thick round.... I was not only going to hide a treasure—I meant also to bury a grief. That grief over which I had lately been weeping, as I wrapped it in its winding-sheet, must be interred. (328)

Though Methusaleh's improbable survival gently ironizes the ephemerality of Lucy's infatuation, its advanced age also lends dignity to her human love. Lucy's intimate knowledge of the pear tree, of its own past scars (the hole having formed over a very old wound), and of its companion species (the ivy and creepers no doubt drawing nutrients from Methusaleh's capacious roots) maps a microcosmic geography sacred enough for her mournful purpose. The roll of recent letters, preserved for the future by moisture-repellent oiled silk, then wrapped in an ancient object from a store full of ancient objects, tactfully combines the old and the new into a relic from the present to be discovered by a future excavation. Still, the limits of Lucy's ritualistic tact are reached as a cool hint of perfunctory abstraction routinizes the solemn ceremony:

> Well, I cleared away the ivy, and found the hole; it was large enough to receive the jar, and I thrust it deep in. In a tool shed at the bottom of the garden, lay the relics of building materials, left by masons lately employed to repair a part of the premises. I fetched thence a slate and some mortar, put the slate on the hollow, secured it with cement, covered the hole with black mould, and, finally, replaced the ivy. This done, I rested, leaning against the tree; lingering, like any other mourner, beside a newly-sodded grave. (328–29)

Carefully stratified layers of letters, silk, oil, jar, tree, rock slab, cement, soil, and ivy materialize a private grief hidden in Lucy's heart, forming a hybrid composite of man-made and natural materials hidden in the depths of the garden where roots and soil meet. Wielding masons' tools, Lucy in mourning becomes a builder, transforming the physical space around her.

By contributing a new knot of human disturbances to rock, earth, flora, and fauna, Lucy Snowe contributes to Villette's development from low-lying marshland into a modern, industrial metropolis lined with broad avenues artificially lit. Lucy deposits a new stratum of history to a space already deeply veined with human and natural histories, for Brontë bequeaths to Villette the urban geology of Brussels, where Charlotte attended and taught at the Pensionnat Héger-Parent. Located on the Rue d'Isabelle, which followed the original city walls and their fortified trenches, the school straddled the vertical and horizontal boundaries between the medieval Basse-Ville, or Lower Town, and the modern Haute-Ville, or Upper Town, constructed in the late eighteenth century. The now-sunken space could be accessed by descending the Escalier de la Bibliothèque, a long flight of stairs, such that the Rue d'Isabelle was literally below the new town, occupying a deeper stratum of Brussels. Confirming that

Charlotte knew this history, Elizabeth Gaskell, whose account emphasizes the organisms that flourished there, wrote,

> In the thirteenth century, the Rue d'Isabelle was called the Fossé-aux-Chiens; and the kennels for the ducal hounds occupied the place where Madame Héger's pensionnat now stands. A hospital (in the ancient large meaning of the word) succeeded to the kennel. The houseless and the poor, perhaps the leprous, were received, by the brethren of a religious order, in a building on this sheltered site; and what had been a fosse for defense, was filled up with herb-gardens and orchards for upwards of a hundred years. (160–61)

Throughout the neighborhood's diverse history, each repurposing of the space organized living beings and building materials atop superseded infrastructures, only to deposit eventually its own seam of lithic and organic markers. A common thread of refuge unites these uses. Confirming this portrait of seclusion, Helen MacEwan notes that the school's walled garden protected it from the street, and that the land had been used by the guild of crossbowmen who guarded the city and maintained a secret passage in case of siege. McEwan concludes, "All these layers of history and legend surrounding the site of the Pensionnat and its garden—the medieval convents, the crossbowmen's exercise ground, the story of their secret underground escape passage—must have contributed to the Gothic atmosphere of Charlotte's novel" (80). Charlotte's decision to rename the Rue d'Isabelle the Rue Fossette certainly adds a morbid touch to her rendition of Brussels. Typically translated as "Little Ditch Street," connecting it to its ancient role as a trench for defense, it could also be translated as "excavation" or "grave," which vividly dovetail with Lucy's excavation of Methusaleh's hidden hole to dig a grave for her beloved's correspondence.

If she lives in "Little Grave Street," is Lucy buried? Such an interpretation is borne out by the legend of a nun haunting the school. As MacEwan explains, the slab covering the crossbowmen's passageway in the real-life Pensionnat Héger-Parent inspired *Villette*'s legend that a medieval anchorite was buried alive beneath Methusaleh (79). Cool and skeptical, Lucy contextualizes the supernatural tale within Villette's history of urban development:

> The ghost must have been built out some ages ago, for there were houses all round now; but certain convent-relics, in the shape of old and huge fruit-trees, yet consecrated the spot; and, at the foot of one—a Methusaleh of a pear-tree, dead, all but a few boughs which still faithfully renewed their

perfumed snow in spring, and their honey-sweet pendants in autumn—you saw, in scraping away the mossy earth between the half-bared roots, a glimpse of slab, smooth, hard, and black. The legend went, unconfirmed and unaccredited, but still propagated, that this was the portal of a vault, imprisoning deep beneath that ground, on whose surface grass grew and flowers bloomed, the bones of a girl whom a monkish conclave of the drear middle ages had here buried alive. (117–18)

This richly textured garden sediments the living atop the dead, the flourishing below the dying, the organic beside the inorganic, tied together by soil composed of inert minerals capable of supporting life. The garden physically preserves histories of life and death at multiple scales: the biblically ancient tree, dying at a rate so slow as to be nearly imperceptible; the novitiate, whose death centuries ago seems more swift and certain than the tree's but is called into question by the ghost; the flowering and fruiting plants, with their annual rhythms of hibernation and resurrection; Lucy's love for Dr. John, newly deceased. Despite Lucy's unbelief, the nun visits her three times—as well she might, as Lucy's epistolary ritual may have desecrated her grave.

The sexual symbolism of the pear tree and the nun, killed for a "sin against her vow" (118), betrays Lucy's unease at her unfaithfulness as she falls in love with fellow teacher M. Paul Emanuel. Not coincidentally, the nun's first visitation occurs immediately after Lucy buries the letters—an act that unearths links between her recent past and the nun's distant past, itself linked to a still-deeper past tied to the ancient pear tree. Apparitions suggest that past is not past, which is why, even after the apparition is unmasked as a flesh-and-blood beau of a student, this discovery neither deflates Lucy's fears that the past will reanimate nor restores her faith that the school is a sanctified refuge. This fear and this profanation haunt her perambulations of the garden, which she now perceives as a graveyard whose organic contents are capable of rising again:

Pausing before Methusaleh—the giant and patriarch of the garden—and leaning my brow against his knotty trunk, my foot rested on the stone sealing the small sepulcher at his root; and I recalled the passage of feeling therein buried; I recalled Dr. John; my warm affection for him; my faith in his excellence.... Was this feeling dead? I do not know, but it was buried. Sometimes I thought the tomb unquiet, and dreamed strangely of disturbed earth, and of hair, still golden, and living, obtruded through coffin-chinks. (401)

Lucy's foot, virtually descending her personal "Escalier de la Bibliothèque" into the written record of her romantic history, plumbs pasts both earthly and human, written in rock and in ink.

The horror of "dream[ing] strangely of disturbed earth" is the threat of the Anthropocene. The recognition that humans have been the most powerful force influencing the Earth's geosphere, that we have been so for two hundred years, that we are realizing it belatedly—all are contained in the drama of Lucy's epistolary sepulcher. Lucy must face that her personal past persists though she buries it in the ground, where it interacts with the garden's other organic and lithic inhabitants. Sudden revelations that her actions and material traces will shape the future in ways she cannot predict, and that her life is intimately affected by the human and natural histories of the ecosystems she inhabits, reproduce at the microcosmic scale of a single human being the Anthropocene concept: the thesis that we live in a new geological epoch dominated by human activities that cause climate change, pollution, ocean acidification, biome destruction, mass extinctions, and increased incidence of catastrophic weather events. Following biologist Eugene Stoermer (who coined the term in the 1980s) and atmospheric chemist Paul Crutzen (whose publications popularized the term at the dawn of the twenty-first century), geologists, climatologists, and environmental scientists argue that the Holocene ended at the beginning of industrialization, which ushered in the new "human age." In 2017, the Subcommission on Quaternary Stratigraphy Anthropocene Working Group, an advisory unit for the executive committee of the International Union of Geological Sciences, published its formal confirmation that sufficient evidence exists to establish a distinct geological epoch. It also reported that the precise moment and location of its onset—a consensus for its temporal onset, the Global Standard Stratigraphic Age (GSSA), and its spatial onset, the Global Boundary Stratotype Section and Point (GSSP), commonly referred to as the "golden spike"—could not yet be determined. The quarter century it took for the subcommittee to confirm the Anthropocene's existence indicates how hard it is to locate links that tie ecological shifts to human actions. The slow pace of geological change makes it difficult for some individual humans to perceive the causal networks that trace contemporary climatological and ecological disturbances to human actions two centuries ago. But, in the tapping of Lucy Snowe's foot at the base of an ancient pear tree, we can discern a glimmering of just such an awareness.

Charlotte Brontë wrote the Anthropocene at the scale of a lifetime. Beyond *Villette*, each of Brontë's novels offers a human-sized glimpse into the end of the Holocene and the beginning of a new era. Brontë's protagonists are canaries in the coal mine of the Anthropocene, barometers whose experiences register multiple temporal scales of anthropogenic change, from the murky depths of geological deep time to the prehistoric processes by which humans began to reshape their environments permanently (including their degradation of forested uplands to produce the moors with which the Brontës are associated), and from the lived memories handed down by one generation of survivors to another to the constricted chronological palette of an individual human life or single annual cycle of seasonal changes. Individually, each of her novels depicts a protagonist becoming aware of, or actively resisting her awareness of, ecological change as she struggles to describe a newly toxic Earth. Collectively, Brontë's oeuvre charts an author who, clinging tenaciously to Holocene narratives of triumphant, beneficial human mastery over the nonhuman world, mourns the fall of an Edenic Earth but gradually constructs narrative techniques appropriate for representing human–nature interactions in impure, often dangerous landscapes. Brontë was perfectly positioned to do so because she grew up in a mill town in Yorkshire in the early nineteenth century. A clergyman's daughter, she was in contact with the families of factory hands. An inveterate walker, she would have seen the changes to the flora, fauna, and rocks of the moors around her. Indeed, she was a keen observer; as family friend Ellen Nussey recalled of her long walks, "Every moss, every flower, ever tint and form, were noted and enjoyed" (quoted in C. Brontë, *Letters* 1:598). These experiences are crucial for interpreting Brontë as a theorist of human-caused ecological change because the moors are anthromes—anthropogenic biomes[1]—created by prehistoric deforestation, then shaped by grazing, hunting, resource gathering, afforestation, and enclosure, which were actively changing Haworth Moor during her life.[2] Consequently, she was one of the first novelists to witness and record the early environmental changes wrought by the Industrial Revolution. Scientific consensus first pinpointed the new epoch's GSSP and GSSA at the turn of the nineteenth century in England's industrializing North. Because Brontë lived at the most widely accepted temporal and spatial turning point at which humans became Earth's most powerful force, she constructs some of the first literary ecosystems animated by anthropogenic (human-caused) change. An attentive witness of the Anthropocene, Brontë synthesized her personal experiences of this new epoch with the warnings and images articulated by early ecologists and with local and national folklore about human interactions with the natural world. This mix of direct and indirect experiences of the nonhuman world were then subjected to Brontë's idiosyncratic mixture of literary genres and inherited tropes—including the descriptive patterns and progressive teleologies of realist fiction; the mutually constitutive links between nature and imagination posited by Romantic poets; and the plot devices of female danger, spatial claustrophobia, and supernatural apparitions typical of the Gothic mode—and adapted them for a variety of fragile ecosystemic settings, including industrializing villages, urban gardens, diseased valleys, and devalued moors.

The rise of Anthropocene theory allows us to reexamine Charlotte Brontë as a keen observer of ecological change whose texts connect human actions and fates with those of nonhuman species and spaces. It reveals that Brontë's novels theorize how individual lives influence and are influenced by "natural" phenomena such as pollution, deforestation, urbanization, extinction, geological mass movements, and adverse weather events. By exploring the links between these ecosystemic events and her characters, Brontë's authorship practices constitute what Anna Lowenhaupt Tsing et al. consider the "arts of living on a damaged planet" and argue (in their collection of the same name) are vitally necessary:

> Our era of human destruction has trained our eyes only on the immediate promises of power and profits. This refusal of the past, and even the present, will condemn us to continue fouling our own nests. How can we get back to the pasts we need to see the present more clearly? We call this return to multiple pasts, human and not human, 'ghosts.' Every landscape is haunted by past ways of life. (2)

To assert that Brontë knew how to live in and write about a damaged planet, that her protagonists are haunted by the ecological ghosts of the past, is not to assert that Brontë was an ardent environmentalist—her novels and letters were as likely to deprecate the moors as to rhapsodize over them—but to insist that she drew connections between the Earth's deep and recent past with such an agility that those who accept the Anthropocene hypothesis may want to pay renewed attention to her oeuvre. My insistence intends to ameliorate Jessie Oak Taylor's observation: "The most striking thing about reviewing the field of Victorian ecocriticism is that there is so little of it" ("Ecocriticism" 877). It also responds to Barbara T. Gates's call for "greening" literary studies by "broadening our scope of interest to include more works by women and more science writing" ("Greening" 13). Gates explains: "Since Charles Darwin sits so firmly at the middle of our century, it is primarily in scholarship on evolution that we Victorianists have led the way in green studies"; she praises recent works interested in animal studies, in amateur natural history, and in the "darker side of the picture," including the speciesism that pervades much nineteenth-century literature (11). I adopt this position by centralizing Victorian science writers who were not focused on evolution as key interlocutors for Brontë and by underscoring the troubling anthropocentric elements of her fiction. Charlotte's literary ecosystems have fascinating dark sides: rather than craft perfectly pure landscapes, her texts unflinchingly include the banal, the ugly, the dangerous, and the anthropogenic. Just as Jeffrey Jerome Cohen's *Prismatic Ecology* insists that ecology should not champion only the green— the normative color of ecology associated with thriving organic life—Brontë's landscapes are gray, brown, and purple, some flourishing but many weakened or endangered. Some of them are toxic, aesthetically displeasing, subject to bad weather, or uncomfortable to occupy in ways peculiar to the Anthropocene.

Drawn to what is "poor, plain, obscure, and little," like *Jane Eyre*'s heroine (292), Brontë did not fall into the trap of paying attention only to charismatic or marquee species dripping with anthropomorphic appeal.[3] As Bruno Latour cautions, "everything perceived is nature. We may not pick and choose" ("Critique" 244). Not being choosy is central to multispecies ethnography, an approach in anthropological fieldwork and research informed by the Anthropocene. Multispecies ethnographers investigate human-nonhuman interdependencies in ways that are sensitive to climate change, biome destruction, and other anthropogenic phenomena that affect nonhuman organisms. They also privilege "[c]reatures previously appearing on the margins" and "new kinds of relations emerging from nonhierarchical alliances, symbiotic attachments, and the mingling of creative agents" (Kirksey and Helmreich 545–46). This is an apt characterization of Brontë's approach to human-nonhuman interaction because Brontë does not essentialize animals but instead traces material networks of interspecies exchange, violence, and protection—necessary work for decentering the human in our planetary histories. As Bailey Kier argues, the point is "not to put animals or other things on a pedestal or to include them, but to begin to map our interdependencies in larger systems of relational re/production" (306). Investigating these systems helps to analyze why and how humans instrumentalize the nonhuman. Consider Jane Eyre's pronouncement: "I am no bird; and no net ensnares me; I am a free human being with an independent will" (293). Rather than express affection or empathy, Jane defines herself against birds to negotiate her own species-being: to clarify the traits of the *Anthropos* so she may claim all of its endowments—in this case, free will.

This and other short-term human-animal interactions are at the heart of Brontë's Anthropocene because they historicize species boundaries, showing them as contested and contingent yet central for human assumptions about the extent to which they can, and should, control the nonhuman world. At the expanded chronological scale of geology, Brontë's oeuvre represents the inanimate world, including rocks, plants, and land formations, as spaces and forces that we "inhabit," rather than simply "observe as landscape or panorama," suggesting that her work can be productively investigated according to the "geological turn" in cultural studies and philosophy. Elizabeth Ellsworth and Jamie Kruse observe this turn in their introduction to *Making the Geologic Now*, which argues that thinking geologically allows scholars to investigate "infrastructures, communities, and imaginations to a new scale—the scale of deep time, force, and materiality" (25). Mark McGurl similarly documents the rise of "a new cultural geology:" "a range of theoretical and other initiatives that position culture in a time-frame large enough to crack open the carapace of human self-concern, exposing it to the idea, and maybe even the fact, of its external ontological preconditions, its ground" (380). McGurl names speculative realism and object-oriented ontology as examples, ultimately tying the rise of cultural geology to the spread of Anthropocene theory from the sciences to the humanities, whose methods illuminate how the concept "exacerbates and magnifies the dilemma of human agency, locating the blowback of the waste products of modernization on the blurry line between intention and accident" (383). *Charlotte Brontë at the Anthropocene* performs cultural geology by showing how Brontë grapples with the problem of human agency, posing questions about what it is, who has it, what its consequences are, how to trace the past actions that produce "these waste products of modernization," and how to prevent their recurrence in the present and future.

WHOSE SPIKE IS RIGHT?
AN OVERVIEW OF THE ANTHROPOCENE CONCEPT

The Anthropocene concept is the proposal that geologists formally declare a third epoch in the Quaternary period of the Cenozoic era. Geologists have argued that there exists enough distinctive stratigraphic evidence to recognize that the Anthropocene has succeeded the two already agreed-upon epochs of the Quaternary period, the Pleistocene and the Holocene. Its etymology, the "age of the human," suggests the rationale for the proposal: that human actions have so decisively altered the Earth's geosphere—its lithosphere, atmosphere, biosphere, and hydrosphere—that the species now constitutes a geological force. Erle C. Ellis refers to humans as "ecosystem engineers," arguing that the "changes in the terrestrial biosphere made directly by human populations and their use of land represent the emergence of a suite of novel geologic processes in the Earth system comparable in scale with those used to justify the major divisions of geologic time" (1010–11). Stoermer has used the term since the 1980s, but Crutzen and Stoermer's short piece in the *IGBP Global Change Newsletter* in 2000 and Crutzen's 2002 piece in *Nature* drew broad attention to it.[4] As Jon Erlandson and Todd Braje note, "It was not until Crutzen and Stoermer explicitly proposed that the Anthropocene began with increased atmospheric carbon levels caused by the industrial revolution in the late 18th century (including invention of the steam engine in AD 1784), that the concept began to gain momentum among scientists and the public" (2). Jill Schneiderman cites the establishment of scholarly journals devoted to the topic, including *The Anthropocene* (2013), *Elementa: Science of the Anthropocene* (2013), and *The Anthropocene Review* (2014), as a decisive sign of the "rapid escalation of engagement with the idea by the scientific community" that the human species had become "a new driver of earth systems" (171). In 2003, Crutzen and Will Steffen claimed, "In terms of key environmental parameters, the Earth System has recently moved well outside the range of natural variability exhibited over at least the last half million years. The nature of changes now occurring simultaneously in the Earth System, their magnitudes and rates of change are unprecedented and unsustainable" (253). But because natural variations in global temperatures and atmospheric carbon dioxide do occur, the burden of proof placed on the Subcommission on Quaternary Stratigraphy's Anthropocene Working Group was steep. As they deliberated, as Schneiderman points out, geoscientists offered other proofs of sufficient change in the lithosphere:

> human-induced erosion and denudation of landscapes through agriculture, construction, and, indirectly, the damming of rivers equates to a distinct lithostratigraphic signal. Mineralogical, biological, and chemical evidence also offers distinct signals of a new geological epoch.... Human modification of the landscape is responsible for significant increases in terrestrial erosion and sedimentation and *has* produced mappable rock units of artificial deposits. Increased extinction rates since the Holocene began *have* diminished certain kinds of creatures in the fossil record. Burning of fossil fuels *has* changed carbon and nitrogen rates globally and caused particles from combustion to appear in sediments worldwide. (185–86)

Though official agreement with such assertive arguments was slow to come from the International Union of Geological Sciences, whose advisory body took until 2017 to publish an affirmative verdict, climatologists and ecologists also identified a number of non-stratigraphic physical markers of profound planetary change, including changes in the terrestrial biome that will eventually leave stratigraphic traces. Ocean acidification, rising sea levels, and loss of sea ice are cited as signs that humans have irrevocably changed the planet, while others suggest that a sixth mass extinction event is occurring or point to increases in extreme weather events.[5]

For humanities scholars interested in the Anthropocene concept, this proliferation of diverse types of physical data and scientific methodologies should not obscure the fact that scientists agree with an insight common in the humanities: that there is no unified "Nature" that can be considered apart from man. One of the most influential pieces on the Anthropocene, Dipesh Chakrabarty's "The Climate of History: Four Theses," opens "with the proposition that anthropogenic explanations of climate change spell the collapse of the age-old humanist distinction between natural history and human history" (197). James Proctor ponders the consequences of "the Anthropocene's challenges to naturalness" for ecologists, who must make a case for action not based on traditional concepts of nature, which "is no longer as natural as it once was (or seemed)" (83), while geographer Jamie Lorimer stresses the profundity of this insight finding public acceptance, writing that the theory "represents a very public challenge to the modern understanding of Nature as a pure, singular and stable domain removed from and defined in relation to urban, industrial society" (593). The Brontë family—who lived at Haworth Parsonage, above them the moors, below them the factories belching smoke that floated upward back toward the parsonage and moors—were certainly faced with such a challenge. Crutzen's 2002 article locates the GSSP and the GSSA very near them, around 1800 in industrial Britain. Terry Eagleton was prescient to claim in 1975 that the Brontës "were quite literally writing at the source of global industrial society. To be provincial writers at this particular time and place, ironically, was to spring from a setting of world-historical significance" (xii). In 2003, Crutzen and Will Steffen examined the climatological histories contained in polar ice to show that "records of atmospheric CO_2, CH_4, and N_2O show a clear acceleration in trends since the end of the 18th century," justifying a location of the GSSA at "about that time, immediately following the invention of the steam engine in 1784" (251). Schneiderman agrees, summarizing,

> Impacts of human activity on earth are discernible in the stratigraphic record going back thousands of years beyond the Holocene. However, extensive and roughly synchronous world changes to the earth system in terms of greenhouse gas levels, ocean acidification, deforestation, and biodiversity deterioration occurred ... from the start of the Industrial Revolution. (190)

E. A. Wrigley elaborates on this link between an industrialization-caused increase in fossil fuel and a panoply of other effects that do not initially seem linked to James Watt's invention of the steam engine. Essentially, massive growths of human populations are possible in industrial economies, putting more pressure on ecosystems. With "the limits to growth inherent in organic economies no longer constrained productive capacity," Wrigley contrasts an industrial with an organic economy—ones whose industries are powered by human and animal labor:

> mineral-based economies created in the wake of the Industrial Revolution were on a different footing. They had gained access to a vast store of energy bequeathed to them by events which had taken place hundreds of millions of years earlier. But, as a result, their economies were consumptible rather than fungible in character. A ton of coal, like a slice of cake, once consumed cannot then be consumed again.... [T]he initial character of the economies created by the industrial revolution makes them vulnerable in the medium term to a degree unknown in organic economies. (24)

Capitalists' solution for this vulnerability—constant growth—translated to a rise in dairy herds, beef cattle, and cereal crops, driving toward the synthesis of artificial fertilizers and the conversion of more land to agricultural uses. In the United Kingdom, Wrigley reports, coal energy consumption rose from 4,295,000 tons in the 1750s to 11,195,000 tons in 1800 (37).

Not all agree that the North of England at the beginning of the Industrial Revolution is *the* golden spike, that "one carefully selected place on earth where the best combination of stratigraphic signals can be found" (Schneiderman 190). Some propose the Paleolithic discovery of fire, the Neolithic growth of agriculture, the domestication of animals, the forest clearances of the Middle Ages, the early-twentieth-century invention of industrial nitrogen fixation, or the Great Acceleration of the mid-twentieth century, with its rise of chemical and nuclear weapons and widespread use of synthetic fertilizers.[6] William Ruddiman's early anthropogenic hypothesis pinpoints preindustrial farming and biomass burning as the original source of anthropogenic effects on global climate, though he acknowledges that industrialization caused a rapid increase in the production of greenhouse gases. Ruddiman later clarified by positing three notable preindustrial increases in atmospheric carbon dioxide and methane: the rise of agriculture seven to eight thousand years ago, the intensification of animal husbandry five thousand years ago, and the genocides and pandemics caused by European exploration of the New World five hundred years ago.[7] Though this latter potential spike is often euphemized as the "Columbian Exchange"—glossing over genocide with a cheerful rhetoric of reciprocal exchange that, at least, emphasizes the importation of new species both ways across the Atlantic—ethically driven reportage cites 1610 because it registers the precipitous change in carbon dioxide levels after the mass deaths of Native Americans.[8] In "The Inhuman Anthropocene," Dana Luciano warns, "Numerous cosmologies hold that the Earth will remember acts of intra-human violence, that the planet itself will testify to the brutality humans have inflicted upon members of their own species," and attributes the Anthropocene to "the global dissemination of a specifically Western idea of humanism that posits itself as universal but endlessly defers the truly universal distribution of the benefits it confers, one that legitimates and covers over the violence, racial, colonial and otherwise, done in its name" (n.p.).

Luciano's dizzying, yet defensible, leap from polar ice to structural racism illustrates why these spikes proliferate: the stakes are so high. Assigning responsibility for planetary collapse is a grim business. It is also multifold: a proliferation of golden spikes results from disciplinary differences. A geoscientist examines different kinds of evidence than an atmospheric chemist, paleoclimatologist, geologist, biologist, geographer, or cultural historian. This different data is then examined through different methods to answer different sorts of questions. When polar ice, fossils, global temperatures, or geochemical records are consulted, different spikes emerge. The theory of the Great Acceleration, for example, builds on empirical evidence related to marine overfishing, shrimp culture, paper production, and water use—variables for which control data does not exist before World War II.[9] Without historical comparisons, the conclusion they draw is not falsifiable, and the evidence for the mid-twentieth-century spike cannot be weighed fairly against the thinner record that persists from two centuries earlier. More worryingly, Braje and Erlandson note, "specific thresholds, tipping points, or developmental indicators used to define the start of the Anthropocene are often directly influenced by the research agenda of the author" (118). Their use of the loaded term "agenda" suggests an unwillingness to acknowledge broader disciplinary limitations, which would unmask the "neutrality" to which scientific research aspires. This threat must feel quite real to skeptics who read verdicts like Luciano's that the "Anthropocene offers climate change not just periodicity but narrativity. And like any well-told story, it relies upon conscious plotting and the manipulation of feeling" (n.p.).

As a result, some scientists believe that "the drive to recognize the Anthropocene is political rather than scientific" (Schneiderman 171). Ellis and Trachtenberg agree that some scientists are wary of a concept that non-scientists find compelling for its emotional and narrative content. It is because the Anthropocene concept has "moral content at its core, rather than being only a scientific concept with a detachable moral significance" that it has gained traction with humanists, social scientists, and the public (n.p.). In their very title, "Is the Anthropocene an Issue of Stratigraphy or Pop Culture?", geologists Whitney J. Autin and John M. Holbrook hint that there is only one possible answer to the question. Other scientists show greater receptivity to approaches deriving from the humanities and social sciences. Schneiderman, declaring that "the term has captivated popular and scholarly imaginations," speculates that "the stratigraphic debate is much less interesting than dialogues about the Anthropocene in which scholars across disciplines are engaged" because the "acknowledgment of a new epoch can enable perception of systems of oppression that have led humanity down this path" (186, 187). Steffen et al. accordingly praise Anthropocene theories' linguistic and social dimensions:

> Virtually no analyses consider the psychological impacts or consequences of global change on individual humans and on their societies. Many in the scientific community may consider these aspects to be irrational and inconsequential. Yet, in the final analysis, it will be the human perceptions of global change and the risks associated with it that will determine societal responses. (*Global Change* 247)

Karl Butzer similarly believes that the risks of ecological disaster means that we should accept the Anthropocene hypothesis rather than wait for consensus settle on a golden spike. "Current popular interest is to be welcomed," he insists, "particularly if it can be channeled into innovative academic nodes with committed students, faculty, and institutional leaders, to provide experienced scientific teaching and address genuine research projects" (1540). Butzer's ultimate goal is to replace the golden spike with "a flexible, time-transgressive concept, rather than a firm time-frame, that should stimulate identification and investigation of centers of early or unusual human disturbance" (1539). And Butzer's disarmingly candid bid for help—"I presume that our wordsmiths can suggest a more elegant way" to express the "divergences and discontinuities" that stymie scientific consensus (1541)—attests that the rise of Anthropocene theory has caused an intellectual crisis.

This intellectual crisis cannot be fully thought through without using the tools of the humanities to understand the risks and suffering associated with environmental change. Julia Adeney Thomas reflects, "it is impossible to treat 'endangerment' as a simple scientific fact. Instead, endangerment is a question of both scale and value" (1588). Consequently,

> biology is not going to ease our responsibility to understand the human figure on the scales at which we can transform the political and social structures currently ratcheting up global warming. Instead, historians and others in the humanities and social sciences bear the responsibility of describing the values, political institutions, and economic activities that have pertained in past societies so that we can denaturalize present conditions and expand our thinking about possible options. (1605)

Doing so will not only help to resolve problems related to locating the GSSP and GSSA, but also to scale down Anthropocene theory and the phenomena it describes. This difficulty in scale motivated Timothy Morton's *Hyperobjects* (2013), which deems climate change to be so large in both physical size and temporal existence that it defies understanding. Andreas Malm also characterizes it as a concept whose complex temporality resists thought. Relating the millions of years it took for fossil fuels to form both to the centuries of infrastructural development that enabled the Industrial Revolution and to the narrow timescale of a momentary crisis is difficult because the effects of fossil fuel dependence are delayed, making climate change "a messy mix-up of time scales. The fundamental variables of the process ... operate over seemingly unrelated temporal spans" (8). Thomas similarly muses, "In considering the Anthropocene, all scales matter, but it is not clear that they all matter equally" (1589). Irresolution around the golden spike is a symptom of this scalar problem; each spike proposes a wildly different age for the new epoch—eight thousand years ago? Four hundred? Two hundred? Seventy? Despite these inconsistencies, the concept of the spike offers a productive way to pose questions about environmental destruction: Who did it? Why? When? Rather than trying to resolve on a single spike once, we should see their proliferation, paradoxically, as a sign that a sophisticated model of Anthropocene temporality is developing. In this sense, the flexible account for which Butzer pleads already exists: debates over the golden spike show that Anthropocene theory is a powerful discourse that, when taken as a conceptual landscape of related theories, allows us to understand that climate change and ecological crises occur over a series of overlapping spatial and temporal scales.

SCALES AND DETAILS: REGIONAL REALISM FOR THE ANTHROPOCENE

Literature offers models for how different scales of temporal and spatial phenomena can be productively crafted into a single cultural object—a narrative—capable of recording local conditions at particular historical moments, registering human attitudes toward nonhuman organisms, and influencing how they view their environment. Stories do not stand apart from the rise of the Anthropocene, whether by that term we mean the intellectual concept or the ecological condition. This is why, to explain why "the humanities also offer virtual conceptual and methodological tools for grappling with ecological catastrophe," Jesse Oak Taylor explains, "[w]ords, images, and stories are among the oldest of human tools" (*Sky* 16). He argues that fiction "helps reconcile the expansive timescales of evolution, climate, and geological change with those of human history and everyday life" (11). Tsing also reasons that "a rush of troubled stories is the best way to tell contaminated diversity" (*Mushroom* 34). Moreover, narrative structures the very concept of the Anthropocene; many consider it *to be* a story. Geographer Holly Jean Buck defines it as "a collection of multiple, related stories ... adding up to something more than its pieces" (369–70). These recent insights refresh Donna Haraway's 1989 dictum that scholars must "insist on value and story-ladenness at the heart of the production of scientific knowledge" and to regard science as "part of the field of practices that make meanings for real people accounting for situated lives" (*Primate* 3). Latour also outlines strategies for making meaning at a time when environmentalist arguments that rely on "producing indisputability" through the universally agreed-upon truths will fail. What is needed is the "slow process of composition" ("Manifesto" 478). Nature is no longer "always already there," but an "assemblage to be slowly composed" by writing narratives that emphasize "discontinuity, invention, supplementarity, creativity" (477). Here, Latour dovetails with Rita Felski, who argues that literary studies should move beyond the hermeneutics of suspicion, which places the meaning of a text always outside of that text. Felski explains, "critics read against the grain and between the lines; their self-appointed task is to draw out what a text fails—or willfully refuses—to see" (1). Both Latour and Felski turn back to reading and writing, asking us to pay attention to the details and patterns that shape powerful narratives. I turn the same way, relying here upon close reading and structural analysis.

Description, the abundance of which is a primary trait of Victorian realism, becomes of paramount importance. For Latour, a well-composed narrative activates public and scholarly interest in climate change by gathering empirical facts into heterogeneous narratives that refuse to resolve into a unity. What is needed is a "*stubbornly realist attitude*" that "reconnects scientific objects with their aura, their crown, their web of associations," thereby acknowledging the importance of enfolding subjective emotion and perception into "realistic" narratives ("Manifesto" 231, 237). Proctor also advises paying "attention less to generalities of nature than the interwoven details that constitute our environment" (83). Haraway's continued commitment to storytelling for withstanding ecosystemic collapse requires "establishing the reality and vivid specificity" of the Anthropocene by carefully situating narratives of ecosystemic change, which must emerge from "*this* place, not just any place" (*Chthulucene* 39). Butzer also values precise accounts of local experiences because "what is apparently true in one sector of a particular environment is not necessarily applicable in another" (1540). These resonant remarks connecting scholars from archaeology, ecology, science studies, and literary criticism suggest that detailed, localized, focused case studies are especially fruitful. This is not to say that it is impossible or uninteresting to connect each atomic unit of ecosystemic storytelling to broader regional trends and historical shifts, but to say that microscopic tools—such as single-author monographs—can contribute powerfully to the creation of multidisciplinary, multi-spike field of Anthropocene scholarship. Constructing locally embedded, historically specific narratives rich in thick description could constitute a genre of literary criticism that is properly Anthropocenic, in which subjective experience is shaped directly by personal experiences of the nonhuman world and indirectly through a variety of written and oral sources that provide authors with imagery and tropes to adopt, adapt, or reject in order to connect a local, individual experience of human-caused environmental stress with the broader spatial and temporal scales of the Anthropocene.

More specifically, investigating Charlotte Brontë provides this kind of deep, regional insight into Anthropocene theory's initial GSSP and GSSA. As Wright observes, during the Brontës' lifetimes, "two-thirds of the European production of cotton textiles took place in the UK," and the "comparable percentages for iron production and coal output were 64 and 76 per cent" (27). Within England, industrial production in the West Riding of Yorkshire "had far outstripped any rivals, causing both relative and absolute decline elsewhere" (115). Distributions of coal usage and steam power funneled migrating workers to particular neighborhoods, for the "impact of explosive growth ... was not general to whole counties but restricted to limited areas within them" (167). These changes disproportionately affected Brontë country, in other words. Andreas Malm notes that the West Riding was ideally situated between woolen and cotton districts and saw a considerable boom when the Brontës were in residence. "Historically speaking, the Anthropocene could well have been called the Anglocene," Malm argues, since England "accounted for 80 percent of global emissions of CO_2 from fossil fuel combustion in 1825 and 62 percent in 1850" (71, 12–13). Malm quotes these statistics in the service of seeking the origins of twenty-first-century climate in the nineteenth century; he concludes, "it is a matter of searching not for climate in history, but for *history in climate*" (6). Wrigley, too, points out, "We are awash in data on the disastrous effects but comparatively poor on insights into the drivers" of climate change (19). Jason W. Moore identifies one such driver by arguing that capitalism is "a way of organizing nature—as a multispecies, situated, capitalist world-ecology" ("Introduction" 6). Moore rightly castigates the "dominant Anthropocene perspective" (5) for ignoring capitalism's ecological effects, but his mode of argumentation perpetuates the kinds of critique that Latour and Felski argue are no longer terribly useful. Labeling an idea or attitude is "bad" is not enough. I turn to Brontë to understand *why* destructive or maladaptive practices seem attractive for her characters, who belong to the British industrial communities that disproportionately hastened the end of the Holocene. As Lucy Snowe's vision of buried letters rising again reminds us, disowning the past will not neutralize its effects on the present. What is needed is to understand how, and why, this "dominant Anthropocene perspective" came to be.

FEMINIST STRATEGIES AGAINST
THE ANTHROPOCENE DISPLACEMENT

Malm refers to one flaw in this dominant perspective as "the Anthropocene displacement": the "category mistake" that reifies the actions of particular populations as simply human nature, thereby "ascribing actions to an entity that could not possibly have performed them" (Malm 270, 267). Correcting it requires "replacing the vague 'anthropos' with the nations and companies, institutions and imaginaries, technologies and ideologies that are the true drivers of the Anthropocene" (70). Indeed, many accounts disregard how certain populations bear disproportionate responsibility for, or disproportionately bear the burdens of, ecosystemic change. Schneiderman explains that the term "does not acknowledge that some groups of human beings have had greater effects on the planet than others" because *how* the new epoch is written about "has the potential to obscure or reveal the agents of such change" (184). Naming it the Age of Man, moreover, reflects a certain "self-centeredness" (187). This terminological problem also leaves open the perverse possibility of glorying in the apparent triumph of the human as master of the world. Michael Ellis and Zev Trachtenberg observe, "the notion that humanity has attained the status of a force of nature [is] a comparison that some will find flattering, and others appalling" (123). Stacy Alaimo points out that "hand-wringing confessions of human culpability appear coated with a veneer of species pride" ("Shell" 90). Eileen Crist writes that the "poverty of our nomenclature" paints an "Promethean self-portrait" of humanity as

> an ingenious if unruly species, distinguishing itself from the background of merely-living life, rising so as to earn itself a separate name (anthropos meaning 'man,' and always implying 'not-animal'), and whose unstoppable and in many ways glorious history ... has yielded an 'I' on par with Nature's own tremendous forces. That history—a mere few thousand years—has now streamed itself into geological time, projecting itself ... thousands or even millions of years out. (16–17)

Haraway similarly criticizes ways of writing that reduce all non-human organisms to "props, ground, plot space, or prey ... [whose] job is to be in the way, to be overcome, to be the road, the conduit, but not the traveler, not the begetter" (*Chthulucene* 39). To ensure that humanity is no centered as the hero of a drama, slotting non-human organisms always into the predicate position, the human must be redefined so that "human exceptionalism and bounded individualism...become unthinkable" (30). To do so, it is crucial to examine sites, artworks, and texts that speak to the emergence of these attitudes, to their persistence, and to their influences on particular individuals occupying a certain anthrome at a specific historical moment.

Alaimo developed a methodology for doing so in *Exposed*, which "locates subjects as they engage in both ordinary and extraordinary practices" that "seek to make sense of the networks of harm and responsibility that entangle even the most modest of actions." Alaimo's declaration that now "is no time for transcendent, definitive mappings, transparent knowledge systems, or confident epistemologies" (*Exposed* 3) is shared by the contributors of *Anthropocene Feminism*. As its introduction recalls, "Counter to the technoscientific desire for specificity, definition, and fact, we coined the term ... as an experiment of provocation, expressing a survivalist ethos in regard to the masculinist and patriarchal urge to proclaim mankind an agent of major change" (Grusin xi). This collection recovers the intellectual prehistory of climate change to reveal how

> the concept of the Anthropocene has arguably been implicit in feminism and queer theory for decades, a genealogy that is largely ignored, or, worse, erased, by the masculine authority of an institutional scientific discourse that now seeks to name our current historical moment the Anthropocene. By the same token, feminists, especially ecofeminists and feminist science studies have long argued that humans are dominating and destroying a feminized earth, turning it into standing reserve, capital, or natural resource to devastating ends. (viii–ix)

Feminist critics have implicitly developed Anthropocene theory because they reject the disembodied, universal, masterful model of the human being that these feminist thinkers see at work in some articulations of the concept. Lynne Huffer contextualizes these efforts participate in the recent "renaturalization" of feminist philosophy. Turning away from models of a disembodied *Anthropos* and from social constructionist models of gender, they turn toward "animals, the cosmos, subatomic particles and waves, the brain, and the energetic pulse of biological life as objects of feminist concern," which model the world in ways that are "more complete," "more accurate," and "more ethically and politically promising" (65, 69). Kate Singer's recent body of work on Romantic ecologies demonstrates the usefulness of such an approach to analyzing literature. In her identification of an affective materiality in Charlotte Smith's poetry—"an affective flow that moves beyond human sympathy, sentiment, and sensibility, past psychological and even physiological emotion, and into more extensible forms of affect and materiality conversant with those of the nonhuman outer world" (176)—Singer applies new feminist approaches to embodiment as keys to understanding how Smith's depictions of the South Downs provide important clues about the poet's theses on the interrelations of gender, subjectivity, and the past. Emphasizing the materiality of writers' connections with local ecologies is therefore a powerful feminist strategy for reexamining nineteenth-century literature as powerful responses to environmental change.

Anthropocene Feminism shares more strategies for minimizing future damage to the planet, including "the assembling of small-scale systems," "the claiming of a responsibility for all human and nonhuman actants toward a goal of mutually thriving," and "the continued flourishing of speculation and imagination" (Grusin xi)—strategies which can be found in Brontë's fiction. To provide one example, consider Alaimo's concept of "carbon-heavy masculinity." Critiquing Chakrabarty's definition of humans as a *force*, Alaimo argues that "some of the discourses of climate change impose a rather troubling binary between universal (masculine) scientific knowledge and the marked vulnerability of impoverished women," allowing them to "bracket humans as biological creatures" and thus "abstract the human from the material realm and obscure differentials of responsibility and harm" ("Shell" 103). Alaimo explains that "transcendent scientific perspectives," when combined with a "hypermasculine consumerism" that excuses the Earth's destruction with promises of plentiful material goods and endless fossil fuels, yield a "carbon-heavy masculinity" that ignores our responsibilities and vulnerabilities as biological agents (*Exposed* 3). Brontë painted many vivid portraits in which vulnerable women and landscapes encounter a carbon-heavy man who fashions himself to be as stonily strong and eternal as the minerals whose ceaseless extraction enables his way of life. Beyond the clearest candidate—*Shirley*'s factory owner, whose irrational adherence to the tenets of classical political economy leads to multiple attacks on his factory and his person—are more subtle figures. In *Jane Eyre*, Rochester reacts to the failure of his bigamous wedding ceremony with self-combustion: "His whole face was colorless rock: his eye was both spark and flint. He disavowed nothing: he seemed as if he would defy all things" (334). *The Professor*'s Crimsworth is compared to rocks frequently, and his reflection about his student, Frances, "I believe she thought I was like a smooth and bare precipice, which offered neither jutting stone nor tree-root, nor tuft of grass to aid the climber," betrays a satisfied pride in his abstracted invulnerability (134). When he wishes to escape the Continental perplexities of the garden belonging to his female boss—an anthrome she tends into a space of erotic enchantment to maintain power over male employees—he retreats to a quiet cemetery, where he finds Frances, "my lost jewel dropped on the tear-fed herbage, nestling in the mossy and moldy roots of yew-trees!" (194). Crimsworth recovers his masculine pride by casting Frances as damsel in distress.

This scene illustrates Claire Colebrook's claim that the classic feminist axiom, "the personal is political," needs updating. Indeed, "the personal is geological" ("Counterfactual" 2), and feminists need to explore how gender and sexuality influence and are influenced by webs of power that degrade global ecologies. Gendered behaviors have powerfully shaped the Anthropocene, no matter how trivial or self-preserving they seem. Alaimo explains,

> Modes of thinking, being, and acting may arise from a political recognition of being immersed in the material world, as they contend with the conceptual challenges of shifting time scales and traversing geocapitalist expanses where one's own small domain of activity is inextricably bound up with networks of harm, risk, survival, injustice, and exploitation. ("Shell" 103)

In *The Professor*, for example, Crimsworth's objectifying behavior functions as a compensatory mechanism to repair the damage done to his ego by his wealthier, stronger, and abusive brother, who ridicules his insufficient virility. Physiologically intimate with the "tear-fed herbage," Frances is materially and emotionally intertwined with the Earth as her tears nourish the grass beneath her feet. Crimsworth may treat her as a gem mined out of the earth to be admired for his own pleasure, but her body is no "jewel." The "mossy and moldy roots" deposit bits of soil on Frances as she crouches, rendering her a very different type of *Anthropos*, one that, as Alaimo argues, "immersed and enmeshed in the world" ("Shell" 103). Frances plays the earth to Crimsworth's stone, inhabiting the enmeshed, immersed life rather than a transcendent, mastering carbon-heavy masculinity. Her body is "inextricably interlinked with circulating substances, materialities, and forces," an example of why "agency must be rethought in terms of interconnected entanglements rather than as a unilateral 'authoring' of actions" (104, 102).

The Professor's image of an earthily entangled Frances mourning the family members buried underneath her anticipates *Villette*'s stratified vignette of Lucy Snowe kneeling at the old pear tree, digging through the soil to bury her letters under the stone marking a medieval grave. By getting her hands dirty with the soils, rocks, and roots that her own actions are transforming, Lucy performs the necessary work of seeking out "contact with the materiality of the past," which, Lynne Huffer argues, can be understood by way of the fossil, whose presence disrupts beliefs that in linear, progressive time (80). As the "monstrous materialization of the untimely," fossils reveal that humans are not apart from nature, but instead "part-animal, part-mineral" (82). Encounters with the past in the form of bony, rocky things dug from the ground can "articulate an ethics that takes seriously the dissolution of the human" but, Huffer warns, can also generate "fantasies of resuscitation" (84). When Lucy's excavations generate a vision of the nun's corpse rising up with a rattle of bones, she reacts with fear. Seeing ghosts—perceiving the past's persistence into the present—is good in the Anthropocene, but necromancy is not. Lucy's job as a companion for a sickly lady prepares her well. One evening, the lady says she will recuperate, citing the reappearance of "Memory," who "is just now giving me a deep delight: she is bringing back to my heart, in warm and beautiful life, realities—not mere empty ideas, but what were once realities, and that I long have thought decayed, dissolved, mixed in with grave-mould" (44). She dies hours later, decisively handed over to the realm of decay and dissolution.

Similar images of graves and cemeteries wind through Brontë's novels, which treat earth-embedded traces of the human past as frankly alarming, even as their heroines reconcile themselves to the losses that make their present a continual exercise in mourning and their future a rocky, dirty dissolution in the ground. Some of her heroines, like Jane Eyre, however, refuse this reconciliation—a reminder that technologies developed for seeing the past, including realist novels and scientific discourses, must be applied with discretion. These visions of humans as powerful agents of biological and climatological change could, after all, provoke species pride instead of resolutions to take action. Elizabeth Povinelli demonstrates that this danger existed at the onset of the Anthropocene: when geologists "uncovered large stratified fossil beds that helped spur the foundation of modern geologic chronology, it created a massive increase in resource extraction, and it released unheard of tons of hydrocarbons into the atmosphere," attesting to the "entanglements of knowledge, capital, and biological processes that provide conditions for the very idea of the Anthropocene" (55–56). Exploring the circulation of Victorian science in Haworth Parsonage will show why it is useful to link these dangerous entanglements to fictions written by a clergyman's daughter growing up in a remote English village.

SCIENCE IN HAWORTH PARSONAGE, ANTHROPOGENESIS IN VICTORIAN SCIENCE

The sciences figured prominently among the Brontës' intellectual pursuits. Barbara Goff, who has written extensively about the family's interest in natural theology, theorizes that "it is probably a persistent sentimentalism (and possibly sexism) regarding the Brontës' intellectual isolation that has prevented us from seeing them relatively aggressively pursuing scientific interests" (489). Yet the family read medical, natural historical, and geological texts in their home library, in friends' and neighbors' libraries, and circulating libraries, and they attended lectures about medicine, galvanism, phrenology, and other sciences at the Keighley and Haworth Mechanics' Institutes, whose mission of self-help was reflected in their shelves being stocked with works of chemistry, astronomy, physics, geology, and natural history (Barker 169–77). Juliet Barker, characterizing Haworth Parsonage as a "vibrant powerhouse of intellectual activity," records that Patrick Brontë and his curates lectured at the Keighley Mechanics' Institute and that Charlotte presided over the Haworth Mechanics' Institute Easter tea in 1853 (31, 385, 855). Marianne Thormählen theorizes that Patrick, who was mostly self-taught and entered Cambridge at a late 25 years of age, desired to supplement his education in classics and therefore "took a lively interest in the arts and sciences throughout his life" and eagerly consumed general education textbooks (*Education*, 18–19). Barbara T. Gates classifies Patrick as one of many Victorian clergymen who were eager amateur natural historians ("Natural History" 250), and Ronald Berman asserts that Charlotte inherited this love of natural history (271). Patrick's interest in medicine and Charlotte's and Anne's in phrenology are also well documented. Sally Shuttleworth argues that the "Reverend Brontë and his family were involved in the local network of the intelligentsia who were devoted to the idea of self-improvement and control through the acquisition of knowledge and the principles of science" (24). Shuttleworth writes that Charlotte

> did not explicitly record her indebtedness to contemporary scientific theory. Nor, as far as we know, did she commence writing her fiction armed by extensive reading in scientific and medical texts. Yet ... [for] anyone interested in the inter-penetration of literature and science, Bronte's work offers an interesting challenge: to trace the interconnections with wider psychological discourse one must move outside the mainstream of intellectual culture to plot the subtle pathways of exchange and appropriate which operate within the wider textual economy. (11)

Lying along these "subtle pathways," I argue, are images, etiologies, and modes of attention that Charlotte Brontë adapted from nineteenth-century natural history and geology—tropes no less interesting because they did not require a deliberate booster of "extensive reading" before writing each novel. Like the Yorkshire gritstone under their feet, this scientific knowledge accreted slowly, from daily contact with sources familiar to Brontë scholars, including periodicals (especially *Chambers' Edinburgh Journal* and *Blackwood's Edinburgh Magazine* but also including newspapers, such as the *Leeds Mercury* and the *Leeds Intelligencer*) that reviewed scientific monographs, summarized meetings of scientific societies, and covered scientific expeditions. In this respect, the Brontës resembled other middle-class families who joined the increasingly large body of literate readers with the leisure time and motivation to explore the latest scientific theories and discoveries published in central works of Victorian science, such as Robert Chambers's *The Vestiges of the Natural History of Creation*, Humphry Davy's *Consolations in Travel*, and Oliver Goldsmith's *A History of the Earth and Animated Nature*.[10]

Charlotte Brontë read, or was familiar with, many key texts of Victorian science. Danielle Coriale argues that *Shirley*'s eclectic structure borrows from Chambers's *Vestiges* (125); Kerrow Hill's *The Brontë Sisters and Sir Humphry Davy* examines that scientist's influence; and a letter from teenage Charlotte advises her friend to "read Bewick and Audubon and Goldsmith, and White's *History of Selborne*" (*Letters* 1:131). Brontë's study of natural history is reflected in the profound influence that Thomas Bewick's *History of British Birds* and Gilbert White's *The Natural History and Antiquities of Selborne* had on her art. She and her siblings regularly copied drawings from *Bewick's*, which features in the first scene of *Jane Eyre*. In *Shirley*, natural history is a pastime enjoyed by multiple characters: Josephine McDonagh argues that this novel repurposes White's nature walks (471). In a similar vein, Marianne Thormählen avers that the "emphasis on 'minute observation' in the Brontës' references to the study of natural phenomena is a characteristic that recalls White's exactly recorded evidence of his own senses" and exemplifies how the "natural world plays a major role in all of the Brontës' novels, its manifestations ranging from mystical forces acting powerfully on leading characters to detailed and informed observations on flowers and birds" (*Education* 95). Coriale affirms "Brontë's passionate interest in natural history and her experimentation with it in her fictional writing," which reflect "a green sensibility that has yet to receive serious critical attention" (119). That Charlotte shared the tendency of *Agnes Grey*'s heroine to "botanize and entomologize" (106) is confirmed by Deborah Lutz, who describes Charlotte's scientific pursuits, which included collecting and pasting ferns into an album (227). These accounts place Charlotte among the ranks of the women who, Barbara T. Gates explains, participated in scientific activities like collecting scientific data, formed animal protection societies, and wrote children's tales, travel narratives, and other popular science genres. These works invented new ways to speak about nature that eschewed masculine rhetorics of mastery and created "new narratives of science and of women" well before the middle of the nineteenth century (*Kindred Nature* 105). Charlotte's lifelong interest in natural history is notable even though, as Thormählen notes, "there seems to have been a presumption that natural history was somehow 'science lite,' an effeminate kind of part study, part history" (*Education* 96). Resisting this stereotype, she explains its "modern counterparts" include "zoology, botany, geology, and biology," noting, too, that Charlotte's education in geography familiarized her with "the parts of the world and their interrelations; the various European countries and their distinctive characteristics and boundaries; geological facts and conditions; different climates all over the world and the factors that influence them; and the branches of industry and agriculture that created the wealth of individual nations" (95, 81).

The early reception of Charlotte Brontë's works acknowledged the accuracy of her descriptions of nature and affirmed their value as accounts of regional flora and fauna that acquainted a broader audience with Yorkshire topography. Nineteenth- and early-twentieth-century critics and scientists who celebrated the scientific accuracy of Charlotte Brontë's works, believing them to be integral components of her realist aesthetic, included paleontologist Louis Compton Miall, geologist James Spencer, and literary critics like G. H. Lewes, Leslie Stephen, and early Brontë specialist J. Horsfall Turner. Miall, Spencer, and Turner single out for praise *Jane Eyre*'s comparisons of the geological features of Yorkshire and Derbyshire. In addition to her personal experiences of these landscapes, her knowledge of geology also contributed to this accuracy. Buckland has shown that the Brontës were familiar with geological texts and incorporated their themes and images, suggesting that geology served Charlotte as a repository of images, vocabulary, and other stylistic tools from which she liberally drew. Buckland reveals that the family had close ties to Adam Sedgwick, the Yorkshire geologist who defined the Devonian, Cambrian, and Silurian periods and taught Charles Darwin (45). I would also name the Reverend Scoresby as a similar influence. Scoresby, the Vicar of Bradford—Patrick's boss from 1839 to 1847 and Elizabeth Gaskell's primary informant about Haworth—was a prominent scientist and explorer who served as vice president of the Yorkshire Geological Society (then the Geological and Polytechnic Society of the West Riding of Yorkshire). Its findings were publicized since 1839 in the *Proceedings of the Yorkshire Geological Society*, as well as in regional and national newspapers, including two read at the parsonage, the *Leeds Intelligencer* and the *Leeds Mercury*, which printed submissions from Patrick and Branwell Brontë, reviewed *Villette*, and regularly reported on new scientific publications, gatherings, and lectures. Scoresby's particular interest in electricity and its applications for local industries is reproduced in the images and language of galvanism and magnetism that permeate

Charlotte's novels. The Brontës also eagerly consumed *Blackwood's Edinburgh Magazine* and *Chambers's Edinburgh Journal*, during which time the periodicals featured regular and lively scientific reportage. In such venues, Ralph O'Connor has established, geology was "publicized in spectacular and theatrical forms." O'Connor summarizes, "it was in their literary productions—in books, journals, magazines, and newspapers—that these geologists and their followers reached most of their increasingly variegated public . . . by giving their public a tantalizing glimpses of an earth history far longer and stranger than the story of a literal six-day Creation" (2). The influence of *Blackwood's*, *Chambers's*, and the Leeds newspapers is as important as it is subtle because they published clearly scientific articles about geology and natural history alongside histories, travelogues, expeditionary and missionary accounts, political discussions, and satirical columns that also referenced important trends and controversies in Victorian science. *Blackwood's* reviews of new scientific publications drew out (and often ridiculed) new discursive tropes in these texts, reviewing them as part of a distinct style whose scope, structure, and vocabulary could be isolated and appropriated. Charlotte Brontë, who meticulously copied *Blackwood's* in her earliest writings and read *Chambers's* eagerly during the period she wrote her mature novels (Barker 184–93), learned this lesson thoroughly, as I show in my readings of her novels, whose depictions of industrializing Yorkshire incorporated tropes of Victorian science writing to construct an eclectic Anthropocene realism that meditated on ecological change not in and of itself, but as it was embedded in the everyday life by laypeople struggling to survive and understand historically new types and intensities of human-caused ecosystemic degradation.

The stylistic eclecticism characteristic of Brontë's realism was not wholly foreign to science writing. The contexts in which Charlotte encountered Victorian science (from periodicals and library books to lectures and social discussions) and the texts themselves flexibly intertwined narrative structures with observed facts and new theories. Practices of topography—the "place-writing" that tells the history of a region's people, industries, and landscape—combined scientific data with the colorful anecdotes and narrative pull of social history. Richard Grove's account of Alexander von Humboldt's *Cosmos* (1845–62), volumes of which were released at the same time as Brontë's novels, attributes its success to its rejection of the strict positivism that "increasingly separated [the sciences] from literary or artistic preoccupations." Grove shows that Humboldt develops an "artistic and literary treatment to the subject of natural science" full of "evocative descriptions" designed to "promote a love of the study of nature, by bringing together in a small space the result of careful observations on the most varied subjects" (373, 372). James Secord's account of the reception of Chambers's *Vestiges* attributes its success to its being a "hugely ambitious synthesis" of "astronomy, geology, physiology, psychology, anthropology, and theology" that was as "readable as a romance" (*Sensation* 1). If the Anthropocene is a kind of story, so too were the new sciences that were proposing a radical departure from natural theology by discovering the planet's "deep history," by which "it turned out that *nature has had a history of its own*" (Rudwick, *Deep History* 3). In other words, the boundary between nature and history that Anthropocene theorists say began crumbling in 2000, with Crutzen and Stoermer's publication in the *IGBP Global Change Newsletter*, has its own prehistory in Victorian geology that proposed the Earth to be far older than the 6,000 years stipulated by the Bible, developed the theory of the evolution of species, and substituted the Uniformitarianism of William Whewell, James Hutton, and Charles Lyell for the Catastrophism of Georges Cuvier. Lyell's Uniformitarian *Principles of Geology* (1830–33), which proclaimed the past to be the key to the present, tastes of the backward-looking temporality of the Anthropocene concept, with its difficult-to-perceive timescale and the delayed emergence of ecological effects of human actions. Moreover, the turbulence in stratigraphic science introduced by Lyell's 1833 proposal that geologists recognize the presence of humans on the Earth as justifying the naming of a "Recent" or "New" period, ratified in 1867 with the formal adoption of Paul Gervais's term—the "Holocene" (wholly new) epoch—means that the Victorians, too, believed they lived in a brand-new geological epoch. Martin Rudwick's *The Great Devonian Controversy*, on the proposed insertion of a new period between the Silurian and Carboniferous periods, further suggests that the time period in which Charlotte Brontë lived was an era of stratigraphic redefinition as contentious as our own.

Brontë also lived at the same time as the founders of ecology—formally named by Ernest Haeckle in 1866—including von Humboldt, Alfred Russel Wallace, and George Perkins Marsh. Marsh's influential *Man and Nature: The Earth as Modified by Human Action* (1864) was published a decade too late for Charlotte to have read, but its warnings about mankind's devastating impacts on many natural biomes are anticipated by works she read, such as Gilbert White's *Selborne*, which condemns the uncontrolled burning of moorlands. Other early accounts of human-caused environmental devastation included Charles Babbage's thesis in *On the Economy of Machinery and Manufactures* (1835) that fossil fuel usage increased levels of carbonic acid in the atmosphere;

theories of climate change by Joseph Fourier in the 1820s, Louis Agassiz in the 1830s, and John Tyndall in the 1860s; concerns about human-caused extinctions of animal species in Lyell's *Principles of Geography* and Wallace's *The Geographic Distribution of Animals*; and recognitions that farming and deforestation were denuding soils around the globe by James Hutton and the Comte de Buffon. Brontë encountered Buffon's desiccationist arguments about the desertifying effects of deforestation in Goldsmith's *History of the Earth and Animated Nature*. These parallels between Victorian and contemporary science are acknowledged by Anthropocene theorists. Marsh's *Man and Nature*, for example, is commonly cited as a forerunner, as are Eugene Hazard's *The End of the World by Science* (1855), Antonio Stoppani's proposal of an "Anthropozoic era" in 1873, and W. I. Vernadsky and Pierre Teilhard de Chardin's "noösphere" (1945 and 1966, respectively).[11] These texts warn that humans were creating a series of unstable anthromes that endangered nonhumans, while others focus on geological change and stratigraphic dating. It is the combination of *both* trends—the challenge to traditional understandings of the Earth's age that destabilized geological dating schemes and deepening ecological concerns about anthropogenic environmental destruction—that make it plausible to investigate Charlotte Brontë as a writer of the Anthropocene.

Laura Dassow Walls draws such a parallel between our early twenty-first-century moment and this nineteenth-century moment quite strongly. Arguing that Victorian science contained early articulations of the Anthropocene concept, Walls concludes that, "in hindsight,"

> the Anthropocene came into visibility in the mid-nineteenth century through the agency of natural historians.... [T]hat revolutionary insight was disguised, denied, and resisted at various levels, even as it powered the dramatic syntheses of modern natural science around the foundational insight that nature has a *history* of its own—that is, that Planet Earth is not the natural embodiment of nature's eternal laws, but the sedimented product of historical processes that are directional, contingent, highly specific, intensely local, constantly operating, and profoundly unpredictable. ("Natural History" 187–88)

Just as much as the Anthropocene, as an empirically verifiable physical phenomenon, emerged in fits and starts, with sudden accelerations and multiple spikes, so too did the recognition of the Anthropocene's existence. This is why being a cultural geologist of Charlotte Brontë's fiction requires no time-traveling anachronism. Not only was Brontë's life directly and intimately affected by the ways prehistoric and contemporaneous human actions shaped the moors (she lived *within* the Anthropocene, was part of the *condition* of the Anthropocene), but also her writings are intertwined with the dawning awareness that humans had been reshaping their environment (they engaged with the Anthropocene *concept*, were part of the rise of the *theory* of the Anthropocene). Brontë's novels are useful for illuminating the ways in which nascent recognitions of the Anthropocene were (as Walls asserts) "disguised, denied, and resisted," for her career charts a trajectory by which, thinking in tandem with her father's natural theology and her sisters' representations of human/nature interaction in moorland environments, Brontë initially resists this dawning cultural awareness but gradually comes to terms with the fact that there is no pure Eden left and that we must figure out how best to live on this damaged planet.

Charting such literary prehistories of the Anthropocene concept is important because we must, as Malm argues, "infuse a bit of modesty in the Anthropocene revelation" because "it would be self-indulgent to judge our current environmental concerns and theoretical categories ... as the only way to be 'environmentally conscious' " (71–72). David Higgins, in his work on literary responses to the eruption of Mount Tambora in 1815—which, like my own, investigates the "global catastrophe" of ecological collapse "as a textual phenomenon" (2)—agrees that Anthropocene theorists should not overstate the newness of contemporary arguments about ecological change from earlier enunciations. Higgins warns that "attempting to make our work relevant by suggesting a breach between past and present thinking" (13) is to be avoided. Indeed, it would be a grievous oversight not to restore connections between contemporary geology and climatology to the earlier science writing. It is not merely a problem of being incomplete or inaccurate, though, for there are severe political consequences to exaggerating this break between then and now: "The problem with any prophetic narrative centered on a sudden ecological awareness," Malm explains, "is that by obliterating the reflexivity of past societies, it tends to depoliticize the long history of environmental destruction" (71). This in turn disempowers living individuals by making positive action seem impossible, given that it is, apparently, *human nature* that causes such destruction (71). By recovering these past reflexivities, possibilities for positive action emerge, especially through figures like the Brontës, whose works inspired activism that prevented the installation of windfarms along their moorlands. As Tom Whitehead reported in *The Telegraph* in February 2013, "The literary significance of the Brontë moorlands has been used for the first time to curb the onslaught of wind farms, in a key victory for campaigners" (n.p.). Attesting to the power of literary ecosystems, Buck suggests that practices of enchantment can effect such positive change:

> Enchantment is drawn from the roots of 'enchant' and 'charming,' *incantare*, to sing, reflecting its linguistic or discursive process.... This provokes this question: Who are the enchanters? Capitalists are not the sole enchanters in the Anthropocene: Anyone can enchant an object, a habitat, a landscape, although people are not generally taught processes by which to do this, and there are not necessarily equal opportunities for these enchantments to blossom into widespread material changes. (371)

Charlotte Brontë was precisely one such enchanter.

THE ANTHROPOCENE AS CRISIS AND CONDITION IN BRONTË'S OEUVRE

Charlotte Brontë's lithic characters figure the Anthropocene as a complex temporal phenomenon unfolding at multiple scales, including sudden cataclysms that alter lives in a moment, slow processes of gradual degradation that appear over the course of a lifetime, and deep-time shifts that are normally imperceptible to humans. Living at the time and place considered by many theorists to be the new epoch's temporal and spatial point of emergence, Brontë herself resolves on no single golden spike, instead tracing subtle, sometimes contradictory, networks of causation. Meshes of plants, animals, rocks, and humans resolve kaleidoscopically into constantly changing moors, manors, seas, and cities that endanger and are endangered by her characters, allowing environmental degradation to emerge through individual disasters and to persist as an ongoing state of toxicity. In her oeuvre, the Anthropocene becomes visible as both a crisis and a condition. This dual vision is helpful not only for dismantling assumptions about time, causality, and humanity at the root of cruxes in Anthropocene theory, but also for identifying a useful suite of strategies for living on our damaged planet. Each chapter of this book isolates a particular Brontëan axiom for the Anthropocene, examining its dual operation as a momentary response to a crisis and a habit for surviving toxic conditions. Sometimes, these strategies prove adaptive, salutary for the nonhuman organisms and landscapes around the characters who deftly deploy them. At other times, they prove maladaptive or are incompletely realized, their implementation compromised by entanglements of class, race, gender, and species politics. Either way, Brontë highlights the necessity of perceiving, ameliorating, and pinpointing responsibility for ecosystemic failure, while foregrounding the difficulties of doing so.

Chapter 1, "Bog Burst at the Dawn of the Anthropocene: Observing the Moors under Crisis," establishes how Charlotte's ecological imaginary triangulated her experiences of the moors, her knowledge of science writing, and her father's and sisters' representations of peat, bogs, marshes, and moors. It is within this context that she began her own lifelong engagement with questions about human contributions to environmental degradation. I open with the most alarming moment in which the family's early history intersected with the Anthropocene: the bursting of Crow Hill bog. In September 1824, the three youngest children were walking the moors when the bog suddenly exploded, nearly drowning them in a torrent of peaty sludge. The event caused considerable damage to the local landscape and led Patrick and Emily Brontë to represent the rare geological phenomenon in letters, sermons, and poems. Analyzing these texts reveals that Patrick's natural theology engaged substantively with early Victorian science writing about humans' impact on the environment and how Emily's "High Waving Heather" sets the stage for Charlotte's divergences from her father's approach to ecosystemic change. To illuminate the place of the bog burst within Victorian science, I explain why bursts are anthropogenic and how scientific theories and cultural myths known to the family represented the moors as spaces of pervasive human-caused environmental change. To show how the Brontës engage with these scientific and folk approaches to moors as anthromes, I analyze other representations of the 1824 burst in biography, criticism, and literary tourism to show, conversely, how assumptions about moor ecologies and environmental change profoundly shaped the Brontës' reception history. The legacy of Crow Hill bog, ultimately, is that it instilled in Haworth Parsonage the importance of grappling with the intellectual and ethical tasks of accurately perceiving and minutely describing the ecological crises of the present in order to survive them and to prevent future ones. Carefully, responsibly witnessing catastrophes and developing lifelong habits of recording local conditions, the Brontës suggest, are necessary for surviving the Anthropocene and answering fundamental questions necessary for discussing it: "What is going on?" "How can we tell?" "What details matter?"

Chapter 2, "Three Days on the Moors with Jane Eyre: Defining *Anthropos*," zeroes in on the question, "What are humans?" Charlotte Brontë's first published novel, *Jane Eyre* (1847), revolves around the problem of species-being.

Jane Eyre's embattled journey from isolated orphan to married heiress prompts her to interrogate what counts as a human being, what qualities make it human, and whether one should want to be included in its ranks. Crises compel her to resist definitions of *Anthropos* that isolate her and to redefine the human in terms that allow her to claim her right to thrive in toxic landscapes. Threatened and vulnerable, Jane clings to corporeal exceptionalism—the idea that the human is a special sort of animal, apart from nature. To Jane, her desire to be recognized as *Anthropos* justifies any action that will preserve her fragile body and her belief that her actions are freely chosen and effective. After her corporeal exceptionalism is roundly challenged, Jane experiments with alternate models of *Anthropos* that are better for the landscapes around her. However, the gendered constraints that limit her range of possible responses pressure Jane to side with older models that endorse her triumphal self-formation. Comparing *Jane Eyre* to Emily's *Wuthering Heights* and Anne's *The Tenant of Wildfell Hall* reveals the alienating austerity of Jane's rejection of her own naturalness: Emily converts her romantic leads into bog bodies, immersing them permanently in the moors, while Anne pairs two *Anthropoi* adept at estate management to fashion an ecological allegory of moor reclamation. *Jane Eyre* emerges as a tale of conflicted anthropocentrism as its narrative structure alternates between multispecies frameworks that emphasize complex dependencies and anthropocentric ones that rely on a hierarchical vision of humans mastering nature. Jane ultimately chooses the older, antagonistic framework, rejecting more radical understandings of humans as enmeshed in their environments and showing how her proto-feminist efforts at self-determination compromise her nascent ecological awareness.

By contrast, *Shirley* (1849), Charlotte Brontë's second published novel, consistently challenges these hierarchies by proliferating perspectives on human/nonhuman interaction. Chapter 3, "*Shirley*'s Tale of Valley, Factory, and Lioness: Gathering Multispecies Romances of Ecological Degradation," argues that *Shirley*'s dual heroines, third-person narrator, and proliferation of tales about environmental degradation challenge normative beliefs about the human species. *Shirley*'s setting, a remote Yorkshire valley over a half-century of industrial development, matches the original golden spike of Anthropocene theory, allowing the novel to reconstruct the fabled emergence of the epoch in Britain's industrial North. This self-reflexive novel knows that it is fabled, for *Shirley* juxtaposes—but refuses to reconcile—incompatible perspectives on industrialization and human influences on the nonhuman world. Though *Shirley*'s reception history has been dominated by aesthetic critiques of its formal eclecticism, I argue that the novel's polarizing stylistic oddities recover deep and recent histories of regional ecologies to tell personal, regional, and national stories of loss. A multispecies, multigenerational framework for recording short- and long-term shifts in a particular Yorkshire landscape gathers myths, folklore, essays, stories, gossip, science writing, and literary realism. In this way, the tropes of science writing that Jane Eyre anthropocentrically toys with are elevated from theme into form. Whereas Jane Eyre flees each denuded landscape she encounters, *Shirley*'s characters inhabit a single, history-laden space that they thoroughly explore with sexual experiments in species hybridity, intellectual courses of natural history, empathetic attempts at ecological stewardship, and financially canny strategies of land management. Some of these pursuits are as compromised as Jane Eyre's *Bildung*, but *Shirley* unflinchingly identifies particular individuals as culpable for ecological degradation and maintains an acute awareness of what has been lost. *Shirley* cares how women's goals for equality, freedom, and financial stability contribute to the Anthropocene, but its questions are slightly different: "Who can say when it happened?" "Whose stories can be recorded?" Like paying attention to local biomes and redefining the human, storytelling the Anthropocene also operates on two temporal dimensions: *Shirley* affirms the importance of individuals testifying about their experiences of crisis and toxicity, and gathers testimonies into a complex narrative of habit and survival by incorporating multiple perspectives and time scales.

Jane Eyre is positioned at the end of the Holocene, when the catastrophic effects of human actions on the nonhuman world are becoming visible but a variety of avoidance behaviors allow privileged *Anthropos* to escape spaces they have destroyed, while the fifty-year span of *Shirley*'s frame narrative places one foot in the Holocene and the other in the Anthropocene. Brontë's final novel, *Villette* (1853), is set solely in the Anthropocene. Chapter 4, "Provisional Survivors in Postnatural *Villette*: Learning to Love the Storm," focuses on stormy, polluted, urbanizing Villette, where nature can only be accessed through mediation, commodification, or hallucination. Through *Villette*, Charlotte reworks the garden-filled town of her first mature novel, *The Professor*—completed in manuscript form in 1846 but published after her death in 1857—into a postnatural topography of crisis. This unstable, dangerous ecology is connected to global Anthropocenic environments and phenomena that cause waves of death and exile to shape Lucy Snowe's life, climaxing with the presumed death of her fiancé in stormy seas. Amid these threats, Lucy's task is to answer the Anthropocenic question, "How do we protect life?" In moments of crisis, she must maintain her psychological equilibrium and focus on finding practical solutions so she can survive and protect other vulnerable humans around her. In the longer term, she learns how to tend the non-human environment around her—how to garden and how to love people whose resemblance to storms, animals, and plants would have, in Jane Eyre's eyes, invalidated their rights to such protection. The success of Lucy's strategies of surviving and tending is due partly to her oligotrophism: her ability to thrive in unpropitious conditions and without ample resources. Her resolution not to take more resources than is necessary matches M. Paul's own, as his marked penchant for tending provides an alternative model of heterosexual romance that is more ecologically friendly than the carbon-heavy masculinity underpinning *Shirley*'s couples.

That Lucy must also survive the death of her fiancé indicates that successes will always be partial, always haunted by the losses sustained by survivors. This Anthropocenic question—"How do we cope with the acceleration of loss and death?"—is at the heart of the conclusion, "Climates for Mourning, Editing, and Scholarship." I examine bluebell imagery in the Brontë sisters' novels and poetry (including Charlotte's textual labors in editing Emily's bluebell poems for publication in 1850) to show how Emily and Anne bequeath suggestions for surviving the loss of home ecosystems and how Charlotte herself used writing to process the deaths of her siblings and the changes undergone by the moors. Coping with loss occurs in the short term as momentary outpourings of grief and as long-term habits of mourning. I link bluebells to these human-scaled griefs—for the flowers' annual rebirth and death forces the Brontës' poems to address loss as both cyclical and final—and global losses by discussing how bluebells flourish in two particular biomes: in liminal ecosystems destroyed by humans thousands of years ago and in rare patches of surviving ancient forests. Focusing on some of the last manuscripts worked on by the Brontë sisters, the conclusion shows how, at the end of Charlotte's career, *Jane Eyre*'s affirmation of anthropocentrism is no longer possible, subsumed by the necessary tasks of living in the Anthropocene. From *The Professor* and *Jane Eyre* to *Shirley* and *Villette* to her editing tasks, Brontë traces a wide range of responses as her protagonists witness environmental catastrophe and make decisions that exacerbate or ameliorate the negative effects of humans on the landscapes they live on. Sometimes her protagonists resist the ecological truths coalescing in front of them and focusing on saving themselves. Sometimes they generate creative strategies for responding capably to this new epoch and helping other organisms survive catastrophes and toxicities. Her approaches in different texts sometimes reinforce each other, at other times contradict one another. At no time are they rendered wholly compatible. But what emerges is a narrative of an increasing awareness that the Anthropocene has begun and can no longer be ignored. It is both a lived experience and a theory of environmental history, made legible as a series of crises and as an abiding condition, to all of which we must respond by paying attention to our ecosystems, questioning our species-being, telling our stories (and gathering those of others), protecting life where we can, and mourning the lives and the spaces that have been irrevocably lost. Writing Anthropocene fictions at the scale of a human life, Charlotte Brontë recorded the dawn of the new epoch, along with the difficult questions it provoked, the strategies for survival that it necessitated, and the grieving processes it engendered.

ONE

Bog Burst at the Dawn of the Anthropocene

OBSERVING THE MOORS
UNDER CRISIS

Around six o'clock in the evening of Thursday, September 2, 1824, a curious phenomenon rocked Crow Hill, perched at the top of the moors looming above Haworth. In the West Riding of Yorkshire, late summer is associated with the riotous empurpling of blossoming heath. During that summer, however, observers noted that the annual profusion of color was dimmed by a period of dry, hot weather. These unusual conditions broke in the last half of August, when days of fierce storms saturated the ground and struck it with frequent bolts of lightning that cost the lives of humans and pastured animals. Documenting this meteorological turn, the *Edinburgh Journal of Science* reported that "a most alarming storm of thunder and lightning ... occurred, accompanied with a vast quantity of rain, and spreading destruction over a great extent of country." But, in an anomaly that the journal deemed one of 1824's "rarer atmospherical phenomena," Haworth and its surroundings enjoyed a sudden break between cloudbursts as August shaded into September. On the first day of the month, stifling "clouds preventing radiation from the earth at night, caused the heat to be particularly oppressive." On the second day, "the clouds increased, and much rain fell, but here there was no electrical discharge." During the stifling afternoon, high temperatures were "the greatest evil" (Brewster 54). But for three local children who were recovering from prolonged illness (and, moreover, had been denied their accustomed moorland exercise by the stormy weather and were mourning the recent departures of their older sisters for a boarding school nearly fifty miles away), the abrupt arrival of warmth and clear skies must have seemed a respite from boredom and confinement, a propitious extension of their recovery rather than an omen of imminent ecological disaster.

These were the conditions under which Haworth Parsonage servants Nancy and Sarah Garrs embarked on a late-afternoon walk with their young charges: seven-year-old Branwell, six-year-old Emily, and four-year-old Anne Brontë. Taking advantage of the momentary spell of fine weather, the group squelched up the waterlogged moorlands above the village, heading along the commons toward Stanbury. Unspent electricity crackled in the "unusually close" atmosphere, with "scarcely a breath of air stirring" underneath an ominous canopy of "copper-colored, gloomy, and lowering" clouds (P. Brontë, *Letters* 51). Having scrambled nearly four miles, the children followed a pathway that skirted around Crow Hill, which, their father, the Reverend Patrick Brontë, would write to the newspaper, was crowned by "a flat for a great way around," in the middle of which was a bog "about the distance of half a mile." The area featured "rising grounds that overtop this flat considerably, and from whence waters lodge continually," making it "generally moist" though "not altogether a quagmire" (53). As the walkers came into view of Ponden Hall—the stone farmhouse often identified as Thrushcross Grange in Emily's *Wuthering Heights* and the eponymous estate in Anne's *The Tenant of Wildfell Hall*—a booming noise shattered the oppressively tense atmosphere. More reverberant than the thunder that rolled through the skies in late August, the noise disrupted Patrick miles away and shook the window to which the loud sound had drawn him. Crow Hill bog's tight, convex covering of interlocked peat fibers had suddenly ripped open. The pressurized bog waters underneath the walkers' feet were released with such a violence that the Brontës barely escaped being drawn into a seven-foot-high flood of water, peat, and rocks gushing down into the Worth Valley below. Sarah Garrs, using her cloak as a temporary refuge, shepherded the children beyond the rushing torrent to the sheltering porch of Ponden Hall, where their father found them after a frantic search.

What had occurred was a bog burst, a rare geological movement that scientists classify as a mass wasting. These mass wastings (also known as mass movements) are geomorphic phenomena in which tons of sand, rocks, or mud suddenly shift downslope. Along the spectrum of mass wastings that collapse moors, bog bursts are the most extreme; their geomorphically gentler cousins include bogflows, bog slides, peat slides, and peat flows. A peat bog is formed when dead vegetation accumulates in an area of high rainfall and poor drainage. Under these wet conditions, mosses, heathers, and other dead plants form an anaerobic slurry of water and vegetable matter. Within the swampy, oxygen-deprived mixture, the dead plants are prevented from decomposing fully. As the liquid slurry is compressed under the pressure of successive waves of newer mosses and heathers settling down over previous years' harvests, layers of progressively darker, harder peat develop underneath more recent deposits. As William Atkins explains, "Under normal conditions, the bulk of the peat blanket, known as the 'catotelm', is impermeable to water, while the top, 'active' layer, called the 'acrotelm' and formed of vegetation in various states of decomposition, continues to absorb water until it is saturated, at which point further water either pools on the surface or flows off into the moorland streams" (176). Certain conditions—like the drought experienced by Haworth in the summer of 1824—can cause a dangerous situation. In a drought, dry peat masses with "lower water contents and lower liquid limits" undergo a "decrease in particle size," which triggers "the closer packing of the organic particles and the consequently smaller pores and higher bulk density." Consequently, it "would take a smaller increase in water content to bring about significantly higher water pressures or even a change of state" (Dykes and Kirk, 391). In other words, rainfalls less torrential than those swamping Crow Hill in early September 1824 could have spelled disaster.

Sudden changes in moisture content are devastating because peat is "a low density, organic-rich, nonmineral soil, which has a high water content, significant fiber content, high voids ratio, high compressibility, and low shear strength" (Warburton 159). If this fragile, ropey, porous honeycomb is dried, then inundated, its structural integrity is compromised. In *The Moors* (2014), an eclectic work of ecology, travel narrative, and literary criticism, William Atkins names Crow Hill as a paradigmatic example: "In the various historical accounts of bog bursts, including Patrick Brontë's, the phenomenon is usually reported as occurring during or immediately after a violent rainstorm, following a long period of exceptionally dry weather. During such drought periods the acrotelm may dry out and shrink, so that deep vertical fissures form in it" (176–77). If it does shrink enough that its dense mesh of mosses cracks,

> When torrential rain comes, these fissues allow water to penetrate into the catotelm, destabilizing the peat's layers and lubricating the interface between the peat base and the underlying shale or clay on which it sits, until the whole liquefied bog suddenly slides downhill as if tipped from a dish, a black tide rated with blocks of surface peat and carrying vegetation, boulders, everything, in its wake. (177)

Atkins's lively, action-packed description is typical of descriptions of the Crow Hill burst. Brontë biographer Juliet Barker radiates this excitement when she announces, "Two huge areas of moorland bog had sunk without a trace" (152). In 1948, Ernest Raymond declared that "earth mutinied and uprose" before developing a striking metaphor of parturition: "the great hill, after a terrible gestation and labor, had heaved with a life of its own and delivered itself of the intolerable bog, which, bursting its confining walls, rolled down the valley, a mass of mud, water, boulders, uprooted vegetation, and broken trees" (205). Victorian biologist Louis Compton Miall dramatically crafted passages in which blocks of compressed peat rush downward, leaving a trail of destruction that uncannily resembles lava flows after volcanic explosions. "The contents of a hillside" are evacuated during bog bursts, during which the "vast spongy accumulation of peat and water ... pours forth an inky flood, deluging whole parishes" (*Geology*, 622).

Scurrying to the porch of Ponden Hall, the Brontë children witnessed precisely such an inky flood in the aftermath of the explosion as blocks of peat, small rocks, and large boulders were sent flying into the air, some traveling the distance of a mile before falling back to earth. The wide and deep flow of brackish mud felled trees, flooded homes, destroyed bridges, and drowned the cattle and sheep caught in its wake (Lock and Dixon, 248–49). To quote Patrick's summary, delivered as a sermon on September 12, "two portions of the moors sank several yards during a heavy storm of thunder, lightning, and rain, and there issued forth a mighty volume of mud and water, which spread alarm, astonishment, and danger along its course of many miles" (*Brontëana*, 211). In another account, a twelve-page pamphlet designed as a twopence Sunday school prize for children, Patrick elaborates for his target audience all of the awe-inspiring details. "To my young readers," he intones, "I have here written to you in the most interesting manner I could, on a subject which is itself very interesting" (*Brontëana*, 202–3):

> During the time of a tremendous storm of thunder, lightning, and rain, a part of the moors in my chapelry ... sunk into two wide cavities; the larger of which measured three hundred yards in length, about two hundred in breadth, and was five or six yards deep. From these cavities ran deep rivers, which uniting at the distance of a hundred yards, formed a vast volume of mud and water, varying from thirty to sixty yards in breadth, and from five to six in depth; uprooting trees, damaging, or altogether overthrowing solid stone bridges, stopping mills, and occasionally overwhelming fields of corn, all along its course of ten or fifteen miles. (203)

Patrick's first letter to the *Leeds Intelligencer*, published on September 9, repeated this information restrainedly. A "black moory substance ... mixed occasionally with sand and rocky fragments, pieces of timber," while "uprooted trees" had tumbled down the moors in an "overwhelming flood" ranging from "from thirty to forty yards in width, sometimes sixty, and seldom less than three or four yards in depth." But a sense of fear develops as Patrick reports that conditions at the site continued to change. A "great crater" appeared, "surrounded by many smaller pits" (*Letters*, 51). At eight o'clock the next morning, a further eruption occurred.

These fears of future eruptions testify to the terror that the burst inspired in the region, whose denizens were concerned about the long-term consequences for downslope ecosystems and their industrial and agricultural activities. In the brief accounts of the burst given in Brontë biographies and scholarship, further disruptions of the Crow Hill bog are not generally noted. In 1879, however, J. Horsfall Turner recorded four separate eruptions occurring on the Thursday after the initial burst, sending forth "fresh accessions of mud and peat" that "rushed over the steep with a tremendous noise ... at the distance of four miles" (151). Patrick's prediction that, because "the ground is already sunk to a great extent, and riven and shaken for a considerable distance, there will be a more than usual conflux of water to the place; which may, from time to time, produce other sinkings of the earth, and other eruptions of mud and water, upon a less extensive and less destructive scale," was borne out (*A Sermon*, 214–15). His second letter to the *Intelligencer*, published on September 16, confirms that the largest cavity had "extended itself" over the two weeks succeeding the eruption, ultimately reaching over a mile in circumference as a result of multiple eruptions and of the mass "sinking, principally by its own weight." By this time, the wide, peaty, rubble-strewn torrent had subsided to a "rivulet" of mostly clear water "above the thickness of the body of a man of ordinary size" (*Letters*, 54). Local witnesses who confirmed the increasing size of the two cavities generated by the first burst further observed "a body of peat moss loosened by these disruptions to the extent of a mile in circumference." They also predicted future aftershocks, the newspaper reporting that the "prevailing opinion on the spot" was "that this enormous mass will come away before the discharge from Crow Hill will finally close" (J. Turner 151). Patrick agreed that "there may be other muddy eruptions for a considerable time; but it is to be hoped they will comparatively small and neither very extensive nor injurious" (*Letters*, 54).

Through these predictions, Patrick's direful tone creeps into the sober newspaper and scientific accounts. The effects of the burst did compound as currents of water full of sand, peat, and vegetable matter flowed for days, polluting nearby rivers, "coloring" them and their distributaries "with a peaty stain as far as to the Humber," as well as suffocating their fish (Miall, *Geology* 623). Five miles from Leeds, "1,270 kilos of dead perch and trout" were trawled from the Aire (Atkins 177). Water at least as far downstream as Leeds was rendered non-potable after the "7-foot high torrent of mud, peat and water had swept down the valley," making it "so filthy" that, "when taken into a glass, [it] appeared nearly as black as ink" (Barker 151). Yorkshire topographer William Keighley recounted that mud and debris "kept the water of the river Aire in such a turbid state that for some time it could not be used at Leeds or any other place, either for culinary or manufacturing purposes" (109). The *Intelligencer* reported that the "quantity of peaty mud" arriving there was so vast "as to induce the manager of the Water Works to stop the pumps which supply the reservoir" (quoted in P. Brontë, *Letters*, 52). Nearer to the burst site, slurry clogged waterways, flooded fields, stopped watermills, and stilled factories for days, upending the region's economy. Patrick's sermon attests that these effects were severe and widely acknowledged. Describing spectators drawn to the scene, he hears farmers mourn the loss of the crops "so lately their hope, but now laid prostrate and ruined." He also reports hearing out-of-town visitors "lament in pathetic terms the great expense that must be incurred by the different townships" (*Brontëana*, 217). Though Patrick despairs that parishioners and visitors downplayed the event's spiritual lessons in favor of calculating its earthly costs, the infrastructural damage, was, as Claire Harman drily concludes, was "indeed catastrophic" (51).

For the Brontës, the burst would have been far more catastrophic had not Sarah Garrs's quick thinking prevented the injury or death of up to three of the four children who survived to adulthood. Their survival may have occasioned the earliest public reference to the children—that is, the first written or printed record beyond private correspondence or routine notations on parish registers and school records. On September 11, the *Leeds Mercury* concludes its account with gratitude that children playing nearby escaped the peaty deluge:

> A stone bridge was also nearly swept away at this place, and several other bridges in its course were materially damaged; we feel happy, however, in being able to state that it was not fatal to life in a single instance. The torrent was seen coming down the glen before it reached the hamlet by a

person who gave the alarm, and thereby saved the lives of several children who would otherwise have been swept away. The torrent at this time presented a breast of 7 feet high. (quoted in Parsons 440)

The unnamed children play an important role in the *Mercury*'s account. Their appearance marks a logical and emotional transition around which the journalist pivots from reporting verified facts to speculating about the likelihood of future bursts. This speculation quotes two eyewitnesses (including Patrick, who is identified by name), reflecting the children's rhetorical usefulness as a pathetic appeal justifying the article's turn to educated guesswork and lending exigence to the journalist's plea that action be taken to avert future ecological disasters. Atkins argues that it is "possible that those children were the Brontës," adding, "We can in any case be confident that they were nearby" (176). Harman reports Atkins's judgment without weighing in (51), while Barker embeds the *Mercury* passage in such a way that strongly implies that it is them (151). Only Patrick's biographers, Lock and Dixon, imply they were *not* the Brontës; they link the *Mercury*'s reference to the second eyewitness instead (249). Regardless, their presence at an ecological crisis that spurred debates about how to prevent future ones shows that the family's experiences illustrate what it was like to be present at the Anthropocene's emergence.

What is indisputable, though not previously acknowledged, is that the Brontë children survived an ecological disaster. Nor is it known that they were central to an early debate about whether human actions cause such catastrophes. Patrick's explicit identification of his children in his sermon and poem, both published by Bradford printer Thomas Inkersley, drew them immediately into the written record of the affair. The Brontë children thus appear as survivors of the bog burst in articles in the *Mercury* and *Intelligencer*; in scientific accounts in the *Edinburgh Journal of Science* and the *Proceedings of the Royal Institute of Great Britain* (1898); and in regional histories, such as William Keighley's *Keighley, Past and Present* (1879) and J. Horsfall Turner's *Haworth: Past and Present* (1879). Perhaps it is because Patrick's narrative makes Branwell, Emily, and Anne central figures of the burst that biographies leverage the natural disaster as a flash point for debating his efficacy as a father, rather than emphasizing the circulation of Patrick's scientific speculations beyond his parish. His burst writings are scoured for the paternal affections that Elizabeth Gaskell pointedly withholds in her formative portrait in the *Life of Charlotte Brontë* (1857). Counter to its sketch of a distant and mercurial patriarch, his bog sermon displays deep concern. After having "sent [his] little children, who were indisposed, accompanied by the servants, to take an airing on the common," he hears ominous noises and recalls, "My little family had escaped to a place of shelter, but I did not know it, and consequently watched every movement of the coming tempest with a painful degree of interest" (*Brontëana*, 212). His use of *painful, consequently*, and *little* emphasizes the children's vulnerability, as do his aside that they were convalescing and his aside, "but I did not know it," which crackles with dramatic suspense. Specifying that "servants" (plural) accompanied his children clears him of neglect, while the detail about the "common" suggests that he scrupulously instructed them to obey property laws. His correction of details published by the *Intelligencer*—including his defensive rejoinder that Crow Hill was "not altogether a quagmire" before the burst (*Letters*, 53)—also shows concern.

In line with this analysis, Barker concludes, "The picture of an anxious father looking out for his children because they were late and then fearing dreadfully for their safety ... should forever dispel any suggestion that Patrick was a cold and uncaring parent" (151). Barker accordingly uses the bog burst to debunk Gaskell's "sensational stories" of a "half-mad and violent eccentric" who discharges guns, shreds his wife's dresses, and starves his children on a vegetarian diet (124). A more skeptical Harman writes, "The Reverend Brontë didn't notice how long they had stayed out," concluding that this is "in itself a telling detail" (50). Where Harman merely raises a skeptical eyebrow, Lyndall Gordon reproduces Gaskell's portrait, deeming him "proud and self-sufficient" and "not partial to little ones," before remarking unconnectedly that "the long low moors, with its fringe of stunted copse, are neither grand nor romantic" (11, 8), echoing Gaskell's implication that he contributed to his wife's and children's early deaths by rooting them to a wasted ecosystem with an inhospitable climate and unsanitary arrangements. By contrast, Ann Dinsdale, in an interview about the bog burst, approvingly notes that he was "fascinated by the natural world and encouraged his children to walk on the moors every day" (Penman). Whether or not Patrick is pronounced a good father, these judgments assume that his attitude toward the natural world is intimately related to his love for the children and that their experiences of the moors are firmly related to their writings. Ultimately, what is under interrogation is the siblings' exposure to an ecosystem seen as insalubrious, unstable, and stern yet also grand, dynamic, and inspirational. I conclude, then, that the bog burst distills into one dramatic episode the moors' appeals and dangers, providing insight into the family's scientific interests and into the ecosystem that figures so prominently in their texts.

Yet, beyond the fact that the three youngest members witnessed the bog burst, there is very little consensus about its significance for the family. Most accounts of Brontës and the phenomenon exist in travel narratives and handbooks, rather than criticism, and even Barker's magisterial group biography declines to proffer a theory:

> If the bog-burst caused such excitement and trauma to Patrick, one wonders what effect it had on his children, particularly as the apocalyptic interpretations could not have been lost on them. None of their writings for this period are extant, however, and only one poem by Emily, written twelve years later, even approaches the experience, so we cannot tell what they felt about their own brush with death. (154)

The poem in question, "High Waving Heather," is frequently cited as the sole representation of the burst by the children. Dinsdale asserts that though "we can only speculate how this event shaped Emily's attitude to nature," this particular poem is haunted by "echoes of the event she'd witnessed," causing her to stop viewing nature as a force neutral to human interests and instead seeing it as "violent and willful" (Penman). Winifred Gérin claims that the "spectacle appears simply to have delighted the six-year-old Emily," who "never quite succeeded in hiding her contempt for those mortals who shrank before nature's fury" (6). Stevie Davies muses, "It is likely that Emily ... put the incident into store in her mind as an emotional and spiritual resource" (*Free Woman* 13). Katherine Frank pronounces that Emily saw "literally 'wuthering heights'" as the burst heaved the moors' surfaces, provoking "a deep affinity for the harsh rugged landscape surrounding her home" (49). Raymond theorizes that the burst motivated her to model Peniston Crag after Ponden Clough (207). Edward Chitham notes that routes taken by Heathcliff and Catherine in *Wuthering Heights* retrace the September 1824 walk and repeats an anecdote from one of Inkersley's assistants to argue that Emily corrected the proofs of the bog-burst sermon (*A Life* 31). If true, this must have occurred just before Emily joined her sisters at Cowan Bridge, and her father's language shaped the account she relayed to them.

If there is any consensus, it is in supposing that they took from the bog burst lessons about the moors' power and violence. With Anne a mere four years old and Charlotte having left Haworth three weeks before, this is a sensible conclusion. Atkins nevertheless links the burst to Anne through her contributions to the literary world of Gondal, "a bone-strewn place" imbued with "a history of bloodshed" inspired by her experience of bogs as violent and unpredictable (184). Nick Holland speculates that this would have been the first time she saw Ponden Hall and concludes that "the power and devastation ... would have been a memory that stayed with her" (40). Indeed, her selection of Ponden Hall for Wildfell Hall may position the burst as an explanatory prehistory for Wildfell's derelict grounds. But most accounts do not venture that far: Raymond observes, "Clearly the Crow Hill bog-burst was a family story among the Brontës" (207), and Harman deduces reasonably that the older sisters "surely would have heard about it when their father and Emily joined them in November, and in later years Charlotte would have become familiar with the moralizing poem Patrick published on the subject" (51). Charlotte also joined her siblings for the walks they later took along the burst site (Chitham, *A Life* 67; Gérin 30), so though she would have had secondhand knowledge of the initial event, she would have had repeated firsthand encounters with its long-term effects: its scars and debris, its lowering of the bog, and its disruptions to flora and fauna. Furthermore, she would have been familiar with Patrick's sermon and poem. On a more symbolic register, Harman links Charlotte to the burst by using "Extraordinary Disruption," from the title of Patrick's poem about the burst, as a metaphor for her residence at Cowan Bridge (52). Harman also uses it as a metaphor for Charlotte's digressive style. Harman (quoting Patrick) lists "fascinating moments, when the narrator is diverted into some tirade ... like a bog bursting and bringing up 'black moory substances' from deep below the surface" (218). "Another bog burst from Charlotte's seething substratum" occurs in *Shirley*, and her letters designate political crises as "moral earthquakes" (271, 268). Harman's bog-burst metaphorics equates Charlotte with her landscape: both are sudden releases of power from a remote moor that capture attention far beyond Yorkshire. These equations are central to the Brontë legacy, which rests on a series of material and symbolic links that triangulate the family, their texts, and their moors.

What is less familiar is what the uncertainty surrounding the burst can tell us about the family's relationship to their landscape. Misinformation abounds (John Sutherland adds hailstones to the atmospheric mix for good measure [13]), as does guessing (the verbs "speculate" and "wonder" are oft invoked). Certainly there are gaps in the record. We cannot confirm which illness the children had; it is reported variously as whooping cough, scarlet fever, or the measles. J. Horsfall Turner, amid meticulously accurate descriptions of the moors, places Charlotte on the scene (152). Blake Morrison's play *We Are Three Sisters* (2011) knowingly reproduces this error, pushing the burst forward two decades so that the three sisters are present and brainstorming their first novels. Portraying the burst as a humanitarian crisis, Morrison credits Charlotte for gathering blankets for exposure victims and Anne for arranging a benefit concert for those whose "cottages on Butt Lane were flattened," whereas Emily protests, "Doing good and helping others! . . . If that's all life holds, then make an end of me now" (44, 52). Morrison's counterfactual illustrates tensions between expectations for ministers' daughters and the Brontës' literary ambitions, but what interests me here is how twinned threats of uncertainty and mortality—contemporary threats to our knowledge of the Brontës, historical threats to the Brontës' bodies—dominate representations of the bog burst. Errors and guesses show that the bog burst's uncertainties are productive: they produce multiple narratives to provide the information whose absence so discomfits us.

In spite of Morrison's good reasons for shifting the date, it is not strictly necessary for proving the burst's importance: 1824 was itself a formative period for the family. Then, the fragile equilibrium brought by Aunt Branwell's residence at the parsonage after their mother's death in 1821 was disrupted by the eldest sisters' departures. At Cowan Bridge, famously, their safety was again assailed, curtailing the lives of the eldest two sisters. But 1824 was also filled with artistic and intellectual milestones. It was the year Branwell received his first set of toy soldiers, to which he added a new set roughly each year until 1828 (Moon 51–53)—inaugurating the "Plays" that, as the tales of the "Islanders" and "Young Men" coalesced into the story-worlds of Angria and Gondal, made the children into writers. It is also the year of the "Mask" incident, oft invoked to prove the children's precocity, in which Patrick asks them profound questions, providing a mask so they could answer with intellectual courage and moral maturity (Gaskell 39). Just as the burst undoubtedly occurred at a key moment in the family's psychological, intellectual, and aesthetic development, so too did the Brontës occupy the moors at a crucial transition moment during which debates about moors proliferated: their mutability, their fragility and resilience, their aesthetic and economic value. To reconstruct this moment, I adopt the 1824 Crow Hill bog burst as a focal point because it is one of the earliest moments in which the family's history intersects with the Anthropocene. I examine Patrick's bog writings in the context of Victorian scientific debates about environmental change and natural disasters and explore moorland ecology and cultural constructions of the moors to illuminate how the family's relationship to local biomes shaped their literary investigations of humans' moral responsibility for the nonhuman organisms and landscapes around them. To appreciate how their texts engaged with Victorian debates over the negative impacts of humans on the environment, we must take a closer look at the moors as anthropogenic biomes. Let us take our own walk in Brontë country—one under far less dramatic circumstances than those of September 2, 1824.

A TOUR OF BRONTË COUNTRY:
THE ANTHROPOGENESIS OF BOGS AND THEIR BURSTS

Brontë country radiates outward from Haworth Parsonage and the village that trickles downslope from St. Michael's Church at the foot of the graveyard facing the parsonage's front door. Named for its origins as a "hedged enclosure" or "hawthorn enclosure," Haworth perches atop the steep ridges of the Worth Valley, a position propitious both to the water-powered factories and to the squat and hardy flowering shrubs for which the area is known. The Worth Valley runs north and south in the western section of the historic county of the West Riding of Yorkshire, just where it abuts Lancashire's eastern border. As the northernmost spur of the South Pennines, this valley is defined by broad, stone-bordered moors, cut short like plateaus and comprising the mudstone, siltstone, and limestone strata that peeked out in the Brontës' day and are exposed today by two additional centuries of erosion. These geological features are equally as perfect for leisure walks as for quarrying the dark stones that, so crucial to Haworth's moody aspect, formed the building blocks of the parsonage, churchyard, graveyard, and village, and of the dry stone walls penning sheep, attesting to histories of enclosure and marking spent agricultural grounds long since released from tillage. The Pennines, a group of fells too low to be mountains but prominent enough to be called the backbone of England, were formed by glacial retreat in the Carboniferous period. Climbing north from the Peak District to the Scottish border, the Pennines give shape along the way to the West Riding, burdening it with bitter temperatures, fierce winds, and abundant precipitation. A prominent ridgeline, they precipitate numerous watersheds, including the becks burbling around Haworth Moor coalescing into the Aire and Calder rivers before emptying eventually into the Irish, North, and German Seas.

The flora that can survive this environment are oligotrophic organisms, capable of surviving unfavorable conditions. Around Haworth, these include climactic extremes of temperature and precipitation, as well as a dearth of the nutrients needed by most flora. As the Victorian biologist Miall, professor at Yorkshire College, wrote of the region's oligotrophs,

Some thrive both on peat and on sand, in bogs and on loose gravel. They may range from sea level to a height of several thousand feet. They can endure a summer glare which blisters the skin, and also the sharpest cold known on this planet. Some can subsist on soil which contains no ordinary ingredient of plant food in appreciable quantity. ("Moor" 639)

The upland moors' oligotrophs must thrive in acidic soils, for the landscape is stripped by flows of fast-moving waters of the nutrients needed by copiotrophic species, which weaken or die in their absence. Brontë country's most iconic oligotrophs include *Erica* and *Calluna* heathers, used in dyeing, tanning, brewing, and broom-making, consumed by grazing sheep, and valued for their purple blooms. They also include the *Sphagnum* mosses that transform into peat as they incompletely decay in the upland soil, whose mixture of millstone grit, shale, and clay forms a water catchment. When waters from the area's heavy rains are detained from their downward course by this gritty soil, the capacious bladders of the *Sphagnum* mosses trap the waters. The waterlogged mosses, pushed down with each annual deposit of leaves, stems, and rhizoids, slowly succumb to the anaerobic environment to form the peat bogs whose dominating presence is the moors' defining trait. Their presence makes moors, which cover 8% of the world's surface, spongily absorbent wetlands (Gladwin 29). In Brontë country, the moors are "treeless with flat to undulating vistas" and "littered with rock formations (granite and limestone) and accentuated with mountain ridges," along which are blanket bogs filled with the "remains of plants, trees, and animals that once flourished on the surface of peatlands" but, once submerged this anaerobic environment, remain suspended in a state of partial decomposition (32).

Moors' lack of stately trees, their preponderance of quaggy bogs full of decaying vegetation, and their resistance to agriculture contributed to the cultural devaluation of this landscape, commonly referred to as a "waste." Keighley's topography, for example, describes "a wild waste of moor and fell grazed by sheep" (104). Though the term suggests wildness, moors are not a fully natural space apart from human activity. Derek Gladwin notes that capitalist attempts to render all lands "productive" deemed the moors wastelands because incomplete decomposition interrupts cycles of production into which all dead organisms must be profitably reinserted (28). Attempts to "improve" moors by draining bogs to reclaim the "wasted" land thus proliferated in the sixteenth to nineteenth centuries. Yet, as Ian D. Rotherham points out, despite being called "wastes," peatlands were in fact "a contested resource," "highly productive" economically because they "provided fuel, food and building materials" (*Peat* 4, 15).

The Brontës were well aware of the value and contested nature of peatlands. Patrick's childhood in Ireland brought him into close contact with peat. Chitham concludes that Patrick collected peat as a boy (*Western Winds* 102), while William Wright claims that his father constructed sod fences from peat and engaged in a decades-long quarrel over a "piece of exhausted bog," for "for nothing in Ireland is supposed to test a man's honesty like a piece of waste land lying contiguous to his own land" (67, 119). Wright's frontispiece features a young Patrick carting peat in a barrow. Though this fanciful work reports unsubstantiated tales, more reliable biographers similarly stress Patrick's encounters with bogs. Erskine Stuart alleges that Patrick "used to delight to frighten his little fledglings by recounting many a ghostly legend of the Irish bogs" (108–9), some which servants repeat in *Jane Eyre*. In Haworth, peat mattered. Atkins notes that Brontës frequented the many turbary roads for peat cutting that crisscross Haworth Moor (167). Steven Wood and Peter Brears note that turbary roads also connect Top Withins to three peat pits (72), and Dudley Green notes that social unrest in 1839–40 partly resulted from the failure of the peat crop (121). Emily's diary paper for 1841 records pets "ensconced in the peat-house" (Orel 42). Harman reports that Ponden Hall and the parsonage had peat stores (29), Chitham affirms that the parsonage used peat fire (*A Life* 17), and Barker notes that Charlotte had the peat loft converted into Arthur Bell Nicholls's study after their marriage (885).

Bogs continue to provide valuable resources—peat-preserved organic matter and man-made artifacts are vital evidence for scientists and historians, while peat itself provides an ideal medium for horticulturists, fuel for industrial purposes, and activated carbon, used in the medical and cosmetic industries and for cleaning oil spills—making them as "contested" a space now as they were in the Brontës' time (Joosten and Clarke 56). At that point, enclosure had eroded traditional commons rights to pasturage and resource extraction, particularly of peat, but also bracken, broom, furze, gorse, gravel, herbs, ling, rush, sand, and stone. This economic shift was supported by a corollary discursive devaluation. Rotherham links the term "waste" to the enclosure movement, blaming "perceptions of wealthier land-owning classes that these areas were not productive for them directly and by the nature of their terrain were dangerous places. They harbored unrest and disease and, for those living outside, the great fens or heaths were strange and fearful places"

(*Peat* 15). Rotherham's 1869 source calls them "useless and unsightly excrescences, growing over and covering up ... good land" (*Peat* 19). Gladwin lists important texts with dim views of moors: Edmund Spenser's *A View of the Present State of Ireland* (1596) leverages Ireland's association with bogs in the English cultural imaginary to justify imperialism; William King's address to the Royal Society in 1685 demands Parliament drain the bogs that debase "every barbarous ill-inhabited country"; and Maria Edgeworth's *Castle Rackrent* (1800) features conversations about bog improvement between landlord Sir Kit and his English bride (41, 44, 46). These stereotypes concerned Charlotte, as seen in an 1840 letter she wrote to her friend Ellen Nussey about lectures given by her father and his curate:

> both are spoken of very highly in the Newspaper and it is mentioned as a matter of wonder that such displays of intellect should emanate from the Village of Haworth 'situated amongst the bogs and Mountains and until very lately supposed to be in a state of Semi-barbarism.' Such are the words of the newspaper. (*Letters* 1:214)

Charlotte's sarcasm contests this "barbarism" and prefigures *Shirley*'s proud pro-Yorkshire passages. Yet the heroine of *Jane Eyre*, after sleeping on the moors, must be "purified" from the "traces of the bog" that "degrade" her (391). And the peat loft's conversion—part of the larger renovation project that Charlotte funded with royalties—suggests an ambivalence toward moorlands. By implying that the Brontës were no longer so dependent on this cheap, smoky, and odorous fuel, the conversion distanced the parsonage from its boggy surroundings (and the family from its peasant Irish origins) and marked Charlotte's authorial success and upward mobility.

Gaskell's *Life of Charlotte Brontë* depends heavily on these negative views of moorlands as inhuman spaces requiring improvement. The *Life*'s infamous portrait of Haworth is perfectly in keeping with Gladwin's trio of texts. Its opening describes a harsh space devoid of "patches of arable land" and critiques the parsonage's inadequate garden, where "only the most hardy plants could be made to grow" (6). Gaskell's account deftly isolates Haworth Parsonage as an island amid lonely moors, distanced from the village below. Unlike the valley floors dotted by unattractive, poorly constructed buildings, the parsonage appears as a place apart, "crowned with wild, bleak moors—grand, from the ideas of solitude and loneliness which they suggest, or oppressive from the feeling which they give of being pent-up by some monotonous and illimitable barrier, according to the mood of mind in which the spectator may be" (5). Depicting the region as a graceless entanglement of moors, villages, and factories, she concludes that there, life "does not flourish" but "merely exists" (4, 5). By contrasting the lifeless, timeless moors with the modernizing, overpopulated valley floors over which the parsonage towers, Gaskell's bleak, Romantic topography neatly attributes Charlotte's literary genius to her confrontation with her environment. Charlotte heroically transcends both the inhuman moors and the banal human landscape below. Gaskell's hyperbolic vision of the savage village, though influential, has been roundly challenged.[1] Even unreliable Wright condemns "Mrs. Gaskell's dreary moorlands and dismal surroundings." He opines, "Genius of the Brontë kind would not be so rare if grey and somber surroundings could produce it, or if it could be stimulated by chilling repression and cramped circumstances" (2–3). More recently, Harman deflates this myth of lifeless inhumanity:

> The moors around Haworth ... were not quite the semi-wildernesses of today, carefully preserved for walkers, shooting parties and the water industry; they were places of work for quarrymen and peat-cutters, hill farmers and smallholders. The route to what are now the isolated ruins of Top Withens ... passed by at least seven small homesteads in the Brontës' day, and walking on the moor would have had to take into account the dangers of trespassing, as well as large areas of permanently boggy and impassable terrain. (31)

Harman's correction of stereotypes militates against inaccurate accounts of the moors' inhuman barrenness. Accounts like these help explain why bogs were an object of the Brontës' aesthetic representation—which I argue is particularly significant in the context of the Anthropocene, for such accounts acknowledge how human motives and interests shaped the moors.

Moors, after all, are *human* environments. About the Pennines, Andrew Bibby warns that the "idea that this landscape is a primeval one is a deeply appealing one," but "historically completely inaccurate. The moorlands have been shaped by human activity from the earliest days, and continue to be shaped in both minor and major ways" (85). Bibby's warning is timely: the moors that seem to be wild are carefully managed to *appear* as wild. Paths are maintained, trash cans and restrooms provided, and heather burned. Ironically, this assiduous management of Haworth Moor brings it into greater conformity now with Gaskell's portrait than it was then—reflecting the lasting appeal of her bleak vision. After invoking these myths, Bibby confesses,

> I have used a number of highly subjective adjectives in the last few paragraphs in my description of the moors—words such as wild, hostile and savage—which frankly, should not pass without comment and challenge. We have become so familiar with this way of viewing moorland landscape, however, that the likelihood is that their use did not seem striking or inappropriate. We have accustomed ourselves to the idea that the moors do possess a sort of innate wildness about them. (82)

Bibby connects the rise of this moor ideology to the rise of the picturesque, Edmund Burke's sublime, and domestic tourism in England after the Napoleonic wars. Gaskell's castigations thus contribute to this tradition—or seem to. Her disapproval reveals a nascent awareness of the Anthropocene's intensification of human-caused transformations of nature. Complaining about the lack of rural scenery between Keighley and Haworth, Gaskell remarks, "what with villas, great worsted factories, rows of workmen's houses, with here and there an old-fashioned farmhouse and outbuildings, it can hardly be called 'country' any part of the way" (4). When humans and nature intersect, Gaskell laments it as an absolute, and final, absence of the natural—registering the pain and resistance often felt when confronting signs of climate change.

Gaskell's lamentation registers her anxiety to protect Charlotte's personal and literary reputation. The links she forges between the Brontës and the moors also link her ecological and literary fears: if their legacy relies on their landscape, then the moorlands' mutability threatens links among readers, writers, and texts. Little wonder that Lock and Dixon betray anxiety about the gaps in Haworth's history. "Just how long there has existed some kind of chapelry on the present site," they fret, "it is not possible to tell." Resisting this indeterminacy, they seek an alternate certainty in the "natural" spaces surrounding the church. There,

> around village and hamlet, farm and crag, around the very stones themselves, stretch the miles and miles of heather and bracken, ling and bilberry, grass and moss-crop—the moors themselves. They are the oldest of all, for they were here before there came the humans to build their houses of the local millstone grit, and they will remain long after man and stone have crumbled into dust. (208)

Lock and Dixon's stoicism would appeal to the clergyman in Patrick, but their confidence in the moors' immutability arises more from a desire to establish Haworth's singularity than a desire for accuracy. Whether we see the moors as eternal or mutable matters because the Brontës' reception rests on our assumptions about moors. And the moors do change. Crow Hill (either the peaty morass or the body of writing about it) eloquently testifies to that effect. In the *Life of Charlotte Brontë*, a strange chiasmus develops in response to unwelcome evidence that Gaskell cannot ignore: the remnants of natural spaces are too civilized for her hagiographic purposes, yet the region's urbanizing spaces are not civilized enough. Gaskell's insistence upon the wild inhumanity of Yorkshire's windswept uplands is not scientifically accurate, but her paradox accurately reflects a particular historical moment in which growing knowledge about the human origins of ecosystemic change inspired fear, disgust, and a longing to see beauty and aesthetic inspiration in these altered spaces. Her frustration at these (to her) ugly combinations of the human and the inhuman, the civilized and the uncivilized, the built and the natural, arises from bewilderment at the profound ecological shifts that marked the dawn of the Anthropocene.

Though Gaskell resists overtly acknowledging the causal relationship between Haworth's ungraceful penumbra of human structures and the moors' putative lack of abundant life, Victorian scientists drew these connections. It is not that the moors were newly *becoming* human environments over Charlotte's lifetime (though new evidence was making it clearer). Rather, moors *always* were human environments. The excavations that spurred geology's dramatic extension of the Earth's age also uncovered evidence of periods of acute ecological crisis caused by prehistoric human activities. It was not in the valleys, the modern center of human populations, but in the uplands that humans first settled. Yorkshire moors bear physical evidence of Mesolithic, Bronze Age, Roman, Celtic, Viking, and Saxon settlements, providing early examples of anthropogenic ecological degradation.[2] Remnants of root systems in the peat attest that these landscapes were originally densely forested, and man-made rock formations (such as Crow Hill's Alcomden Stones) and pollen embalmed in peat prove that these landscapes had been eminently arable. Extensive deforestation during the Mesolithic period and mismanaged agriculture during the Bronze Age acidified the sandy soil, which, no longer protected by trees from wind and water, lost nutrients to the harsh winds and waters to which it was continually exposed.[3] Eventually, the denuded soil could not support crops—only the moors pushing humans down the valley. In the ensuing centuries, unregulated burning, grazing, and draining ensured that any would-be pioneer saplings catered the preferred snack of game species, instead of contributing to the succession of climax vegetation (that is, to the land's eventual reversion to forest). Even if we accept the early anthropogenic hypothesis—that the dawn of the Anthropocene was not at the Industrial Revolution in the North of England, but, instead, that "land clearing and agriculture caused emissions of greenhouse gases to begin to alter climate as early as 7000 years ago" (Ruddiman et al. 147)—that is the very time when humans were transforming Yorkshire's forests into moors, so the Brontës were still living in an anthrome. Upland moors like those over Haworth are therefore anthropogenic environments in two senses: they were originally created by human actions, and successive periods of human action maintained them as moors.

Though contemporary advances in palynology, radar imaging, and carbon dating have considerably advanced knowledge about the submerged histories of wetlands, nineteenth-century conversations about reclaiming heaths, moors, and bogs—"improving" them by draining them into profitable plantations or fields—addressed their anthropogenic origins. Sir Humphry Davy hypothesized these origins in a series of lectures gathered as his *Elements of Agricultural Chemistry* in 1814. Advising the "scientific farmer" how to improve crop yields from moors, Davy explains why the soil is so poor: waterlogged, "spongy" soils housed fluids that "gradually rendered [the soil] incapable of supporting the nobler classes of vegetables" (169). But how did they become waterlogged in the first place? Davy, examining extant root systems and signs of Mesolithic inhabitation, reasoned that deforestation was the origin of bog formation:

> Many peat-mosses seem to have been formed by the destruction of forests, in consequence of the imprudent use of the hatchet by the early cultivators of the country in which they exist: when the trees are felled in the out-skirts of a wood, those in the interior are exposed to the influence of the winds; and having been accustomed to shelter, become unhealthy, and die in their new situation; and their leaves and branches gradually decomposing, produce a stratum of vegetable matter. In many of the great bogs in Ireland and Scotland, the larger trees that are found in the out-skirts of them, bear the marks of having been felled. In the interior, few entire trees are found; and the cause is, probably, that they fell by gradual decay; and that the fermentation and decomposition of the vegetable matter was most rapid where it was the greatest quantity. (169)

Even partial clearance encourages bog formation because trees "in the center of woods are sooner or later destroyed, if exposed in their adult state to blasts, in consequence of the felling of the surrounding timber" (233). Bogs can form, in short, under conditions created by humans.

The Brontës were well acquainted with Davy's theories. While Kerrow Hill has written at length on this acquaintance, a few intersections are quickly sketched. Patrick owned Davy's *Elements of Chemical Philosophy* (1812), whose effects on Emily Stevie Davies traces in *Wuthering Heights* (*Emily Brontë* 71, 41). In Anne's *Tenant*, the heroine reads *Consolations in Travel; Or, The Last Days of a Philosopher* (1830). Clare Flaherty sees Davy's mark in the "articulation of the intersections of faith, science and love" in Anne's unpublished work (31). Flaherty also notes that Davy's combination of literary and scientific interests would have interested the Brontës and that they would have been familiar with discussions of Davy in periodicals like *Blackwood's*. I would add *Chambers's*, another family favorite, to Flaherty's list, as it published a comprehensive "Biographic Sketch" on his death. Patrick and Charlotte enthusiastically approved of Davy's pioneering research into the use of nitrous oxide for anesthesia (Snow 53–68). Though there is no direct evidence that the Brontës read *Agricultural Chemistry*, Davy's interest in human-caused changes to the Earth permeated all his works, including ones we know they read. Moreover, Davy's theory of bog anthropogenesis was widely reported in venues they did access. It figured prominently in the parliamentary *Report of the Commissioners Appointed to Enquire into the Nature and Extent of the Several Bogs in Ireland* (1810–1814). The second *Report*, paraphrasing *Agricultural Chemistry*, reasons that

> if these spots were the seats of timber trees, formerly, there can be no good reason assigned why they should not resume that character. We learn, in fact, that some of them have sustained that character three times; and that three distinct growths of timber, covered by three distinct masses of bog, are discovered on examination. Some Naturalists suppose that forests were the predecessors and causes of these formations. The subject is, at least, curious, and interesting as an addition to the History of the Earth. (188)

To marshal support for bog reclamation, the Commission adopts Davy's conclusions about bog formation. Two affectively charged phrases—the qualifier *at least* and the use of *interesting* as an appellation for a theory of nothing less than the "History of the Earth"—register the Commission's unease with acknowledging human-caused ecological destruction. "Whether these morasses were at first formed by the destruction of whole forests, or merely by the stagnation of water," the *Report* hedges, is "a question that cannot now be determined" (188). Plumbing the depths of human culpability is not in its interest (which is to recommend taming Irish "wilds" for the profit of Anglo-Irish settlers), yet the *Report*'s hedging registers how deeply anxieties about anthropogenic ecosystemic shifts shaped technical and popular discussions of wetlands.

Other popular Victorian science-writing texts that engaged in these nascent conversations about short- and long-term human impacts on the environment include the family's beloved volumes of natural history, particularly early ecologist Gilbert White's *The Natural History and Antiquities of Selborne* and Thomas Bewick's *History of British Birds*, whose "profound effect" on the family, Christine Alexander argues, "cannot be overestimated" ("Educating" 13). We know the lasting importance of these works for Charlotte not only because her fiction incorporates them (*Jane Eyre* opens with the heroine reading *Bewick's*), but also from an 1834 letter that concludes a course of self-improving reading for Nussey with works by Bewick, White, John James Audubon, and Oliver Goldsmith (*Letters* 1:131). White's *Selborne*, a classic of natural history structured as a series of letters, depicting human-animal interactions in the landscapes around his Hampshire vicarage, profoundly influenced Bewick. Just as White's letters embed phenological observations about plant and animal life cycles within a framework of village life, using interpersonal and interspecies interactions as a context for scientific inquiry, Bewick's vignettes set wild birds among domesticated animals and human activities or at boundaries where natural and man-made spaces meet. Of particular interest for the Brontës, whose works reflect Yorkshire's specific conditions, is the fact that *Selborne* "established both a literary genre and the scientific validity of close study of a single region in details over many years by a generalist" (Walls, "Natural History" 190). Josephine McDonagh argues that Charlotte adapts White's signature trope—the nature walk—as a platform for introspection, sociopolitical commentary, or supernatural visitations, "rather than as an unmediated experience of the natural world" (471). Indeed, they are not unmediated, for Bewick or White or the Brontës, who contextualize "nature" within human histories. Bewick and White narrativize scientific observation through a multispecies lens that foregrounds human-nature interaction. Like Davy, White considers historical bog formation, affirming that in Hampshire bogs there "formerly abounded ... subterraneous trees," long since extracted as "fossil-wood" for home construction (26). He condemns walkers for crushing birds' eggs, pet owners for allowing cats to terrorize fish, and gardeners for destroying the "secret nurseries" of mole-crickets (213, 212).

As suggested by Jane Eyre's favorite parts of *Bewick's*—vignettes set in inhospitable climes and sensational scenes of death and crime—such an approach does not result in a sentimental pastoral espousing the benefits of human protection over nature. White's gentle natural history waxes dark when it considers anthropogenic ecological destruction. Letter VII warns that the wetlands need better protection. After extolling moors for being "of considerable service to neighborhoods that verge upon them," he argues against unnecessary human interference that would attempt to improve them by converting them back into the more directly remunerative agricultural lands (29). Controlled burning each decade has long been an integral part of the temporal rhythms binding humans, animals, and biomes in the moors, but when overgrazed or incompletely burned, the moors are jeopardized, their biodiversity reduced and their resilience threatened. White reserves his most severe chastisement for those who, ignoring folk tradition and the law, burn so extensively that the fires cannot be controlled:

> Though (by statute 4 and 5 W. and Mary, c. 23) 'to burn on any waste, between Candlemas and Midsummer, any grig, ling, heath and furze, goss or fern, is punishable with whipping and confinement in the house of correction'; yet, in this forest ... such vast heath-fires are lighted up, that they often get to a masterless head, and, catching the hedges, have sometimes been communicated to the underwoods, woods, and coppices, where great damage has ensued.... [W]here there is large old fume, the fire, following the roots, consumes the very ground; so that for hundreds of acres nothing is to be seen but smother and desolation, the whole circuit round looking like the cinders of a volcano; and the soil being quite exhausted, no traces of vegetation are to be found for years. (30)

These images of "whipping" and imprisoning malefactors who stoke fires with the power of a "volcano" sit uneasily between lyrical passages on generative cycles of leafing, blossoming, hatching, and fledging. Setting aside his descriptive style of delighted curiosity and patient tolerance for the vagaries of man and animal, White prescriptively champions what we would now call an environmentalist program of biome preservation and interspecies harmony. By the time the Brontës began walking Haworth Moor and gleaning literary inspiration from it, it was already threatened by pressures of modernization and industrialization to put the supposed wastelands to good (profitable) use. The Brontës, their home poised between one of England's first rapidly industrializing towns and moorlands whose "naturalness" bore signs of generations of human interference, occupied one of the first Anthropocenic environments, one in which the warnings given by the natural historians they read would have been immediately relevant.

The unease betrayed by Davy, Bewick, and White climaxes in George Perkins Marsh's *Man and Nature: or Earth as Modified by Human Action*, published a decade after *Villette*. Marsh assembles an archive of evidence of ecological destruction, focusing on the ancient Mediterranean but supplementing with global data from the past and the present. After listing human actions that, "on a large scale, interfere with the spontaneous arrangements of the organic or inorganic world" and alter "the physical conditions of the globe we inhabit," Marsh concludes that mankind "has brought the face of the earth to a desolation almost as complete as that of the moon" (3). Because the preexisting "arrangements of nature" are "highly desirable," any "transforming operations" to render a space habitable by man "should be so conducted as not unnecessarily to derange and destroy what, in too many cases, it is beyond the power of man to rectify or restore" (34). But human actions do tend to "subvert the relations and destroy the balance which nature had established between her organized and her inorganic creatures" (31, 21, 43). Marsh concludes, "The earth is fast becoming an unfit home for its noblest inhabitant, and another era of equal human crime and human improvidence ... would reduce it to such a condition of impoverished productiveness, of shattered surface, of climatic excess, as to threaten the depravation, barbarism, and perhaps even extinction of the species" (44). Due to such alarming prognostications, *Man and Nature* is identified as an attempt to establish "a new ethic of global stewardship" (Walls, *Passage* 285) and "the first modern environmental treatise" (J. Taylor, *Sky* 2).

The urgency of preventing irreversible derangement causes Marsh to recruit moors, as Davy and White did earlier, as examples of human-caused destruction. After surveying causes of bog formation—geological (stratigraphic shifts), animal (locusts, beavers), and hominal (lumberjacks, shepherds, engineers, poachers)—he zeroes in on the latter. Included in this category is Davy's theory about the removal of trees that served as protective barriers: "the entrance thus afforded to the wind occasions the sudden overthrow of hundreds of trees which might otherwise have stood for generations" but whose stumps molder in bogs, mere "monuments of its former vegetation" (*Man and Nature* 32, 241). Despite his praise for bogs' biodiversity, provision of fuel, and historical evidentiary value, he shudders at their creation by deforestation. Likewise, his account of mass movements is as intense as those by Atkins, Warburton, and Davy. One passage ceases to represent nature as a codependent network of multispecies agents; instead, it is an aggressor facing a vicious foe. Continuing to castigate the human actions that desertified formerly lush forests, Marsh declares that Nature

> avenges herself upon the intruder, by letting loose upon her defaced provinces destructive energies hitherto kept in check by organic forces destined to be his best auxiliaries, but which he has unwisely dispersed and driven from the field of action. When the forest is gone, the great reservoir of moisture stored up in its vegetable mould is evaporated, and returns only in deluges of rain to wash away the parched dust into which that mould has been converted. (43)

Marsh piles on examples of natural disasters to which deforested lands are especially vulnerable, including droughts, floods, mudslides, and eruptions. Documenting the effects of erosion caused by deforestation and overgrazing, Marsh describes the "seas of mud and rolling stones that sometimes lay waste, and bury beneath them acres, and even miles, of pasture and field and vineyard" in France (50). In Switzerland, "terrible discharges of rain" coalesce along heaths and moors into "a deluge mighty enough to sweep down the largest masses of gravel and of rock" (250). In the US, landslides result in "appalling calamities" because, long afterward, the "earth still remains mixed with the rocks and gravel it heaps up at its point of eruption" (294). Surveying the wreckage, Marsh declares that Nature is responding to intensified human rapaciousness by releasing "destructive energies hitherto kept in check" (43).

Marsh's anthropogenic theory of "natural" disasters is borne out by contemporary science. Dykes and Kirk blame "inappropriate human actions," including unrestricted peat cutting, bog draining, burning, grazing, digging, tipping, and building boundary markers, roads, embankments, or agricultural fields, which "eliminate downslope support" or cause a "loss of structural integrity of the peat mass normally provided by the tensile strength of the peat." These activities shift water pressures, rupture acrotelms, vibrate peat masses, strip layers of peat, or increase shear stress. In essence, though mass movements might be triggered by natural events (typically high-magnitude rainfall), "anthropogenic causes of failures ... change the overall condition of the peat deposit so that it becomes more susceptible to failure if subjected to a natural trigger event" (388). Rotherham agrees; though a given burst "might be the result of the bog simply outgrowing itself," it is "usually the consequence of human interference, frequently resulting from attempts to drain or cut the bog," which "destabilize all or part of the bog with dramatic and devastating consequences" (*Peat* 12). Such interference proliferated in Victorian Yorkshire, where air pollution from mining and industrial production posed new threats to moors, including erosion, that increased the risk of flooding, landslides, earthquakes, and new cycles of intensified erosion (Goudie 174, 160). While the South Pennines—Brontë country—saw considerable peat cutting in higher grounds in the medieval period, and intensified cutting downslope in the sixteenth to eighteenth centuries, the nineteenth century was a particularly vulnerable period for moors because unsustainable rates of extraction resulted from the industrialization of peat cutting. Moreover, "demands for new and 'improved' agricultural land meant peatlands came under direct assault, and in two to three hundred years were almost totally obliterated. Those remaining are fragile and vulnerable environments" (Rotherham, *Peat* 16). In Victorian Yorkshire, Marsh's concerns were ignored as "peats and turf on low-level moors were stripped away with extensive 'turf-cutting' and 'paring and burning' in upland landscapes" (Rotherham, *Peat* 20, 21).[4]

Also in line with Marsh and Davy, Rens van Beek et. al observe that though some mass wastings are "natural," their frequency and intensity are "exacerbated" by human actions that remove or add materials. They argue that these exacerbations over the last two hundred years were "strongly influenced by human activity due to land use change and vegetation removal" (17). Among these changes are mining and wind farm erection, which cause bursts and slides by developing new shear planes.[5] In addition to local interferences (individual instances of wind farm erection, road construction, peat dumping, gravel filling, and mining), Dykes and Warburton conclude that the "consequences of climate change cause widespread instability in high-latitude peatlands following local or regional melting of the permafrost" (91). Van Beek et al. cite global warming as a source of increases in extreme weather events that trigger bog bursts and slides (19). Because bogs have already been compromised by human activities, this means that both distal (long-term) and proximal (immediate) causes of mass movements are anthropogenic: humans destabilized bogs, which are, as a result of climate change, subject to a far greater frequency of triggering events than they were during the Holocene. Thus, in their investigation of the 2003 slide of a Derrybrien bog destabilized by the construction of a wind farm, Richard Lindsay and Olivia Bragg conclude that "almost invariably," recent bog failures "can be linked to human disturbance" (x).

Increased incidence of bog failure is worrisome for many reasons. From these muddy waters emerge ugly scars that last for decades or centuries. Bursts and slides "cause significance environmental impacts at-a-site, and their runout is far traveled causing considerable downstream devastation to infrastructure and stream ecology" (Warburton 159). Erosion is intensified, rivers are polluted, revegetation is slow, and "scars will persist in the landscape for decades resulting in the loss of agricultural land, reduction in the upland carbon store, and a loss of valuable ecological resource" (173). A series of peat slides in the early 2000s "brought the issue of peat instability into sharp public focus" because they destroyed highways and incurred costs exceeding multiple millions of dollars per burst (161). But bog loss is, in itself, a problem. Rotherham explains that the "destruction of peat bogs must rank as one of the greatest environmental disasters in Great Britain: loss of peat and peatlands contributed to climate change by releasing masses of carbon dioxide; and frequent flooding occurred owing to the removal of extensive areas of water-absorbent sponge" (Rotherham, *Peat* 7). The release of peat-sequestrated CO_2 by the denudation of bogs is a dire prospect.[6] Devastating floods in winter 2015–16 in the North of England dramatically illustrated what happens when moors can no longer neutralize flash floods. Moreover, there are cultural and historical losses because bogs "are one of the main tools we have for 'reconstructing' images of past landscapes and ecologies to help understand long-term environmental changes" (Rotherham, *Peat* 14). In addition to this information, rare organisms may be lost, as these "wastes" support a wealth of biodiversity within a patchwork of bogs, mires, heaths, grasslands, and pastures. Beside the moss, gorse, and heather grow rare aquatic plants, while underneath them nest a variety of rare birds, including the skylarks, curlews, and lapwings flying through the Brontës' texts.

The value of moorland biodiversity was acknowledged by the natural historians the Brontës read—Gilbert White and George Perkins Marsh acknowledge and praise it—as well as by those who read and valued the Brontës. Many scientists confirmed J. Horsfall Turner's assertion of the scientific value of *Jane Eyre*, whose

> word-pictures of these purple-heathered moorlands and upland valleys will be familiar to most readers. Here the geologist, in particular, may find ample interest. The millstone grit, the Cobling coal pit, the cold springs, the lateral valleys, the scattered boulders—each has a history for him. He traces the cold water to the hidden reservoir, the formation of the valleys to the remote glacial period, the coal to some great dislocation, and so on. (152)

James Spencer's essay of literary tourism, "A Geological Ramble from Halifax to Haworth" (1872), displays this "ample interest" as he uses the Brontës to add interest to his nature walk:

> Those who have read the works of Charlotte Brontë, will be familiar with the beautiful word-pictures of these moorland and upland valleys which abound in her works; and we who have traversed these moorlands, in season and out of season, can fully testify to the faithfulness of her descriptions (76–77).

Spencer's assertion that readers who tour Brontë country will be gratified by seeing fiction come to life and locals by faithful novelistic renderings shows how the beauties of the Brontës' novels were used as evidence of the beauties of the moors they depicted, and vice versa. Miall, too, refers readers to Charlotte's word-pictures as accurate yet appealingly vivid:

> The dull brown of a Grit moor, varied with pink when the heath is in bloom, distinguishes it at a glance from the short, fresh turf of the Mountain Limestone, thickly strewn with yellow pansies, orchids, and primroses.... In Charlotte Brontë's novels the Millstone Grit scenery is vividly described, in its beauty as well as in its desolateness; and the unimportant change of one word—sandstone for granite—renders the sketches of 'Jane Eyre' faithful pictures of the moors of South Craven. (*Geology* 603)

In enfolding *Jane Eyre* into his account of Craven Moor's flora and fauna, Miall's topography provides another example of how perceptions about Yorkshire moors and the scientific accuracy of the Brontës' representations of them always played a role in their reception history.

Miall's address to the Royal Society twenty years later, "On a Yorkshire Moor," clarifies the stakes of these conversations by addressing the problem of extinctions. Human-caused extinctions were known in Charlotte's day; in 1848, Hugh Edwin Strickland explained that "innumerable tribes have perished ... entirely from the inroads which the human race—that is, the increase of population, and the progress of agriculture and commerce—necessarily made upon their numbers" ("Dodo" 82). Miall is particularly interested in Yorkshire moor quadrupeds: the elephant, hippopotamus, rhinoceros, cave hyaena, European bison, true elk, and reindeer. Like Strickland, Miall blames humans for reducing Yorkshire's biodiversity:

> The disappearance of so many conspicuous species is commonly attributed to the glacial period, but I think that the action of man has been still more influential.... As men gradually rooted themselves in what are now the most populous countries of the world, the fauna and flora underwent sweeping changes. The forests were cleared, and trees of imported species

planted here and there. The land was drained, and fenced, and tilled. During the long attack of man upon wild nature many quadrupeds, a few birds, some insects and some plants are known to have perished. ("Moor" 638–39)

He also notes that Victorians continued to endanger moorland species by overstocking game and erecting dams (637). Worse still, humans threaten the moors themselves. "In our own time and country the moors waste faster than they form" (625), Miall writes, using *waste* not for the connotation that lets Gaskell heroize Charlotte at the expense of Haworth Moor, but to invoke the sense of loss in the term *mass wasting*. "Even the wastes are shrinking visibly," he observes:

> The moors themselves cannot resist the determined attack of civilized man. Thousands of acres which used to grow heather are now pastures or meadows.... The last defenses of the old flora are now being broken down; it is slowly giving ways to the social grasses, the weeds of commerce, and the broad-leaved herbs of the meadow, pasture, and hedge-row. The scale has been turned, as I think, not so much by climatic or geographical changes, as by the acts of man. (639)

Like Marsh, Miall synthesizes data collected and communicated in the Brontës' time to argue in favor of conservation efforts and to draw attention to human actions that hasten the negative conditions of the Anthropocene, particularly mass extinctions, increased numbers of extreme weather events and catastrophic mass movements, and the decay of biodiverse biomes:

> Every lover of the moors would be glad to know that they bid fair to be handed down to our children and our children's children without diminution or impoverishment. The reclaiming of the moors is now checked, though not arrested, and some large tracts are reserved as open spaces. But the impoverishment of the moors goes on apace. The gamekeeper's gun destroys much. Enemies yet more deadly are the collectors who call themselves naturalists, and the dealers who serve them. (639–40)

Miall's warnings have been heeded since the 1970s, when a tangle of bureaucratic classifications began to emerge that privileged Brontë country as a Special Protection Area (SPA), a Special Area of Conservation (SAC), and a Site of Special Scientific Interest (SSSI). The supporting documentation for these designations prominently features the family, using the moors' literary fame to justify conservation efforts (Natural England, "National Character

Area Profile"). Brontë country tourism has therefore brought attention to the value and fragility of the moors, even as, ironically, the tens of thousands of pilgrims annually trekking there place their own strains on the landscape.

TOURISTS, SCIENTISTS, AND CLERGYMEN: CROW HILL AS A SITE OF GEOLOGICAL DEBATE

I consider the 1824 Crow Hill bog burst the first instance of Brontë country tourism because it was Patrick's first letter to the *Leeds Mercury* that attracted visitors to the site (Lock and Dixon 252)—showing that fears about ecological change have always played a role in the cultural history of "Brontë country." Reacting to Patrick's letter, the *Mercury* editor sent investigators to determine if the burst signaled a larger geological instability that would destroy the woolen industry. This team, Barker notes, quoting from the *Mercury* and the *Intelligencer*, "joined the supposed 10,000 sightseers who came from all over Yorkshire to view the dramatic sight," though the *Intelligencer* later retracted this figure because only "200 horses passed through the Stanbury toll-bar" (152, 1014fn68). However, a foreman from a nearby mill reported that "several thousands of people in Coaches, Giggs, Horsemen, and on foot visited Crowhill" (quoted in Dewhirst 14). Though counting sightseers who did not pass to toll-bar would still not yield ten thousand rubberneckers, these figures emphasize the excitement the event generated. Rather than focus on correcting this figure, let us explore why it seemed as plausible to a skeptical investigative team as to the local observers who spread the figure. These locals voices are channeled by Atkins on his visit to Crow Hill. Abandoning precise numbers and technical terms, he conveys the rare geomorphic event in human terms:

> Two hundred years ago, when the bog burst, the moor here had been stripped down to the underlying shale; people came to look ... not only from the nearby villages, but from miles around. Ten thousand of them, it was said. Nothing like it had been seen in living memory.... The land had unsheaved itself, had shucked off its peat mantle. It was a sore, still streaming. But it settled, and scabbed, and today there was nothing to be seen of it; only the dip of the wet land that might, one torrential day, after a hot summer, release itself again. This was what we had come to look at: nothing. (183)

This passage combines homely metaphors to evoke the rhythms of rural daily life (the stripping down of laundry day, the sheaving and shucking of harvest) with anthropomorphic imagery of wounding (comparing this discharging of literally tons of peat to blood loss through a cut on a human body) to reduce the burst's incomprehensible scale to a human-sized one. Using indirect discourse to evoke village gossip and suddenly shifting from sober recitations of known facts to images of chaos, Atkins portrays the burst first and foremost as a *story* handed down from one generation to the next. Macbeth is not more shocked at the trees of Birnam Wood marching to Dunsinane Hill than tourists are witnessing the liquid tons of "black moory substance" miraculously transporting the contents of Haworth Moor to Leeds. Land is not supposed to act that way.

Atkins's homey, anthropoid images symbolically capture the mysterious bog burst, while also capturing the difficulty of finding the burst's material traces—or, more accurately, perceiving the burst through what is *not* there. The passage pulses with a frustrated awe at two fantastical acts of disappearance: the disappearance of the "peat mantle" that the land, taking on a surprising amount of power and intention, "unsheaved itself," and the disappearance *of that disappearance* as the bog gradually reconstituted. The "nothing" that Atkins hikes so far to see represents the disappearance of the evidence he so desires. Like the coverage found in Patrick's burst writings, scientific annals, and regional histories, Brontë tourism guides are preoccupied by conclusive physical evidence. Guide writers intrepidly hunt the most visually compelling evidence to link the burst to the real-life settings of the sisters' novels.[7] Visitors are exhorted to examine Crow Hill for telltale concavities and displaced boulders while walking from Ponden Kirk ("Penistone Crag") to Ponden Hall ("Thrushcross Grange") and thence to Wycoller ("Ferndean"). Signs of the desiccated bog are welcomed because tourists can physically encounter what was experienced by the Brontës, also superseded phenomena from two centuries ago. In 1824, this evidence was disturbingly apparent, as is attested by Patrick's letter in the *Intelligencer* on September 16—the burst's "extraordinary effects," the reverend claims, "are become so manifest to the most superficial observers" (*Letters* 53). In 1888, they were still perceptible to non-scientists, when Stuart's tourist guide, *The Brontë Country: Its Topography, Antiquities, and History*, identified the site by the stony signs remaining sixty-four years later. Stuart notes that the site now housed Keighley Corporation's reservoirs, where "a splendid water-shoot was showing to great advantage" and a "strong west wind was tossing the little lake into a wild confusion of miniature waves." A beck that "rushed along with full-toned vehemence" continues to pulse with the violence of the 1824 explosion (166). Still clearer signs of geological change surrounded Ponden House, where the children sheltered: "Huge boulders scattered around this hamlet testify to the extraordinary results occasioned by the bursting of the Crow Hill bog, which took place during Mr. Brontë's incumbency, and was the cause of his preaching a sermon, and writing a poem" (166–67). A footnote tips readers that both sermon and poem could be purchased as a twopence pamphlet at Brown's booksellers in Haworth village—another sign of the burst's significance for Brontë fans (167fn1). In 1894, Harwood Brierley's tour of real-life models for Wuthering Heights included the still-unstable bog, which "shakked like a jelly" (n.p.).

The bog burst continued to shape Brontë tourism in the twentieth century. In 1913, Whiteley Turner notes that Patrick's sermon and poem were exhibited as relics alongside Charlotte's boots and Keeper's collar at the Brontë Museum located above Haworth's Yorkshire Penny Bank (222). In 1948, Ernest Raymond informed prospective pilgrims that Emily was

> fascinated by Ponden Clough where she could see—as you may today—in the boulders along the glen, the traces of that old catastrophe. Secure, then, in our identification of Ponden Kirk with Peniston Crag, we had a mid-point on which to hang the wild moors of *Wuthering Heights*. We have found the desolation we can divide with Emily. (207)

Raymond's allusion to *Wuthering Heights*'s opening (in which Lockwood writes, "In all England, I do not believe that I could have fixed on a situation so completely removed from the stir of society.... Heathcliff and I are such a suitable pair to divide the desolation" [3]) uses the bog burst to link Emily and tourists by equating her with Heathcliff and Lockwood with tourists. The persistence of physical traces forges an emotional bond between Emily and fans eager to encounter her ghostly presence.[8] In 1969, Nancy Brysson Morrison's *Haworth Harvest* echoes Atkins's disbelief. Triply defining the explosion as "this upheaval of the earth itself, this shaking of the foundation, this moving of the immovable" (19), Morrison's waves of appositives attest to the burst's impossibility. In these Brontë country guides—Stuart in 1888, Brierley in 1894, Turner in 1913, Raymond in 1948, Morrison in 1969, Lemon in 1993, and Atkins in 2014—the rarity, severity, and suddenness of bog bursts, combined with lingering questions about their causes, foreclose a complete account of Crow Hill. This is true for scientists as well as Brontëans. In a 2007 paper, Dykes and Warburton decry the lack of scientific consensus about bursts while supporting their new scheme for classifying mass movements with a photograph from 2005 displaying the lingering effects of a 1989 bog burst at Crow Hill. Their interpretation of this photograph echoes the language of "manifestation" that Patrick uses to characterize the damage seen by the 1824 tourists (82). Moreover, the 1989 burst has Brontëan ties beyond this link. Charles Lemon notes that what became known as the Brontë Bridge on Sladen Beck was damaged by the 1824 event, and by floods in 1907 and in 1989, the latter of which is the most well-known example of the bridge's destruction (109). As the differences between Lemon's account and Dykes and Warburton's account indicate, though the 1989 event is known by Brontëans as a flood, it is characterized more accurately as another mass movement of Crow Hill bog—the one that Patrick predicted, showing the continued relevance of his bog-burst texts.

PATRICK BRONTË'S IMPROBABLE EARTHQUAKE: A SERMON OF GLOBAL ECOLOGICAL COLLAPSE

If the 1824 Crow Hill bog burst is central to the Brontës' cultural legacy, so too are the Brontës crucial for understanding the burst. Patrick's testimony, including his letters to newspaper editors and friends, his sermon, his poem, and the prefaces written for the two latter publications, continues to be of historical and scientific significance. These mass movements pose problems because the muddy, unstable sites remain difficult to analyze—so difficult that, for instance, the paper by Dykes and Warburton that included a photograph of Crow Hill was the first to propose a "formal classification scheme" for bursts. Discussing the 2003 Derrybrien bog burst, Lindsay and Bragg wryly admit, "It is difficult to say exactly what happened, partly because evidence was washed away" (x). Surprisingly few eyewitness accounts exist. Dianne Meredith writes, "Because most bog bursts happen at night, in the dead of winter, and in remote places, only a few have been witnessed" (323), and Matthias Jakob and Oldrich Hungr grumble, "Assembling historical accounts of debris flows is a bit like collecting postage stamps—the accumulation of unconsolidated trifles," which, in spite of their scientific worth, "often do not appear to be newsworthy except locally" (46). Like a rare stamp, Patrick's evidence is valuable. Lindsay and Bragg, for example, create their Table 4.2 from the "substantial detail of the 1824 bog burst on Crow Hill ... available from records made by and associated with the Reverend Patrick Brontë" (29). They cite Patrick's sermon and poem, as well as literary biographies and journal articles—an interesting instance of scientific citations of humanist scholarship.

Though literary critics have had far less use for Patrick's observations, especially his claim that an earthquake caused the burst. But their derision is largely unwarranted. Newspaper accounts, witness memoirs, and secondary sources float a number of plausible-sounding theories for the Crow Hill burst, including earthquakes, which appear as a potential cause alongside above- or below-ground flooding, a lightning strike, a waterspout, or the draining, creation, or collapse of an underground chamber. In the nineteenth century, earthquakes were known to trigger bog bursts; the *Second Report* on Irish bogs, published a decade before Crow Hill, mentions them while surveying the "various causes [that] have been assigned for this phenomenon," such as flooding or the "falling in of a subterranean vault," before agreeing with the "idea [that] generally prevailed among people on the spot": that earthquakes elsewhere caused "partial earthquakes" in England (190). It is also important to remember that the *Mercury*'s investigative team was primarily concerned with assuaging fears about the woolen industry and thus predisposed to contest theories that would compound that fear. The disparagement with which literary scholars treat Patrick's hypothesis is therefore unearned. Bob Duckett alleges that "his views on earthquakes were ridiculed" (245), while Barker quotes an anonymous *Mercury* letter that calls Brontë's account "really preposterous" and scoffs that the burst "alarmed our worthy minister" (153). Barnard and Barnard allege that "few were convinced then or later" of Patrick's burst writings, which it describes as merely an example of "his preaching style at its most vivid" (84). Gordon only pursues the burst's spiritual meaning (24), and Barker hypothesizes that he "obstinately refused to change his opinion" because his parishioners resisted the "spiritual thoughts the had hoped to inspire" (152). The scientific content of his burst writings is regarded solely as proof of his irascibility and impracticality.

But Patrick's account is, on balance, far more right than wrong. His explanations concerning the influence of groundwater, soil pipes, electricity, gas, and water pressure were in keeping with scientific consensus at the time. Geologists today, by pursuing both proximal and distal causes, still approach bog-burst etiology in a twofold manner and continue to use classification (as he does) to analyze bog bursts. Because bog bursts are poorly understood, contradictory conclusions circulate—sometimes in the very analyses that deride his obliviousness. Harman pinpoints methane gas as triggering of the mass movement (51), while John Sutherland says it was from "an eruptive subterranean water spout" (14) and Nancy Brysson Morrison from flooding alone (18). As Keighley wrote in 1879, his ethos benefiting from the distance of time,

> With all deference to the opinions of the Rev. P. Bronte and [Edward Baines of the *Leeds Mercury*], we think that the cause of the disruption is to be ascribed neither to an earthquake nor a waterspout, but simply to the pressure of the accumulated waters having become too great for the stability of their mossy embankment. (112)

Indeed, the conditions prevailing at Crow Hill offer a sufficient explanation: the bog was unstable for decades because a combination of natural and anthropogenic forces weakened the peat mass's tensile and shear strengths. In the drought of summer 1824, the upper networks of fibers holding in the liquid slurry dried and ripped at a few sites. (A local poet's lines that "the summer's heat the heaps of peat / Had dry'd in many a gaping chink" substantiate this deduction [Nicholson 42]). During the same period, the catotelm was critically weakened by fluctuating levels of water seepage through soil pipes and underground springs. Flooding in early September triggered the event by oversaturating the fragile bog. The virtue of this explanation is that it sounds reasonable, unlike the more sensational earthquake theory. But this explanation, as certain as I am of it, is not sufficient for understanding the burst's cultural and rhetorical richness; we must also appreciate why skilled writers draw contradictory lessons from it.

The confusion around the 1824 Crow Hill bog burst is the result not of Patrick's personal failings, but of a far more general—and generative—response to mass wastings. To establish a "lack of consistent terminology to describe peat failures," Warburton points to the proliferation of terms to describe them, including "debacles," "cloudbursts," "peat flow," and "peat slide," explaining that "[t]his confused terminology has partly arisen due to the difficulties in determining the particular type of failure" (166). A century before Warburton, Whiteley Turner's *A Spring-Time Saunter Round and About Brontë Land* (1913) addresses this terminological ambiguity. Describing "a birds-eye view of Ponden Valley," he identifies it as "the first recipient of the great bog-slide ... locally referred to as a 'Phenomenon,' 'Crow Hill Earthquake,' 'Crow Hill Bogburst,' and 'Crow Hill Flood'" (176). "Phenomenon," a term also used by Patrick in the title of his poem, renders the event inexplicable. The public's shock is emphasized. "Earthquake" prioritizes active debates about its etiology, emphasizing its causes. "Flood," a term also used by Atkins to describe the 1824 burst, foregrounds the peaty deluge's effects. This proliferation of monikers echoes the generous salting of hearsay in Turner's glib account and preserves the uncertainty generated by contradictory explanations. This is one reason why the burst presented, and presents, a rich topic for analysis: these tenacious but "inaccurate" explanations create a compellingly nuanced portrait of the event's broader significance. Patrick participates in a wider tradition of theorizing bog-burst etiology, inserting the Brontës into significant, ongoing scientific debates about the causes of geological change and natural disasters.

Patrick's vacillations therefore typify public and scientific responses to bog failures. After the *Mercury* printed his account, supplementing it with its editor's alternate theory, he wrote back on September 18 with some vehemence that "the phenomenon in question was what justly deserves the appellation of an earthquake" but admits humbly that his first letter was "written at an Inn, in great haste, and without the requisite premeditation" (quoted in Lock and Dixon, 252). This subtle step back accords with the measured clarification he sent to the *Intelligencer*:

> Owing to the damage that has already been done, and might possibly occur, it becomes a matter of no small moment to ascertain ... both a remedy and an antidote.... [T]he first step towards curing or preventing diseases, is a thorough knowledge of their cause. This knowledge, however, is not always easily acquired; nor is it easy in the instance under consideration, fully to ascertain the cause of all these extraordinary effects. (*Letters* 53)

Despite Patrick's humility, the *Intelligencer* article that concludes by rejecting his earthquake theory ("It seems, however, to have been merely the bursting of a large bog") begins by affirming his account, explaining that "we have since then had opportunities of ascertaining that it is perfectly correct" (51). The *Mercury* is equally appreciative. Both papers quote him extensively, concur that future bursts will follow, and echo his concerns about burst prevention. Notably, a *Mercury* article from September 11—which forms the sole or primary source on which most biographical and critical accounts rely—reiterates the difficult of ascertaining facts:

> No human being was on the spot to witness the commencement of this awful phenomenon, and of course we cannot arrive at an absolute degree of certainty as to its cause: the most probable one is the bursting of a waterspout. The suddenness and violence of the disruption strongly favors this supposition. It would evidently require a power acting with a great degree of momentum to move and break in pieces the large and almost solid masses of peat and turf which were forced down the hill, to say nothing of the detached rocks which were moved. (quoted in Keighley 111)

The article repackages Patrick's accurate observations as proof of a competing theory, lending through a multitude of numbers—distances, altitudes, and circumferences—an empirical air to their "supposition." The writers respond to the difficulties of communicating the burst's intensity by crafting a powerful emotional report: a "most amazing quantity of water was precipitated with a violence and noise of which it is difficult to form an adequate conception," and it is "impossible to form any computation of the quantity of earthy matter which has been carried down into the valley" (110). As a result, despite the paper's fastidious attention to numbers, the overwhelming impression left by their coverage is frustration at their lack of knowledge.

The journalists' frustration at inadequate conceptions and impossible computations cannot be relieved, yet the norms of reportage demand the authority that bog bursts resist. Into this vacuum of knowledge Patrick steps, making Crow Hill all the more fascinating as a historical event of scientific and literary consequence. A Cambridge graduate occupying a respectable position, the Reverend Brontë was the right person at the right place at the right time. The respect afforded to his account by newspaper editors (in the immediate aftermath), by historians (in the five decades after), and by scientists (both then and now) reflects the rarity of his proximity to the event and the sophistication of his scientific knowledge. It is due to Patrick's moral authority and intellectual credibility that scientists know so much about this bog burst. After all, it was his letter that drew the *Mercury* editor and his team, as well as thousands of sightseers, to Crow Hill in the first place. His sermon betrays some anxiety about his role in making the event a platform for sensationalized disagreement: "Several graceless persons," he recalls in horror, "wrangled and disputed with each other, even in the very bottom of the cavities, and on their edges" (*A Sermon* 217). The prefatory note to his verse account also signals discomfort with his role in setting the terms of the debates about (and in) Crow Hill. After having crafted a long scientific discussion that his "young readers" could understand, he abruptly ends the preface with the curt dismissal, "Whether this may be called the disruption of a bog, or an earthquake, is of no great consequence, either as it relates to the interest it may excite, or the effects it has produced" (*The Phenomenon* 203–4). But it was too late. Patrick, in initiating the flurry of bog-burst writings by himself and others, had already set the terms of the discussion. Without Patrick's writings about the burst, very little would have been known about this natural disaster, and the debates that resulted from the burst would have not have occurred.

Patrick Brontë is therefore, as I argue elsewhere, a popularizer of science whose bog-burst writings reflect a proto-Anthropocenic awareness of human responsibilities for local environmental shifts.[9] He also occupies the important hybrid role, somewhere between naturalist and artist, that Jesse Oak Taylor identifies as first defined by the early environmentalist George Perkins Marsh (1801–1882), who "compared the observer of ecological change to the poet, the painter, and the sculptor" (*Sky* 2). Taylor further knits together science and literature by arguing that Victorian literature actively engaged with human-caused climate change. As Marsh and Taylor recognize, both naturalists and artists make the Anthropocene apprehensible, pushing audiences to perceive ecological change where they had not. Indeed, one recurring trope in Marsh's *Man and Nature* is his visualization of the imperceptible to support his pioneering articulation of the Anthropocene. In one passage, Marsh observes that spaces "untrodden by man ... are subject to change only from geological influences so slow in their operation that the geographical conditions may be regarded as constant and immutable" (34). But he then reconstructs these influences with his assemblage of minutely observed details that reveal these microscopic changes. Like Marsh, Patrick assembles an archive of global examples from the past and present to emphasize the current ecological change common to all. In addition to "Etna, Vesuvius, and other burning mountains," which he calls "earthquakes on the grandest and most appalling scale," he names more recent ones, including some cited by Marsh (*A Sermon* 213).

Like Marsh, Patrick's sermon assembles a prehistory of ecological destruction narratives to make his audience to feel culpable, listing the destruction of Korah, Dathan, and Abriam, the phenomenon that "quaked" Mount Sinai "at the delivery of the Ten Commandments," and "the horrid opening which swallowed up the Israelitish rebels in the wilderness" as examples of natural disasters by which God smote sinners (215). His sermon's epigraph—from William Cowper's "The Task," inspired by the unusual weather patterns of 1783 resulting from volcanic pollution—inserts Patrick's bog-burst productions in a lineage of authors (including Jane Austen and the Lake Poets) influenced by these 1783 events (Cowper 86fn57–64). In the lines Patrick quotes, a stunned Cowper surveys these earthquakes, heat waves, fogs, floods, fireballs, meteors, and thunderstorms, questioning, "When were the winds / Let slip with such a warrant to destroy? / When did the waves so haughtily o'erleap / Their ancient barriers deluging the dry?" (85). An Anthropocenic awareness of extreme weather flickers in his inference that "th' old / And crazy earth has had her shaking fits / More frequent, and foregone her usual rest" (86). Patrick's use of *wrangle* for the pugilists in the collapsed bog may stem from lines elsewhere in "The Task," which shares his interpretation of natural disasters as God-given signs demanding moral reform:

> Is it a time to wrangle, when the props
> And pillars of our planet seem to fail,
> And nature with a dim and sickly eye
> To wait the close of all? But grant her end
> More distant, and that prophecy demands
> A longer respite, unaccomplished yet (86)

Because the "dim and sickly eye" of a nature no longer pure does not indicate immediate apocalypse, Cowper, rather than fixate on individual spiritual salvation, advises interpersonal and international cooperation to ensure that nature's "end" will be "more distant": "Sure there is need of social intercourse / Benevolence and peace and mutual aid / Between the nations" (85). In quoting Cowper and biblical disasters, Patrick's bog-burst writings construct a global, textual history of environmental disaster that places the 1824 Crow Hill bog burst within that genealogy to leverage his authority as a curate and witness to advocate for both spiritual and earthly reform.

When Patrick hedges or blusters about his contested theory about the origin of the burst, he does so to protect the integrity of his *moral* classification of the event as an earthquake, which allows him to construct a global history of natural disasters and set the 1824 burst within that history. Having set Crow Hill at the end of this genealogy of natural disaster narratives, using them as keys for interpreting his own, Patrick reverses this rhetorical move in his sermon's survey of the bog site. Using his local phenomenon to generalize about global populations, he recalls,

> On the day after the earthquake, when the fame of it had reached the inhabitants of Haworth and surrounding parishes, motley groups of people from all quarters, hastened in to view the scene; and exhibited, in miniature, a picture of the world—a picture not merely of the inhabitants of Haworth, and Keighley, and Bradford, but of England, and France, and Spain, and the four quarters of the globe. (*A Sermon* 216)

The sermon extends Haworth's fifteen minutes of boggy "fame" by reporting details about local environmental conditions to the "motley groups" whom he hopes will read his pamphlets. Among causes of earthquakes, he lists the industrialization of mining operations. "The dreadful effects of these fire-damps when kindled," he deplores, "are but too well known in this country to need an illustration; sometimes in deep and extensive coal-pits, where there is not a free and continual flow of air, explosions take place, that scorch and force all things round them; and, in an instant of time, hurry numbers of souls into eternity" (214). Just as the sermon's tour of the collapsed bog trains his readers' attention to the peaty soil, so do these details about local conditions emphasize the physical earth. Not solely a convenient symbol of the Second Coming, the bog is palpable and linked to present-day human actions. Immediacy and culpability also animate Patrick's verse account. In the "Extraordinary Disruption," Patrick depicts a modernizing rural space, Anthropocenic in its endangered fragility and interspecies intimacy:

> Pale, trembling mortals, flee on either side.
> The clanking engines, and the busy mill,
> In thick obstruction, deep immersed, stand still.
> Grim devastation lords it o'er the plain,—
> The gardens bloom, the mead, the yellow grain,
> The green plantation, and the brambly wood,
> Lie deeply buried in the murky flood. (207)

Blanketing humans, flora, fauna, and machines, the "murky flood" unites its human and nonhuman victims in their common Anthropocenic fate. As Patrick recounts, the "thick obstruction" of bogwaters smeared "black moory substance" across the region (*Letters* 51), coating it with industrial byproducts because the ash-absorbing *Sphagnum* mosses in the top three centimeters of peat bogs trap carbonaceous substances made airborne by burning fossil fuels (Le Roux and Shotyke 204). Like White, Marsh, Bewick, Davy, and Miall, Patrick depicts moors as hybrid, emergent Anthropocene spaces—both natural and artificial, human and nonhuman—but his telescoping between local and global contexts and juxtaposing of literary, biblical, and historical catastrophes makes the role played by industrialization uniquely visible.

TWO BRONTË POEMS, TWO APPROACHES TO ANTHROPOCENIC RESPONSIBILITY

Patrick's "Extraordinary Disruption"—its full printed title, with the burst date marred by a printer's error, is "The Phenomenon; or an Account in Verse of the Extraordinary Disruption of a Bog, which took place in the Moors of

Haworth on the 12th day of September, 1824"—divides 184 lines of heroic couplets into ten verse paragraphs of unequal lengths. It opens with a mannered description of a beautiful moorland at twilight: "The scene is passing fair," but for "a red halo, whose portentous glare, / Or said, or seemed to say to all—'beware!'" (204). This "red halo" translates the copper-colored sky of Patrick's technical letters to the *Mercury* and *Intelligencer* into poetic language that foreshadows his imagery of cherubs guarding the Garden of Eden with flaming swords after Adam and Eve's fall. Ever the clergyman, he takes Genesis 3.24 for his text—"So he drove out the man; and he placed at the east of the garden of Eden Cherubims, and a flaming sword which turned every way, to keep the way of the tree of life"—figuring the 1824 bog burst as another fall. Like his sermon, the poem alludes to many catastrophes caused by human sin, including Noah's flood, which one expects (due to the hydraulic similarities uniting deluge and burst) to occupy pride of place. But by ordering them chronologically, Patrick emphasizes how human sin causes multiple exiles: we are always being booted from paradise, always losing ecosystems. This simultaneity breaks down the linearity implied by his chronology, giving the impression that man and earth mutually pollute one another. In his description of Adam and Eve's fateful pomegranate, it is polluted—"the poison ran / Of that fair fruit infernal, the whole man / Polluting; the bad juice, with subtle flow, / Diffused itself throughout"—but it is only after their snack that "death's dark gloom, / Usurp'd the seat of Eden's lovely bloom" (205). This sense of continuous loss and confused causality are constitutive tropes of the Anthropocene. As my Introduction argues, the scientific search for a single "golden spike" will likely never end. Newly proposed times, spaces, and agents continue to offer new, contradictory accounts of human-caused environmental change. Patrick's archive of disasters similarly proliferates golden spikes, showing again his natural theology's affinity with scientists and their methods. This technique also shapes *Villette*, which, chapter 4 argues, is a sequence of golden spikes to depict a continuously embattled ecosystem.

Further parallels can be drawn in the stern declarations that open and close Charlotte's second novel, *Shirley*. It begins by warning that no romance can be found on its pages and ends by describing a pastoral valley's industrialization, whose costs are symbolized by local folklore that alleges that fairies went extinct when the first mill was erected. Patrick's preoccupation with man's first fall similarly allows him situate ecosystem loss as a narrative problem—as an issue of readers, writers, and storytelling. To critique writers' nostalgic desires to depict an Eden no longer accessible, Patrick punctures the bucolic peace of his own poem's twilight scene:

> Where are those days, alas! by poets feign'd,
> Those spotless days, when every virtue reign'd;
> When Eden bloom'd without one tree of sin,
> And no fell serpent, guileful, lurk'd within:
> Those days, where are they? In the poet's brain,
> Whose warm fancy taught the flattering strain;
> Who painted what he wish'd, not what he knew,
> Deluding, and deluded as he drew.
> E'er since the flaming sword, in heavenly strife,
> With fiery circles coped the tree of life (204)

By insisting that "spotless days" exist now only "in the poet's brain," this passage unmasks soothing pastorals as self-serving and illusory. Patrick alleges that poets delude readers with this self-service, emphasizing human responsibility and supplementing the advice for sound reading found in his preface with rules for good writing. His reference to coppicing—"the flaming sword ... coped the tree of life"—also touches on post-Edenic ethical human action. This traditional practice, rather than fell centuries-old trees, annually harvests fast-growing shoots that emerge from stumps to provide a sustainable source of firewood. This culling of young branches from a mother tree coped by "flaming sword" recapitulates the temporal logic of periodic natural disasters that reenact the ur-disaster of man's first fall in worlds that have already fallen. Though his natural theology looks backward to the original fall and forward to the apocalypse, Patrick gathers biblical and historical disasters coppiced from the first fall into multiple branches (letters, sermons, poem, prefaces) that analyze the burst.

Through such gatherings, Patrick's body of bog-burst writings trace a pattern of returns to familiar touchstones. Reusing the same historical disasters and the same details from Crow Hill does not degenerate into barren repetition; differences in each iteration demonstrate intensifying degeneration. His poem's four epic lists of moorland fauna perform the theme of extinction. With each return to the list, the number of species and living organisms diminishes. First, pre-burst descriptions display the gamboling of larks, linnets, blackbirds, fish, hares, moorcocks, and cattle guarded by swain and milkmaid. In second epic list, just before the eruption, cats, crickets, rooks, "frighten'd" gulls, "sagacious" bees, along with a heron and a "conscious" heifer, "scream" as they attempt to flee "their lov'd home, the safe sequester'd grove" (205). As sludge rockets into the air, the third catalog emphasizes animals endangered by humans: "startled moorcocks" attempt to escape "fleeing gunners" while "peasants" (no longer solicitous swain and milkmaid) callously ignore their "bleating sheep" and "cattle," who expire with "a loud, last dismal low" (206). The land too is drowned: "trees and rocks, and earthy mounds / . . . in dread confusion, tumble in the waves" (207). By the fourth epic list, species that can flee have disappeared. The few that remain are dying. The "finny tribe" that "sunk in muddy suffocation die," as do "snowy geese, that crop the grassy brim" and "motley ducks, that gabbling, featly swim / With unsuspecting joy, await the roar / Of that thick flood" (207). Drawing on his intimate knowledge of the moors to incorporate natural details that other burst writings overlook, Patrick describes total extinction: "All nature sinks, and dies beneath the sway / Of those black waves, that ponderous force their way" (207). His biodiverse litanies dwell on the intimate relations between human and nonhuman to condemn the disruption of Crow Hill's fragile equilibrium by the human actions that unleash God's wrath upon it as collateral damage.

Yet Patrick's overt interspecies sympathy is meant to inspire readers' sense of personal guilt instead of a disinterested love for the sacrificed animals. This is evident when he compares the 1824 burst to the biblical deluge: if this event inspires horror, then, he wonders, "How dread the horrors keen, that thrilling ran // When the vast deluge, fathomless, was hurl'd / A shoreless ocean, round a guilty world!" (207). Patrick reserves his most dramatic diction for imagining the hypothetical loss of human lives "had not God, who stills the ocean's roar, // Said to the wide, the deep disporting hill— / 'Restrain thy foaming fury'" (206). Privileging the human and the afterlife over the nonhuman and earthbound, his anthropocentric focus decenters his multispecies sympathies precisely when he contemplates the near deaths of his children. He draws parallels between Noah's paternal role and his own without mentioning the animals saved inside Noah's ark or lost outside of it. When his review of 2 September reaches the moment when his children were most in danger, running toward Ponden Hall, Patrick sighs in relief, "Even when he seems to roam without a rein, / God counts the links of his eternal chain" (207). Without divine mercy, the "country round had swum one murky sea; / Whilst Albion loud had rais'd her plaintive wail, / And he who writes had never told the tale" (207). Like the sermon, the poem telescopes between the local and the national by allegorizing a domestic drama, thus affirming the scientific value of lay witnesses—if they are keen observers. Accordingly, this reference to "he who writes" the "tale" diverts attention from the scene of crisis to the scene of writing. Survivors—if they are skilled writers, he suggests—can document ecological crises, trace their causes, and advocate ethical responses.

That Patrick Brontë's children were internalizing, adapting, rejecting, or otherwise responding to his suggestions at the time of the burst is affirmed by critical consensus about the "mask episode," also in 1824, when Patrick asked his children to don a mask to respond honestly to difficult questions. Caldwell and Goff both affirm that young Charlotte echoed the bitextual structure of her father's natural theology when, asked to name her favorite book, she answered the Bible, and when asked for her second favorite, responded with "the Book of Nature" (Gaskell 39–40). I argue that, later, she responds to Patrick's call to *writerly* action for expressing humans' fallenness and responding to environmental catastrophe. Chapters 2 to 4 document how Charlotte's novels become less anthropocentric as she recorded the increasing damages levied on the Earth by human actions, making her heroines intent on tending their fallen world. This worldly determination differs from Patrick's anthropocentrism, which privileges the salvation of all human souls in the Second Coming. For his desired end requires the Earth's total destruction. Patrick's attitude is not uncommon, even for one concerned about the ecological health of his surroundings; James McKusick diagnoses an anthropocentrism in Gilbert White's work, for example, as the Hampshire clergyman (like his counterpart in Yorkshire) believed and preached "traditional Christian doctrine that the Earth was created for human purposes" (26). Regarding nature as "a source of scientific knowledge and aesthetic pleasure," White blithely pursued various "intrusive activities"—such as hacking through woody obstacles during his walks or collecting and pinning insect specimens—leading McKusick to conclude that White's "love for the natural world remains anthropocentric at a deep ethical and emotional level" (27). It is the same for Patrick Brontë. In his final verse, he forgets his empathy in anticipation of the "heavenly joy" of the faithful, who will sing "Hosannah to the King of kings" until "the new earth and heavens wide echo round, / The sweet, triumphal, immortal sound!" (208). Here, the poem swerves from multispecies empathy to anthropocentric indifference. Like the *Mercury* article that skillfully positions the near-tragic loss of children playing on Crow Hill as a pathetic appeal to advance the journalist's agenda, Patrick's awed reflections on his family's near destruction pivot from distressing descriptions of drowned animals, uprooted trees, scarred fells, and polluted rivers to celebrations of the perfect new world God will provide after the apocalypse. The salvation of Patrick's parishioners requires ecological destruction—an exchange troubling not only in its willingness to sacrifice the nonhuman, but also in its cognitive sleight-of-hand, which strategically conflates scientific phenomena and moral states.

Twelve years later, Emily would reverse Patrick's anthropocentric pattern by celebrating her experience of the burst while deploring its ultimate ecological consequences. Though "High Waving Heather" (1836) does share many similarities with Patrick's "Extraordinary Disruption," and though Atkins argues that Patrick's poem directly influenced her rendition of the bog burst (178), Emily's anthropocentric celebration of human strength and determination differs from the clerical complacency with which Patrick stoically accepts the denudation of Crow Hill bog, the contamination of local rivers, and the sacrifice of trees and animals as a fair exchange for reminding his parishioners to think seriously about saving their own souls. "High Waving Heather" opens with a verse declaring that joy is to be found not in the hereafter, but in the burst's earthly violence. This misanthropic attraction to dangerous natural forces does not admit of the joyous farewell with which Patrick rejects the degraded post-Edenic Earth in favor of the perfect new world to come. Patrick's language of compulsion and helplessness—twice he specifies that the storm is "resistless" and indicates that the correct response to is to flee the fallen world (*Brontëana* 207)—could not differ more from Emily's resistant speaker, whose identification with the storm frees her soul from its hated restraints:

> High waving heather, 'neath stormy blasts bending,
> Midnight and moonlight and bright shining stars;
> Darkness and glory rejoicingly blending,
> Earth rising to heaven and heaven descending,
> Man's spirit away from its drear dungeon sending,
> Bursting the fetters and breaking the bars. (*Complete Poems* 34)

Willingly thralled by the storm, fetters burst and bars broken, the staunch speaker imagines Earth and Heaven converging. Patrick disentangles two separate events from the feared burst; as Barker notes (153), his sermon dwells on the judgment of souls and Earth's destruction in the apocalypse, whereas *The Phenomenon* revolves around the creation of a new Earth. For Emily, a single event is occurring, it is happening *now*, and it is desired. We need no new Earth, no matter how fallen this one may be. In this poem, as Marsden argues of her other works, Emily "rejects the redemptive potential of a wholly otherworldly heaven in favor of an eschaton based on resurrection and recreation." Caring more about each human being's "sacred bond with the earth," the speaker uses the storm to show how this bond can survive "the final collapse of boundaries between the human subject and the numinous life that animates the whole of creation" (Marsden 125). Indeed, in "High Waving Heather," all natural forces are welcomed, whether tending toward "darkness" or "glory;" in the immediate context of stormy chaos, they collapse the psychological and material boundaries between man and earth. Goff writes that the *devoirs*, the philosophical essays written in French when she and Charlotte attended the Hegers' pensionnat in Brussels, eschew natural theology's anthropocentrism (482). Ivonne Defant argues that for Emily, "nature 'spoke' its own language," as Patrick believed, "but that nature interfered with human matters without being exclusively conditioned by a supreme divine will" (39).

The idea that nature "spoke" is similarly central to "High Waving Heather," whose soul-freeing storm is constructed largely of sound. "Rejoicingly blending" the bog burst's constituent noises of wind, rain, river, and thunder, the poem bypasses the anthropocentric assumption that human salvation requires the Earth's destruction. Like Emily's best-known poem, "No Coward Soul Is Mine," it inspires courage, not fear, and affirms the value of earthly life in the face of death, explaining the second verse's characterization of life-threatening forces as "life-giving":

> All down the mountain sides, wild forest lending
> One mighty voice to the life-giving wind;
> Rivers their banks in the jubilee rending,
> Fast through the valleys a reckless course wending,
> Wider and deeper their waters extending,
> Leaving a desolate desert behind. (*Complete Poems* 34)

The bog burst's unifying force blends the shrieks of "wild forests," the "life-giving wind," and the "jubilee rending" of rivers into "one mighty voice." Equally as effective as the storm at blending sounds is the poem's incantatory repetition of the present participle suffix, -*ing*, to end twelve of the poem's eighteen lines. The dying falls of these shared present participle endings unite these clanging, disparate sounds, softening the violence of the trochaic feet beginning each line with a bold bang. Father and daughter both create brash sonic palettes, but whereas Patrick showcases cacophony, using onomatopoeia to inspire pious fear, Emily develops euphony to craft a more ambiguous moral message. Her speaker merges humans with nature in a single event, a celebration of power unleashed. A restrained but not monotonous rhyme scheme—abaaab acaaac deddde—lends sinuous movement the poem, whose tidily stark division of eighteen lines into three verses of six lines apiece is softened by subtle variations in line lengths. Lines of ten, eleven, or twelve syllables roughly alternate longer with shorter lines but proceed in no fixed order. Where Patrick's stalwart heroic couplets march the reader with military precision toward a biblically foregone conclusion, the reader of Emily's poem dizzily follows the unpredictable "wending" path of the peaty morass. The fastidious elisions and halving caesurae that maintain the iambic pentameter of the "Extraordinary Disruption" are eschewed in the unbalanced "High Waving Heather," where caesurae are offset and elisions inactive.

Rather than metrically correct the bog burst's unpredictability, Emily retains it—all the better to underscore the primary themes of the poem's final verse, change and uncertainty. Paradoxes abound as the storm is both "roaring like thunder" and "like soft music sighing":

> Shining and lowering and swelling and dying,
> Changing for ever from midnight to noon;
> Roaring like thunder, like soft music sighing,
> Shadows on shadows advancing and flying,
> Lightning-bright flashes the deep gloom defying,
> Coming as swiftly and fading as soon. (*Complete Poems* 34)

Sharp contrasts jump out from the cushioning cloth woven by the verse's susurrating sibilance and the extra unstressed syllables produced by polysyndeton through Emily's repetition of "and" in lieu of commas. Antitheses—lowering/swelling, midnight/noon, roaring/sighing, bright/gloom, shining/fading—proliferate visual, aural, and conceptual opposites, allowing the storm, the speaker, and the soundscape of the poem to "change for ever" during its brief disturbance. Ten percent the length of Patrick's poem and lacking the explanation-filled prologue and epilogue that, like the ooze of peaty sludge slowing down in its path from Stanbury to Leeds, swell her father's poem to nearly two hundred lines of trudging pentameter, "High Waving Heather" is as brief, violent, and irregular as the initial explosion. Its galloping rhythm rushes readers past the squeezed-in extra syllables, while the abrupt end of the storm itself constitutes the poem's own end, refusing to resolve the paradoxes generated by the previous lines. A poem of pure change, it breathlessly revels in nowness, in crisis. Its sheer musicality seduces the reader into sharing the speaker's fierce affection for the storm and cool disregard for the dangers she exposes herself to—as well as for the ecological damages that the still-cooler morning light would bring.

But should we love a storm-filled world? Should our identification with the non-human revolve around power? And should human freedom be so reliant on natural disaster? There is a whiff of anthropocentrism in the poem's idea that humans can unleash their own power by absorbing natural forces. But a slight twist in vowel sounds works subtly against this anthropocentrism. The short "e" harmonies of the first two verses' multiple end rhymes, which glossily slip from one word to another through the change of a single letter or addition or deletion of a syllable within a shared *-ending* suffix—bending, blending, descending, sending, lending, rending, wending, extending—sharpen in the third verse. Here, the hard "i" of dying, sighing, flying, and defying trimly snip the drawl of the near monorhyme curtailing the dreamy fugue of circulating *sh-* and *n-* sounds to prepare the reader for the storm's sudden cessation in the final line, "Coming as swiftly and fading as soon." The repetition of the hard "i" in the third verse harmonizes with the second verse's "behind," tightening the transition between the second and third verses and calling attention to "wind/behind," the end rhyme connecting the second verse's second and sixth lines. Visually, this combination initially scans as a perfect rhyme, but the third verse's harder sounds reframe it as exclusively an eye rhyme. Distinct from "stars/bars" and "noon/soon," the perfect rhymes in the corresponding second and sixth lines of the opening and closing verses, it forms the poem's sole slant rhyme. Reexamining this special case of "wind/behind" after having read the third verse reveals that the wind, though "life-giving," is left without a completing assonant partner. Sonically left out in the cold, the "wind" at the end of the line jarringly disrupts the "one mighty voice" of the line's first two feet. Retrospectively, we see that "behind" is a turning point at which the soft, multiple *-ending* rhymes of lines one, three, four, five, seven, nine, ten, and eleven yield to ones based on the hard "i" vowel. To put it differently, the rhyme scheme—abaaab acaaac deddde—places emphasis on the second "c" because this is where the "a" rhymes are replaced by "d" rhymes. The upshot is that the poem pivots around the twelfth line, "Leaving a desolate desert behind"—not coincidentally the poem's only line about the storm's damages. The hard "i" shared by "behind" (ending the last line of the second verse) and "dying" (ending the first line of the third verse) invites the reader to speed callously past this melancholy pause to maximize the thrilling power of the driving perfect rhymes that resume in the third verse. In terms of the poem's anthropocentrism, this mismatched rhyme inserts the thin end of the wedge. "High Waving Heather" tempts its readers to be seduced by excitement of witnessing the ecological catastrophes by which nature, as Marsh warned, would rise up to avenge the wrongs of man, certainly "leaving a desolate desert behind."

Readers must choose between vicariously adopting the narrator's identification with the powerful storm that frees her soul and excavating the vein of loss whose subterranean presence is indicated, much like a gritstone outcropping on Haworth Moor, by the off-key rhyme penetrating the smooth surface of *-ing* suffixes. Emily does not make a choice but merely poses the dilemma, combining polysyndeton and antithesis to amplify the poem's unresolved contradictions. Unlike Patrick, who makes the moral he concludes from Crow Hill abundantly, even overdeterminedly, clear through his use of multiple genres, stark binaries, classificatory schemes, and disaster archives, Emily quietly encodes the moral compromise that secures the speaker's joy at the cost of the desolation and desertification of the ground beneath her. She suspends the interpretations, dividing this desolation between her speaker and her reader.

Other poems dwell more fixedly on this dampened note of sadness for the desert left behind. Emily's Gondal poems, with their emphasis on grieving survivors, exile, battles, and imprisonment, foreground environmental devastation through their common motif of homesickness. While my conclusion chapter addresses this nostalgia for lost ecosystems in the Brontës' poetry, comparing two versions of "Why ask to know the date—the clime?" will show how Emily's other poems unambiguously criticize humans' complicity in destroying their landscapes. In the first draft of September 1846, a soldier recalls with revulsion his own violent participation in civil war. His opening question (the poem's title) reflects this shame. Even while confessing to his own complicity, he secures his anonymity by refusing to name the time and place of his most savage behavior. This landscape's destruction is tripled: the soldier's poem erases its destruction from history by refusing to identify the denuded land for posterity; the military campaign scars and strews the battlefield with its wreckage, a mixed burden of bodies, buildings, and weapons; and the wasted harvests, neglected farm animals and machinery, and bloodied fields disrupt the pastoral rhythms and practices that had, according to the speakers, harmonized man, animal, plant, and lands over previous cycles of agricultural production. "It was the autumn of the year, / The time of labouring peasants dear," yet, "Week after week, from noon to noon," the work of harvest is first ignored, then perverted by war, "Trod out and ground by horses' feet," or "kneaded on the threshing-floor / With mire of tears and human gore" (*Complete Poems* 183). These unholy mixtures desanctify the land—"Some said they thought that heaven's pure rain / Would hardly bless those fields again" (183)—enacting another fall from Eden as man's action spiritually pollutes his landscape.

Watching the slaughter of soldiers and the decimation of fields, civilians and veterans begin to devalue life. Having "learnt, from length of strife / of civil war and anarchy, / To laugh at death and look on life / With somewhat lighter sympathy" (*Complete Poems* 183), they are desensitized to the acts of violence that caused such losses. These early lines serve as a thesis statement that brings coherence to Emily's unfinished draft, which clocks in at 264 lines. Her second draft of May 1848 retains the original speaker and scenario but may be considered a full rewrite, its twenty-five lines occupying 90 percent less space than the first draft. In this condensed field for poetic action, Emily omits a scene of wartime treachery in which the speaker steals from a comrade and breaks his promise to take care of the dying man's young daughter. Emphasis shifts from human to nonhuman victims, as the 1848 version maintains the original lines about the ruined fields and stipulates that this ruination occurs both at home and in "foreign sod." Four revised lines, "Our corn was garnered months before, / Threshed out and kneaded-up with gore; / Ground when the ears were milky sweet / With furious toil of hoofs and feet" (190), shift attention to violent verbs ("threshing-floor" becomes "threshed out" and moves to prominence as the line's first foot) and interspecies mixing ("hoofs and feet" together destroy the harvest, replacing the first draft's uniting of "tears and human gore"). Whereas the personal narrative at the heart of the first draft, like Patrick's burst writings, draws readers to consider the moral responsibility of each individual, Emily's second draft asks what such violence means for our understanding of humanity in general—a question that, chapter 2 shows, is central to *Jane Eyre*. Pointing to the gory aftermath of battle, the speaker ironizes, "There dwelt our own humanity / Power-worshippers from earliest time, / Foot-kissers of triumphant crime / Crushers of helpless misery" (190). More than the storm-chaser of "High Waving Heather," the disillusioned soldier critiques human tendencies to glorify power, to relish in its forceful manifestations and to desire to take part in them, sounding the same wary note that Miall and Marsh sound to prophesy the destruction of valued landscapes by human action.

Sir Humphry Davy also named warfare as a force of anthropogenic ecosystemic degradation. *Consolations* condemns "the devastations of war, the effects of the destructive zeal of bigotry, the predatory fury of barbarians seeking for concealed wealth under the foundations of buildings and tearing from them every metallic substance" (273–74). He links these examples to less overt forms of anthropogenic change, characterizing agriculture, settlement, and deforestation as processes by which man "converts her rocks, her stones, her trees into forms of palaces, houses, and ships; he employs the metals found in the bosom of the earth ... imprisons air by water, and tortures water by fire" (274). Davy's personifications, making nature a "she" (as does Marsh), water and air capable of being "tortured" and "imprisoned," solicits interspecies empathy in the same way Emily transforms horses into weapons and sheaves of grain into trampled gore in "Why ask to know the date—the clime?" These startling depictions of human/nonhuman interactions destabilize strict boundaries between the human and nonhuman and complicate theories of agency—a destabilization Charlotte experimented with in her second published novel, *Shirley*. This interspecies redistribution of agency also seems to cause disturbances in the flow of time: the monitory red halo of Patrick's "Extraordinary Disruption" signals the erasure not only of landscapes but also of clearly defined moments, as in "Why ask to know the date—the clime?" The textual conjuring of bad weather as temporal aberrations will be seen again in *Jane Eyre* and *Villette*, whose heroines, like Emily's speakers, face their own anthropocentrism when they survey the physical damage wrought by the storms whose useful prophecies they heed.

The aberrant temporalities that the Brontës construct for testing their characters' willingness to face their complicity in environmental degradation can be seen in the moors themselves. Time slows in bogs, whose anaerobic conditions uncannily preserve organic materials and form the peat that is prized for its slowness of burn yet, as Rotherham notes, was referred to as "combustible earth" during the Renaissance both because peat could be used as fuel and because the bogs from which it came were known to burst suddenly (*Peat* 9). Atkins elaborates, "Moor time is stone time, tectonic time" because each moor is shaped slowly by "epic processions of ice, million-year cataracts, molten injections, marginal hardenings, piecemeal exposure," whose slow movements make the moors seem timeless. "But the moor is not always gradual," he notes, contrasting stone time—the deep time of geology—first to the three-hundred-year chunk of time required to produce twelve inches of new peat and then to the very short duration of bog bursts (172–73). The Crow Hill burst taught this temporal paradox to Emily:

> The moor had become, for Emily, not just fugitive and perilous, but a forum for divine communication. Even in this land they knew so well, the ground beneath your feet might be made to give way, might 'erupt' and liquefy and send a punishing wall of sludge into the peopled valleys below.... [T]he moor's timelessness had been rudely skewed; it was a signal to her not of nature's indifference but rather its wilfulness, its deep-lying violence. And yet they had been spared. The moor, which might have drowned them all, had not. (176–78)

Indeed, Patrick and Emily stress the suddenness of the burst, finding its precipitous appearance and its brevity equally shocking. Emily compares the phenomenon's end to a lightning strike. "Coming as swiftly and fading as soon" (*Complete Poems* 24), the speaker observes nostalgically, ending the poem with an abruptness rivaling the burst's own. Patrick, by contrast, exclaims with unmixed relief, "But as the fiercest passion soonest dies, // So this vast flood, that foam'd with loudest roar, / Was, self-exhausted, soonest heard no more" (*The Phenomenon* 207). But though the "vast flood" recedes, its ecological effects do not. Writing of traces of the 1824 event, Patrick recalls how rocks were dislodged from the strata underlying the bog:

> So, rocks on rocks, pil'd by the foaming flood,
> All its vast force with trembling base withstood;
> Till the indignant waves collecting fast,
> Form'd a dark lake, urged by the incumbent blast;
> And push'd at once, with wide resistless sway,
> The mighty mass, 'midst thund'ring sounds, away (206)

Certainly, moor time is tectonic time, but the Crow Hill bog burst showed the Brontës that it is a paradoxical sort of time, both long and short. Not all geological changes occur over deep time.

It is important to linger over representations of sudden, catastrophic geological changes during events like 1824's extraordinary disruption because so much scholarship on science in nineteenth-century literature is concerned with representations of deep time that responded to the geological excavations revealing the Earth to be substantially, almost unthinkably, older than previously thought. But significant changes in the Earth happen at a variety of speeds. Some are so slow as to be invisible, while signs of change can be misinterpreted as permanent conditions if examined at the wrong time scale—such as the length of an individual's residence at a particular place, which in

Patrick's case allowed him to believe that Crow Hill bog was "not altogether a quagmire" and posed no danger to his children. Some are so fast that they appear to be temporary crises, and witness accounts appear to focus on ephemeral conditions—such as Patrick's foamy tide and Emily's lightning-fast deluge. But the rocks of Crow Hill, formed at the scale of deep time until the swift eruption displaced them to the new spaces that they have occupied for nearly two hundred years, reveal that the bog burst is geological phenomenon both slow and fast. Reporting on this swift shift in a passage as breathless as "High Waving Heather," the *Leeds Mercury* reported that "the contents of the two bogs which have been excavated" have left "concavities [that] have been emptied not only of their water, but also of their solid contents." Evidence of this remained for rubberneckers in the form of "a precipitous range of rocks which presented the appearance of a gigantic staircase" (quoted in Keighley 110). Exposing the bog's shale foundation, the burst vividly demonstrated for tourists new scientific theories about the Earth's mutability with unwonted, and largely unwanted, speed. This pedagogical power excited Miall, who, despite his conservationist concern over the dwindling of moorlands, vibrates with excitement when he rhapsodizes those moments (such as in the aftermath of a bog burst) when "we are lucky enough to see the bed of a Sphagnum swamp." At such moments, geology manifests: "Then we may see that the peat rests upon a sheet of boulder clay, and this upon the sandstones and shales. Between the peat and the boulder clay there is sometimes found an ancient seat-earth, in which are imbedded the moldering stumps of long dead trees" ("Moor," 623–24). This horizontally layered image of seat-earth (rock strata over a seam of coal), punctured vertically by the remains of ancient forests felled by humans, offers a compelling image of Anthropocene change: ecological crisis proves, again, to be seductive as a thrilling experience, a narrative challenge, and a form of knowledge.

When modeled as either momentary crisis or permanent condition, the Anthropocene fails to materialize palpably to the humans who have created it. Short-term crises place emphasis on individual or familial survival, while long-term conditions are difficult to perceive. Human-caused biome degradation therefore became a narrative problem at the dawn of the Anthropocene. Positioned at the temporal and spatial emergence of this new epoch, the Brontës responded to this problem by writing about anthropogenic change through the lens of ecological crises, in which storms, lightning strikes, droughts, and mass movements proliferate, along with their attendant human tragedies of shipwrecks, deaths, crop failures, and eruptions, which are carefully interwoven into fiction as both plot mechanics and psychological symbols. Charlotte in particular merges threads of crisis, with their themes of extinction and survival, with threads of a vastly different time scale: of toxicity, of languishing, of slowly worsening conditions. The Anthropocene becomes textually visible as *both* crisis and condition. Brontë solves the problem of making climate change, mass extinctions, ocean acidification, weather destabilization, and other signs of human-caused environmental destruction visible by rendering it within the narrative frame of a realist novel and within the time frame of a single human life. The Anthropocene becomes tangible to human readers, too, as her protagonists' lives are profoundly shaped by environmental change and as Charlotte works through her own multiple and changing answers to the questions posed by Emily and Patrick, about how to witness, survive, respond to, and write about anthropogenic devastation in ways that are both ethically and aesthetically productive.

TWO

Three Days on the Moors with Jane Eyre

DEFINING *ANTHROPOS*

What happens the day after a bog burst? As chapter 1 shows, Patrick Brontë's bog-burst writings and Emily's storm-loving poetic speakers foreground the moral and scientific value of witnessing a catastrophic event unfold. Charlotte's first published novel, *Jane Eyre* (1848), however, calls attention to the day after. Individual crises are decentered within a longer narrative of *Bildung*, whose representations of ecological (and personal) change include the shorter timespan of individual crisis and the longer one of the lingering condition. As Jane's peripatetic autobiography relocates from Gateshead Hall to Lowood School to Thornfield Hall to the moors beyond it to Moor House to Ferndean Manor, her answer is clear. Waking up outside of the Garden of Eden for the first time, what does one do? One flees.

Jane instinctively leaves inhospitable spaces, her keen instinct for survival prevailing over the fascinated attraction to power that drives Emily's adrenaline-fueled poetry and over the single-minded desire for the world yet to come that governs Patrick's bog-burst writings. Each dramatic set-piece depicting the crisis of ejection from home and admission into a new sanctuary yields to descriptions of the recurring tasks and choices that rebuild her life—until the slow changes lurking imperceptibly underneath the stable conditions of her new life cause a crisis to erupt. Uniting her manifold struggles to secure love, freedom, self-control, and financial prosperity in a stable home is the need to be recognized as a human being. Emblematic of this need is the passionate speech that leads to her engagement to Rochester, which climaxes with her insistence, "I am no bird; and no net ensnares me; I am a free human being with an independent will, which I now exert to leave you" (293). Uncertain of her own humanity, Jane must repeatedly rediscover and reassert it. Along Jane's journey to secure her rights as a human being, the novel investigates this mysterious category, *Anthropos*. Who qualifies as a human being? Why should one want to be human? What are the operative differences separating humans from animals, plants, and rocks? How much control should humans exert over these nonhuman organisms and their environment?

Because definitions of the human rely upon knowing these species differences and the environmental factors that influence one's categorization inside or outside *Anthropos*, they powerfully influence her movements across the world. She may count as a human being only in the right space, explaining why she threatens to "exert" her human "independent will" to leave Rochester's walled garden, where she senses danger despite its resemblance to the Garden of Eden. Her revelation on the moors—"I would fain at the moment have become bee or lizard, that I might have found fitting nutriment, permanent shelter here. But I was a human being, and had a human being's wants: I must not linger where there was nothing to supply them" (374)—also links her survival to fleeing inhospitable spaces and articulating her human divergences from animals. Unsurprisingly, she is intent on dividing the human from the inhuman, though the novel repeatedly attests to the difficulty of maintaining the integrity of these taxonomical designations. In Bertha Mason, any latent desire for a flexible species designation—to feel a family resemblance to bee, bird, or lizard—dissolves into horror. "What it was, whether beast or human being, one could not, at first sight, tell," Jane puzzles; "it groveled, seemingly, on all fours; it snatched and growled like some strange wild animal: but it was covered with clothing, and a quantity of dark, grizzled hair, wild as a mane, hid its head and face" (338). With organisms exhibiting such contradictory evidence, every meeting is a taxonomic identification. Meeting Rochester is a frightening amalgam of dog, horse, and rider until she is satisfied with her designation: "The man, the human being, broke the spell at once. Nothing ever rode the Gytrash: it was always alone; and goblins, to my notions, though they might tenant the dumb carcasses of beasts, could scarce covet shelter in the commonplace human form" (133). Jane's wry estimation of man's metaphysical value draws from schoolmate Helen Burns's critique of Jane's temperament, "you think too much of the love of human beings," and her reminder that "the sovereign hand that created your frame, and put life into it, has provided you with other resources than your feeble self, or than creatures feeble as you.

Besides this earth, and besides the race of men, there is an invisible world and a kingdom of spirits" (82). For Rochester, however, who needs Jane's help to enact his "final re-transformation from India-rubber back to flesh" (155), the human form is not so commonplace after all, and valuing and preserving one's own humanity is a precondition of spiritual enlightenment, not a diversion from it. Jane does offer the needed help. Though her instinct for physiological and moral preservation leads her to leave this office after the aborted wedding ceremony, the fact that she later opts to return to Thornfield and its particular human mission (rather than accept St. John Rivers's request that she move to India and fill a more traditional missionary post) reveals that these questions about defining the human, assessing its value, and determining its responsibilities had always remained open.

Jane Eyre's contested definitions of the human offer a powerful case study for Anthropocene theory because many scholars who accept that humans have become the primary force affecting the Earth's geosphere take exception to the neologism's first term. Rory Rowan insists that *Anthropos* should "be understood not as a pre-constituted identity but rather as the object of political contestation in the struggle to define the terms of future human existence on the planet" (449). Stacy Alaimo—alongside other contributors to *Anthropocene Feminism*—queries, "Who is the 'anthro' of the 'Anthropocene'?" This essay argues that "some accounts of the Anthropocene reinstall rather familiar versions of man," particularly the Enlightenment "disembodied, rational subject" critiqued by second- and third-wave feminists (89). Reinstating this model rejuvenates "all too familiar formations, epistemologies, and defensive maneuvers—modes of knowing and being that are utterly incapable of responding to the complexities of the Anthropocene" (90). Whereas theorists like Dipesh Chakrabarty represent "man as a bounded being endowed with unilateral agency," feminist theorists "offer cautionary tales, counterpoints, and alternative figurations for thinking the Anthropocene subject," ones that do not "abstract the human from the material realm and obscure differentials of responsibility and harm" but reveal how deeply the "Anthropocene subject [is] immersed and enmeshed in the world" (89, 103). Realist fiction, with its emphasis on causality, description, character development, and social and material environments, traces the immersions and enmeshments that reflect how *Anthropos* is "a material being, subject to the agencies of the compromised, entangled world" (104). *Jane Eyre* in particular embodies this alternative model by revealing how individuals' journeys to maturity are hampered by the toxic bodies and landscapes they inhabit. *Bildung* is transformed from a linear progression in time to a spatial navigation of entangled networks. As Jane navigates them, ecological, taxonomic, and personal crises co-occur, attesting to the interdependence of environment states and definitions of the human.

Still, Jane is no model Anthropocene feminist. She never takes *Anthropos* for granted, but her desire for Enlightenment personhood leads her to think of humans as transcendent instead of physical, objective instead of compromised, and controlling instead of entangled. Jane oscillates between epiphanic experiences of immersion and reactionary retreats from the precarity of enmeshed life in damaged landscapes. In spite of suffering at the hands of those who reserve the title of "human being" for certain people, Jane retreats into the narrow definitions that underwrite the comfortable conclusion of her embattled campaign to achieve full personhood, which succeeds in the secure berth of "Reader, I married him" (517). The compromises of Jane's romantic fulfillment have interested critics at least since the 1960s. If Sandra Gilbert and Susan Gubar inaugurated the interpretation that unites Jane and Bertha as victims of gender-based inequalities, and if Gayatri Spivak has shown that empire and race introduce a wedge into this presumed unity, contemporary feminists' recognition of differentials of Anthropocenic responsibility offers a further refinement: that Jane's feminist bid for freedom has profound ecological consequences. Embedded in her campaign is an oppositional model of humanity—one that pits humans against each other, against nonhumans, and, in the struggle for self-control, against themselves. These struggles illustrate Claire Colebrook's revision of the second-wave feminist rallying cry, "the personal is political," into "the personal is geological." As Colebrook clarifies, "to understand the sexed subject, [we] need to take the emergence of the human species, and the domination of the planet (and other humans), into account" ("Counterfactual" 2). The Anthropocene may "require us to shift our scale of narration away from human generations and history to species' emergence and deep time," but it also requires us to "confront a sudden event of geological impact with an intensively human timeline," thus returning to "the classically feminist question of the *scale of the personal*" (1). *Jane Eyre*, subtitled *An Autobiography*, is narrated precisely at this personal scale.

To pursue the links between the personal and geological, this chapter links Jane's protofeminism to environmental degradation by exploring the intersections of gender and conceptions of the human that reach back to the dawn of the Anthropocene and have culminated in the explicit postulation that a new geological era began where and when *Jane Eyre* begins. This chapter unpacks how Jane's shifting grasp on humanity—both her definition of it and her admission into the category—influences her relationship to the real and imagined nonhuman organisms she encounters. Bewick's engravings, Jane's surveilling visions of the countryside, the freezing and toxic environs of Gateshead and Lowood, the tales Jane internalizes about the animals around her, the crisis landscapes of Jane's paintings, the biodiverse but (apparently) inhospitable moors from which Jane escapes, the ruins of Thornfield's horse-chestnut, and finally the ruins of Thornfield itself: all show how Jane's self-concept flickers between being a subject constituted by will, abstract thought, and control over the nonhuman world, and an entangled material being as likely to be affected by the nonhuman world as to affect it and cognizant of the necessity of linking human activities with the health of particular ecosystems. Interpreting these key scenes through this Anthropocenic lens reveals these critical moments in Jane's life as ecological crises that clarify the stakes for defining the human—its rights and responsibilities, its powers and limitations—and identify obstacles impeding the adoption of new definitions necessary for changing the behaviors that cause ecological degradation. By showing that what is good for Jane's personal narrative arc is not always what is good for the environment she traverses along the way, this chapter will demonstrate how the volatility of the human as a taxonomic category inflects our perceptions of ethical action in the Anthropocene.

ON NOT GOING ON A WALK THAT DAY: TAXONOMIES OF POWER

Jane Eyre's abrupt first line—"There was no possibility of taking a walk that day"—strikes a note of negation that is decisive yet ambiguous. No possibility remains, but the reason why the environment is unsuitable for exposure remains unspecified. Jane's next utterance, "I was glad of it," defiantly relates a personal triumph rather than lamenting a lost opportunity to commune with nature (9). Critics accordingly focus on Jane's individualism in this passage, which depicts her efforts to avoid her unsympathetic Reed cousins by removing herself from Gateshead Hall's public spaces to ever more snug and secure spaces. An antagonism is posited between Jane and her environment, amounting to a "topography of withdrawal" that illustrates Jane's "self-marginalized uniqueness" (Spivak 246). Critics interpret her retreat to the breakfast-room window-seat as either a reassuring indication of her ability to thrive in isolation or as troubling evidence that her surroundings exclude and entrap her. What unites these perspectives is their treatment of space as chiefly symbolic (Ewen; Hennelly; Locy).

But we should not collapse the distance between Jane's natural environment and her social one, emptying out the former's physicality. When Jane recalls, "I never liked long walks, especially on chilly afternoons: dreadful to me was the coming home in the raw twilight, with nipped fingers and toes, and a heart saddened by the chidings of Bessie, the nurse, and humbled by the consciousness of my physical inferiority" (9), her body registers its material continuity with the inhospitable conditions of Gateshead. Jane's "nipped fingers and toes" matter, as do the novel's other immersions and entanglements, which, as Alaimo argues in *Exposed*, connect bodies, social practices, and outside spaces. Jane's disempowerment is an amalgamation of material and social factors (her "physical inferiority" and her orphan status) that increase her vulnerability to intraspecies violence and harsh landscapes. Whether one *likes* the outdoors—whether one actively expresses an unalloyed affection for a biome—is beside the point. Jane's exposure to vulnerable environments renders *her* vulnerable. Her tenuous grasp on the "double retirement" provided by the window-seat's curtains and "panes of glass, protecting, but not separating [her], from the drear November day" (10) evaporates the moment her cousin John Reed, the family's heir, drags her from the window-seat to attack her. Throughout the novel, Jane is forced to expose herself outdoors regardless of weather conditions, creating a narrative of exposure that incorporates both singular moments of crisis (including this confrontation, which leads to her imprisonment in the Red Room and her removal to Lowood) and habitual exposures, such as the Sunday walks during her decade at Lowood, walks that take her over "an exposed and hilly road, where the bitter wind" penetrates her body through her "ungloved hands" and unbooted feet (72). Prompted by Rochester's bigamy to wander the moors, Jane is repeatedly expelled from secure, comfortable spaces. Even more inhumanely, Bertha's imprisonment in an insalubrious space demonstrates how safety is differentially allocated in the Anthropocene.

These differentials adjust individuals' exposures to unstable, depleted, or toxic landscapes, making it crucial to construct, Alaimo argues, "an ethics that is not circumscribed by the human but is instead accountable to a material world that is never merely an external place but always the very substance of ourselves and others" (*Bodily Natures* 158). This ethics includes strategic exposure, Alaimo argues, studying activists who perform voluntary exposures to Anthropocene toxicities. They activate an "insurgent vulnerability" allowing them to "perform material rather than abstract alliances, and to inhabit a fraught sense of political agency that emerges from the perceived loss of boundaries and sovereignty" (*Exposed* 5). *Jane Eyre*'s narrative of exposure depicts a series of exiles and migrations, most involuntary but some voluntary, and all linked to politicized definitions of the human. Nipped by the cold, Jane hosts the weather in her very body, living proof of the bidirectional causal links that contravene definitions of *Anthropos* as self-enclosed and self-determining. Understandably, Jane often reacts to the physical and psychological sufferings of exposure, caused by the gendered and classed social hierarchies deeming some *Anthropoi* less worthy of protection, by claiming her full status and rights as a human being. Consequently, while some of her attitudes and behaviors in moments of exposure open up the possibility of redefining the human in more environmentally and socially just ways, others perpetuate the definitional constructs that rationalize her own victimization.

Treating weather solely as a metaphor—treating, for example, the storm that destroys the horse-chestnut as an abstract symbol of her passionate nature flaring up after a period of prolonged self-control—also perpetuates these constructs. Metaphor, even as it draws disparate phenomena together, relies on a prior assumption of conceptual distance between tenor and vehicle. Metaphors delight and surprise because they presume the objects' essential dissimilarity. In this case, characterizing the relationship between Jane and the weather as figurative assumes that it is primarily conceptual. These limits postulate the human as exceptional: triumphantly *outside* the outside. Yet Jane's body materially indexes outside conditions, making *Jane Eyre* an ideal text for an "atmospheric reading," theorized by Jesse Oak Taylor. Analyzing novels that thematize smog and other urban forms of pollution, Taylor explains how atmospheric reading bypasses literary-critical consensuses on the relationships among plot, setting, and subjectivity:

> Atmospheric reading revises the common notion that the novel is a genre predicated on (and formative of) the human individual as the key locus of agency, ethics, and subjectivity. This emphasis on subject formation produces a series of assumptions about how novels work and are to be read, including the primacy of character and plot over such features as setting.... Foreground becomes background and background becomes foreground. Character development, once the central question of the novel, becomes merely a device to narrativize a set of atmospheric 'readings,' by which I mean that the text registers atmospheric effects in a matter akin to a meteorological instrument. (*Sky* 14–15)

The present chapter also inverts foreground and background while considering many Anthropocene effects, including deforestation, mass extinction, ocean acidification, and disruptions of geological strata. Thomas H. Ford also reads *Jane Eyre* for its atmosphere, which he asserts is "a medium of literary self-reference," making Jane "an artist" whose "chosen medium" is air (88). *Jane Eyre* responds to atmospheric reading because it thematizes divergent models of humanity and their impacts on local ecosystems: Jane's oscillations between models of the human show how the narrative patterns linked by atmospheric reading to environmental change are indissolubly linked to the definitions of *Anthropos* that interest feminist scholars.

Taylor's insight that the conditions of reading contribute to realism's "atmosphere" can be applied to *Jane Eyre* metatextually. It opens, after all, with a scene of reading as Jane's rejection of uncongenial exposure gives way to fascinated absorption in the multispecies vignettes of Thomas Bewick's *History of British Birds*. Following good scholarly practice, she quotes and then interprets Bewick's representations of

> "the vast sweep of the Arctic Zone, and those forlorn regions of dreary space,—that reservoir of frost and snow, where firm fields of ice, the accumulation of centuries of winters, glazed in Alpine heights above heights, surround the pole, and concenter the multiplied rigors of extreme cold." Of these death-white realms I formed an idea of my own: shadowy, like all the half-comprehended notions that float dim through children's brains, but strangely impressive. The words in these introductory pages connected themselves with the succeeding vignettes, and gave significance to the rock standing up alone in a sea of billow and spray; to the broken boat stranded on a desolate coast; to the cold and ghastly moon glancing through bars of cloud at a wreck just sinking. (10–11)

Bewick's teaches Jane how to interpret image through text and vice versa and provides scientific and aesthetic tools for transforming her actual surroundings into far more stimulating visions. Jane's perusal transfigures her immediate atmosphere (her momentarily secure nook overlooking the wet, chilly park) into the "the multiplied rigors of extreme cold" and "the accumulation of centuries of winters, glazed in Alpine heights." Trading the physical risks of forced exposure for the thrills of imagined exposure, she recalls, "With Bewick on my knee, I was then happy: happy at least in my way." Reading controls her interactions with the environment—or, at least practices controlling imagined episodes of exposure. As Jane's lofty perch is transfigured into one of Bewick's "solitary rocks and promontories," and she herself into "the black horned thing seated aloof on a rock, surveying a distant crowd surrounding a gallows" (11), the scene establishes the significance of nonhumans to her assertions of individuality and to her love of narrative. Crafting stories amounts to an "ontological affirmation of self" for Jane, Brenda Silver agrees (102). Similarly, Carla Kaplan explains that Jane "measures human relationships by a yardstick of narrative exchange" (10). What is less understood is how these exchanges are contingent on Jane's species affiliation. Regarding Bewick's "black horned thing," for example, James Buzard briefly considers the implications for Jane's ambivalent identification as a human: "Jane herself—rough beast—might *be* that strange creature," but if Jane "escapes in imagination to a state of uncompromised animal purity achievable, if anywhere, only on a landscape as barren to human purposes as those barren ice floes" (212), this purity is as specious as her escape is imagined. Bewick's North Atlantic is not timeless or inhuman; it reflects centuries of active human management of the islands' wildlife. Domesticated pigs were fattened on the islands; birds' eggs were collected at unsustainable rates. Today, as Seth Brewington and other anthropologists have established, these populations are endangered by Anthropocenic changes (Brewington et al.).

Certainly, young Jane may know nothing of these eggs or pigs. And in Brontë's next novel, *Shirley*, the titular character proposes a holiday at the Faroe Islands, "those lone rock-islets where the sea-birds live and breed unmolested." To distract her friend Caroline (who, like the Brontës, lives in a parsonage abutting a graveyard) from "musing about remnants of shrouds, and fragments of coffins, and human bones and mold," Shirley imagines "seals lying in the sunshine on solitary shores, where neither fisherman nor hunter ever come." Yet her next utterance, "We shall be on the track of the old Scandinavians" (231), acknowledges the area's human history. Just as the isolation of Bewick's birds is subtly punctured by signs of humans, Brontë's Faroes are subject to human contact yet inhumanly pure. Such imagery takes humans' mastery over nature for granted while erasing signs of their impact—an impossible equilibrium that embodies

> the logic of the Anthropocene: the idea of a life that could develop to its utmost potentiality without incurring debt or death to itself is both what drives technological-industrial investment *and* generates the delusional idea of a life without expense, loss, or misprision; the notion of generating more (in the final instance) than one initially takes, the dream of a pure

ecology in which everything serves to maximize everything else and in which there is no cost. (Colebrook, "Counterfactual" 17).

The site of this delusion of a costless, perpetual purity in the Brontë canon is the North Atlantic. *Jane Eyre* and *Shirley* fix the region at one moment in time when the North Atlantic is poised carefully at the ecological moment of first contact—a poise achievable insofar as it is imagined. A bystander overhearing Shirley and Caroline objects, "Does it not strike you that your conversation for the last ten minutes has been rather fanciful?" (232). Their projected holiday does remain a projection. Jane too experiences these spaces only vicariously, and this is precisely the point: it is easier to maintain the useful fiction that human action is ecologically costless when the action is a fanciful story. Yet even these fictions normalize anthropogenic ecological change. One tale, "The Cooper of Thorsund and His Family," published in 1827 in *Blackwood's*, which the Brontë children were eagerly absorbing at the time, is narrated by a lovestruck sailor on a man-of-war cruising the Faroes with a baronet completing a mineral survey. The story begins when they approach the sheer granite cliffs of Diamond Islet. The sailor proclaims that, "though cursed with the most perfect sterility, and from its situation inaccessible to the wants to either man or beast," it is "the settlement and impregnable citadel of millions of the fowls of Heaven, who had abode and flourished there, generation on generation, since the flood, and are likely to do so, unmolested by man, till time shall be no more" (692). But the man-of-war does not leave this "impregnable citadel" wholly "sterile" and "unmolested":

> The gentlemen were highly delighted with the view, and by way of having some idea of the amount of the feathered population, the knight suggested that a small nine-pounder carronade, which was used for an enemy's tops, should be shooted and fired at the rock. . . . . This was speedily done, and was instantly followed by such a novel scene as absolutely beggars description. The boom of the gun, followed next moment by the crash of the shot on the rough centre of the solid mass, so terrified the simple and unaccustomed inhabitants of this lonely and silent rock, that immediately forth issued old and young of ducks, geese, gulls, gluttons, kittywaiks, and mews, in endless battalions, with such an intermixed screaming of terror and despair as was really deafening. (692)

The sailor's aesthetic pleasure in the "novel scene"—"the sight was sublime" (692)—derives from the very eventuality that he denied would ever occur to the Faroese avian population. An imagined moment of contact, the story does not directly incur ecological costs, but its rhetoric transfigures birds into "battalions," enemy combatants by virtue of their contact with armed humans, and excuses interspecies violence when its purpose is scientific. Impossibly, the man-of-war vicariously penetrates, yet preserves, the islands' purity, reproducing that paradoxical impression of first contact that animates Brontë's North Atlantic imagery. Violence also accompanies human-nonhuman contact in Bewick's vignettes, in which birds supervise ships sinking, criminals fleeing or being hanged, and churchyards scattered with tombstones.

Jane Eyre condemns such cruelty to animals, although it similarly posits that humans and animals meet at moments of death or endangerment. Jane deems tyrannical John Reed's wanton exercises of his Adamic right of mastery over animals, and she distinguishes her own uneasy relationship to the outdoors and her aesthetic appreciation of them from John's predilection for interspecies violence. Jane suggests that the boy's inversion of man's duty foreshadows future attempts to control, devalue, and exert violence against other humans:

> John no one thwarted, much less punished; though he twisted the necks of the pigeons, killed the little pea-chicks, set the dogs at the sheep, stripped the hothouse vines of their fruit, and broke the buds off the choicest plants in the conservatory: he called his mother "old girl," too; sometimes reviled her for her dark skin, similar to his own; bluntly disregarded her wishes; not unfrequently tore and spoiled her silk attire; and he was still "her own darling." (18)

The novel's unequivocal condemnation of John and related practices of intraspecies violence is prefigured in *The Professor*, which opens as narrator William Crimsworth reunites with his brother after a decade of separation. William warily observes his brother's driving: "a vigorous and determined application of the whip from the ruthless hand of his master soon compelled him to submission, and Edward's dilated nostril expressed his triumph in the result of the contest; he scarcely spoke to me during the whole of the brief drive" (14). The semicolon's parallel between William and the horse is revealed as foreshadowing when he quits his job in Edward's factory. Edward responds, "I wish you were a dog! I'd set-to this minute, and never stir from the spot till I'd cut every strip of flesh from your bones with this whip," before disregarding the subjunctive mood of his pronouncement and flaying him with the same instrument used on the horse. Recalling Jane's tyrant allusions and showing that he too finds interspecies cruelty a sound reason to alienate family, William protests against "the most nauseous slavery under the sun" (35).

The interspecies politics of Charlotte's *Jane Eyre* and *The Professor* align with Anne's *Agnes Grey*, in which Maggie Berg discerns a "feminist opposition to speciesism" (193) and in which Judith Pike finds a correlation between "the lack of empathy for animals and the abuse of animals" and "the corrupted sensibilities of the upper classes" (143). As Ivan Kreilkamp shows, although it may seem that the Brontës, "in the midst of this culture of animal cruelty, appear strikingly eccentric and at odds with their surroundings," their anti-cruelty was not be lost on readers "at a moment when a nascent 'animal rights' movement—not yet called by that name—was taking its place as a powerful social force in England" (88). David Perkins, who argues that for Romantic poets, "sympathy with animals and radical politics were intertwined" (930), excavates literary precursors for the Brontës' anti-cruelty. But beyond the unquestionable horrors of animal cruelty lay questions about the patterns of representation that underpin the political affordances of feeling for animals. Jane invokes animals as figures for her disenfranchisement, illustrating how, as Cary Wolfe argues, identifying with animals is often a "self-serving abstraction," simply "another sign of the very privilege and mobility enjoyed by those ... at the top" of the "social ladder," allowing them to define humanity as "the subject of freedom" (xii). As a human being, Jane is positioned near the top, but lower than other *Anthropoi*, explaining why her interspecies identification fluctuates with her political fortunes: her material entanglements with nonhumans dissolve into the "self-serving abstraction" that preserves her self-worth throughout her struggles.

The Brontës' novels illustrate how deeply attitudes toward nonhumans depend on definitions of the human—and how these attitudes are strategic, contingent, and inconsistent. At times, *Jane Eyre*'s dog imagery lauds canine loyalty. The lovelorn Rosamond Oliver complains to her dispassionate beloved, "Your dog is quicker to recognize his friends than you are, sir," and when Jane is reunited with Rochester, she recalls that, in sharp contrast to his unresponsive master, "Pilot pricked up his ears when I came in: then he jumped up with a yelp and a whine, and bounded towards me" (417, 499). Yet when Jane, roaming homeless on the moors, compares herself to a dog ("I thus wandered about like a lost and starving dog" [377]), she does so to display neither her loyalty nor her sagacity, but deep shame at her compromised humanity. Abandoned by her species ("not a charm or hope calls me where my fellow-creatures are" [371]), Jane's taxonomic designation temporarily resembles that of *Shirley*'s mill-workers, whose suffering "left scarcely anything but animal wants" and made them "desperate as famished animals" (508). In *Shirley*, animalization results in violent acts to reclaim one's humanity or to resist another's re-humanization; it causes the Luddite revolt during which "the fighting animal was roused in every one of those men there struggling together" (326). Jane, however, is allowed to exploit her degraded designation to arouse empathy in those who could provide shelter: "If I were a masterless and stray dog," she cannily ventures, "I know that you would not turn me from your hearth to-night" (388). Repeating this sentiment in a register less beseeching than aggrieved, Jane "rather severely" chastises the servant (lower on Wolfe's social ladder) for having "wished to turn [her] from the door, on a night when you should not have shut out a dog" (393). Shame settles on those who rate Jane's status as equal to or lower than animals.

This expression of barely concealed rage, so unusual at this late moment in *Jane Eyre*, reflects the fact that being identified with animals is the surest way to lose one's status as a human. John calls her a "bad animal" as a justification for assault. His full invective—"'Boh! Madam Mope!' ... 'Where the dickens is she! ... Lizzy! Georgy! (calling to his sisters) Joan is not here: tell mama she is run out into the rain—bad animal!'" (11)—associates exposure with animals. Labeling her "Madam Mope," an allegorical title he revises to "animal," exercises his Adamic right of naming, as does his adoption of diminutives (Lizzy, Georgy, Joan) used at no other time. Aunt Reed's classification of Jane as not "natural" similarly emphasizes how taxonomy functions to deny rights: because Jane does not exude "a more sociable and child-like disposition ... lighter, franker, more natural as it were—she really must exclude me from privileges intended only for contented, happy little children" (9). This flexible use of indexicals within inverted commas substitutes subject positions: "she" for "I" and "me" for "you." Like John's diminutives, these floating referents are unique in the novel, revealing the slipperiness of the outlines of Jane's identity—and its political consequences. Jane's classification is up for grabs, distinguished from the clearer taxonomies by which, for example, Eliza Reed justifies her decision to disown her sister: "Georgiana, a more vain and absurd animal than you was certainly never allowed to cumber the earth. You had no right to be born" (271).

If species determines rights, conversations about animals are also about determining which living beings are eligible for which kinds of rights. In *Jane Eyre*, sometimes it's good to be an animal, and sometimes it's not. Put less simply, Jane's attitude toward animals reflects her changing perceptions of her current access to power and self-determination, indicating that Jane's interspecies and intraspecies relations are mutually interdependent. Taxonomic comparisons reflect and affect ontologies of the human in ways that, through their connections to the materiality of bodies, activate, but exceed, the power of metaphor. As a result, *Jane Eyre*'s taxonomic designations are not disinterested, predestined, and fixed, but strategic, contingent, and inconsistent.

Postmodern though it may seem, such uncertainty around the species concept flourished before Charles Darwin's *On the Origin of Species* crystallized the principle of mutability by identifying an organic mechanism for variation. "No one definition has satisfied all naturalists," Darwin allows, "yet every naturalist knows vaguely what he means when he speaks of a species" (38). As Richard A. Richards explains, approaches to isolating species shift functionally on the context, and "there are multiple, inconsistent ways to divide biodiversity into species on the basis of multiple, conflicting species concepts, without any obvious way of resolving the conflict" (5). Beyond this species problem, the recognition of variation between and within species dates at least to the first formal biological definition by John Ray in 1686 or to Linnaeus's retraction of his claim in *Systema Naturae* (1735) that species categories were permanently fixed and discrete. Since the 1960s, biologists have increasingly been critiquing the "essentialist story" by which Darwin is conceived to have unilaterally disrupted universally accepted essentialist accounts of the species concept (Wilkins), and since 1984, with Barbara Goff's work on *Wuthering Heights*'s anti-anthropocentrism, literary critics have rejected oversimplified accounts of the species concept. Goff notes that before this time, though "virtually all critics ... addressed themselves to the rhetoric of animality in the novel," few were "willing ... to grant animality more than a metaphorical status" (479). Animal imagery has been investigated non-figuratively by Theresa Mangum, who emphasizes the physical presence of dogs in Emily's life and relics, and by Karen Rowe, who unpacks Rochester's animality. Deborah Denenholz Morse and Martin Danahay have noted, "The effect of Darwin's ideas was to make the human more animal and the animal more human, destabilizing boundaries in both directions" (2). Analyses that directly challenge the "essentialist story" are more common in scholarship on Emily as the archetypical Brontëan who theorizes humanity as a species. For Goff, *Wuthering Heights* "is a hypothetical experiment in the breeding of human beings, conducted to suggest how the breed has been corrupted from its 'native state'" (480); for Joseph Carroll, its "emphasis on the primacy of physical bodies in a physical world" allows Emily to forge alternatives to the pre-Darwinian "folk concept of human nature" that governed commonsense accounts of humanity (242, 244).

Jane Eyre's species politics are equally interesting. Whereas Emily's proto-genetics explores the intrafamilial inheritance of species traits, Charlotte explores familial dissimilarities, from *The Professor*'s ominous fraternal variation ("As an animal, Edward excelled me far" [14]), to *Jane Eyre*'s provision of a cousinly antithesis to John Reed ("Physically, [Diana] far excelled me.... In her animal spirits there was an affluence of life and certainty of flow, such as excited my wonder" [403]). The physiological differences between Edward's and Diana's animal spirits exemplify Charlotte's anti-essentialism, by which floating taxonomies acknowledge intraspecies variation and interspecies affinities. Hoeveler's observation that by the time Jane marries, "The cormorant that was the hungry and angry heart of Jane has now become a meek and mild sparrow," at which time Rochester is identified as an eagle, nullifying his earlier designations as a toad and an ape (41). For Charlotte, radical personality change—sufficient progress along the path of *Bildung*—amounts to a species shift. Intraspecies variation from Richard Mason to Rochester multiplies the distance between John Reed and Diana; dividing them is the taxonomic gap "between a sleek gander and a fierce falcon: between a meek sheep and the rough-coated keen-eyed dog, its guardian" (221).

Meanwhile, for Charlotte Brontë, female anger triggers hybridization. About Bertha, Jane asks, "What creature was it, that, masked in an ordinary woman's face and shape, uttered the voice, now of a mocking demon, and anon of a carrion-seeking bird of prey?" (243). When Aunt Reed experiences Jane's outbursts "as if an animal that I had struck or pushed had looked up at me with human eyes," Jane also manifests hybridity (275). Despite Aunt Reed's simile ("as"), hybridization in the novel is not entirely figurative. Grammatically, Jane's possession of an animal's body is figurative; what she recoils from is the material manifestation of species hybridity. Charlotte's fiction frequently posits such interspecies affinities—the possession of traits classed with organisms from other species—to express the *Anthropos*'s non-figurative diversity. While *Shirley* does so by way of interpreting Shirley's manifestations as lion, tiger, and panther, *Jane Eyre* reveals not only that differences in species can manifest as personality differences, but also that the ontology of species is a crucial intellectual framework for delineating character in realist fiction. The servant Bessie, presumably ignorant of the phrenological vocabulary that Jane might employ, confides that the Reed sisters "lead a cat and dog life together; they are always quarrelling" (108). By understanding personality through the species concept, Charlotte concurs with Anna Tsing's observation that "human nature is an interspecies relationship" ("Unruly Edges" 144). Another way in which narrative practices of characterization represent humanity as an interspecies relationship is by elaborating human-animal relationships as proxies for intraspecies interactions that are rebuffed, sublimated, or extradiegetic (interactions that do not occur within the temporal boundaries of the primary story layer). Jane's recollection, "Georgiana would chatter nonsense to her canary bird by the hour, and take no notice of me" (268), reveals that Georgiana interacts with literal animals to avoid interacting with figurative "bad animal" Jane and that her species-identity is closer to her canary than her cousin because her personality brings her into more intimate contact with nonhumans.

Heartbroken Rosamond Oliver, by contrast, channels love, not animosity, through animal mediumship. Resuming her caresses, she complains, "'*He* is not stern and distant to his friends; and if he could speak, he would not be silent.' ... As she patted the dog's head, bending with native grace before his young and austere master, I saw a glow rise to that master's face" (419). St. John's blush physiologically inscribes this oblique endearment. The triangulated pats are received, as is the semi-public shaming that shows how frequently interspecies practices become figures for human morality. When Jane conveys an intraspecies tenor by way of an interspecies vehicle, using language to classify the nonhuman as human, moral judgment is sure to follow. Here, St. John's inflexibility makes him saintly, but inhuman. Later it will absolve Jane of guilt for refusing his proposal, showing how Jane will stoop to condemning individual humans for possessing impure species identities when doing so justifies her own behaviors and decisions. Still, *Jane Eyre*'s strategic, contingent taxonomies float many definitions of the human as she alternately embraces and fights her predisposition to, as Helen Burns cautions, "think too much of the love of human beings" (82–83). Rochester shares Jane's species ethics, daring those who interrupted their bigamous wedding ceremony to "judge whether or not I had the right to seek sympathy with something at least human" (337). Gazing alternately at Bertha and Jane, he conflates three sorts of judgment (species discernment, spiritual judgment, and legal decision) by commanding, "Compare these clear eyes with the red balls yonder—this face with that mask—this form with that bulk; then judge me, priest of the gospel and man of the law, and remember with what judgment ye judge ye shall be judged!" (339). Jane's recollection corroborates Rochester's position: "it snatched and growled like some strange wild animal: but it was covered with clothing, and a quantity of dark, grizzled hair, wild as a mane, hid its head and face" (338). Jane's taxonomic indecision marks her privilege over Bertha, who is a "carrion-seeking bird of prey," a "clothed hyena," a "dog quarrelling," and a "tigress" (243, 338, 241, 245). Having earned, by dint of her discipline, purity, and trauma, a dose of John Reed's Adamic power in her narratorial right to label, she exercises it to fashion from Bertha's dehumanization a pleasurable Gothic thrill that routes readers' sympathy toward herself. Sometimes it's good to be an animal, and sometimes it's not.

In *Jane Eyre*, taxonomy determines survival. As Wolfe argues, in a society that grants animals a kind of subjecthood, "membership in a given species should have no bearing on thinking the subject of freedom and rights," but even if "the category of the subject was *formally* empty . . . it remained *materially* full of asymmetries and inequalities" (xii). After Spivak, critics have investigated this paradox through Bertha Mason. Most grant the centrality of animality to her disempowerment; Hoeveler argues that Jane "juxtaposes the human/domestic against the animal/Gothic" in order to "triumph over a woman coded as 'colored' and animalistic" (38). Jane's indecision in classifying Bertha resembles Aunt Reed's own while classifying Jane, but Bertha's extreme case requires turning to a taxonomical last resort: the supernatural, whereby she is a "specter," a "vampire" and a "demon" (327, 339). The novel's Gothic horror arises from internalizing how the taxonomic designations carrying so much power are mutable, overlapping, and indeterminant. Rochester routinely exploits their persuasive powers; trying to prevent Jane from retiring, he calls her "a curious sort of bird [seen] through the close-set bars of a cage: a vivid, restless, resolute captive," and in proposing—putatively an offer to share socioeconomic power—he orders her not to "struggle so, like a wild frantic bird that is rending its own plumage" (162, 293). How quickly verbal persuasion slips into physical is demonstrated when Jane decides to leave Thornfield: " 'Jane! will you hear reason?' (he stooped and approached his lips to my ear); 'because if you won't, I'll try violence' " (349). Maintaining close proximity, he muses, "I could bend her with my finger and thumb: and what good would it do if I bent, if I uptore, if I crushed her?" Locked in his grip, Jane is first a "she," then an "it"; the palpability of her presence recedes, and Rochester perceives only a drama between his desire and his reason. By deciding that "it is you, spirit . . . that I want: not alone your brittle frame" (366), Rochester invokes the mind/body duality of Enlightenment philosophy to define *Anthropos* as primarily spiritual, burdened by a physicality that must, in the end, be dismissed as incidental.

But *Jane Eyre* very much cares about Jane's body. Living within flesh alternately starved and nourished, beaten and caressed, frozen and warmed, Jane cannot afford to dismiss her own physicality. She must actively resist being animalized by those whose definitions of *Anthropos* minimize corporeality. This includes Rochester, whose avian similes provoke her resistance, climaxing in the rallying cry, "I am no bird; and no net ensnares me; I am a free human being with an independent will" (293). That this cry precedes his proposal indicates that species seems powerful enough to sanction Rochester's bigamous proposal. For Jane, the reward for having her authenticated species-being is an advantageous marriage. She learns this lesson so well that she wields this drama of taxonomic discernment as a technique of seduction between the proposal and the failed wedding. Rochester, "his face all kindled, and his full falcon-eye flashing," is "worked ... up into considerable irritation" and thus into withholding her human identification and reverting to the "fierce favours" she "decidedly preferred": his equivocal endearments of "elf," "sprite," and "changeling" (314, 315). Her technique succeeds in its patently erotic ends—Jane smugly notes that "he was excellently entertained"—and feminist ends, for had she exhibited "a lamb-like submission and turtle-dove sensibility, while fostering his despotism more, [it] would have pleased his judgment, satisfied his common-sense, and even suited his taste less" (315). Jane triumphs in their romantic game of taxonomy, skillfully suppressing Rochester's "despotism" and physical violence through discourses of rationality. But ushered in with Bertha come revelations that the game is risky and Jane's victory temporary.

ECOLOGOCENTRIC EXPOSURES:
GOD'S-EYE VIEW IN JANE EYRE'S WORD-PAINTINGS

Surviving in *Jane Eyre* being appreciably a matter of taxonomy, it is unsurprising that scenes of classification feature organisms whose lives are, like Bertha's, precarious. Brontë therefore populates scenes of danger with animals; crises are set in pointedly multispecies spaces, revealing that vulnerabilities depend on particular dispensations of multiple human and nonhuman organisms. Morse, who theorizes Bertha's attic as one of the novel's many "animal places," has argued that "Jane is fascinated by the interaction of people with non-human animals in animal environments," especially ones that exhibit "animals vying for survival" (162, 157). Given this plethora of animals, I adopt the language of "contact zones" used by multispecies ethnographers. These liminal spaces are positioned between a (predominately or perceivedly) natural environment and a (predominately or perceivedly) man-made environment. At contact zones, Jane's species politics are most precisely delineated. From the opening, where *Bewick's Birds* represents spaces of human-animal interaction as sites of death, crime, and danger, contact zones are seen as threatened by (and threatening to) human beings. Jane's position in the window-seat recapitulates the thrilling drama when species meet at contact zones and reiterates that the site of natural history, of learning about the nonhuman, is geographically and philosophically a contact zone. As Buzard observes, "only glass divides Jane from the domain of 'the natural,'" while "only a curtain divides her from that of 'the social'" (217). Despite the abstraction implied by Buzard's scare quotes and the customary elision of "British" and "history" in scholarly references to *Bewick's Birds*, these superimposed environments—the ones in which and about which Jane reads—are not generic, but precisely located in space and time. Readers of *Jane Eyre* should attend closely to the historically specific ecological implications of particular spaces.

We do not always do so because Jane does not want us to. Narrating, she toggles back and forth between description and generalization, nudging the readers to rush to their symbolic freight: Jane's character. To elicit sympathy, the opening scene shifts from describing one fight with John to his habitual patterns of bullying. Jane *herself* depicts contact zones in terms that warrant Buzard's use of "the 'natural'" and "the 'social.'" She strategically stylizes the natural world in ways that display what Timothy Morton would call her ecologocentrism:

> *ecologocentrism* underpins most environmentalist philosophy, preventing access to the full scope of interconnectedness. Thinking, even environmentalist thinking, sets up "Nature" as a reified thing in the distance, "over yonder," under the sidewalk, on the other side where the grass is always greener, preferably in the mountains, in the wild. "Nature" ... is a function of distance. ("Ecologocentrism" 75).

Morton advises that "society can no longer be defined as purely human" because humans and ecosystems are linked by a "genuine interdependence" that trucks with no "illusory boundary between inside and outside" (75). *Jane Eyre* vividly demonstrates the appeal of rejecting Alaimo's assertion that humans are fundamentally entangled in nature. Narratologically, this reification is a powerful tool of *Bildung*. By distancing herself from the landscape beyond the window yet maintaining a connection to it by reading *Bewick's*, Jane vicariously masters the physical threats posed by her social and physical surroundings and consumes the latter as an object of sublime aesthetic appreciation. In *Bewick's*, Jane finds her trials dramatized in morbid vignettes and verified through the scientific authority of taxonomy. The abstractions of the scientific and the sublime soothe her bruised self-respect, gratify her taste, and inspire her resistance against John Reed, whose response—he throws the heavy ornithological volume at her—recapitulates the use of science to justify violence. This is the same trope seen in the *Blackwood's* tale that deems the shelling of Diamond Islet an acceptable price for learning about Faroese avian life. John rationalizes Jane's assault because she is a "bad animal." Even Jane's voluntary relations with nature are marked by separation and power: she identifies in passing with lonely waterfowl to compensate for her isolation but resists internalizing this identification. Ecologocentrically, she deactivates her interspecies empathy when, terrified, she turns from birds to her uncle's ghost as a means of avenging unjust treatment, and, eventually, escapes it through further intellectual abstraction at Lowood.

The placement of *Bewick's Birds* at the novel's opening is the first suggestion that taxonomy mediates human species-identity, but throughout the novel, Jane's self-knowledge is mediated by personal experiences of nature and scientific discourses about it, which offer her raw materials for assembling a self-concept that differs from the one offered by the Reeds. The stakes of the ecologocentrism by which Jane alternately identifies with and defines herself against the nonhuman are revealed in the structural rhythms by which exposure scenes (during which Jane is either vulnerable or invulnerable to threatening natural forces) function as a barometer for her rising or falling social status. Such moments foreshadow victory or defeat against a human antagonist, such as John Reed, Reverend Brocklehurst, Blanche Ingram, and, of course, Bertha Mason. But because these scenes stimulate her to strengthen her piety, discipline, and self-confidence (all necessary weapons for intraspecies skirmishes), Jane's exposures operate as causal mechanisms as well as foreshadowing. For example, after confronting Mrs. Reed and being "left alone—winner of the field," her pleasure in "vengeance" recedes, prompting her first episode of voluntary exposure (45). Desiring self-control—"I would fain exercise some better faculty than that of fierce speaking"—she exits the human space she has conquered and crosses the boundary of the "glass-door in the breakfast-room" to the hostile outdoors she had avoided:

> I covered my head and arms with the skirt of my frock, and went out to walk in a part of the plantation which was quite sequestrated; but I found

> no pleasure in the silent trees, the falling fir-cones, the congealed relics of autumn, russet leaves, swept by past winds in heaps, and now stiffened together. I leaned against a gate, and looked into an empty field where no sheep were feeding, where the short grass was nipped and blanched. It was a very grey day; a most opaque sky, "onding on snaw," canopied all; thence flakes felt it intervals, which settled on the hard path and on the hoary lea without melting. I stood, a wretched child enough, whispering to myself over and over again, "What shall I do?—what shall I do?" (46)

Jane atones for her loss of self-control through a period of voluntary exposure climaxing in her arrogation of her right to control her future (the repeated "shall" of her closing query). Again she retreats from human society, but this time, it is penitential; she finds "no pleasure" in identifying with the nonhuman. Whereas the quotes from *Bewick's* emphasize Jane's pleasurable consumption of inhuman images, her quote from Walter Scott fulfills the poetic rhythms of her own creation as the assonant five-syllable pair ("a very gray day; a most opaque sky") yields to a tightened four-syllable pair (" 'onding on snaw,' canopied all") whose slant rhyme softens the harder assonance of the first pair. Unlike the "nipped" grass, she covers herself by adjusting her clothes. Unlike the "congealed" and "stiffened" leaves, she moves flexibly (Jane may "lean," but the pathway is hard) through a biome where nonhuman life is locked in suspended animation and where the only member of a charismatic species ("no sheep were feeding") is Jane. Her nonplussed observations of nature prompt her epiphany about self-control. Regretting her outburst to Mrs. Reed and having been duly chastened by her rebellion again John's control, she no longer seeks this opposition in the human community, but in nature, whose difference constitutes her selfhood, in the manner of "persistent Western models of objectivity and mastery" (Alaimo, "Shell" 107), as rational, dynamic, self-disciplined, and transcending her environment.

Jane regards entanglement as a voluntary act of imagination or brief period of penance, not an abiding characteristic of *Anthropos*. The oppositional nature of her self-constitution can be seen in moments when she looks out of a window, literalizing the "epistemological position of 'God's-eye view,'" which Alaimo argues "dominates many of the theoretical, scientific, and artistic portrayals of the Anthropocene" (107, 90). *Jane Eyre*'s views adopt this perspective, which emphasizes "the colossal scale of anthropogenic impact by zooming out—up and away from the planet" and urges "viewers to shift scales" and "safely view [the Earth] from a rather transcendent, incorporeal perspective, not from a creaturely immersion in the world" (91). "Nonhuman agencies and trajectories are absent" in these views, as are "winds, tides, currents, and the travels of birds, cetaceans, or other creatures," with the result that, like Gateshead Hall's congealed, stiffened, and sheepless plantation, the Earth appears as "an eerily lifeless entity, devoid of other species, as if the sixth great extinction had already concluded" (92, 91). The proofs of biodiversity and opportunities for creaturely immersion offered by Bewick are processed as dead landscapes whose sterility underscores Jane's vitality. Even her word-paintings (most of which describe spaces she wants to leave) do not celebrate the landscapes so much as they do Jane's transcendence of them. On the day Miss Temple leaves Lowood, she lingers at her chamber window and decides to leave because her mentor "had taken with her the serene atmosphere [she] had been breathing" (101). This atmospheric reading admits of only human influence. Miss Temple creates the atmosphere, and the details Jane records here are man-made:

> There were the two wings of the building; there was the garden; there were the skirts of Lowood; there was the hilly horizon. My eye passed all other objects to rest on those most remote, the blue peaks; it was those I longed to surmount; all within their boundary of rock and heath seemed prison-ground, exile limits. I traced the white road winding round the base of one mountain, and vanishing in a gorge between two; how I longed to follow it farther! ... I desired liberty; for liberty I gasped; for liberty I uttered a prayer; it seemed scattered on the wind then faintly blowing. I abandoned it and framed a humbler supplication; for change, stimulus: that petition, too, seemed swept off into vague space: "Then," I cried, half desperate, "grant me at least a new servitude!" (101–2)

Jane's dominant perspective purchases a glimpse of political freedom by expunging the landscape's nonhuman features and possibilities for creaturely immersion. Her roving eye restricts her contact with the landscape, and her pen applies layers of the liberty thrice-mentioned atop her brush's patterns of color and light. It is through such word-paintings that Jane conforms to "the doctrine of prudential restraint" and the "vision of human progress" that George Stocking identifies as part of a shift in the meaning of "civilization" in England after the 1830s. Because "the ability to delay gratification [and] to exercise rational control over one's baser instincts, was in turn the basis for individual liberty and political responsibility," her word-paintings disavow her materiality and thus the "baser instincts" of her intemperate passions so she may claim her status as a fully entitled *Anthropos* (Stocking 36). Critics have long noted the affective structure, by which *Jane Eyre* alternates between periods of self-control and passionate, undisciplined release. But put in the context of the Anthropocene, it is also a classificatory structure that requires Jane to prove, repeatedly, her membership in the sole species putatively capable of rational control.

By rejecting her creaturely connections with her environs (Gateshead, Lowood, Thornfield, Moreton, and Ferndean), converting them into objects for her eye alone to perceive and her pen to convert into markers of personal growth, Jane enacts a curious paradox identified by Colebrook, by which the "very eye that has opened up a world to the human species, has also allowed the human species to fold the world around its own, increasingly myopic, point of view" (Colebrook, "Extinction" 22). Alexis Shotwell agrees that many are compromised "simply by living, buying things, throwing things away" because "we implicate ourselves in terrible effects on ecosystems and beings both near and far away from us. We are inescapably entwined and entangled with others, even when we cannot track or directly perceive this entanglement" (8). Soon after Jane is granted her new servitude, her visit to Thornfield's leads recapitulates these refusals of interspecies identification. Moving through rooms in which she "by no means coveted a night's repose" because they feature "wrought English old hangings crusted with thick work, portraying effigies of strange flowers, and stranger birds, and strangest human beings," she ascends until she stands "on a level with the crow colony, and could see into their nests" (125). Surrounded by admixtures of the human and nonhuman, she ignores or rejects these admixtures as menacingly nonnormative (despite physically occupying the crow colony's view). Peering past the rookery down with a painterly eye on the lands owned by her employer and future husband,

> I surveyed the grounds laid out like a map: the bright and velvet lawn closely girdling the grey base of the mansion; the field, wide as a park, dotted with its ancient timber; the wood, dun and sere, divided by a path visibly overgrown, greener with moss than the trees were with foliage; the church at the gates, the road, the tranquil hills, all reposing in the autumn day's sun; the horizon bounded by a propitious sky, azure, marbled with pearly white. (125–26)

Jane reinforces her surveying position by constructing an orderly palisade of punctuation. Semicolons and colons in this long sentence typographically divide the entangled objects into separate phenomena, a grammatical austerity that creates order from the visual complexity presented by the overgrown, vibrantly green, intensely lit scene, whose mixture of fully artificial structures (mansion, church, gates, road) and human-cultivated multispecies spaces (lawn, field, park, path) positions Thornfield at the commanding center of a contact zone. Over this zone, Jane enjoys a dominant position—the position she habitually seeks when chafing against her limited sphere for activity—placing her on a level with (not below) the "propitious sky," dramatizing *Anthropos*'s desire for hierarchical control and her own propitious campaign for gender equality.

This campaign is indicated by the succeeding passages, which feature the first instance of the imprisoned Bertha's laughter and one of Jane's most oft-cited feminist reflections:

> It is in vain to say human beings ought to be satisfied with tranquility: they must have action; and they will make it if they cannot find it. Millions are condemned to a stiller doom than mine, and millions are in silent revolt against their lot. Nobody knows how many rebellions besides political rebellions ferment in the masses of life which people earth. Women are supposed to be very calm generally: but women feel just as men feel. (129).

In expounding women's similarities to "their more privileged fellow-creatures" (130), Jane claims rights for women by virtue of their common species-identity. Her blend of taxonomic and political terms—originating from "tyrant" John Reed's classification of Jane as a "bad animal"—negotiates a bargain that Alaimo argues is typical of eighteenth- and nineteenth-century feminism. This bargain "accepts the nature/culture hierarchy in order to transfer women into the elevated category," for if "woman's perceived proximity to nature is responsible for her oppression, then her liberation, it would seem, is contingent on her distance from nature" (*Undomesticated* 3–4). For these early feminists, "woman, too, needs to rise up from her degraded bestial position and embark on the same route to transcendence" (4). The trouble with this position is illustrated by Jane Eyre's own conspiracy to make Bertha's bestiality a foregone conclusion. Jane's bourgeois white feminism complicates her *Bildung* by means of an anthropocentric taxonomic transfer that displaces a conflict between the sexes to a rivalry between women, then refiguring it as an interspecies contest. A similarly careful management of narrative tension—one that subtly combines solid causal analysis with hazier but symbolically rich speculation while comparing the relative powers of the human and the nonhuman—occurs in the dénouement of George Perkins Marsh's *Man and Nature*. After cataloging a range of negative changes in natural environments and meticulously linking them to human actions, Marsh gnomically concludes, "Every new fact ... is another step toward the determination of the great question, whether man is of nature or above her" (549). Marsh's equivocation recalls the subtly self-congratulatory contemporary art and science writing about climate change that Anthropocene feminists critique as paradoxically rehabilitating speciesist discourses that helped to create the Anthropocene. In a letter, Marsh performs this paradox of faux modesty when he calls *Man and Nature* a "a little volume showing that whereas Ritter and Guyot think that the earth made man, man in fact made the earth" (*Life and Letters* 422). Although Jane's fate depends on the answer to this "great question," due to her gender, the question is doubled: Is man above nature? And does Jane count as a man?

Jane tries to circumvent this process, anthropocentrically taking the former question for granted to adjudicate the latter. But the novel reopens the first question each time Jane believes she has settled the second. Recurrent crises of survival (her exposures, her moor wanderings, Bertha's attacks, the Lowood epidemic) force Jane to confront her own body's vulnerability, physicality, and animality—confrontations because her campaigns for equality are irrevocably connected to her desire for continuous transcendence. Surmounting Thornfield cannot satiate this desire; from the roof, she sighs, "I longed for a power of vision which might overpass that limit" (129). When she does overpass it, the price is high (her trial of moorland exposure) and the reward uncertain (the scene set inside Bertha's third-story attic ambivalently foreshadows both the short-term defeat of exile and the long-term victory of marriage). With the outcome of her intraspecies struggles unsettled, Jane shifts her attempts at transcendence to interspecies relations—hence Bertha's dehumanization. Yet reminders of her physicality pull her down to nature's level, as when her enrollment at Lowood is dogged by a literal hunger that she learns to master when Miss Temple rewards her diligence with drawing lessons. That night,

> I forgot to prepare in imagination the Barmecide supper of hot roast potatoes, or white bread and new milk, with which I was wont to amuse my inward cravings: I feasted instead on the spectacle of ideal drawings, which I saw in the dark; all the work of my own hands: freely pencilled houses and trees, picturesque rocks and ruins, Cuyp-like groups of cattle, sweet paintings of butterflies hovering over unblown roses, of birds picking at ripe cherries, of wren's nests enclosing pearl-like eggs, wreathed about with young ivy sprays. (88)

This substitution of an aesthetic feast for a material one teaches Jane that representation can powerfully intercede in battles between her all-too-natural body and her will to transcend her physicality. Locating the "free," the "ideal," and the "spectacular" in the skill of drawing grants Jane the power to surpass any view. Jane answers Marsh's question, "whether man is of nature or above her," not by gathering "new facts" about anthropogenic environmental degradation, but by producing unlimited "inward" views of ever-thriving roses, cherries, eggs, and ivy that can never decay or die, fixed forever by her artistic touch at the peak of their robustness and beauty.

In *Jane Eyre*, artistic representation seems to affirm man's transcendence of nature, as well as the illusion of "pure ecology in which everything serves to maximize everything else and in which there is no cost" (Colebrook, "Counterfactual" 17). When stymied, Jane turns her "mind's eye to dwell on whatever bright visions rose before it" and her "inward ear to a tale that was never ended—a tale my imagination created, and narrated continuously" (129). In addition to the solipsistic pleasures of autobiographical narration, Jane paints scenes whose style is modeled after Bewick (as Susan Taylor has established) but whose content is self-referential. Like Brontë, who copied Bewick's "Palm Squirrel" not out of "zoological curiosity," but out of technical appreciation for its "composition," which she found "suitable for a needle-case" (Alexander, *Art* 199), Jane adapts scientific techniques for representing contact zones in ways that suit her human needs. Her description of the watercolors she exhibits to Rochester diminishes their nonhuman features. In the first, "all the distance was in eclipse; so, too, was the foreground; or rather the nearest billows, for there was no land," while the "second picture contained for foreground only the dim peak of a hill, with grass and some leaves," and the "third showed the pinnacle of an iceberg piercing a polar winter sky: a muster of northern lights reared their dim lances. . . . Throwing these into distance, rose, in the foreground, a head,—a colossal head" (147). Only one, which shows a woman's corpse near a shipwreck, retains Bewick's birds; in it appears "a cormorant, dark and large, with wings flecked with foam," but only because "its beak held a gold bracelet set with gems, that I had touched with as brilliant tints as my palette could yield" (147). The bracelet offers better scope for her talents and "brilliant tints" than the bird. The two remaining paintings show female figures transcending the looted corpse's vulnerable materiality. In one watercolor, a woman is "rising into the sky" among the clouds, "crowned with a star" and lit up by "a pale reflection" that is "like moonlight." But it does not require the moon's help: "this vision of the Evening Star" is lit from within (147). She overcomes the limitations of organic bodies and the savagery of interspecies competition by becoming a spirit or goddess, her transcendence of materiality unchecked by cormorant or bracelet. Bewick offers a grim account of contact zones that mirrors both her social position, but Jane sublimates its organic, multispecies content and abstracts scientific techniques in order to visualize, validate, and exhibit her desires.

Jane's third watercolor, which personifies death, "the shape which shape had none," most clearly underscores that her paintings are flagrantly not taken from the life (148). When Rochester asks, "Where did you get your copies?" Jane's answer, "Out of my head," emphasizes her allegorical style, by which the distances maintained in Bewick's contact zones are collapsed by superimposition (146). Jane's finesse in blending color dissolves discrete subjects of representation into a two-dimensional wash of liquid color "where tint melts into tint" (132). Rochester's surprise that Jane can "paint wind" fixates on her art's immaterial aspects. The tangibility of enmeshment recedes further as Jane manages to "mix [her] freshest, finest, clearest tints" (187). Colors coalesce in a "suffusion of vapor" capable of "catching golden gleams from the sun, and sapphire tints from the firmament," of revealing a corpse through green seawater or superimposing a translucent goddess over a midnight sky (147, 462). The technical difficulty of this task promises further isolation to Jane, for whom painting provides an alibi for introspection:

> I used to take a seat apart from them, near the window, and busy myself in sketching fancy vignettes, representing any scene that happened momentarily to shape itself in the ever-shifting kaleidoscope of imagination: a glimpse of sea between two rocks; the rising moon, and a ship crossing its disk; a group of reeds and water-flags, and a naiad's head, crowned with lotus-flowers, rising out of them; an elf sitting in a hedge-sparrow's nest, under a wreath of hawthorn-bloom. (268)

Despite the predominance of conjunctions ("and") and prepositions ("between," "in," "with,"), which entangle and immerse, the colons and semicolons rigorously separate a heterogeneous assemblage of natural and supernatural objects, which are synthesizable exclusively inside Jane's "kaleidoscope of imagination." Compared to Jane's sweeping rooftop visions, the restricted palette of her intimate vignettes values fancy over mastery, though both engage in the anthropocentric practice that Alaimo argues is constitutive of those artistic renderings whose attempts at critiquing anthropogenic climate change are compromised by their adoption of the anthropocentric God's-eye view. In these renderings, "the world is rendered into a kaleidoscopic vision you may hold in your mind like a toy in your hand. Brilliantly, its aesthetic pleasures are the selfsame as its critique, as its visual delights repeat in solipsistic symmetries" (Alaimo, "Shell" 94). In this passage, "kaleidoscope" may be serendipitous, but what is not is Jane's habit of perceiving the world as a toy for her painterly eye. The novel's preponderance of words like "bright," "shine," "piece," "fragment," "glisten," "glittering," and "brilliant" transfer this kaleidoscopy to her verbal arts. She is, as Nancy Armstrong deems, a "bricoleur" whose "power to transform cultural objects" manifests first in her manipulation of *Bewick's Birds* (211). Jane's relationship to this volume is indeed indicative: used by Jane as she ages more for its repository of artistic techniques than its provocations to Deleuzo-Guattarian becomings-animal, it shows that for Jane, nature is *over there*, a storehouse of materials for creating one's art—and oneself.

Jane's impulse to emulate Bewick's "black horned thing" is motivated less by a love for feathered creatures than by a desire to be a solitary figure dominating a hostile landscape from above. Her relations' dislike responds to this desire. Aunt Reed's deathbed rambles fixate on Jane's

> sudden starts of temper, and her continual, unnatural watchings of one's movements! I declare she talked to me once like something mad, or like a fiend—no child ever spoke or looked as she did; I was glad to get her away from the house. What did they do with her at Lowood? The fever broke out there, and many of the pupils died. She, however, did not die: but I said she did—I wish she had died! (267)

Jane rationalizes this hatred as a product of "natural antipathies"—she can "see it clearly" now that they were "opposed ... in temperament"—but this explanation cannot fully account for Aunt Reed's reaction (266, 19). Behind this clash of temperament lurks a profound disagreement in the way they would answer Marsh's query whether man is of or above nature. As a result, Aunt Reed's entreaties for Jane to behave "more natural as it were" are not wholly discredited by her narrow conception of the *Anthropos* juvenile (9). This disagreement over transcendence reappears in Elizabeth Rigby's infamous critique of *Jane Eyre* in the *Quarterly Review*. Rigby, who charges Jane with impiety and unfemininity, has been critiqued as reactionary and normative, but her discomfort with Jane's boundless appetite for transcendence is worth reconsideration:

> It is by her own talents, virtues, and courage, that she is made to attain the summit of human happiness, and, as far as Jane Eyre's own statement is concerned, no one would think that she owed anything either to God above or to man below. She flees from Mr. Rochester, and has not a being to turn to.... Of course it suited the author's end ... to exhibit both her trials and her powers of self-support—the whole book rests on this assumption—but it is one which, under the circumstances, is very unnatural. (590)

It is "unnatural" that Jane "flees" and seeks a "summit" on her "own": what lay at the heart of Rigby's allegations is Jane's drive to be alone and above. Preferring the restrained naturalism of Currer Bell's word-painting to the allegorical transcendence of Jane's canvases, Rigby proclaims, "Let him describe the simplest things of nature—a rainy landscape, a cloudy sky, or a bare moorside, and he shows the hand of a master; but the moment he talks of art itself, it is obvious that he is a complete ignoramus" (593). For Rigby, a "master" artist masters not nature, but the "first principles" of his chosen medium (593). By contrast, Jane indiscriminately masters nature through representation, painting, and word-painting to signal milestones along her path of *Bildung*. Perhaps Jane *is* unnatural, after all.

EPIDEMICS, BOG BODIES, AND POLLUTED WATERS: MAPPING THE TOXIC ORDINARY

Despite Rigby's moralizing, Brontë does not always grant Jane transcendence. Jane's corporeal entanglements periodically reemerge: blood trickles down her forehead after *Bewick's* hits it, her trial in the Red Room induces a faint and a fever, and her first year at school witnesses a typhus epidemic. But at Lowood, her body develops a robustness that the older, narrating Jane flaunts by prefacing it with a lush word-painting. The question that concludes the word-painting ("Have I not described a pleasant site for a dwelling?") and her answer ("Assuredly, pleasant enough: but whether healthy or not is another question" [91]) introduce a rare conscious irony to Jane's narration. Retroactively casting ominous overtones over her descriptions of natural beauty, the passage throws into relief how Jane "thrives in the very natural environment that breeds the typhus infecting over half of the Lowood girls" (Morse 158). Though "disease had thus become an inhabitant of Lowood, and death its frequent visitor," Jane lives:

> But I, and the rest who continued well, enjoyed fully the beauties of the scene and season; they let us ramble in the wood, like gipsies, from morning

till night; we did what we liked, went where we liked: we lived better too.... Besides, there were fewer to feed; the sick could eat little; our breakfast-basins were better filled; when there was no time to prepare a regular dinner, which often happened, she would give us a large piece of cold pie, or a thick slice of bread and cheese, and this we carried away with us to the wood, where we each chose the spot we liked best, and dined sumptuously. (91)

Jane's Barmecide supper has materialized into a very real feast, as has her imagined birdlike freedom and isolation. Her rhetorical questions, reversals ("but," "besides"), and repetitions ("all this I enjoyed often and fully, freed, unwatched, and almost alone," with "unwonted liberty" and "unlimited license" [91]) amplify Jane's victory. Meanwhile, her use of scrupulously accurate word-paintings to highlight her health places representational fidelity at the service of human exceptionalism. One such passage opens, "My favourite seat was a smooth and broad stone, rising white and dry from the very middle of the beck, and only to be got at by wading through the water; a feat I accomplished barefoot" (92). This attitude pointedly differs from the opening chapters that detail her physical vulnerabilities to emphasize her lack of mobility and privacy.

Jane's response to Brocklehurst's catechism, "I must keep in good health, and not die" (39), may blaspheme, but as a description of her future tasks, it is perfectly correct. The landscapes she portrays pose considerable threats, ones the Brontës encountered at the real-life Clergyman's Daughter's School at Cowan Bridge, whose miasmatic valley claimed the lives of Maria and Elizabeth Brontë in the epidemic that Charlotte relocates to Lowood. The legendary insalubriousness of Haworth Parsonage has been a touchstone since Gaskell's *Life of Charlotte Brontë*. For example, Robert Polhemus memorably intones, "In their small world, beloved inhabitants keep dying, and the survivors live in the parsonage like disaster refugees" (156–57). Charlotte's life was indeed marked by waves of loss: of her mother in 1821, Maria and Elizabeth in 1825, Branwell and Emily in 1848, and Anne in 1849. In Brontë biography, a relentless pattern of mortality emerges from a combination of the annual rhythms of winter colds, the ever-present threat of tuberculosis, and the periodic crises of individual deaths. Toxicity settles over Haworth Parsonage, invariably described in terms of its unsheltered situation facing the bleak moors at the back door; its dubious water supply, contaminated by decaying bodies in the graveyard facing the front door; and its proximity to "smoke-dark houses clustered round their soot-vomiting mills" (C. Brontë, *Letters* 1:72). Like the artists who, Alaimo shows, regard "the toxic Anthropocene as unnervingly commonplace" and "imagine the domestic as linked to toxic networks of industrial production, consumer use, and disposal," for Brontë, the ordinary world "has unexpected, injurious agencies" ("Shell" 105, 104). Lowood's charity cases, into whose bodies the landscape's toxicity is transferred, testify to Shotwell's assertion that "[r]ich people have an easier time" in their "avoidance of poison" (85). More subtly, Alaimo suggests that thinking about toxicity "allows us to reimagine human corporeality, and materiality itself, not as a utopian or romantic substance existing prior to social inscription, but something that always bears the trace of history, social position, region, and the uneven distribution of risk" ("Trans-Corporeal" 261). In toxic, ordinary places like Haworth and Cowan Bridge, exposure has serious consequences, ones not evenly distributed across populations.

Though Jane expresses her attraction to the "doctrine of the equality of disembodied souls" that Helen Burns so powerfully preaches, the uniqueness of Helen's death testifies against this equality (273). She dies during the epidemic—but from tuberculosis, not the typhus that infects the "forty-five out of the eighty girls" left unnamed (91). Why focus on Helen, whose death is not representative of a tragedy that, in reality, claimed dozens of lives? The anonymity of the epidemic casualties ironically underscores the extent of their victimization; their toxicity being less romantic and more ordinary than Helen's tuberculosis, Jane spends her grief—and her words—on Helen. This narratively expensive death establishes Jane's immunity to toxicity. A survivor twice over, Jane accumulates the "resurrective" aura that Deborah Denenholz Morse argues is proof of her evolutionary fitness (158). Jill Treftz's argument that Helen displays "symptoms consistent with a neurodevelopmental disability" further suggests that she functions to accentuate Jane's able-bodiedness (444). Helen introduces temporal complexity into the condition of survivorship: to resist acute, transitory threats (typhus) and longer-term toxicities (tuberculosis). Emphasizing Helen does what Mel Chen calls "thinking with toxicity," and placing her in a miasmic valley is a "toxic worlding" that recognizes toxicity "as a *condition*," not only a momentary crisis (207, 197). Yet Jane's desire for transcendence prevents Lowood's toxic worlding from provoking her to "think more broadly about synthesis and symbiosis, including toxic vapors, interspersals, intrinsic mixings, and alterations, favoring inter-absorption over corporeal exceptionalism" (197). Only intermittently does Jane, characteristically striving to be corporeally exceptional, "turn aside from narratives organized around an expected line of descent, denaturalizing 'fitness' and modeling something more interesting about what it might be to survive and thrive in disrupted landscapes" (Shotwell 86). There *is* something interesting in the fact that Jane must survive over and over: it suggests that "fitness" is an ongoing process, not a wholly static or inherited condition, during the Anthropocene. Living at the beginning of an era in which "corporeal exceptionalism cannot be sustained" (85), Jane shows how difficult it is to withstand the physical threats of crises and conditions, how difficult it is to locate and gain entry into spaces that seem less toxic—and how temptingly at-hand are anthropocentric definitions of the human that underpin her resolve her survive.

It is when Jane wanders for three days on the moors after the thwarted wedding ceremony that she radically rethinks her anthropocentrism. In fleeing, she responds to Rochester's betrayal with the one option she will always have: voluntary exposure. This interlude of exposure between her escape from Thornfield and her entry into the safety of Moor House provides Jane an opportunity to revise her definition of *Anthropos* because her physical suffering shows her corporeal exceptionalism to be "temporary and illusory," while her psychological sufferings puncture her anthropocentrism as she realizes that "we cannot in the end be separate from the world that constitutes us" (Shotwell 85). As *Anthropos*'s vulnerability returns with a vengeance, Jane's ability to police the boundaries between herself and her environment and between humans and animals evaporates. Morse too emphasizes the physical presence of hunger and pain in this interlude, though it has been chiefly interpreted as a symbolic "dark night of the soul" (163). Katherine Montgomery sees in it evidence of Jane's non-exceptional animality:

> immediately [before] her crisis, Jane is described in terms that are far more wild and nature-based than human. Her flight from Thornfield and her subsequent wandering, however, throw this natural characterization into a deadly crisis. Jane nearly dies from exposure; the poetic language that had turned her into a creature of nature is swiftly undermined, and any romance in Rochester's characterization of her as a bird is undone when, starving, she eats porridge meant for a pig. (103)

These scenes of exposure painfully literalize the nature-themed "poetic language" that Jane uses to blur species boundaries figuratively while continuing to claim corporeal exceptionality. This crisis tests the efficacy of Jane's skillset for mastering a human-degraded "natural" world whose threat peaks in this moorland episode. She engages with this acidic, upland ecosystem with a degree of physical intimacy unmatched in the novel, but even at this nadir in her path of *Bildung*, she reaffirms her accustomed model of *Anthropos* as above and apart from nature. When the coach drops her off in a "a north-midland shire, dusk with moorland, ridged with mountain," she begins recalling her perilous perambulations with an extended description that abruptly shifts from her habitual past-tense narration into the present. Recalling, "There are great moors behind and on each hand of me; there are waves of mountains far beyond that deep valley at my feet" (371), Jane surveys the land into which she soon becomes entangled—an entanglement that will challenge the philosophical and material differences upon which her understanding of her humanity rests.

Boggy moors provide the ideal setting for unwonted thoughts because the moors' indeterminacy allows Brontë to spatialize the decisions Jane must make: to revise (or not) her understanding of *Anthropos* and to relinquish (or not) her claim to corporeal exceptionalism. "There is something fundamentally contradictory about bogs," Karin Sanders writes:

> They are solid *and* soft, firm *and* malleable, wet *and* dry; they are deep, dark, and dangerous; but they are also mysterious, alluring, seductive. Neither water nor land, bogs are liminal spaces, thresholds between surface and depths, ambiguous sites of origin. As landscapes of nocturnal obscurity they bring about spatial and temporal dislocation: here, one can get easily lost; here, time is eerily suspended. (7)

Accounting for the moor's centrality to Gothic literature, Derek Gladwin agrees that moors are culturally associated with indeterminacy because they are "neither exclusively water nor land"; a bog "appears to be firm land" but "does not provide solid footing" (1). Consequently, these spaces "complicate the oversimplified nature/culture binary often applied to them" and offer authors "an *in-between* place to explore" that "resists categorization" (9–10, 2). Gladwin's hypothesis that moors are used by writers to create "certain slippages, or purposeful confusions" because they are "visually deceptive, physically volatile, and conceptually elusive" with "unclear demarcations between the known and the unknown," explains why Charlotte places Jane in a bog (2, 4). The landscape she struggles through is both a physical and symbolic medium for these decisions. Physical pain, cold, and hunger will influence them, while her aesthetic judgment and verbal representations of the landscape will symbolically reflect the values that she will privilege or subordinate to make them. As soon as the coach drops Jane off at Whitcross, thus beginning her wanderings, she seems to embrace eagerly her opportunity to reevaluate her membership in the human species. The crossroads, "all cut in the moor" so that "the heather grows deep and wild to their very verge," are a contact zone, and she immediately abandons the man-made road (371). She follows instead the moors' natural pathways: "I struck straight into the heath.... I waded knee-deep in its dark growth; I turned with its turnings, and finding a moss-blackened granite crag in a hidden angle, I sat down under it. High banks of moor were about me; the crag protected my head" (372).

As Jane sinks into heather and underneath crag, becoming embedded in the landscape, she relinquishes the normative perception of linear, progressive time of her anthropocentric *Bildung*. The insulating moor shifts the timescale of her narration, which slows considerably as Charlotte uses a wealth of detail to make the reader slog as slowly through the prose as Jane strains to push herself through gloppy swells of bracken. If, as Gladwin writes, "Very little life can exist in anaerobic zones, a characteristic producing a Gothic world of the decomposed un-dead, with much hidden from the scope of society" (32), Jane elects to join this hidden colony of slow death. Time in a bog is slow because its anaerobic conditions retard natural processes of decomposition to make them imperceptible at the scale of a human life. The presence of acidic *Sphagnum* mosses intensifies the mummifying properties of the deoxygenated morass. As living mosses grow over dying ones, and those die over ones long dead, each bog stratifies with a slowly but unceasingly deepening range of living and non-living mosses embedding organic objects that become preserved in the bog, from pollen to butter to trees to human bodies. In bogs, life and death are not mutually exclusive conditions turning off and on as unambiguously as one might flip a light switch; they occupy a single spectrum, an altered temporality of living and dying that prompts Jane's reevaluation of her species-being. Here, human history lingers. Bogs "collect and record memories," and, compared to other archaeological dig sites, "preserve these artefacts with greater accuracy in terms of their origins, thereby containing and producing cultural memory, a way of accessing multiple and often conflicting forms of history through society and culture" (Gladwin 34). So, too, is deep time accessible to an unusual degree:

> One of the many enticements of bogs is their 'slow' or 'deep' geologic time, spanning thousands of years. The micro-geography of bogs is constantly in flux, but the change is too slow for the human eye to observe the constant and intricate rearrangement of textures and colors over time and space. Such a spatio-temporal existence, often outside of immediate human perception, is what contributes to the protean nature of the bog. (29)

Through their powers of preservation, bogs manifest history at multiple timescales at once, from the annual blooming of heather to the centuries-long preservation of cultural artifacts to the millennia-long preservation of flora and fauna, including remnants of ancient woodlands that the bogs displaced after deforestation. Because of these multiple timescales, "bogs destabilize a sense of historical and spatial order," rendering them useful for Gothic narratives that "manifest both natural and also human chaos (that is, fear of death or the end of the world)" (4, 7).

Bogs' protean, heterochronic nature and their intimate relationship to death, decay, and history were well-known by the Brontës, who spent a significant portion of their lives traversing these overlapping frames of seasonal, historical, and geological time. Though these timescales seem unthinkably different, scaled beyond the power of humans to compare and contrast them meaningfully—from the violently short timeframe of ecological crisis (the bog burst) to the deep-time scale of geological condition (the moors' gritstone outcroppings)—novels like *Jane Eyre* forge techniques to narrate their intersections with each other and influence on characters' fates. Crises make putatively imperceptible historical changes perceptible, as well as the role played by humans in these shifts; as I show in chapter 1, Patrick and Emily Brontë wrote about these changes through the medium of a bog burst. *Jane Eyre* addresses swift shifts in scenes of destruction (including the lightning striking the horse-chestnut and Bertha Mason burning down Thornfield), but in the novel's moorland interlude, the short timeframe of Jane's three-day personal crisis intersects vividly with the longer timeframe of bog formation, a combination of slow natural and man-made processes. Jane wades into this slow process of deep time when she sinks herself into the *Sphagnum* mosses and imagines dying and decomposing within it. Having walked through "knee-deep" heather to settle in "banks of moors" under a natural rock ceiling, Jane essentially buries herself alive. As she fashions a "low, mossy swell" into a pillow, she uses the language of burial: "Beside the crag the heath was very deep: when I lay down my feet were buried in it; rising high on each side, it left only a narrow space for the night-air to invade" (373). The next morning, another significant shift of verb tense imagines, hypothetically, that she died: "Hopeless of the future, I wished but this—that my Maker had that night thought good to require my soul of me while I slept; and that this weary frame, absolved by death from further conflict with fate, had now but to decay quietly, and mingle in peace with the soil of this wilderness" (374). In the fluctuation of verb tenses describing her night sleeping comfortably in the moor, Jane explores the many timeframes encoded in her boggy slumbers, blending the temporary oblivion of sleep with the more permanent one of death, which she imagines as a twofold temporal event occurring over the course of a single night and over centuries of decomposition.

By sinking into the mosses and decomposing alongside them, her physical body merging softly with the slowly decaying vegetal masses of the peat to become one with the material of the moors themselves—one of the building blocks of a peaty morass—Jane envisions no general death for herself, but one quite specific to the biome: she imagines becoming a bog body. In *Jane Eyre*'s moorland interlude, Charlotte Brontë employs her firsthand knowledge of bogs' unusual temporal rhythms and physical properties to create an accurate portrait of what would happen to the bodies of humans who fall into bogs or whose bodies are thrown into bogs: they must cease all anthropocentric claims to be corporeally exceptional. Like all organic materials trapped inside the peaty slurry, they yield to the anaerobic conditions. Uncannily preserved, they become natural mummies. Most are from the Iron Age, the time during which deforestation created the bogs, and most are assumed to be the bodies of criminals or suicides, denied traditional burial. While the Tollund Man is the most famous bog body—discovered in 1950, perfectly preserved after two thousand years' suspension in the Bjældskovdal peat bog—other famous bog bodies excavated closer to the Brontës' lifetime include well-publicized discoveries in 1700, 1773, 1797, 1818, and 1835 (Sanders 10). In August 1823, the publication of James Hogg's letter, "A Scots Mummy," in *Blackwood's* likely drew Charlotte's attention to bog bodies at an early age. Sanders writes that all these "entropic" discoveries challenge "chronological models" of life—the time I have characterized as that of anthropocentric *Bildung*—because they are "corporeal time capsules in which the presence of the past is quite literally palpable" (Sanders 10). Jettisoned "out of time," bog bodies constitute "corporeal contact zones between things that historically have been separated" (10, 11). Bog bodies epitomize the moors' heterochrony, inscribing physically onto the human body their conceptual challenges to linear time. Discovering a bog body rediscovers that "the past can be *corporeally* preserved and rediscoverable," that "things can disappear as if gulped down by strange forces and reappear as if 'frozen in time.' Bogs are unhomely homes for whomever is placed in them; they are a loci of paralysis, but also of explosive volatility" (7). The surreal slowness of Jane's period in the bogs between Thornfield and Moor House is one such paradoxically "explosive" locus of "paralysis." The moors' superimposition of violent crises and lingering conditions, which is preserved in the text through its shifting verb tenses, branches two distinct paths in *Jane Eyre*: one in which Jane converts the crisis of her flight from Thornfield into the gentle, protracted conversion of her struggling self into a bog body, and one in which she reboots her flight by overcoming her weakened body's desire for permanent sleep.

In "A Scots Mummy," Hogg presents this same choice to his interlocutor, *Blackwood's* personality Sir Christopher North. Suffering from writer's block near the boggy Altrieve Lake, Hogg complains, "I hae naething to write about." Sir Christy answers, "For shame! Have you not the boundless phenomena of nature constantly before your eyes?" He harangues the jaded Hogg, invoking the word "phenomenon" (the same word used by Patrick for the Crow Hill bog burst just over a year later) so insistently that Hogg teases him for using the "French word" and commits a deliberate solecism, referring to "one of the greatest natural phenomenons" (188). Hogg obliges nevertheless, recounting in graphic detail a nearby bog body excavation and concluding his letter to Sir Christy with a recommendation: "leave orders that you are to be buried in a wild height, and I will venture to predict, that though you repose there for ages an inmate of your mossy cell, of the cloud, and the storm, you shall set up your head at the last day as fresh as a moor-cock." This cheeky banter attempts to neutralize the horror of the preceding account, which dramatizes why one should *not* want to become a bog body. "On the top of a wild height, called Cowanscroft, where the lands of three proprietors meet all at one point, there has been, for long and many years, the grave of a suicide," he begins, spinning an absorbing tale of innocence impugned (190). Jane, too, is an innocent who flees to a moorland crossroads, her flight savoring of the suicidal in her willingness to plunge into wetlands without resources. Hogg dismisses such desires, punctuating his tale with disgusted interjections such as "it never once occurred to me as an object of curiosity, to dig up the moldering bones of the culprit, which I considered as the most revolting of all objects" (190). But intermingled with disgust is fascination at the violent process by which two peat-cutters excavate the bog body. "Not much more than a foot from the surface," it is subject to attack as the two men "tore...open" the cloth wrappings and "pulled and pulled" at the hay-rope, which, still tight around his neck, "would not break." After the body yields, the peat-cutters physically violate the corpse with their fingers and knives and morally violate the suicide by interrupting the peaceful rest of the dead:

> One of the lads gripped the face of the corpse with his finger and thumb, and the cheeks felt quite soft and fleshy, but the dimples remained, and did not spring out again. He had fine yellow hair about nine inches long, but not a hair of it could they pull out, till they cut part of it off with a knife. They also cut off some portions of his clothes, which were all quite fresh, and distributed them among their acquaintances, sending a portion to me among the rest, to keep as natural curiosities. Several gentlemen have in a manner forced me to give them fragments of these enchanted garments; I have, however, retained a small portion for you, which I send along with this, being a piece of his plaid, and another of his waistcoat breast. (190)

Dug up, cut into parts, and distributed in pieces across the United Kingdom, the bog body is rudely ejected not just from the bog, but from slow time. The excuse of scientific interest ("natural curiosity") cannot dampen the story's horror, partly because the revolted Hogg himself becomes a willing party to these circulations ("I have ... retained a small portion for you") and partly because this horror derives from disrupting moor temporality. The peat-cutters violate the temporality of deep-time death and decomposition that Jane believes would offer her peace. For once the body is exposed to oxygenated air, it is endangered: as Hogg laments, they "digged up the curious remains a second time, which was a pity, as it is likely that by these exposures to the air, and from the impossibility of burying it up again so closely as it was before, the flesh will now fall to dust" (190). In the sudden dispersal of preserved body into dust, "A Scots Mummy" performs Sanders's argument that though "[r]econnection with the past is frequently intended to *stabilize the present* ... bog bodies, uncanny and liminal, more often than not refuse to be constant; indeed, they *destabilize*" (xvi). Were Jane to become a bog body, she would become one with nature, but an easeful death would cede her place in human history—the timeframe of history normally perceivable to humans—unless she was rudely dug up, like Hogg's bog body.

Though Jane escapes this fate, Catherine Earnshaw is, like the Cowanscroft suicide, a bog body whose grave is twice disturbed. A later iteration of the moldering corpses filling the innumerable turfy graves of the Brontës' juvenilia, *Wuthering Heights*'s central heroine persists as both physical object and as memory well into the next generation, exerting a destabilizing force on the narrative's chronology. Catherine is, as Jane imagines herself to be, buried in peat:

> The place of Catherine's interment, to the surprise of the villagers, was neither in the chapel under the carved monument of the Lintons, nor yet by the

tombs of her own relations, outside. It was dug on a green slope in a corner of the kirk-yard, where the wall is so low that heath and bilberry-plants have climbed over it from the moor; and peat-mold almost buries it. Her husband lies in the same spot now; and they have each a simple headstone above, and a plain grey block at their feet, to mark the graves. (170)

By means of bilberry and heather plants growing over the low wall, the moor encroaches upon the churchyard to embrace Catherine's body, over which new layers of peat have already begun to accumulate. It is because she has become a bog body that Heathcliff's second, and successful, attempt to open her coffin discloses the same vision as if he had succeeded in his first attempt, on the evening after her burial: "I got the sexton, who was digging Linton's grave, to remove the earth off her coffin lid, and I opened it. I thought, once, I would have stayed there: when I saw her face again—it is hers yet!—he had hard work to stir me" (288). Her fate is foreshadowed when she discovers Thrushcross Grange. Heathcliff reports to Nelly Dean that part of her is already buried in the bog: "We ran from the top of the Heights to the park, without stopping—Catherine completely beaten in the race, because she was barefoot. You'll have to seek for her shoes in the bog to-morrow" (48). Bizarre though it may seem, the phenomenon of the bog body is ubiquitous in *Wuthering Heights*—so ubiquitous that readers learn from one of the novel's earliest passages (likely its most famous one) that even its naïve newcomer narrator, Lockwood, knows they proliferate in the region. Lockwood's vision of Catherine's bloodied hand cracking his chamber window to gain admittance accompanies a nightmare that, like her lost shoe, foreshadows her corporeal fate. Recalling his nightmare about listening to the fire-and-brimstone sermon of pastor Jabes Branderham, Lockwood identifies the Chapel of Gimmerden Sough as a colony of bog bodies: "I have passed it really in my walks, twice or thrice; it lies in a hollow, between two hills: an elevated hollow, near a swamp, whose peaty moisture is said to answer all the purposes of embalming on the few corpses deposited there" (23). In addition to these bog bodies given a Christian burial in boggy grounds are the unintentional ones made of pedestrians who lose their way along the marshes. This is an ever-present possibility to Lockwood even before his nightmare about Gimmerden Sough; earlier that evening, he pleas to Catherine Linton, "Do point out some landmarks by which I may know my way home: I have no more idea how to get there than you would have how to get to London." When she responds, "Take the road you came. . . . It is brief advice, but as sound as I can give," Lockwood scolds her lack of sympathy:

"Then, if you hear of me being discovered dead in a bog or a pit full of snow, your conscience won't whisper that it is partly your fault?" (16). A compromise is reached—he will stay safe from the bog by staying overnight—but it is there, in Catherine Earnshaw's room, that Lockwood comes in the reach of her perambulating, preserved corpse and her nightmare-provoking Bible. Ironically, his attempts to avoid the bogs merely mires him further within them.

The bog's entanglements with the human population of *Wuthering Heights* are inescapable because they are manifold: physical, narrative, and cultural. They are physical because of the material exchanges twining humans and landscapes together. They are narrative because the bogs structure the novel; Lockwood's fear of disappearing into the bog functions as a plot device because it traps him periodically at Wuthering Heights, making him a captive audience for Nelly Dean's reminiscences and for the domestic dramas unfolding in the kitchen. They are cultural because representations of bogs encode ideas about life and death, as Sanders shows. Lockwood's fears do not arise *ex nihilo*; Gladwin notes that, historically, bogs are seen as "foul" homes of mischievous elves who "lure men into a watery grave" or evil creatures who "seduce innocent men into a certain death" (7). Folklore and gossip spread these ideas. For example, when Heathcliff imprisons Nelly and Catherine Linton before Edgar Linton's death, Nelly is rumored to be "sunk in Blackhorse marsh." Zillah, while freeing them, reports Heathcliff's instructions to her: "If they have been in the marsh, they are out now, Zillah. Nelly Dean is lodged, at this minute, in your room. You can tell her to flit, when you go up; here is the key. The bog-water got into her head, and she would have run home quite flighty; but I fixed her till she came round to her senses." Heathcliff's pretense to offer protection activates the politics of species identification: if Jane as a bad animal can be denied rights, so too can Nelly be disempowered, a creature of the marshes left imprisoned until the bog-water in her skull disperses. Continuing her report, a titillated Zillah divulges, "They tell that in the village—about your being lost in the marsh" (278–79). The villagers' chilling indifference and Zillah's enjoyment in spreading the rumor echo the failure of Lockwood's strategy for withstanding the corporeal dangers presented by the moors' hydraulic instability: to reach out to fellow humans for aid. That Wuthering Heights's residents refuse to lead him back to Thrushcross Grange exemplifies how wetlands are sites of evolutionary pressure that can be wielded as intraspecies weapons. The ones who can survive are those who have known them intimately and who possess robust enough bodies to withstand the inhospitable environment—or those who ally themselves with those who do, leaving the weak and unallied struggling alone to stay out of the sticky sloughs.

Unlike Jane, Heathcliff survives and thrives because of, not in spite of, his impure species-being. Isabella Heathcliff's parting shot as she flees the Heights for the Grange—"He's not a human being" (174)—allows her to claim her freedom by disavowing his humanness (thereby recuperating her own), but it underscores the limitations of conceptualizing human independence apart from material conditions. Isabella's freedom is the freedom to risk dying in the marsh. Goff's exploration of these links between species and survival concludes that Emily, even "more aggressively than Darwin, had come to conclusions about the literal descent of Victorian man from his essential animal nature" (479). Contrasting narrator Lockwood as the anthropocentric archetype against Heathcliff's embodiment of evolutionary fitness, Goff concludes that the novel "is about the colossal stupidity, arrogance, even impiety of anthropocentrism" (506). *Wuthering Heights* bypasses *Jane Eyre*'s nervous insistence on species boundaries, definitions of the human that rely on purity and exceptionality, and *Bildung* based on characters' abilities to transcend their ecosystems. *Wuthering Heights* insists on immersion. Unlike Jane, who desires to be recognized as a human being, Heathcliff "confound[s] categorization" (483), embraces his orphaned animality, and intensifies it by embracing his entanglements with the material earth. For example, after reporting the loss of Catherine's shoes, Heathcliff recalls, "We crept through a broken hedge, groped our way up the path, and planted ourselves on a flower-plot under the drawing-room window" (48). After the shoes enter their deep-time path of bog preservation, Heathcliff continues to define their activities in terms of immersion: through hedge, up path, and over flower-pot. As she spends more time with the elegant Lintons, he deepens his immersion:

> Heathcliff was hard to discover, at first. If he were careless, and uncared for, before Catherine's absence, he had been ten times more so since. Nobody but I even did him the kindness to call him a dirty boy, and bid him wash himself, once a week; and children of his age seldom have a natural pleasure in soap and water. Therefore, not to mention his clothes, which had seen three months' service in mire and dust, and his thick uncombed hair, the surface of his face and hands was dismally beclouded. (54)

In life, Heathcliff is already entangled with the bog, as "hard to discover" and "beclouded" in "mire and dust" as the Cowanscroft body. A weekly dousing in soapy water prevents his total submersion, sloughing off each week's accumulation of peaty soil, but the prolonged timespan of his outfits' "three months' service" suggests that he already belongs to the bog's slow time.

Both Cathy's and Heathcliff's temporary and permanent immersions in the bog—the transient condition of dirtiness and the abiding one of their bodies preserved side by side—exude the porous confusion of the physical and conceptual species boundaries that Jane Eyre reaffirms by her decision to seek human help instead of burying herself prematurely amid the moors' mosses and heather. In the novel's final passage, Lockwood intuits the advantages of accepting this porosity: peace and unity. Noting that Cathy's grave is "half buried in heath" and over Edgar's are both "turf and moss creeping," he concludes, "I lingered round them, under that benign sky: watched the moths fluttering among the heath and harebells, listened to the soft wind breathing through the grass, and wondered how any one could ever imagine unquiet slumbers for the sleepers in that quiet earth" (337). If the moors are a bad place to live in, they are a good place to be buried in, with the cushioning verdure and slow time of the bog mollifying the corpses whose lives were so brief and whose deaths were so violent. Stevie Davies also reads in the novel an exchange of anthropocentrism for the moors' rhythms of life and decomposition:

> Each grave is involved in a different stage in the process of reversion to the moor, which is also claiming the derelict church. When the process is complete, each grave will be equally and wholly covered over with heath. The deletion of individual identity is felt as positive and recreative.... At the point where the moors have reclaimed the graves entirely, and rubbed out the writing on the headstones so that human identity is deleted, the code which has characterized this novel will finally be broken. (*Free Woman* 150)

This reading dovetails with recent criticism that highlights the materiality of the bodies circulating in *Wuthering Heights* and connect this materiality to the novel's curious temporalities. Sarah Ross points to "Heathcliff's brutal rigor mortis," arguing that his physical condition allows the "release" of his soul "to wander the moors for eternity" (176). By arguing that his graveside "reunion" with Catherine "does not negate Messianic time, but stands apart, providing relief to the agony of loss in the corporeal present" (178), Ross excavates yet another timescale into the bogs' entangled temporalities. Carol Margaret Davison pursues these links between Emily's bodies and biblical time, asserting that her corpses are "strategically used as mirrors to reflect back the eschatological ideas and moral, judgmental sensibilities of their viewers" (155).

As we have seen in chapter 1, this eschatological sensibility is Patrick Brontë's own—making the ways that Emily and Charlotte write about bog temporalities, from the momentary crises of bog bursts to the annual cycles whereby plants sprout, blossom, and wither to the changes visible only at the scale of geological deep time, part of a longer conversation among the Brontës about whether, as Marsh asks, man is of or above nature.

The force of Catherine's and Heathcliff's love rockets past the conceptual brambles that waylay both Patrick and Charlotte's moor texts addressing the relationship between man and nature. Their orthodoxy—Patrick's intellectually formidable but stylistically sticky combination of scientific debates and biblical eschaton; the dramatic extremes of Jane Eyre's embattled *Bildung*, which shuttle her from one biome to the next as she attempts to reconcile her spiritual and earthly needs—is wholly rejected by heretic Catherine, who differently values Earth and Heaven. On her deathbed, she wishes to hasten death, asking Nelly to open the window—to Nelly's conventional response, "I won't give you your death of cold," Catherine counters, "You won't give me a chance of life, you mean"—and she hallucinates an ultimatum to Heathcliff, "I'll not lie there by myself: they may bury me twelve feet deep, and throw the church down over me, but I won't rest till you are with me. I never will!" (126). For Heathcliff, too, his eventual burial in the peat is a consummation devoutly to be wished; at Edgar Linton's burial, Heathcliff bribes the sexton to bury him next to her and open up the adjacent sides of their coffins ensures that they will be embalmed in peat side by side, corporeally together forever. When he attempts to convince Nelly that he "disturbed nobody" by this successful, second attempt to open her grave, Nelly taunts him with the possibility that "she had been dissolved into earth, or worse," and asks, "What would you have dreamt of then?" His answer, "Of dissolving with her, and being more happy still! ... Do you suppose I dread any change of that sort? I expected such a transformation on raising the lid—but I'm better pleased that it should not commence till I share it" (288). This conversation is temporally complex; his impassioned speech toggles chaotically between two occasions when he disturbed Catherine's grave. It is therefore easy to miss the fact that he *does* see, in this second disruption, her perfectly preserved bog body: he had merely "expected" her corporal dissolution. It was during the *first* attempted exhumation that he encounters instead an immaterial ghost. He recalls, "There was another sigh, close at my ear.... I appeared to feel the warm breath of it displacing the sleet-laden wind. I knew no living thing in flesh and blood was by" (289). Though he reports, "I was consoled at once," the ghost mocks him by leading him "home," where, though he feels "sure ... [to] see here there," he recalls, "I looked round impatiently—I felt her by me—I could *almost* see her, and yet I *could not*! I ought to have sweat blood then, from the anguish of my yearning ... to have but one glimpse!" (289).

Her immaterial ghost only frustrates him; her bog body, eighteen years later, calms him: "Now, since I've seen her, I'm pacified—a little. It was a strange way of killing: not by inches, but by fractions of hairbreadths, to beguile me with the specter of a hope through eighteen years!" (290). "Fractions of hairbreadths" encapsulates bog's slow temporality, which will reduce nearly to zero the eighteen-year distance between their deaths, just as the dual temporality of this monologue dissolves the two decades-apart exhumations, and Catherine's two corpses—the ghostly breath above ground and the bog body below—into one another. By embracing the inevitability of his body's dissolution, by being unafraid of Catherine's "transformation" and wishing to "be dissolved in earth" with her, he abjures any claim to corporeal exceptionalism. But because they are buried in peat, his openness to decay paradoxically ensures that he and Catherine will be preserved together—and at the scale of deep time. The bog will materially accomplish the entanglements that Heathcliff's ambiguities foreshadow at the level of narrative. Catherine's slow transformation into a bog body and Heathcliff's violent disruptions of her languorous decomposition most vividly exemplify how Emily Brontë takes advantage of the moors' uncanny temporality to collate narratives that proceed at different paces. By uniting the many threads of Emily's chronologically convoluted novel, the bog body provides a material analog of the frame narration by similarly intertwining the lives of two generations.

FROM SOUTH CRAVEN MOOR TO MOOR HOUSE:
THE RETURN OF ANTHROPOCENTRISM

The bog body has this power because, as Sanders points out, the uncanny lingering of bog bodies lends a sense of "urgency to the reality of the physical body" and highlights the "stubborn materiality of the body's corporeal existence" (xv). In *Wuthering Heights*, even ghosts bleed. But like Lockwood, Jane Eyre struggles to retain her anthropocentrism during trials that challenge her species-being. This is why, though Jane seriously desires to become a bog body in the middle of her moorland exile, Charlotte Brontë does not centralize the bog body as a narrative linchpin for *Jane Eyre*. As Jane refuses to acknowledge humanity's essential physicality, the novel's temporal structures decenter challenges to orthodox definitions of *Anthropos*. The unwonted verb tenses make the moorland episode stick out, jaggedly, from the narrative's temporal fabric, and her refusal, at the novel's end, to tell Rochester about her struggles on the moor also isolates the incident. This is why, as Jane shelters under crag and among bracken, she suddenly refashions her chosen death as one of quick, violent dismemberment, not deep-time decomposition: "Well, I would rather die yonder than in a street or on a frequented road.... And far better that crows and ravens—if any ravens there be in these regions—should pick my flesh from my bones, than that they should be prisoned in a workhouse coffin and molder in a pauper's grave" (379–80). Her curious interjection ("if any ravens there be in these regions") digresses into natural history, shifting the matter of survival into one of representation, just as her imagination of becoming pieces willingly accepts the gruesome violence it would to reinsert herself—like the peat-cutters' portioning of the Cowanscroft suicide—into the narrower scale of human history.

Jane contemplates becoming not a bird singing in a pastoral landscape, but a morbid *Bewick's* vignette set in a violent nature/culture contact zone. These two fantasies, being eaten by birds or interred by generations of decaying mosses, allow Jane to envision herself wholly incorporated within nature, without even an insubstantial "workhouse coffin" separating them. The grimness of this episode suggests that only in death can Jane metaphysically embrace the multispecies tableaux that delight her aesthetically. Ultimately, her desire to refigure her species-being is weaker than her desire for transcendence. For many characters, she is already dead (her aunt acts like it, her uncle in Madeira has been told it, Rochester fears it), so leaving the moors facilitates her rebirth. She keeps nature's physicality at arm's length by retreating into the comfortable rhythms of word-painting, by which she exerts control over nature and asserts her corporeal exceptionality. Her painterly eye resumes its habitual position surmounting all to reduce this complex ecosystem to a desolate but tame view on a two-dimensional canvas. She does acknowledge, however, that this contact zone's lonely liminality offers a chance at reinvention:

> I see no passengers on these roads: they stretch out east, west, north, and south white, broad, lonely; they are all cut in the moor, and the heather grows deep and wild to their very verge. Yet a chance traveler might pass by.... I might be questioned: I could give no answer but what would sound incredible and excite suspicion. Not a tie holds me to human society at this moment—not a charm or hope calls me where my fellow-creatures are—

one that saw me would have a kind thought or a good wish for me. I have no relative but the universal mother, Nature: I will seek her breast and ask for repose. (371–72)

Forced to avoid human contact, Jane must for first time follow Helen's advice not to think too much of human beings, but in place of the afterlife her friend has in mind, Jane fills this vacuum of intraspecies social interaction with Mother Nature and contemplates reconfiguring herself as a living organism akin to (and kin to) the animals and plants around her, not above them.

For a time, this multispecies experiment prospers, and Jane demonstrates "what it might be to survive and thrive in disrupted landscapes" (Shotwell 86), such as the moors, whose anthropogenic degradation I elucidate in chapter 1. In reminiscences such as "I saw ripe bilberries gleaming here and there, like jet beads in the heath: I gathered a handful and ate them with the bread," Jane's physiological and aesthetic needs dovetail (372). The analogy between bilberry and jet beads highlights Mother Nature's generosity in providing resources, some of which are easily plucked but others, like the jet seams mined under Yorkshire, require far more human labor and disruption to the landscape. This gemological reference echoes the real-life inspiration for Jane's moors: Brontë's 1845 stay at Hathersage Vicarage, home of her friend Ellen Nussey and model for Moor House. Charlotte explored North Lees Hall (the real-life Thornfield), attended a church where the name "Eyre" is etched, and toured the "famous caverns where the semi-precious mineral Blue John was mined," an experience that Charlotte, who "liked to contemplate the beauties of nature in silence," would have preferred without her fellow tourists' loud chatter (Barker 533, 534). By paralleling migrations of rocks and organisms between Yorkshire and Derbyshire—Jane and Charlotte, jet and fluorite, the coal for which jet is a precursor and the lead whose seams are veined with Blue John—this mineral imagery reflects Jane's desire that the nature should nourish the body and the eye. With no voluble tourists around, she can contemplate natural beauty without her ears disrupting her eyes. She can appreciate the diminutive spectacle of bee and lizard migrations in a way that embodies Anthropocene feminists' "loving attention to our proximal ecosystems and coinhabitants" (Shotwell 86):

What a still, hot, perfect day! What a golden desert this spreading moor! Everywhere sunshine. I wished I could live in it and on it. I saw a lizard run over the crag; I saw a bee busy among the sweet bilberries. I would fain at the moment have become bee or lizard, that I might have found fitting nutriment, permanent shelter here. But I was a human being, and had a human being's wants: I must not linger where there was nothing to supply them. (373–74)

In this passage, Jane's recurrent flirtation with empathic multispecies identification intensifies into a desire to shift species entirely, before pivoting abruptly back to human exceptionalism. Despite the movements of bee and lizard, Jane describes this quiet space as if it were a still life. Her language of lights and tints returns (she cannot "live in" and "on" sunshine) and, with it, her insistence on the taxonomic distance between human and nonhuman. Nature becomes again primarily an object to delight Jane's visual perception and test her virtuosity as a word-painter:

> My glazed eye wandered over the dim and misty landscape. I saw I had strayed far from the village: it was quite out of sight. The very cultivation surrounding it had disappeared. I had, by cross-ways and by-paths, once more drawn near the tract of moorland; and now, only a few fields, almost as wild and unproductive as the heath from which they were scarcely reclaimed, lay between me and the dusky hill. (379)

As the "dim and misty landscape" resists her "glazed" eye, the village ("quite out of sight") eludes her painterly vision altogether, and (as in her paintings) the landscape is reduced to "only a few fields," all but Jane's raw subjectivity has "disappeared." The temporal clarity of her verb tenses begins to reconstruct her sense of a distinction between the past and the urgent "now."

Sighting an *ignis fatuus* inspires her to extricate herself from the enveloping marshland. By its light, she is led "aslant over the hill, through a wide bog, which would have been impossible in winter, and was splashy and shaking even now, in the height of summer" (380). The *ignis fatuus*—a spontaneous combustion of marsh gases, produced when methane and phosphine combine—is as elusive as its fanciful nickname, the "will-o'-the-wisp," implies. "Because ignis fatuus appears to hover, recede, vanish, and then reappear," Dianne Meredith explains, "the term is also used figuratively for any delusion that leads one astray" (329). Readers familiar with British folklore will find its appearance ominous because only a few traditions "claim the will-o'-the-wisps are benevolent fairy lights that appear in order to help people who are lost or in danger. Those who can see them have the gift of foreknowledge. Usually, however, the lights are cast in malevolence, which is ascribed to the work of devils or evil elves" (328–29). The uncertainty introduced by these contradictions—is Jane a clairvoyant being helped along by fairies, or is she being duped by supernatural foes?—is compounded by the fact that *ignes fatui* are often witnessed before bog bursts, like the natural "phenomenon" observed by Emily, Branwell, and Anne in 1824 at Crow Hill. That the bog Jane crosses is "splashy and shaking even now, in the height of summer" is a further sign that the conditions for such a crisis are brewing. Patrick's account of Crow Hill's conditions just before the eruption—the bog itself being unusually soft for the summer and the atmosphere being full of electrical charge—tally with Jane's observations. But Jane does not pursue the image of the *ignis fatuus* as an empirical sign of a potential ecological disaster. The folk tradition that holds the will-o'-the-wisp to be a harbinger of a bog burst also maintains that these eruptions are caused by fairies blowing hot winds across the moors. This latter account is Jane's preferred framework for writing about her ordeal. Having declined to identify with bees and lizards, Jane (who learns these tales from Gateshead Hall servants) sees the moors as potentially full of fairies and elves, grappling imaginatively with a landscape constructed by folklore rather than a biodiverse mire constructed atop rocks and decaying organisms.

Doing so allows Jane to add dramatic interest to her narrative; as Gladwin argues of literature written about bogs, the "uncanny qualities associated with bogs ... enable creative representation" precisely *because* their physical indeterminacy makes them "difficult to write about or discuss in definitive terms" (3). Brontë deftly employs this ambiguous space to elicit anxiety for a narrator who readers know must have survived the ordeal in some way. Scrambling through a bog at this transition point from Thornfield Hall to either death or an as-yet-unknown destination makes folkloric sense, furthermore, because bogs are "considered to be gateways to other worlds," as a result of their "transitional and interstitial" positioning as buffers between other biomes (2). Tradition holds that the fairies positioned along these boggy gateways open supernatural realms—a superstition that shapes Jane's early imprisonment in the Red Room after her confrontation with John Reed over *Bewick's*. Just before she encounters the apparition of her dead uncle, she misrecognizes herself as a different creature altogether, as a

> strange little figure there gazing at me, with a white face and arms specking the gloom, and glittering eyes of fear moving where all else was still, had the effect of a real spirit: I thought it like one of the tiny phantoms, half fairy, half imp, Bessie's evening stories represented as coming out of lone, ferny dells in moors, and appearing before the eyes of belated travelers. I returned to my stool. (18)

Jane cannot classify her species-being ("half fairy, half imp") and interprets her reflection as an inhuman "it," and the fear she feels at this alienation prompts her obedient return to the stool she was told not to leave. After her release from the Red Room, Bessie attempts to soothe her by singing, "Why did they send me so far and so lonely, / Up where the moors spread and grey rocks are piled? / Men are hard-hearted, and kind angels only / Watch o'er the steps of a poor orphan child" (27). These folktales and songs position the moors as a nebulous, inhuman space of danger and homelessness—touchstones of bogs' folkloric associations—and teach Jane to manage her emotions and species identification through narrative representation, while foreshadowing her real-life enactment of these imagined scenes. She *will* become that orphan exiled to the moors; she *will* emerge out of them to appear before the belated traveler St. John Rivers. Jane's rejection of *Gulliver's Travels*, "that cherished volume" used by Bessie to soothe her at the same period, similarly foreshadows Jane's uneasy travels after leaving Thornfield, for young Jane shudders at Gulliver's fate as "a most desolate wanderer in most dread and dangerous regions" (26). His exploits exemplify the fears, disappointments, and vulnerabilities that accompany multispecies engagement in a rapidly changing landscape. It signals that she will ultimately refuse to valorize nonhuman organisms or wish to become one, both of which Lemuel Gulliver chooses at the Land of the Houyhnhmns. When the "poor, obscure, plain, and little" are classed as inhuman, experimenting with the species-being of *Anthropos* augurs isolation, pain, and death (292). She must always transcend traits and states defined as nonhuman, including physicality, and to convey this transcendence to her dear readers, her narrative draws heavily on cultural devaluations of moors as physically impoverished but spiritually suggestive wastelands.

As the sticky bog rouses her—"Here I fell twice; but as often I rose and rallied my faculties" (380)—it rouses her commitment to her oppositional model of humanity. Regardless of the "exhausted limbs" and the clingy bits of mud and moss that attest instead to *Anthropos*'s vulnerability and permeability, she desires transcendence. After this physical trial, perceptual trials multiply, allowing Jane an orderly transition from animal to human artist:

> Having crossed the marsh, I saw a trace of white over the moor. I approached it; it was a road or a track: it led straight up to the light, which now beamed from a sort of knoll, amidst a clump of trees—firs, apparently, from what I could distinguish of the character of their forms and foliage through the gloom. My star vanished as I drew near: some obstacle had in-

> tervened between me and it. I put out my hand to feel the dark mass before me: I discriminated the rough stones of a low wall—above it, something like palisades, and within, a high and prickly hedge. I groped on. Again a whitish object gleamed before me: it was a gate—a wicket; it moved on its hinges as I touched it. On each side stood a sable bush-holly or yew. (381)

In this passage, Jane recalibrates her perception, which initially proves as misleading as the folk tradition would regard the *ignus fatuus* to be. A mere "trace of white" may be "a road or a track," which follows a "sort of knoll" capped by trees of undetermined species and number (they are a "clump"), while the light is blocked by "some obstacle" that is faintly "like palisades" and leads to a "whitish" (not white) object. As Jane's eyes strain and she attempts to classify the trees ("bush-holly or yew"), dashes indicate the depth of her confusion and the length of time it takes for moor, bog, stones, and bushes to resolve into wall, gate, palisades, and hedge. Beyond the quaking bog, the boundaries between ground and sky solidify, and the whitish gleams stabilize from flickering, deceptive lights into stable, touchable objects.

The flanking bush-hollies (or yews) are less an indication of thriving natural world than an architectural element, evidence of human control over nature, indicating that Jane will soon regain admittance into a domesticated world of human sociability. In a reversal of her position at the Gateshead Hall window-seat, she looks into a house through a low casement:

> Entering the gate and passing the shrubs, the silhouette of a house rose to view, black, low, and rather long.... In seeking the door, I turned an angle: there shot out the friendly gleam again, from the lozenged panes of a very small latticed window, within a foot of the ground, made still smaller by the growth of ivy or some other creeping plant, whose leaves clustered thick over the portion of the house wall in which it was set. (381)

As Jane looks through this window, the "ivy" or "creeping plant" provides her with a symmetrical frame for human domesticity. This aesthetic framing of familial intimacy by plants that are barely controlled continues as Jane moves a "spray of foliage," a painterly phrase that marks her return to aestheticizing and controlling natural organisms:

> The aperture was so screened and narrow, that curtain or shutter had been deemed unnecessary; and when I stooped down and put aside the spray of foliage shooting over it, I could see all within. I could see clearly a room with a sanded floor, clean scoured; a dresser of walnut, with pewter plates

ranged in rows, reflecting the redness and radiance of a glowing peat-fire. I could see a clock, a white deal table, some chairs. The candle, whose ray had been my beacon, burnt on the table; and by its light an elderly woman, somewhat rough-looking, but scrupulously clean, like all about her, was knitting a stocking. (381)

The moor recedes; the wild *ignis fatuus* becomes a candle, and Mother Nature a servant knitting. A tree becomes a dresser, ore becomes plate, and *Sphagnum* becomes orderly blocks of fuel. The moor's Gothic properties are tamed as the foreboding folktales of evil elves and catastrophe-causing fairies are replaced by quotidian images of domestic order and comfort. As Jane approaches Moor House, the benefits of intraspecies bonding—the safety, comfort, and companionship of family life—come into focus. Brought to a point of precarity so extreme she will die if she cannot secure shelter immediately, Jane is so absorbed in the spectacle of the Rivers sisters through the window that she forgets her physical pain and waits patiently before applying for shelter. Jane's choice between curtain and window, between the "natural" and the "social," is again staged. The strange, stubborn repetition in her later announcement to St. John Rivers, "I like Moor House, and I will live at Moor House; I like Diana and Mary, and I will attach myself for life to Diana and Mary," reveals her ultimate decision to reject Helen's warning not to exaggerate the significance of *Anthropos* (446). The allure of intraspecies sociability, naturalized as genetic filiation with the discovery that the sisters are her cousins, triumphs over Mother Nature's too-slender offerings and her damaged ecosystems. Only her paintings are left to suggest that her strength of vision relies on the interspecies empathy and identification that, like the mud and peat clinging to her dress, she sloughs off as she enters Moor House.

Domesticity offers its own dramas. To be home requires constant vigilance, a heroic separation from a wet, dirty landscape. Having been covered in peaty sludge, Jane finds extreme satisfaction in seeing "all my things, clean and dry," in seeing her silk dress now "quite decent" because "traces of the bog were removed," and in seeing her "very shoes and stockings . . . purified and rendered presentable," with "no trace of the disorder I so hated, and which seemed so to degrade me, left" (391). This cleansing completes the restoration of Jane's species-being and of her anthropocentrism. Syntactically, the lonely position of "left," separated from its referent ("trace") by appositions and commas, performs the dangers of dirt—of objects not in their proper place, like Jane herself, lately in exile on the moors. As Eithne Henson observes, "Her destitute wanderings have involved her with the moorland landscape at an unacceptable level; she is sodden and 'bemired' in the bog, and there can be no layer of literary or religious text between her and sensory experience" (52). Only ritual purification can overcome this horror—a cleansing of her person and her surroundings. Upon inheriting her uncle's fortune and learning the Riverses are her cousins, she determines,

> My first aim will be to *clean down* (do you comprehend the full force of the expression?)—to *clean down* Moor House from chamber to cellar; my next to rub it up with bees-wax, oil, and an indefinite number of cloths, till it glitters again; my third, to arrange every chair, table, bed, carpet, with mathematical precision; afterwards I shall go near to ruin you in coals and peat to keep up good fires in every room.... My purpose, in short, is to have all things in an absolutely perfect state of readiness for Diana and Mary before next Thursday; and my ambition is to give them a beau-ideal of a welcome when they come. (450–51)

Cleaning down plays a key role in Jane's full investiture as a politically endowed human being. This speech flaunts her physical, intellectual, verbal, and economic powers, forces that she will martial to separate herself from the polluting dirt of the nearby bog. She declares her intent to apply all her effort and cash to protect her human family from the natural forces of slow decomposition that penetrate their porous physical and species boundaries. The glittering, hygienic surfaces of the scrubbed home, the blistering heat of its fires, and its freshly covered walls and floors embody her restored purity, strength, and corporeal exceptionality. "When all was finished," she boasts, "I thought Moor House as complete a model of bright modest snugness within, as it was, at this season, a specimen of wintry waste and desert dreariness without" (452). Pleased with the stark contrast between inside and outside, Jane obsessively maintains a home that materializes and enforces her oppositional model of *Anthropos*.

CLOVEN TREES AND CRUMBLING GRANGES:
ULTRASOCIAL *ANTHROPOS* AMONG THE RUINS

But no matter how much Jane Eyre cleans down, entanglements persist between species and between organic bodies and the non-organic rocks underneath, around, and within them. Describing this hybridity, Alaimo points out that efforts to cordon off the human body from the earth, to use human powers to fight the moors' entropy, will always fail. She argues that "the distinction between biological and geological agency is not tenable because biological and chemical transformations flow through the world in multiple and messy ways." Alaimo lists among these messy ways that oil, carbon, and other fuels—the burning of which features high on Jane's tactics for fighting dirt—bind human and nonhuman as "a matter of chemistry and, on epochal time scales, biology, as fossil fuels issue from decomposed organisms" ("Shell" 95). In the Brontës' time, this concept of fundamental, unavoidable geological and organic messiness circulated in the works of Sir Humphry Davy. In *Consolations in Travel* (1830), read by the Brontës, one passage contrasts the short-term, catastrophic effects of lightning strikes to the lingering, subtle effects of unspent electricity in charged atmospheres (like Crow Hill bog on September 2, 1824, and Thornfield on the night of Jane and Rochester's engagement). Davy catalogs the human and nonhuman causes of the decay of organic matter and man-made objects:

> The chemical agencies of water and air, are assisted by those of electricity; and their joint effects combined with those of gravitation and the mechanical ones I first described, are sufficient to account for the results of time. But, the physical powers of nature in producing decay, are assisted likewise by certain agencies or energies of organized beings.... In the crevices of walls, where this soil is washed down, even the seeds of trees grow, and, gradually as a building becomes more ruined, ivy and other parasitical plants cover it. Even the animal creation lends its aid in the process of destruction, when man no longer labors for the conservation of his works. (272–73)

Davy lists foxes, insects, and humans as examples of the "organized beings" whose "agencies or energies" contribute to the destruction of their environment, but he also acknowledges the less easily observed agencies of nature's non-animal forces. Of man-made buildings, he notes that "in a few centuries they decay and are in ruins," for they must "yield to the operation of the dews of Heaven, of frost, rain, vapor, and imperceptible atmospheric influences; and, as the worm devours the lineaments of his mortal beauty, so the lichens and the moss, and the most insignificant plants shall feed upon his columns and his pyramids" (273–74). In his blending of Romantic imagery of the ruins of past human civilizations with the prophecies of early ecologists (figures like George Perkins Marsh and Louis Compton Miall, discussed in chapter 1), Davy is as concerned as Jane herself at the consequences of natural and human-caused decay over time.

He is, however, far more accepting of the inevitability of decay. In his discussions of the intimate relationships between human activities and the microcosmic and macrocosmic networks that continually construct, assemble, and destroy the building blocks of the Earth, Davy characterizes the boundaries between man and nature that Jane works so hard to maintain as physical impossibilities. Clues of this impossibility pervade the novel, including Brontë's fashioning of Jane's new house and village as liminal spaces positioned between village and moors. When the servant Hannah explains the house's unfixed appellation, "Some calls it Marsh End, and some calls it Moor House," her use of dialect and parallel structure evoke a regional sense of place while making it clear that, for the villagers, the proper "end" of a marsh is a "house" (392). A decided ambiguity lingers in this fluctuating denomination, striking the novel's customary note of frustrated taxonomic uncertainty. The note is also struck by the village's oxymoronic name—Morton, or "moor town"—which recalls, too, the Brontës' own view at the parsonage's back door, poised between village and moor, and Charlotte's own period of "cleaning down" Hathersage Vicarage (the model for Moor House) in 1845. Marsh's *Man and Nature*, in condemning the uncontrolled burning of heather, hypothesizes that these floating classifications arise from indiscriminately applied regionalisms:

> The English nomenclature of this geographical feature does not seem to be well settled. We have *bog, swamp, marsh, morass, moor, fen, turf moss, peat moss, quagmire*, all of which, though sometimes more or less accurately discriminated, are often used interchangeably, or are perhaps employed, each exclusively, in a particular district. (29)

Despite Marsh's and Jane's tribute to the moors' beauty and biodiversity (as I point out in the Introduction, the Brontës' descriptions of the moors were praised for their accuracy by critics and scientists alike), they ignore the hints of the moors' biodiversity encoded in this verbal fecundity. Marsh's account unifies regional landscapes as "English," while Jane repudiates empathic identification with nonhuman species in favor of a starkly imagined opposition between the unclean, unsafe moors and the tidy, secure home reserved for intraspecies relations.

This rejection is a survival mechanism, as Jane's belonging in human communities is tied to the purity of her species identification. In an ominous speech to Jane, St. John Rivers, head of Moor House, clarifies that while *nice* people have interspecies empathy, powerful people have little use for it: "My sisters, you see, have a pleasure in keeping you ... as they would have a pleasure in keeping and cherishing a half-frozen bird, some wintry wind might have driven through their casement. I feel more inclination to put you in the way of keeping yourself" (400). Again identified as a bird, Jane Eyre must reestablish her *Anthropos* status by crossing the contact zone of the window and reasserting her humanity. Having failed to prove to John Reed that she is not a "bad animal," and having successfully crafted an erotic game out of this task with Rochester, Jane must strive once more to exhibit the correct species traits designated by a local patriarch—only this time, frigid St. John withholds the rewards and risks of the erotic excitements proper to *homo ludens* (playing man) as Jane earns the title of *homo faber* (working man). She must labor ("keeping yourself") and strive after continual transcendence ("I hope you will begin to look beyond Moor House and Morton, and sisterly society, and the selfish calm and sensual comfort of civilized affluence" [451]). Jane is content to become *Anthropos* by becoming *homo faber*. During her moorland wanderings, a "wild and unproductive" heath was the place she selects for her death, but she epiphanically chooses life in a valley where she sees "pasture-fields, and corn-fields," as well as a "heavily-laden wagon laboring up the hill" (379, 374). For Jane, to be human is to work: "Human life and human labor were near. I must struggle on: strive to live and bend to toil like the rest" (374). As the land is cultivated, so must Jane cultivate herself.

    John Gowdy and Lisi Krall identify this model of laboring in "The Ultrasocial Origin of the Anthropocene." During the rise of agriculture, humans became one "superorganism," making it difficult to dislodge the anthropocentric attitudes underpinning climate change. Our "faith in human uniqueness and agency"—which informs Jane's definition of *Anthropos* and motivates her will to live—"has blinded us to the evolutionary forces driving human social organization.... Ultrasociality has given human society features that make it extremely difficult to change course even in the face of impending disaster" (138). The combination of Jane's oppositional model of the human, her desire to be loved, and the ultrasociality of agronomics causes her to project onto the landscape—onto a denuded Mother Nature—the resistance she encounters on her path to *Bildung*. This resistance usually emanates from humans whose positions in gendered socioeconomic hierarchies threaten Jane's bid to be recognized as fully human and to inherit the rights and responsibilities attendant upon it. Jane's ascension of the property ladder (inheriting her uncle's fortune and deciding to share it with her cousins), her acquisition of the legal right to bear Rochester's heirs (and thus to influence the future of his property, despite competition from Blanche and Bertha), and her negotiations with powerful men for equality and self-determination (John Reed, the Reverend Brocklehurst, St. John Rivers, and Rochester himself) all reflect entanglements of class and gender with ultrasociality. Ecological consequences follow from these struggles over sexual and economic forms of reproduction, although due to "the constraints on human intentionality imposed by ultrasociality," they are not always straightforward or easy to trace (138). The repeated frustration of Jane's desire for independence by her own contrary impulses toward ultrasociality vividly dramatizes these constraints, and her interactions as an adult with the Moor House, Thornfield, and Ferndean estates illustrate how the speciesism associated with ultrasociality contributes to environmental degradation.

In Anne Brontë's *The Tenant of Wildfell Hall*, the burden of ultrasociality rests on the narrator, the gentleman farmer Gilbert Markham, whose stalwart work ethic matches Jane Eyre's own but whose knowledge of land management far exceeds hers. Marianne Thormählen notes that his namesake, seventeenth-century agriculturist Gervase Markham, indicates that Gilbert is a progressive farmer committed to improving his lands, reading the latest agriculture periodicals, and working closely with his hired hands ("Agriculture" 278). Though his social status is inferior to Helen's, his narrative at times echoes the refinement of Davy's literary style. Davy also appears in the novel through the material form of his books (the heroine Helen Graham owns his works) and through Gilbert's embodiment of Davy's ideas: his agricultural theories, his attention to the complexity of multispecies agencies that shape moors, and his moral certainty of humans' responsibility for environmental change. When Markham first describes Wildfell Hall, a Romantic sensibility colors his scientifically accurate discriminations between profitable and unprofitable lands as he climbs above his fertile lands to Wildfell:

> the wildest and the loftiest eminence in our neighborhood, where ... the hedges, as well as the trees, become scanty and stunted, the former, at length, giving place to rough stone fences, partly greened over with ivy and moss, the latter to larches and Scotch fir-trees, or isolated blackthorns. The fields, being rough and stony, and wholly unfit for the plough, were mostly devoted to the posturing of sheep and cattle; the soil was thin and poor: bits of grey rock here and there peeped out from the grassy hillocks; bilberry-plants and heather—relics of more savage wildness—grew under the walls; and in many of the enclosures, ragweeds and rushes usurped supremacy over the scanty herbage. (22)

In spite of the acidic soils that his professional eye so reliably diagnoses, Gilbert is drawn to these "relics of more savage wildness" as he narrates his upward movement as a temporal journey back in time. Though he indulges in Romantic commonplaces about uncivilized moors, his ensuing description reflects Davy's own understanding of ecosystemic change (due to the "physical powers of nature in producing decay") and the role played by humans ("when man no longer labors for the conservation of his works"). Wildfell Hall is "venerable and picturesque to look at, but doubtless, cold and gloomy enough to inhabit, with its thick stone mullions and little latticed panes, its time-eaten air-holes, and its too lonely, too unsheltered situation,—only shielded from the war of wind and weather by a group of Scotch firs, themselves half blighted with storms" (22–23). The decay of the manor, its stones riddled with "time-eaten air-holes," "broken windows," and "dilapidated roof" over stone walls and protected by an iron gate with granite decorations (23), recapitulates in miniature the historical formation of the moors over decades of exposure after deforestation. *Tenant* performs *Consolation*'s assertion that a "polished surface of a building, or statue" will soon host "the seeds of lichens and mosses, which are constantly floating in our atmosphere," which find in the building or statue "a place of repose," with the result that "from their death, their decay and decomposition carbonaceous matter is produced, and at length a soil is formed, in which grass can fix its roots" (272).

Wildfell Hall not only contains a copy of Davy's *Consolations of Travel*: its exterior and its gardens model Davy's accounts of natural and human-caused decay, of the desertification of deforested lands into heaths (described in chapter 1), and of the entropic encroachment of volunteer species into cultivated spaces when human care lapses. Gilbert Markham, too, observes a dual movement by which the Romantic imagery of moors as bleak, lifeless, and desolate is supplemented by a rhetoric of rugged endurance. Once subject to the ambivalently beneficial care of humans in the form of "the gardener's torturing shears," Wildfell Hall's garden has been

> left so many years untilled and untrimmed, abandoned to the weeds and the grass, to the frost and the wind, the rain and the drought, it presented a very singular appearance indeed. The close green walls of privet, that had bordered the principal walk, were two-thirds withered away, and the rest grown beyond all reasonable bounds; the old boxwood swan, that sat beside the scraper, had lost its neck and half its body: the castellated towers of laurel in the middle of the garden, the gigantic warrior that stood on

one side of the gateway, and the lion that guarded the other, were sprouted into such fantastic shapes as resembled nothing either in heaven or earth, or in the waters under the earth. (23)

Under the natural pressures of decay, Wildfell hybridizes, proliferating new, unnatural, "fantastic" species in the absence of human stewards who will cultivate only "reasonable" flora and fauna within their own territory. Gilbert observes, half-fascinated, half-disgusted, that the Hall's residents cannot successfully maintain the physical divisions required for protecting their property; the species boundaries in the organisms in their care are eroding, as are the grounds' fences, paths, or borders, which are no longer straight and neat. Like Davy's published works, whose accounts of organic decay are intended to help farmers improve their crops, Gilbert's narration operates on two registers simultaneously—the aesthetic and the economic. A single ultrasocial project of improvement unites his desires to marry Helen Graham, to serve as a father to her child, to improve his farm, and to restore Wildfell and its grounds. As Davy's *Elements of Agricultural Chemistry* makes clear, these goals are not impossible to square. The very processes of decay in moorland soils like those of the Hall make them useful for agricultural fields:

> Poor and hungry soils, such as are produced from the decomposition of granitic and sandstone rocks, remain very often for ages with only a thin covering of vegetation. Soils from the decomposition of limestone, chalks, and basalts are often clothed by nature with the perennial grasses; and afford, when ploughed up, a rich bed of vegetation for every species of cultivated plant.... The strata immediately beneath the soil contains materials which may be of use for improving it, a general view of the nature and position of rocks and strata in nature, will not, I trust, be unacceptable to the scientific farmer. (170–71)

A scientific farmer in Gilbert's position, contemplating the dual responsibility of stewarding farmlands and moorlands, would certainly find this situation not "unacceptable."

In terms of ultrasociality, then, Gilbert seems to be a responsible patriarch who models the benefits of agriculture-based human society. After all, he provides a safe haven for a woman alienated from an abusive husband and will recuperate a property that has been abandoned by its owners. At the end of *Tenant*, we have every indication that the Hall, the family inside, and moorlands around it will all be rehabilitated. By contrast, *Jane Eyre* provides examples of less responsible stewards who model ultrasociality's darker side—that it has "given human society features that make it extremely difficult to change course even in the face of impending disaster" (Gowdy and Krall 138). Jane's ultrasocial redistribution of her uncle's wealth ensures that the Rivers siblings can maintain their "sequestered home," to which "they clung . . . with a perfect enthusiasm of attachment" despite its poor (and rapidly degrading) condition (402). St. John's characterization of the degraded property reveals how necessary are Jane's efforts to clean the home, refresh its furnishings, and stabilize the estate with her capital:

> I am poor; for I find that, when I have paid my father's debts, all the patrimony remaining to me will be this crumbling grange, the row of scathed firs behind, and the patch of moorish soil, with the yew-trees and holly-bushes in front. I am obscure: Rivers is an old name; but of the three sole descendants of the race, two earn the dependant's crust among strangers, and the third considers himself an alien from his native country—not only for life, but in death. (407)

With its "crumbling" walls, "scathed" trees, and "moorish" soil, Moor House bears the weight of two timelines of human mismanagement—the long-term degradation of English uplands into moors and the shorter-term neglect of its impoverished heirs—until Jane restores her family's "patrimony." Like Gilbert, Jane foresees the "impending disaster" that the estate faces and attempts to avert it. But St. John, as stubbornly anthropocentric in his ultrasociality as Jane, doubly rejects her attempts at rehabilitation. First, his proposal of marriage attempts to reestablish his (ineffectual) patriarchal control over the family. Class and gender militate against the health of Moor House and its grounds as St. John, filled with "hardness and despotism," robs Jane of her "liberty of mind," and demands she "disown half [her] nature" (469, 459, 460). Second, by moving to India as a missionary, he cedes his ancestral position in a local ecosystem in favor of mastering imperial territory. Unlike Gilbert Markham, he abandons his responsibility to the estate and his neighborhood, just as indifferently has he hastens his own private "impending disaster," the early death that his sisters know will overtake him in India.

At first, Jane condemns St. John's disloyalty to the moors around him. She quizzically reflects, "never did he seem to roam the moors for the sake of their soothing silence—never seek out or dwell upon the thousand peaceful delights they could yield" (404). Yet she, too, treats the terrain as a political battlefield, and she, too, ecstatically leaves it. Anticipating that Thornfield will be in the same good condition she last saw it in, she revels in her return journey to the region, with its "familiar face" and "character," so "mild of feature and verdant of hue compared with the stern North-Midland moors of Morton!" (487). In doing so, Jane abjures her inherited responsibilities. The moors are reduced to a grim backdrop that elicits philosophically and narratively interesting discontent. They become, again, a place to flee rather than tend, a place to fashion into a domestic battleground rather than rehabilitate as a multispecies constellation of humans, animals, and plants embedded inside and around landscapes, rocks, and buildings. Even before abandoning Moreton for Thornfield, Jane resumes her use of her natural surroundings as raw material for self-construction through aesthetic representation—Rosamond is "electrified with delight" by Jane's "sundry views from nature, taken in the Vale of Morton and on the surrounding moors" (425)—and her profession that she shares Diana and Mary Rivers's love of the region employs the language of the disembodied artist, not the embodied heir:

> I saw the fascination of the locality. I felt the consecration of its loneliness: my eye feasted on the outline of swell and sweep—on the wild colouring communicated to ridge and dell by moss, by heath-bell, by flower-sprinkled turf, by brilliant bracken, and mellow granite crag. These details were just to me what they were to them—so many pure and sweet sources of pleasure. (402–3)

Jane's painterly "eye feasted" on "colouring" and on "details," while she chooses "brilliant" to modify "bracken" for its convenient alliteration, not for its scientific accuracy. Jane's early preference of mastering nature through representation—musing over *Bewick's* indoors instead of going on a walk that day—thus survives the shock of ejection from Thornfield. She is converted to Ruskin's characterization of the "desolate moor" as a space whose "sublimity ... depends on its monotony" and will eventually become "uninteresting or intolerable" (177). By changing representational modes to suit her transient symbolic needs, Jane treats nature as standing reserve, equally available for poetic conventions and feminist interventions.

The moors' erasure from the plot is settled when she announces by letter—not in person—that she will never to return to Morton. Jane also uses her representational faculties to downplay the moors earlier, when she reunites with Rochester. Questioned over her wanderings, she dryly remarks, "Well, whatever my sufferings had been, they were very short," to cut the conversation as short as she claims her sufferings were (506–7). She distracts him by weaving a vein of sexual jealousy into her story—"Of course, St. John Rivers' name came in frequently in the progress of my tale" (507)—with a sense of self-satisfaction that comes not only from her retroactive exertion of power over the uncontrollable landscape, but also from the resumption of her sexual power over Rochester. The moors have been linked with sex and danger in their conversations before. For example, when he cryptically informs Jane that he intends to "get sweet, fresh pleasure . . . as sweet and fresh as the wild honey the bee gathers on the moor," he refers to his bigamous desire. Jane returns, "It will sting—it will taste bitter, sir" (160), warning him that nature will thwart his unlawful desires, passing judgment through the bee-sting and the abatement of the nectar's sweetness. Jane's first suspicion that their attempt to wed will be blocked as unlawful also invokes the moors; standing at the altar just before Richard Mason and his lawyer stop the proceedings, she recalls seeing them stand "by the vault of the Rochesters, their backs towards us, viewing through the rails the old time-stained marble tomb, where a kneeling angel guarded the remains of Damer de Rochester, slain at Marston Moor in the time of the civil wars" (333). Moors, it seems, hold as much danger for the Rochesters as they do for poor orphan children like Jane. William Atkins notes that this association of crime and the moors was common in the Brontës' West Riding, where they were seen as "a notorious refuge for criminals, a hideout," an "uninhabitable wilderness" where lurked "death *everywhere*" (153). Sanders notes that most bog bodies are "believed to be Iron Age sacrifices or victims of punishment" (2), a link with criminal behavior seen also in the suicide of "A Scots Mummy," in J. Horsfall Turner's report that Patrick Brontë's brother "escaped being shot at Ballynahinch by hiding in a bog" (*Brontëana* 297), and in Emily Brontë's poem "The Outcast Mother," where a mother exiled to the snowy moors fears for the life of her illegitimate baby. The first novel Charlotte wrote, *The Professor*, includes the recitation of Scott's "The Covenanter's Fate," which describes a deathly battle waged in a bog (240), while her third novel, *Shirley*, parodically reimagines such a battle when the neighborhood's annual church picnic goes awry. When the two heroines' Sunday-schoolchildren march in mock-battle against the Dissenting church's own young parishioners, Shirley reflects with mock bravery, "We know that battle may follow prayer; and, as we believe that in the worst issue of battle, heaven must be our reward, we are ready and willing to redden the peat-moss with our blood" (286). This parody is the exception among the Brontës' works, as their moor symbolism tends to posit with complete sobriety that nature symbolizes, exposes, or avenges unlawful human arrangements through imagery, songs, and artwork and through their physical embodiment in nature/culture contact zones. In *Jane Eyre*, these crimes include not only the intimate betrayals of child abandonment (by Aunt Reed) and bigamy (by Rochester), but also large-scale betrayals of national unity (the Civil War). Rochester is connected to all three: his family participates in the war, and his father and brother cast him out, ordering him to the Caribbean to marry an heiress, whom he, in turn, abandons.

The likelihood that these domestic and political disruptions will continue into the next generation is indicated by the fate of Thornfield Hall, whose destruction (through the death of Bertha Mason) is a precondition for Jane and Rochester's legal marriage. Its fate also registers the likelihood that contact zones will serve as battlefields for these disruptions, for many of Thornfield's outdoor spaces exhibit signs of human management (gardening, farming, mining, road-laying, enclosure, scientific exploration, industrial development, and the like). Long before Bertha's conflagration, the Hall's garden incurs such a disruption when its historic horse-chestnut is destroyed by lightning the night Jane and Rochester become engaged. The appropriateness of this vicarious judgment goes beyond metaphor, for the same lordly attitude that allows him to objectify Bertha and Jane causes him to treat his garden as a space in which "each sense can be indulged," whose "ripe fruit and flowers to be plucked" in the manner of "classic ... images of nubile woman, available to be enjoyed" (Henson 45).[1] Jane recalls,

> No nook in the grounds more sheltered and more Eden-like; it was full of trees, it bloomed with flowers: a very high wall shut it out from the court, on one side; on the other, a beech avenue screened it from the lawn. At the bottom was a sunk fence; its sole separation from lonely fields: a winding walk, bordered with laurels and terminating in a giant horse-chestnut, circled at the base by a seat, led down to the fence. (286–87)

This narration adopts the punctuation of Jane's survey of Thornfield's grounds, but not its propitiousness. Rather than celebrate the ordering powers of human cultivation to create a profitable estate, the semantic enclosures erected by the semicolons and colons suggest Bertha's actual and Jane's potential imprisonment. The scent of Rochester's phallic cigar penetrates the flower-scented air and Jane's isolation; she wishes to "slip away unnoticed" but cannot. A "warning fragrance" tells her she "must flee" (287). In place of her privacy he offers a natural curiosity: directing her to a rare moth, he demands she "come and look at this fellow" to see "his wings," which remind him "of a West Indian insect; one does not often see so large and gay a night-rover in England" (288).

Their romance is always a natural economy (after she nurses Richard Mason, Rochester offers her "a half-blown rose" [249]), but this Caribbean reference specifically links his garden to his sexual treachery. Jane's comparison of Thornfield's garden to Eden, the original ecological paradise from which sinning humans are exiled, prefigures her unwitting complicity and their subsequent exiles—Jane to the moors, Rochester to Ferndean.

It also prefigures the fate of the horse-chestnut in front of which Rochester proposes. As he proposes, Jane recalls, "A waft of wind came sweeping down the laurel-walk, and trembled through the boughs of the chestnut: it wandered away—away—to an indefinite distance—it died" (293). After their betrothal, the storm breaks, but before they can return to the shelter of the Hall, "a livid, vivid spark leapt out of a cloud at which I was looking, and there was a crack, a crash, and a close rattling peal; and I thought only of hiding my dazzled eyes against Mr. Rochester's shoulder" (296). Jane fears for her own safety, but from the perspective of Marsh, White, Miall, Keighley, and other scientists and historians troubled by mounting evidence of anthropogenic environmental degradation, the ruined tree foretells acute ecological crisis. As Erskine Stuart notes, this episode could have been inspired by a real-life event. During one of Charlotte's visits to Ellen Nussey's home, The Rydings—a model for Thornfield Hall—a similar chestnut tree was "struck by lightning and thrown to the ground" (117). But topographically speaking, it is the horse-chestnut's isolation within the garden—in estates like Thornfield Hall and The Rydings, such trees are deliberately placed as aesthetic focal-points in ways that do not occur in undisturbed forests—that makes it liable to lightning strike. Another resonant lightning-blighted tree in the Brontës' history also suggests human culpability for such destruction. In the "Extraordinary Disruption," Patrick's poem about the 1824 Crow Hill bog burst, two symbolic warnings from God are ignored by Haworthians before the ecological disaster: first, the eerie warning light of a red halo hovering over the sky (a warning that also appears in *Jane Eyre* the evening before the aborted wedding ceremony, when Jane looks at the moon and sees "her disk ... blood-red and half overcast" [319]), and second, a lightning-struck tree, which Patrick's verse envisions as a candle that diffuses another warning halo of light across the sky:

> Yet, signs there were to philosophic eyes
> Prognostications sure, that storms should rise
> Ere day's dark close. Late in the previous night,
> The reeling stars shot down with slanting light,

> The crackling blaze hiss'd from the burning wood,
> And a bright halo round the candle stood;
> Whose melting stem unfurl'd a curling shroud (206)

This jarring shift in scale attempts to awe the reader into piously internalizing the relative insignificance of their earthly lives when compared to the afterlife—from God's eyes, the massive tree is but a candle—and recognize the role played by human sin in making the tree's destruction necessary. Patrick drives this lesson home by comparing the stricken tree with the Garden of Eden's own, which, after Adam and Eve are ejected as punishment for their sins, is guarded from further human access by flaming swords. "E'er since the flaming sword, in heavenly strife, / With fiery circles coped the tree of life" (204), Patrick writes, humans on Earth continue to reenact Adam and Eve's sins and their exile. Until the coming of the Savior, "Ten thousand fallen Eves allurements try; / Ten thousand Adams daily eat, and die" (204). As I discuss in chapter 1, Patrick judges the ultimate destruction of the Earth an acceptable sacrifice for saving human souls, just as the destruction of land, plants, and animals during the bog burst is acceptable because his children survived the disaster and his parishioners are warned to save their souls. In Patrick's short novel *The Cottage in the Wood*, a lightning-blast oak convinces his protagonist to reform. In *Jane Eyre*, the lightning-struck chestnut tree operates in a similar way: it is God's message that Jane and Rochester will soon be booted out of their Eden and must reform, Rochester by resigning himself to God's will about their future and Jane by ceasing to make him her "idol," her "whole world," and "almost" her "hope of heaven" (316).

The horse-chestnut is destroyed *for* Rochester and Jane. God smites it in their place. The storm brews as a result of their bigamous blasphemy, and the tree must be sacrificed as a warning that they must reform their souls before death overtakes their mortal bodies just as lightning overtakes the tree. At the same time, just as Patrick's sad litanies of animals and plants actually destroyed in the bog burst are arranged anthropocentrically to call attention to the hypothetical dangers posed by the burst to human beings, the sacrifice of Thornfield's horse-chestnut naturalizes Jane's oppositional model pitting human survival against nature. Charlotte Brontë's combinations of symbolic and material streams of causality—those linking Jane to the destruction of Thornfield's venerable tree and to her ejection from the security and love of her private Eden into the insecurities and discomforts of the moors—may seem to be difficult to reconstruct. But this is very much the point. As Alaimo argues, as a result of the widely distributed (both in time and space) webs of causality that comprise human/nonhuman relationships in the Anthropocene, human actions may "result, unintentionally, in the vast obliteration of ecosystems and the extinction of species" ("Shell" 90). We may experience anthropogenic causality as wholly unrelated to our personal actions, yet our assumption of innocence represents "a retreat from the radical risk, uncertainty, and vulnerability of the flesh, as humans are rendered strangely immaterial" (96). Jane's desire for this invulnerability, this lack of risk and responsibility incurred if one becomes sufficiently immaterial, aligns with Dipesh Chakrabarty's account of humans as a disembodied "force" in the Anthrocene, a "force" which is "neither a subject nor an object" but "simply the capacity to do things" ("Brute"). Alaimo's powerful critique of Chakrabarty's Enlightenment model of the human as a disembodied force suggests that Jane's model of *Anthropos* serves to excuse her personal, material complicity in environmental destruction. Consequently, though Chakrabarty's analysis is certainly as flawed as Alaimo alleges it is, his writings on the Anthropocene usefully demonstrate the difficulties of understanding one's complicity. These flaws show how harmful ideologies work. It is necessary, Chakrabarty argues,

> to view the human simultaneously on contradictory registers: as a geophysical force and as a political agent, as a bearer of rights and as author of action; subject to both the stochastic forces of nature (being itself one such force collectively) and open to the contingency of individual human experience; belonging at once to the differently-scaled histories of the planet, of life and species, and of human societies. ("Postcolonial" 14)

The causality that links Jane with the destruction of the horse-chestnut is precisely the type Alaimo and Chakrabarty describe: actions may have effects that we do not foresee and cannot control. Our inability to assess our effects on nature and to predict the cataclysms that disrupt the pace of deep time makes it possible to isolate human action from its effects and to see those effects as merely metaphorical. Jane's response—ignoring her culpability, she empathizes with the blighted tree while feeling energized by its destruction—epitomizes what it might feel like to witness, but not internalize, the effects of human-caused environmental degradation.

Jane is compromised as a witness particularly because of her emotionally powerful aesthetic response to the lightning-struck tree. The same thrill of survival that lends an anthropocentric edge to Jane's ironically pastoral descriptions of the miasmatic Lowood School trills through the scene when she seeks the blasted tree in the stormy night before her wedding:

> It was not without a certain wild pleasure I ran before the wind, delivering my trouble of mind to the measureless air-torrent thundering through space. Descending the laurel walk, I faced the wreck of the chestnut-tree; it stood up black and riven: the trunk, split down the center, gasped ghastly. The cloven halves were not broken from each other, for the firm base and strong roots kept them unsundered below; though community of vitality was destroyed—the sap could flow no more: their great boughs on each side were dead, and next winter's tempests would be sure to fell one or both to earth: as yet, however, they might be said to form one tree—a ruin, but an entire ruin. (318)

By anthropomorphizing the tree, Jane gives vent to the strong emotions she has had to repress during Rochester's absence in the period preceding their wedding ceremony. At the moment, she is inattentive to the hints that the tree, which "gasped ghastly," symbolizes her immanent separation from Rochester; instead, she exults in the power of her emotions. This exultation recalls that of Emily Brontë's "High Waving Heather," whose speaker, I argue in chapter 1, anthropocentrically fetishizes the thrill of unflinchingly facing the forces of destruction that early ecologists observed were threatening England's moors and heaths. In "natural" disasters like the eruption in Emily's poem and the lightning strike in *Jane Eyre*, the long material history of man's destructiveness reappears, abstracted, as Nature's own in the form of a sudden, violent crisis. An acute tension animates the two desires felt by Jane and by Emily's speaker: to feel one with nature and to feel like a free human being who possesses full control over herself and her life and whose robust health and strength allows her to take unnecessary bodily risks. It is therefore deeply ironic that their desire to feel one with nature—to experience themselves as free, forceful participants in the unleashing of abstract power in the form of the lightning strikes or bog burst—requires them to ignore the catastrophe's true human causes and discount its devastating ecological consequences. Mistaking adrenaline for freedom, seduced by the narrative drama of the fight-or-flight instinct, they come to desire environmental destruction.

Whereas Emily's speaker suspends the question of whether man is of or above nature, transferring onto the reader the moral task of deciding to identify with or condemn the speaker's destructive anthropocentrism, Jane Eyre directly faces the question and answers it in her choice of Moor House over the moors. While facing the sundered, burnt horse-chestnut on her wedding eve, Jane's youthful inclination to interspecies empathy resurfaces. But soliciting the reader's sympathy for the blighted tree is self-serving, for it naturalizes her unlawful relationship. The synoecious *Aesculus hippocastanum*, endowed with hermaphroditic flowers, offers an ideal arboreal symbol in the apostrophe that sets her up as a fellow sufferer:

> "You did right to hold fast to each other," I said: as if the monster-splinters were living things, and could hear me. "I think, scathed as you look, and charred and scorched, there must be a little sense of life in you yet, rising out of that adhesion at the faithful, honest roots: you will never have green leaves more—never more see birds making nests and singing idyls in your boughs; the time of pleasure and love is over with you: but you are not desolate: each of you has a comrade to sympathize with him in his decay." (318–19)

Thornfield's horse-chestnut, its leaves denuded, its bark scarred, is now barred from multispecies networks (no more "birds making nests"), sacrificed by humans in the name of romance—recapitulating in miniature the deforestation that transformed verdant uplands into desolate moors. In regarding the destruction as a personal crisis, Jane, in Elizabeth Povinelli's phrasing, "smuggle[s] a core human drama back into the vitalized world" (62). Her ecologocentric humanization of the tree answers Colebrook's "question of how gendered sexual being emerges from a history that ecologically bound up with violence and depletion" ("Counterfactual" 19). Jane's desire for individual political, romantic, and economic fulfillment purchases her complicity with colonial violence (Bertha's dehumanization and untimely death) and with ecological violence. From her point of view, what matters most is defending her sexual continence, which she needs as proof of her fitness to start a family with the man she loves.

Jane's apostrophe to the horse-chestnut echoes St. John's earlier use of "scathed," making it clear that both connote the archaic meaning to "injure or destroy by fire, lightning, or similar agency" (OED). Fire and lightning are the abstract forces whose paths trace the Anthropocene's distributed causal networks. Both Thornfield and the Riverses' estate are scathed; both are ruined spaces whose caretakers abandon them. Thornfield is in fact multiply "scathed," as Bertha sets Rochester's bed aflame, then afterward burns down the entire Hall. Jane allegorizes the ruined estate as another inchoate bog body, comparing her first vision of the destroyed estate to a lover arriving to arouse his "mistress asleep on a mossy bank" but finds she is "stone dead" (489). This sudden vision of ruin signals the problematic gaps between the Anthropocene's differently scaled stories: Bertha and Rochester's story is on a slightly larger scale, and his with his father larger still—a filial relation at the still-larger scale of hereditary land-ownership and settler colonialism. Jane's shock challenges the useful fiction that human action is ecologically costless; unlike the North Atlantic of the *Blackwood's* and *Bewick's*, with their hypothetical visions of shelling icebergs and of making first contact with pristine landscapes, the ruined Thornfield and its blasted horse-chestnut are entirely real. This useful fiction allows Jane to pursue her positive identification as *Anthropos*, but it has made her complicit in ecological and imperial violence. Nature is again used as Jane's handmaiden to unite the couple when Rochester's disembodied voice, begging her to come, miraculously travels from Ferndean to Moreton just as she needs to decide whether or not to marry St. John and move to India. On the moors, suddenly she senses a tingle that "now summoned and forced to wake" her six senses. In chiding herself, "Down superstition! . . . This is not thy deception, nor thy witchcraft: it is the work of nature. She was roused, and did—no miracle—but her best" (483), Jane finally accesses the humanized Mother Nature who disappointed her during her earlier exile on the moors. As her journey from Morton to Thornfield concludes, she thrills, "I was sure we were near my bourne" (486), but it is pristine no longer. Significant ecological consequences have begun to emerge. Thornfield is anthropogenically denuded space that cannot support life, much less the apotheosis of Jane's *Bildung*. Months after Thornfield's destruction, Jane's belated discovery discloses, finally, what the day after ecological crisis looks like. Not a witness but a survivor, Jane must face waking up for the first time outside of the Garden of Eden. She must decide what to do.

She flees. Having entered Moor House and achieved there her full investiture as a member of *Anthropos*, she is satisfied to leave the patrimony she temporarily tended. Rochester too deserts (rather than rebuild) his destroyed estate, becoming an absentee landlord who refuses to employ locals or center the region's social life. Rather than atone and work on their earthly estates, leaving their recovery of paradise for the afterlife, Jane and Rochester flee, finding in Ferndean a second Eden on Earth. Jane's narrative of continuous exile handily absorbs ecological crisis. Formerly, Rochester had disparaged "the unhealthiness of the situation, in the heart of a wood," whose "damp walls" would have killed Bertha (347), but just as Jane resists Lowood's typhus, she can withstand Ferndean's insalubrious situation. Or rather, once Thornfield is ruined, Ferndean is freshly reinterpreted as hospitable. With the logic of technopositivists who would rather colonize Mars than repair Earth, Rochester, by drawing Jane to Ferndean, essentially fulfills his fanciful plan to "take mademoiselle to the moon" and "seek a cave in one of the white valleys among the volcano-tops" (300). Indeed, *Jane Eyre* figures Ferndean as "green and ferny and fertilized by soft rains ... isolated from society but flourishing in a natural order of their own making" (Gilbert and Gubar 370), a place "of animal survival as well as the place of a happy, fertile married couple whose union is divinely sanctioned" (Morse 161). Polhemus's comparison of Rochester's lunar retreat to "Lot's refuge above the scorched cities of the plain" (163) is also remarkably apt. From scathed *Aesculus hippocastanum* to unscathed *Anthropos*, a transformation affirmed when Rochester laments,

> "I am no better than the old lightning-struck chestnut-tree.... And what right would that ruin have to bid a budding woodbine cover its decay with freshness?"
>
> "You are no ruin, sir—no lightning-struck tree: you are green and vigorous. Plants will grow about your roots, whether you ask them or not, because they take delight in your bountiful shadow; and as they grow they will lean towards you, and wind round you, because your strength offers them so safe a prop." (512)

With a sleight of hand that contextualizes the tree's destruction as part of natural processes of decay, Jane's personification locates a cheerful outcome. Before, she compares the split halves of the hermaphroditic tree to both of them, but now she buries their ecological responsibilities under a refigured metaphor that casts an invigorated Rochester as the horse-chestnut and recodes their relationship as interspecies (his "chestnut-tree" and her languorous, dependent "woodbine"). Their culpability is neutralized, their gender relations normalized, and absolution purchased by her moorland wanderings and his (temporary) injuries.

Gilbert and Gubar conclude their analysis of *Jane Eyre* with a note of regret that Brontë, in her subsequent novels, "was never again to indulge in quite such an optimistic imagining" (371). As subsequent chapters show, the complexity of *Shirley*'s temporality allows the environmental consequences of rapid industrialization in Yorkshire to permeate the entire novel, without offering a second Eden left to fleet to, and *Villette*'s Lucy Snowe lives in a fully post-apocalyptic world. Jane Eyre's desire to be fully, purely human, as little fettered by her gender as possible, shows the terrible ecological consequences of taxonomies that position the *Anthropos* as the rational, disembodied master over the Earth. Yet, as Alaimo points out, definitions of the human develop

> in the messy space where science, history, cultural identities, and politics coincide. Ultimately, whatever it may mean to think oneself as a species will be inextricably bound up with other, more local identities and cultural conceptions rather than separate from them. The Anthropos ... could provoke a sense of species identity quite different from the lofty Western, capitalist humanism, with the recognition that every member of the species is at once part of long evolutionary processes, a member of a species that has had a staggering impact on the planet, and an inhabitant of a particular geographic, social, economic, and political matrix, with attendant and differential environmental vulnerabilities, culpabilities, and responsibilities. ("Shell" 98)

Jane's progress along the path of *Bildung* pivots around vivid confrontations during which Jane's desire to be a human being chafes against her ability to perceive and critique the dense networks of harm binding humans and nonhumans together. Ultimately, her desire to be counted among *Anthropoi* wins out. Nevertheless, Jane Eyre is not *Jane Eyre*: what the former rejects, the latter suspends indefinitely in a series of prophetic visions and multispecies tableaux that are recorded even if Jane renounces them once she acquires an all-human family. Ferndean may beckon with a second Eden, but Thornfield Hall continues to molder dozens of miles away.

THREE

Shirley's Tale of Valley, Factory, and Lioness

GATHERING MULTISPECIES ROMANCES
OF ECOLOGICAL DEGRADATION

Shirley is a problem. Its dual heroines, its third-person narration, and its account of industrialization run counter to Charlotte Brontë's typical authorial choices, frustrating any unified theory of her oeuvre. To preempt readers' dismay at these anomalies, the narrator discloses that her tale offers "something unromantic as Monday morning" (5). This warning was certainly necessary, as evidenced by *Shirley*'s early reception history, which deemed it a deeply flawed, minor "condition of England" novel or a misguided detour driven more by Charlotte's grief at Emily's death than by any serious attempt to grapple with industrialization or to forge a new narrative voice. In such views, *Shirley* is irremediably fragmented by its turbulent composition—interrupted by the deaths of her sisters—and offers, at best, an effective foil for *Jane Eyre* as an outpouring of youthful talent and for *Villette* as the psychologically complex masterpiece of her maturity. Summarizing early reviews, Herbert Rosengarten explains that they charge Brontë with having "failed to impose order on her materials" (46), while Lucasta Miller hypothesizes that the novel's "imperfect aesthetic ... cost her the sympathy of some readers" because its "rejection of aesthetic unity" leaves it without "an overarching dominant idea" ("Introduction" xv). Catherine Gallagher identifies an "incompatibility" between the novel's industrial and romantic plots (121), and Terry Eagleton diagnoses a "disabling duality" by which "spiritual biography is only loosely tied to a dramatic action" (88, 93). By granting the novel's structural inconsistency, such arguments echo the substance (if not the tone) of early reviewers' diagnosis of "Charlotte's failure to achieve ... the realism increasingly demanded by contemporary theories of the novel" (Rosengarten 30). More recent scholarship, however, has sought a hidden unity connecting its industrial themes, romantic plots, and stylistic experiments.[1]

In my attempt to trace Charlotte's career-long engagement with the Anthropocene, it is tempting to seek out a similar unity, to launch a rescue operation against the "criticism" that takes on the vernacular sense of the term when it dismantles *Shirley* as a set of deviations from the generic norms epitomized by industrial novels such as Elizabeth Gaskell's *Mary Barton* (1848) and *North and South* (1855), Benjamin Disraeli's *Sybil* (1845), and Charles Dickens's *Hard Times* (1854). Yet *Shirley* does not linger on the plight of the working class or suggest ameliorations for it—a decision that "precludes the radical ending desired by most readers and critics" (Struve 71). Indeed, the idiosyncratic method by which *Shirley* formally decenters industrialism triangulates its human effects chiefly on characters who are not themselves factory employees or particularly interested in them. I locate the novel's intervention in political economy elsewhere: in its eclectic combination of multiple discourses (scientific, romantic, cosmological) to explore the ecology of industrialization. This eclecticism does not muddle the novel's "stark and uncompromising" nature (Shuttleworth 184) but underscores the knotty process of calculating the impact of industrialization on humans, nonhuman organisms, and landscapes. It also, to borrow Claire Colebrook's phrasing, "raises the problem of intersecting scales, combining the human time of historical periods ... with a geological time of the planet" ("Counterfactual" 1). Not for nothing does Brontë characterize Chartist agitation in her letters as a "moral earthquake" (*Letters* 2:48). Just as her father stubbornly insisted that the 1824 Crow Hill bog burst was an earthquake to craft a global genealogy of anthropogenic destruction, Brontë's representations of industrialization use the state of local ecosystems to test humans' moral responsibility for causing environmental change. This difficulty of doing so, of tracing cause and effect in the Anthropocene, motivates *Shirley*'s stylistic departures from industrial novels and from Brontë's other novels. In *Shirley*, disjunction becomes both form and content.

Shirley represents the political conflicts and environmental changes wrought by industrial development as reconfigurations—some abrupt and violent, some virtually imperceptible—of a regionally specific constellation of linked species and biomes. These changes are understood by individual communities through acts of storytelling, including Caroline Helstone's meticulous engagement with the microcosmic networks of natural history and Shirley Keeldar's feminist cosmology of deep time, both of which reflect Brontë's wide reading in the sciences. These acts of storytelling jostle beside other accounts of capitalism, ecological change, and regional cultures, declining to privilege any one of these modes of representation and causal thinking. The novel constructs an ethnography not on industrialization in general, but on a specific instance of it during a particular historical moment and within a certain locale. The narrator embeds factories within a lush and lushly described Yorkshire valley that does not disappear at the first hint of pig iron but persists as an nature/culture contact zone, defined by ethnographers as spaces "where lines separating nature and culture have broken down, where encounters between *Homo sapiens* and other beings generate mutual ecologies and coproduced niches" (Kirksey and Helmreich 546). The novel's two heroines, centers around whom multispecies tableaux coalesce, move among trees and smokestacks alike. Important scenes are structured around the manifold human uses of plants and animals, and a multilayered temporal framework is developed to reveal a panoply of short- and long-term historical processes of regional environmental change. This approach renders *Shirley* vulnerable to claims of fragmentation and political prevarication, but its layering of many conflicting discourses about ecosystemic change foregrounds these shifts as subjects for representation by scientists, artists, and laypeople alike. Consequently, *Shirley* is a scientific and historical project that renders the end of the Holocene visible and a demonstration of the necessity of forging new methods of telling stories about, and thriving in, the Anthropocene.

PARTIAL WITNESSES: REALISM, ETHNOGRAPHY, AND THE VALUE OF SCIENTIFIC ACCURACY

This chapter builds on other scholars' explorations of Brontë's social-scientific approach of analyzing and describing human cultures in *Jane Eyre* and *Villette* but focuses instead on *Shirley* to show how Brontë's ethnography extends to nonhumans and landscapes, revealing them to constitute a physical medium through which the characters' social, political, and sexual activities occur.[2] I argue that *Shirley* is a multispecies ethnography: it analyzes the mutual imbrication of human and non-human organisms in the Anthropocene. As John Knight explains is characteristic of multispecies ethnography, Brontë represents nonhuman organisms "as *parts* of human society, rather than just *symbols* of it" (1). As Deborah Bird Rose points out, to be "writing in the Anthropocene" in a non-anthropocentric way, one must be sensitive to the "situated connectivities that bind us into multi-species communities" (87). Accordingly, I explore how *Shirley*'s animals and landscapes powerfully shape humans' bodies, emotions, and behaviors, rather than passively reflect characters influenced solely by other humans. The narrator's precise observations of humans within Yorkshire moors, farms, millyards, meadows, gardens, and forests at a specific historical moment, are thus multispecies data. The resulting proliferation of the scientific minutiae contributes to the novel being "unromantic as Monday morning"—so unromantic that to some readers, it is an overcorrection. In an 1877 article, Leslie Stephen blames an overcommitment to empiricism for "the comparative eclipse ... of Charlotte Brontë's fame" and attributes genius to "the poetic as distinguished from the scientific type of mind":

> Genius begins where intellect ends; or takes by storm where intellect has to make elaborate approaches according to the rules of scientific strategy.... To say that a writer shows more genius than intellect may mean simply that, as an artist, he proceeds by the true artistic method, and does not put us off with scientific formulae galvanized into an internal semblance of life. (725)

Shirley suffers from "elaborate approaches," "scientific strategy," and "formulae," even though "the scenery and even the incidents are, for the most part, equally direct transcripts from reality" (726). Stephen's contradiction—How can elaborate formulae yield a direct transcript?—denies the narrativity of science and defines separate criteria for judging science and literature.

What is under question is not Charlotte's accuracy, but the literary value of accuracy. Stephen damns *Shirley* with faint praise by calling it a "continuous series of photographs of Haworth and its neighborhood" (726). A few years later, Erskine Stuart isolates verisimilitude for especial commendation, enthusing, "As we have said more than once, Charlotte Brontë's descriptions of scenery are photographically correct" (151). Despite their disagreement about Brontë's artistry, both treat "photographic" accuracy as passive; neither recognize it as the active collocation of multiple vantage points. As Donna Haraway argues, photography is not passive:

> There is no unmediated photograph or passive camera obscura in scientific accounts of bodies and machines; they are only highly specific visual possibilities, each with a wonderfully detailed, active, partial way of organizing worlds. All these pictures of the world should not be allegories of infinite mobility and interchangeability but of elaborate specificity and difference

and the loving care people might take to learn how to see faithfully from another's point of view.... Understanding how these visual systems work, technically, socially, and psychically ought to be a way of embodying feminist objectivity. ("Situated Knowledges" 583)

Shirley's non-cohesive, multi-perspectival structure epitomizes this feminist objectivity and insists that any discourse is but one of many "partial" ways of "organizing worlds." The narrator weaves ethnographic thick descriptions into scenes to emphasize characters' situated knowledges, periodically inserting passionate judgments that—along with her commitment to the local, the detail, and the fragment—embody the "partiality" and "positioning" that Haraway privileges over neutrality, completeness, and universality. The difficulties of *Shirley*'s task—to demonstrate how to recognize and ameliorate the ecological changes of the Anthropocene, to draw causal relationships across broad swathes of time, to insist on the beauty of the compromised creatures and landscapes that survive without downplaying past extinctions or disregarding future ones—are apparent in Lewes's and Stephen's resistance to Charlotte's mixture of the realistic and the peculiar, the accurate and the partial. *Shirley*'s unapologetic disunities, partialities, and vulgarities are most flagrant in the self-reflexive passages that stress the gap between the events (1811–12) and their narration (1848–49). The novel's chronological spread is defined by two sudden social crises of British industrialization (Luddism and Chartism), which bookend a slower narrative of mounting environmental catastrophe, resulting in structural gaps and tonal shifts that attest to the difficulties of narrating the Anthropocene, creating a pointedly incomplete, multilayered, and partial account that resembles contemporary multispecies enthography.

Though it may seem anachronistic to declare that *Shirley* resonates with contemporary ethnographic practice, chapter 1 has shown that multispecies ethnographers cite eighteenth- and nineteenth-century forebears who share their thematic focus on human/nonhuman interaction, their theoretical blurring of species boundaries, their ethical concerns about human-caused environmental change, and their methodological emphases on small regions and case studies. After generations of nonplussed readers puzzling over *Shirley*'s form, Anthropocene theory provides a new way to frame the novel as emphatically *local* traditions and knowledges are increasingly relied upon for assessing and meeting the challenges of twenty-first-century ecological devastation. Now, Stephen's estimation of Brontë as a "sensitive plant exposed to the cutting breezes of the West Riding Moors" (728) who records, in equal measure, herself and other sensitive plants around the parsonage under threat is less a criticism than a memorable description of the blurring of species boundaries crucial to multispecies ethnography. Stephen believes that positioning Brontë immobile in the "West Riding Moors" erodes her authorial agency because genius is mobile and universal. But in the Anthropocene, rootedness is the primary condition of ecological knowledge, and *Shirley*'s rootedness in an industrializing corner of Yorkshire successfully provides a model for generating that knowledge.

A similar dismissal of Brontë's commitment to the partial and the positioned informs G. H. Lewes's review of *Shirley*—in response to which she penned a single-sentence letter, "I can be on my guard against my enemies, but God deliver me from my friend!" (*Letters* 2:330). Characterizing the novel as "a portfolio of random sketches" because Brontë "never seems distinctly to have made up her mind as to what she was to do; whether to describe the habits and manners of Yorkshire and its social aspects in the days of King Lud, or to paint character, or to tell a love story" (165), Lewes inaugurates a structural critique now familiar, but what makes this review remarkable is how his distaste for Yorkshire informs the putatively formalist basis of his criticism. By demanding that Brontë "learn to sacrifice a little of her Yorkshire roughness to the demands of good taste" and omit the "rudeness," "harshness," and "vulgarities" he judges "inexcusable" (165), Lewes ascribes to a theory of realism that *Shirley*'s narrator critiques as the product of London intellectuals' paradoxical provinciality. She taunts, "Now, let me hear the most refined of Cockneys presume to find fault with Yorkshire manners!" (337). Lewes bites on the proffered bait, asking, "Is this correct as regards Yorkshire, or is the fault with the artist?" (165). He concedes, "let us cordially praise the real freshness, vividness and fidelity, with which most of the characters and scenes are depicted ... with so much life before us, that we seem to see them moving through the rooms and across the moor" (166)—but only after critiquing the novel's fragmented structure, sifting the fragments to declare some authentic and others not. Like Stephen, Lewes employs convoluted transitions and subtle qualifications to deem the novel both realistic and unrealistic, revealing the contradictions that emerge when a particular situated knowledge (learned Londonness) unreflexively encounters a collocation of different situated knowledges.

It also reveals that Brontë's multispecies ethnography is partly motivated by anti-Yorkshire prejudice. In a letter dated 7 April 1840, Brontë addresses this prejudice while recounting how newspapers had praised lectures by Patrick Brontë and his curate, William Weightman, at the Keighley Mechanics'

Institute. Brontë astringently notes, "it is mentioned as a matter of wonder that such displays of intellect should emanate from the Village of Haworth" (*Letters* 1:214). Given Brontë's keen sense that Yorkshire erudition is regularly attacked, her novels' descriptions of her characters' scientific pursuits amount to public outreach similar to the two clergymen's lectures. As Tim Dolin observes, *Shirley* is "preeminently a declaration of what it means to write a novel outside London" (201), and as James Buzard argues, in *Shirley,* "the local or regional acquires greater force, refusing to be simply transubstantiated out of existence in becoming part of the higher-order unity of the nation," making *Shirley* the most pointedly ethnographic of her novels (167). However, *Shirley*'s focus on semi-rural English communities lacks the "controlled self-alienation" Buzard values in metropolitan autoethnography (10), for the novel's partial, positioned narrator fiercely defends provincial culture. Certainly, other scenes resume the "unromantic as Monday morning" tone of the novel's opening. The narrator's position as a participant-observer flickers: sometimes emphasis falls on participation, sometimes on observation. Lewes interprets this flickering as a contradiction, but investigating *Shirley* as an account of how stories about regional histories develop shows that the narrator's oscillation between objectivity and partiality is less an abandonment of literary realism than a reflection of Brontë's interest in exploring the conditions of narrative production.

These shifts in tone and perspective are most obvious when metropolitan transplants, such as the curate Mr. Donne, denounce the social customs under observation. The narrator, impatiently summarizing his "abuse of the people of Briarfield; of the natives of Yorkshire generally; complaints about the want of high society; of the backward state of civilization in these districts; murmurings against the disrespectful conduct of the lower orders in the north toward their betters; silly ridicule of the manner of living in these parts" (111–12), arrays semicolons to construct a syntactically rich list that ironizes Donne's imaginative paucity. At tea with marriageable women, he believes his "strictures must raise him in the estimation of Miss Helstone, or of any lady who heard him," yet Caroline, "a Yorkshire girl herself . . . hated to hear Yorkshire abused" (112). The young ladies react by turning their attention to other marriageable men, just as later, Shirley expels "the lisping cockney" from her garden (and the scene) when he "dare[s] . . . to revile Yorkshire" and calls it "*corse* and uncultivated" (272, 273)—establishing a narrative economy of attention that privileges ethnographic thick descriptions and curtails outpourings of anti-rural sentiment. Passages describing Yorkshire manners, plants, animals, and landscapes engineer ideal opportunities for the partisan asides that both diminish the narrator's objectivity and preempt critical viewpoints that praise accuracy in descriptions of moorland landscapes but decry it in depictions of their inhabitants. Brontë's preface to the second edition of *Jane Eyre* responds after the fact to negative reviews by admonishing the "timorous or carping few" for whom "whatever is unusual is wrong" and "remind[ing] them of a certain simple truths" (5). In *Shirley*, truths are neither certain nor simple, and the carping few are routed in advance. The narrator calls attention to these purposeful gaps in narration to highlight the conceptual slippages of the "natural" in discussions of literary realism, associating metropolitan, anti-Yorkshire attitudes with overly narrow conceptions of nature and of realism. For example, when the narrator refuses to disclose the fate of another prejudiced curate in the final chapter, she justifies her silence by alleging that "discriminating" readers reject "the squeak of the real pig," deeming it "untrue" and "inartistic," and prefer the "sheer fiction," deeming it "sweetly natural" (594).

Shirley's economy of attention lavishes its salvaged space on local dialect. The narrator faithfully transcribes "real, racy Yorkshire Doric adjectives" and "epithets" to convey the "peculiar, racy, vigorous" nature of Yorkshire denizens (346, 147). Chapter 18, sardonically titled "Which the Genteel Reader Is Recommended to Skip, Low Persons Being Here Introduced," features working-class figures and the "racy Yorkshireisms" of "Mr. Hall's sincere friendly homily" (302). Many of the novel's lengthy exchanges are reserved for cozy domestic scenes featuring the conspicuously named Yorke family. Through Hiram Yorke's position as patriarch and Mr. Hall's as a sermonizing vicar, Brontë establishes dialect as a cross-class usage not banned for ladies' and children's ears. Yorke, the "Yorkshire gentleman ... *par excellence*" is an "adept in the French and Italian languages" who possesses the "manners ... of a finished gentleman of the old school" (44, 48). Describing dialect as consciously chosen, the narrator stipulates that "if he usually expressed himself in the Yorkshire dialect, it is because he chose to do so, preferring his native Doric to a more refined vocabulary" (48). The gentle factory-worker-turned-gardener William Farren, who discusses natural history with Caroline and debates political economics with factory owner Robert Moore, code-switches as nimbly as Yorke. Dialect, Brontë's ethnography demonstrates, can articulate scientific exchanges, political debates, refined exhortations of spiritual uplift, and loving murmurings at the domestic hearth.

This account contrasts with Gaskell's use of dialect in the *Life of Charlotte Brontë*, which emphasizes the Brontës' refinement by marshaling regional idioms to depict violence around Haworth: "warching" for "painful," "pawsing" for kicking, and "he'd threap yo' down th' loan" for "he'd beat you down the lane" (14, 20, 16). The Brontës, too, use regionalisms to exploit the North's storied roughness for dramatic effect, most notably in *Wuthering Heights*'s titular adjective. But *Shirley*'s ethnographic precision and historical vision differ greatly from the "lack of topographical specificity" through which Emily creates "an essentialist—even eternalist—vision of Yorkshire ... giving a kind of moral identity to the land, its rocks, and its people" (Buckland 142). Emily's mummification of Catherine Earnshaw and Heathcliff into bog bodies, discussed in chapter 2, slows the decomposition of their organic flesh by such a degree that they seem as abstract, timeless, and immoveable as the rock below the peaty churchyard. By contrast, Charlotte's *Shirley* merges autobiographical references with regional ones, creating a maze of lexical cues that make historical shifts visible through entangling personal and ecological changes. As much as the surnames and place names redolent of the West Riding provide clues for Brontë's real-life inspirations—her father's experiences as the curate of Dewsbury and incumbent of Hartshead, and her own experiences while residing at Roe Head School and visiting friends at Birstall and Gomersal—they also indicate the centrality of the individual case studies, thick descriptions, and participant-observers that lend *Shirley* its ethnographic feel. Meanwhile, the transformations of real-life Oakwell Hall into Fieldhead, Red House into Briarmains, Birstall Church into Briarfield Church, and Hunsworth and Rawfolds Mills into Hollows Mill, combined with the transformations of Patrick's and Miss Wooler's tales about local Luddite unrest (1811–12) into allegories for the renewal of Chartism (1848–49) as Brontë wrote *Shirley*, reveal the importance of personal, local, or lexical details for narrating historical change. The rhythmic syllabic freighting of the Reverend Hammond Robertson (Patrick's predecessor at Dewsbury and Hartshead) in the naming of the Reverend Matthewson Helstone is one example of the merging of autobiography, ethnography, and history.

That *Shirley*'s 1849 ethnographic project about 1812 inspires Stuart's 1888 *Brontë Country*, which instructs readers to follow in his footsteps, affirms the novel's power as a prompt for ever-propagating regional ethnographies. Stuart's catalogue of lexical echoes structures his ethnography ("Rushedge, Whinbury, and Nunneley are all suspiciously like West Riding place-names" [129]) and introduce anecdotes of local culture, from annual events (such as the Christmas ringing of the "Devil's Bell" and the Pancake Bell on Shrovetide) to natural curiosities, such as Liversedge church, on whose tower an ash tree grew and an oak branch was tied to commemorate the Civil War—"a most unheard-of thing" (61). Whereas Stuart celebrates the novel's litanies of Yorkshire customs, Stephen laments them because Brontë

> failed to appreciate fully the singularity of the characters which, in her seclusion, she had taken for average specimens of the world at large. If I take my village for the world, I cannot distinguish the particular from the universal; and must assume that the most distinctive peculiarities are unnoticeably commonplace. The amazing vividness of her portrait-painting is the quality which more than any other makes her work unique amongst modern fiction. Her realism is something peculiar to herself. (727)

Stephen's commitment to the universal destabilizes the value of the vivid particular and thus points to a tension internal to realism: the competing claims of the part and the whole. If the compelling authenticity of Brontë's "portrait-painting" rests upon the "singularity" of her sitters, how does one render an "average specimen" vividly? And having isolated suitable specimens, how does the writer "distinguish" part from whole—particular from universal, village from world—rather than collapse them into a unity? It is this unresolved tension between part and whole that makes Lewes and Stephen both conclude that Brontë is a realist, but a "peculiar" one.

Stephen's and Lewes's discomfort with a realism that decenters the universal underscores the aesthetic consequences of multispecies ethnography's ethical commitments. Defining these commitments, Isabelle Stengers rejects universalism, which depends upon the selection of an objective "external arbiter," in favor of an "etho-ecological" politics "disentangled from any reference to some universal human truth it would make manifest" (998, 1001). Our task is "to design the political scene in a way that actively protects it from the fiction that 'humans of good will decide in the name of the general interest'" (998)—a fiction Stengers explicitly links to the eighteenth- and nineteenth-century political economies that structure more traditional industrial novels. Whereas Dickens's, Disraeli's, and Gaskell's narrators assume the position of the external arbiter of general interest, *Shirley*'s narrator attempts "to 'slow down' reasoning and create an opportunity to arouse a slightly different awareness of the problems and situations mobilizing us" and "to slow down the construction of this common world, to create a space for hesitation regarding what it means to say 'good'" (994, 995). The novel's fragmentation supports what Stengers calls a "ritual assemblage," an exchange of "palaver" (not expert testimony) that accommodates "models of emergence without transcendence" and "imbu[es] political voices with the feeling that they do not master the situation they discuss" (1001, 1000, 995). *Shirley*'s ambivalent ending—"The story is told. I think I now see the judicious reader putting on his spectacles to look for the moral. It would be an insult to his sagacity to offer directions. I only say, God speed him in the quest!" (607)—is a prime example of etho-ecological slowing down. As readers finish the novel, the narrator orders them to prolong the meditative act of reading through reflection, ironically suggesting how long it should take them by identifying God as the only power capable of making the process speedier.

A comparison with the ending of Patrick Brontë's novel *The Maid of Killarney* (1818) will throw into relief *Shirley*'s refusal to claim transcendent mastery. Also a meta-narrative reflection, this ending directly addresses readers with a plea for the same patience that *Shirley*'s narrator requests with her note about the novel's Monday-morning banality:

> When you consider that in one single hour we have surveyed lakes, cataracts, mountains, crossed seas, and travelled over many leagues of land; that we have wandered through the intricate mazes of politics, or journeyed through the more sublime paths of religion; when you think of the hopes, fears, sorrows, and joys of the various personages we have met with—Instead of censuring unreasonably the conciseness or obscurity of your guide's information, let me beseech you to reflect that this, the land of your pilgrimage, is a chequered scene; that your seventy years in retrospect, will seem an hour; and they are truly wise, who sedulously *redeem the time*. (*Brontëana* 199)

The narrators of *Shirley* and *The Maid of Killarney* craft tense, uneasy meta-reflections that are grateful yet aggressive. They dare readers to retract or resent the favor they have granted the narrator: the favor of *slowing down*, the willingly bestowed grant of time, given through the act of reading, along with an openness of mind that Stengers argues is necessary for conversations about ethical action in the Anthropocene. They both call attention to a certain *speeding up*, as well, for the novel compresses into a few sessions of reading a lifetime's worth of experiences and landscapes. The reader's "seventy years" refers to the scale of the individual human life—the scale at which *Jane Eyre*, *Shirley*, and *Villette* all make visible the causal networks of the Anthropocene. But where the forceful narrators of *The Maid of Killarney* and *Jane Eyre* make their opinions abundantly clear and present themselves as masters of their content, *Shirley*'s narrator presents an opaque surface, constructed to resist the penetrating power of readers' spectacles and therefore prolong the etho-ecological moment of slowing down. The novel's structural eclecticism, which creates stylistic inconsistencies and gaps in the readers' knowledge of the characters' lives and the region's local histories, also helps the narrator to resist making readers' decisions in advance on their behalf. *Shirley*'s Anthropocene ethics works precisely through this unstable maintenance of indeterminate relations between the novel's parts and its whole, which creates that "peculiar realism" to which Lewes and Stephen take such exception.

The uncanny temporality of the bog, a central image for the Brontës, re-emerges in *Shirley* without privileging one mode of ecological knowledge over another. Observations, descriptions, and events happen in the veiled slowness of geological deep time and in the cataclysmic violence of ecological disasters—the temporalities of the bog body and of the bog burst—allowing Brontë to narrate the Anthropocene as both crisis and condition. This is where the meta-narrative concerns about constructing and consuming novels intersect with etho-ecological politics. In *The Maid of Killarney*, bogs surface as an image for narrative ethics when an Irish informant, Captain Loughlean, debates the value of novels with his allegorically named visitor, Albion:

> The generality of Novels are what you Englishmen say of us Irishmen, when you liken us to our own bogs—green, smooth, and tempting, on the surface, but concealing underneath, the miry slough, or deadly pool; or, as the Doctor there would tell you in his phraseology, they are so many poisonous boluses, sufficiently incrusted with honey to make them palatable, but in no degree adequate to counteract their pernicious effects on the constitution.... But I must say of my girl, that she subsists on no such food. She reads nothing of the kind alluded to, but what first passes through my hands, and meets my approbation. And there are a few Novels which I have handed over for her perusal, which are not only harmless, but very entertaining and instructive. (155)

The Maid of Killarney thus shares the concerns of the "Extraordinary Disruption," Patrick's poem about the bog burst, which, as chapter 1 shows, lectures its young readers to put their literacy to good use. The degree to which Charlotte takes seriously her father's concerns about the morality of fiction is evident in *Shirley*. Though the conclusion ridicules the idea that only one correct moral could be drawn from any given novel, his concern appears in *Shirley*'s conversation between Caroline, a maid of marriageable age, and Mrs. Pryor, a middle-aged servant of Caroline's friend, Shirley Keeldar. When Mrs.

Pryor suspects that Caroline reads romantic novels, she condemns them by repeating Patrick's marsh imagery:

> "Mutual love! My dear, romances are pernicious.... They are not like reality. They show you only the green, tempting surface of the marsh, and give not one faithful or truthful hint of the slough underneath."
>
> "But it is not always slough," objected Caroline. "There are happy marriages. Where affection is reciprocal and sincere, and minds are harmonious, marriage *must* be happy." (358)

Both Captain Loughlean and Mrs. Pryor compare reading corrupting novels to falling into a bog: penetrating the lacy, bright green acrotelm, becoming mired in the catotelm below, suffocating in the mass of dead and dying peat-forming mosses. *Shirley*'s narrator entertains the same fear about constructing a slough-like narrative—hence her warning about the excitement generated by Monday mornings, which attempts to disavow the romantic content of her narrative. Yet, in another instance of the eclectic novel's refusal to cohere, it includes a double wedding and many courtship scenes. But to criticize *Shirley* as Harriet Martineau criticized *Villette*—to convict it of anti-feminist sentiment because "the female characters, in all their thoughts and lives, are full of one thing, or are regarded in in the light of that one thought" (quoted in Barker 848)—would be to fall into a differently tempting slough. Doing so would ignore the topics that absorb *Shirley*'s heroines and decenter their romance plots, such as natural history, to which I now turn.

DESERTIFIED BODIES IN DEFORESTED LANDS: ILLNESS, FILIATION, AND NATURAL HISTORY

Shirley accomplishes its Stengerian slowing down by juxtaposing divergent approaches to political economy and its relationship to nature in the early Anthropocene, which, in the sections featuring Caroline, are figured in relation to natural history. Caroline regularly engages in this favorite pastime (particularly with Farren and Mrs. Pryor) and directs other characters' attention (particularly Shirley, her love interest, and the children and curates she meets in her duties as the rector's niece) to the condition of the natural spaces around them. In passages redolent of Gilbert White's *History of Selborne*, setting cycles of migration, hatching, flowering, and leafing within the context of human activities, Caroline is established as the novel's moral center. With her empathic, attentive engagement with nonhuman organisms, she is one of the many Victorians who "were in love with natural history" (Gates, "Natural History" 539). Capaciously defining natural history as "overwhelming drive to collect, witness, and catalog nature that occurred during ... the long nineteenth century," Gates notes that it "encompassed a fascination both with local nature and with the animals, vegetables, and minerals of the empire" (540). Recent scholarship pushed back against the tendency that dismisses it "as the quaint pursuit by amateur 'nature-lovers' of such inconsequential outdoor things as bugs and birds, while the real professional science goes on indoors, within the controlled spaces of laboratories" (Walls, "Natural History" 188). Danielle Coriale has written about Brontë's "passionate interest in natural history" and the "wide range of amateur naturalists" woven "into the social fabric of Shirley" (119). Building on these insights, I stress how Caroline's natural history expands the narrator's ethnographic work into the non-human realm to explore the mutually reciprocal relations between Yorkshire's human cultures and its landscapes, animals, and other organisms at the dawn of the Anthropocene.

This reciprocity animates Caroline's walks, which provide more than bucolic imagery: they are structuring devices, indices of human-caused ecological change, sites of multispecies ethnography and scientific investigation. Alexis Shotwell has identified the amateur nature walk as "complementary and perhaps even necessary" for laboratory-based biology because "the projects of ordinary people ... don't fundamentally have an allegiance to the apparatuses of thinking shaped as a practice of dominion over the natural or social world" (99). Having issued an invitation to Mrs. Pryor, who "liked a quiet walk" (352), Caroline joins a woman whose similar scientific proclivities are not a coincidence but a metonym foreshadowing the revelatory unveiling of an occluded secret from the past: the fact that Shirley's ex-nurse is Caroline's mother. Their walks exemplify way that the past exerts unseen pressures on the present; they also exemplify the "ways of placing oneself in community with the objects of care" that Shotwell argues are necessary ethical acts in the Anthropocene (98). Mrs. Pryor accordingly resumes her maternal duties (which are as interrupted as the narrator's peculiar realism) through natural history:

> Mrs. Pryor talked to her companion about the various birds singing in the trees, discriminated their species, and said something about their habits and peculiarities. English natural history seemed familiar to her. All the wild flowers round their path were recognized by her; tiny plants springing near stones and peeping out of chinks in old walls—plants such as Caroline

had scarcely noticed before—received a name and an intimation of their properties. It appeared that she had minutely studied the botany of English fields and woods. (353)

In this passage, the economy of attention that marginalizes characters like Donne also redirects Caroline's attention through Mrs. Pryor's scientific nomenclature. As Shotwell notes, although "practices of noticing and naming are simply parts of Man's God-given right to ... exercis[e] dominion over the natural world" according to some thinkers, for others, they constitute a "form of attunement ... of resisting human exceptionalism while at the same time thinking that humans have responsibilities" (98). This is why, despite this scene's pastoral beauty, hints of struggle, decay, and adaptation quietly fill the scene, including the "tiny" plants surviving in "chinks" of "old" walls, which denote an ecosystem under stress from human activity. As they attempt to reach green space beyond the factory, their outing traces the ever-retreating boundary that must be crossed to access space not yet transformed by a violently encroaching industrialization:

> Here the opposing sides of the glen, approaching each other and becoming clothed with brushwood and stunted oaks, formed a wooded ravine, at the bottom of which ran the mill-stream, in broken, unquiet course, struggling with many stones, chafing against rugged banks, fretting with gnarled tree-roots, foaming, gurgling, battling as it went. Here, when you had wandered half a mile from the mill, you found a sense of deep solitude—found it in the shade of unmolested trees, received it in the singing of many birds, for which that shade made a home. This was no trodden way. (352)

The repetition of "here" marks the passage of time required to cross this boundary, while the diction describing their quest for sylvan quietude ("opposing," "stunted," "broken," "unquiet," "chafing," "fretting," "battling") indicates the intensified flow of an upland mill-stream, its naturally swift waters rerouted for maximum velocity.

The subtext of human-caused ecological change becomes text when the pair reach "the head of the ravine," where the valley is fully visible. Caroline sits and listens as Mrs. Pryor

> looked round her, and spoke of the neighborhood as she had once before seen it long ago. She alluded to its changes, and compared its aspect with that of other parts of England, revealing in quiet, unconscious touches of description a sense of the picturesque, an appreciation of the beautiful or

commonplace, a power of comparing the wild with the cultured, the grand with the tame, that gave to her discourse a graphic charm as pleasant as it was unpretending. (353)

Unlike Jane Eyre's longing gaze from Thornfield's leads, whose primary political import is that women qualify as universal subjects of Enlightenment rationality, Mrs. Pryor's rambling "sense of the picturesque" focuses on "comparing the wild with the cultured" to visualize historical change within local ecosystems. Her hidden past (as Caroline's mother) makes her the perfect candidate for making visible the landscape's own occluded past.

The "graphic charm" of Mrs. Pryor's gaze from the ravine is one of the moments when the picturesque, as Ron Broglio argues, "produces something new: a relationship between humans and the environment that gets generated from within the rules of the picturesque but breaks its normative and normalizing demands" to create "a redefinition of what it means to be human" (*Picturesque* 21, 22). Unlike *Jane Eyre*'s ultimate defense of Enlightenment definitions of the human, *Shirley* pushes back against the picturesque's naturalization of human control over animals and contributes to attempts by forebears of ecology to shift the public's attention to environmental devastation. For example, Alexander von Humboldt, "the first scientist to talk about harmful human-induced climate change" (Wulf 6), also "integrated human beings into natural systems as ecological agents of global change" to argue against any "cyclic, steady-state interpretation of nonhuman history" that "cordons" off man from nature (Walls, *Passage* 199). As chapter 1 shows, George Perkins Marsh accused Victorians of making the Earth "an unfit home for its noblest inhabitants" because "the operation of causes set in action by man has brought the face of the earth to a desolation almost as complete as that of the moon" (44, 43). With her nature walks providing pretexts for recording the kind of local, minute, time-sensitive data that Marsh parses, Caroline's natural history is not simply a symbol of her temperament but an intellectual and ethical activity that traces the transformation of fragile ecosystems under the influence of factories not far from her parsonage doorstep.

Caroline's scientific interests precipitate many of the novel's word-paintings, allowing its settings to chart ecological change over time as the novel traverses from fertile to devastated spaces, from wet to dry ones, from uplands to lowlands. Eschewing clichés about Yorkshire's bleakness, *Shirley* paints a diverse account of multiple biomes that harbor ethnographic and ecological traces of Yorkshire's past. During a walk with Shirley, Caroline previews the biome that awaits if they prolong their "extensive and solitary sweep of Nunnely Common" (199):

> I know all the pleasantest spots. I know where we could get nuts in nutting time; I know where wild strawberries abound; I know certain lonely, quite untrodden glades, carpeted with strange mosses, some yellow as if gilded, some a sober gray, some gem-green. I know groups of trees that ravish the eye with their perfect, picture-like effects—rude oak, delicate birch, glossy beech, clustered in contrast; and ash trees stately as Saul, standing isolated; and superannuated wood-giants clad in bright shrouds of ivy. (201)

Shy Caroline's repetition of "I know," her discernment of moss and tree species, and her offer, "Miss Keeldar, I could guide you" (201), exploit her scientific knowledge as a social commodity for befriending her alarmingly well-dressed and self-assured new acquaintance, suggesting the interdependence of healthy ecosystems and human relationships, as well as the mediation of the two by artistic renderings of natural beauty. This link between scientific knowledge and beauty intensifies when Shirley and Caroline reach the "green brow" of Nunnely Common and look

> down on the deep valley robed in May raiment; on varied meads, some pearled with daisies, and some golden with king-cups. To-day all this young verdure smiled clear in sunlight; transparent emerald and amber gleams played over it. On Nunnwood—the sole remnant of antique British forest in a region whose lowlands were once all sylvan chase, as its highlands were breast-deep heather—slept the shadow of a cloud; the distant hills were dappled, the horizon was shaded and tinted like mother-of-pearl; silvery blues, soft purples, evanescent greens and rose-shades, all melting into fleeces of white cloud, pure as azury snow, allured the eye as with a remote glimpse of heaven's foundations. (200)

This colorful, variegated view discloses in the "sole remnant of antique British forest" a living "remote glimpse" of the region's lush, forested past. Caroline's knowledge of "superannuated wood-giants" and "strange mosses" reveals a thriving, primeval ecosystem flush with rare species and contrasts with the narrator's extensive gaze, which invokes Nunnwood as a focal point accentuating the deforested biomes surrounding it. In his guide to Brontë country, Stuart quotes this passage to affirm that the real-life forest survives eighty years later—"A few clumps of the ancient primeval forest are still to be seen around Dewsbury, some almost surrounded by chimneys belching forth their besmirching smoke" (19)—but, like the narrator, returns to the deforestation of the real-life Calder Valley. Reading ecological cues in place names, he expounds,

> The now dry, sun-baked, smoke-stained banks, almost entirely destitute of trees, were then clothed with an impenetrable forest of oak, birch and hazel, the very river (Calder) taking its name from the latter tree.... Such names as Oakenshaw, Birkenshaw, Heckmondwike, Liversedge, Thornhill and Mirfield have all a sylvan ring about them, and speak of the time when all was forest, moor and marsh. (17)

The degraded ("dry, sun-baked") area surrounding the prehistoric remnant offers a living synecdoche of Anthropocene losses, one environmental historian Ian D. Rotherham would call a "ghost forest." A type of biome found in "upland moors and moorland fringe, and lowland heaths, commons and downs," ghost forests contain "shadows and imprints of an ancient ecology" and indicate anthropogenic deforestation (Rotherham, "Searching" 40). Among these "imprints," Rotherham lists bluebells, wood sorrel, wood anemone, honeysuckle, hawthorn, holly, and hazel—all species that proliferate in Yorkshire and in the Brontës' works.

Shirley's word-paintings are therefore not still lifes; they suspend multiple moments far dispersed in time, bearing signs of the past (ghost forests), the present (patches of pristine forests surrounded by moors, heaths, and developed lands), and the future (lands under development or earmarked for further development). During one walk, Mrs. Pryor and Caroline reach a space that appears untouched by man but illustrates what Rotherham fondly refers to as "grubby landscapes," areas that were incompletely cleared or unevenly developed. This results in unlikely species flourishing and leaving "clues of very different timelines and land-uses" ("Searching" 43). In *Shirley*, flowers in this "grubby" landscape attest to a history of industrial and agricultural development:

> The freshness of the wood flowers attested that foot of man seldom pressed them; the abounding wild roses looked as if they budded, bloomed, and faded under the watch of solitude, as if in a sultan's harem. Here you saw the sweet azure of blue-bells, and recognized in pearl-white blossoms, spangling the grass, a humble type of some starlit spot in space. (352)

The narrator's symbolic invocation of the consciously maintained harem underscores Rotherham's thesis about the cultural construction of "the 'wood'" as "a human creation and a place of long-term interaction" (39). In a paradox common to Anthropocene ethnographies, this landscape is both poor and rich, "abounding" in some beautiful or valued species, such as the wild roses, but simultaneously filled with "humble" ones, the white blossoms (perhaps wood anemone or wood sorrel, common to Brontë country and ghost forests). Charlotte's descriptions of moors, then, emphasize that they are damaged, fragile ecosystems created by centuries of human activity.

Fifteen years before Marsh's dramatic delineation of this damage, *Shirley* anticipates his warning that "another era of equal human crime and human improvidence" would in the foreseeable future "threaten the deprivation, barbarism, and perhaps even extinction of the species" (44) by writing the Earth's condition on its character's bodies. Heather Glen observes that "each of the four main characters is threatened with extinction"—Caroline and Louis by undefined fevers, Shirley by rabies, and Robert by a gunshot—and contextualizes the narrator's "disenchanted perspective" within shifts in Victorian attitudes toward mortality as recurrent epidemics made the end of humanity imaginable (177, 176). In the Anthropocene context, the characters' near-deaths are symbols of and physical extensions of the novel's other threatened extinctions: of non-human species and of entire ecosystems. If "human subjectivity gets defined ... by what assemblages and connections it maintains with the surroundings" and if "meaning emerges from surfaces, contact zones, and associations" (Broglio, *Picturesque* 23), the status of characters' bodies as contact zones in a damaged landscape is dangerously unstable, as is human subjectivity. Tutor Louis Moore, shut in Fieldhead's schoolroom, lacks a meaningful connection to the landscape and pines away like a prisoner in the Brontë juvenilia; industrialist Robert, degrading the valley through processes whose inconsistencies underemploy local workers, is shot by Luddites safely hidden by a hedge; and caninophile Shirley is attacked by a rabid dog. Their own interspecies practices eventually endanger their bodies, and they provide cautionary tales for Stuart's prophecy about *Shirley* country: "if the smoke nuisance and river pollution are allowed to do their baleful work unhindered, a day *will* come when the people of this little island will find that nature has taken its own revenge" (19–20).

Considering that Stuart and Marsh record natural data to compare their late-Victorian present with Charlotte's mid-Victorian past and with the onset of industrialization, enabling them to project the Earth's bleak future, it is Caroline who best embodies the novel's contribution to this dawning threat of extinction. The narrator constructs parallels between Caroline's health and that of individual plants and animals, thus registering through her body the shifting condition of the larger ecosystems around her over the half-century that elapses between the novel's narration and the events it describes. Falling ill, Caroline ceases her nature walks; during her recuperation, the signal that "a genuine, material convalescence had commenced" is the reawakening of her interest in natural history, for "she longed to breathe the fresh air, to revisit her flowers, to see how the fruit had ripened" (414, 415). In the throes of fever, she designates Farren to inherit and care for her plants, and Mrs. Pryor tries to assure her that the "rank grass" and "long weeds and nettles amongst the graves" will be cleared so that "closed daisy-heads, gleaming like pearls" may thrive and "dew glisten among the foliage" in the graveyard (400). Even posthumously, Caroline will help to garden a healthy multispecies biome. Humboldt's *Cosmos* (1845–47) establishes similar links between the health of local landscapes and its human populations by defining climate as "in the most general sense all changes in the atmosphere which noticeably affect the human organs" (quoted in Heymann 587). This approach to climate as a matter of human experience situated in a particular space informs *Shirley*'s depictions of corporeal suffering. Perceiving illness as a climatological displacement, Caroline feels that she resides "in the shadowless and trackless wastes of Zahara, instead of in the blooming garden of an English home" (372). In these anomalous atmospheric conditions, "so long as the breath of Asiatic deserts parched Caroline's lips and fevered her veins," her health is imperiled until "the sun broke out genially" and a "little cloud like a man's hand arose in the west," arriving concomitantly with breezes that "absolved" the neighborhood from the "livid cholera-tint" and "pale malaria-haze" enveloping it (414). The atmospheric disturbance that begins as Caroline's fever-induced hallucination becomes an empirical reality. The sky itself is sick, infected with cholera and malaria. Whether the neighborhood catches Caroline's illness, or vice versa, is left unclear; what emerges is an uneasy, confused, and pained awareness of the ontological and material entanglements among an ecosystem and its stewards. The moors, meadows, and forests depend on the care given by nature-lovers like Caroline, but if she sickens (directly or indirectly) because that ecosystem is compromised, she cannot give it.

The temporary desertification of damp, chilly Yorkshire links Caroline's illness to climatological discoveries about the anthropogenic origins of one form of ecosystemic sickness: deforestation. In 1819, Humboldt, in his study of deforestation in colonial plantations in Venezuela, confirmed the theories of earlier French scientists that deforestation eventually causes desertification.

Humboldt demonstrated that it raises temperatures, decreases atmospheric oxygen, dries up watercourses, and causes erosion, leading to barren lands periodically decimated by flooding.[3] In *Aspects of Nature*, he summarizes, "The wooded region acts in a threefold manner in diminishing the temperature; by cooling shade, by evaporation, and by radiation" (112). Further scientific data emerged from the colonies linking deforestation with hotter, drier conditions. Concerns about deforestation in India and Venezuela led to "frequent and detailed strategic discussion in London," and from 1805 onward, deforestation was a matter of concern to the "British public at large" (Grove, *Imperialism* 393, 395). These results applied to Yorkshire, where Bronze Age humans transformed its densely forested uplands to arable agricultural land and thence to acidified moorlands. From the medieval period through the nineteenth century, deforestation attended the enclosure of the commons, and Humboldt's proofs corroborated arguments that the Brontës read in early scientific texts that posited human-caused environmental change. As chapter 1 details, for example, White documents the results of unregulated moorland burning: "nothing is to be seen but smother and desolation, the whole circuit round looking like the cinders of a volcano; and, the soil being quite exhausted, no traces of vegetation are to be found for years" (26). Desertification was the ultimate consequence of poor stewardship of the moors that the Victorians knew were fragile but crucial to England's ecological health.

Shirley contributes to this politics of desertification a feminist argument that connected corporeal health and moorland stewardship. "Men of Yorkshire!" the narrator apostrophizes, must give unmarried women "a field in which their faculties may be exercised," lest they begin "fading around you, dropping off in consumption, or decline; or, what is worse, degenerating to sour old maids . . . because life is a desert to them" (371). That Caroline's thirst of "Asiatic deserts" begins immediately after this passage, followed by her neighborhood's illness, emphasizes the reciprocity and physicality of the ties between desertified lives and landscapes. This reciprocity is evident when, after Caroline asks her uncle for permission to advertise as a governess, he observes that her "bloom had vanished, flesh wasted" and complains, "These women are incomprehensible. . . . To-day you see them bouncing, buxom, red as cherries, and round as apples; to-morrow they exhibit themselves effete as dead weeds" (183). Helstone thus invokes what Amy M. King calls the "botanical vernacular," the vocabularies of plant sexuality developed by Carl Linneaus and invoked by realist writers to discuss human sexuality discreetly because modern botany "drew on human gender hierarchies and social arrangements," rendering plant taxonomy itself a retranslation of human sexuality (*Bloom* 27). It also exemplifies *Shirley*'s multispecies interdependencies, for this bloom vernacular links Caroline's proto-feminism and scientific interests to the novel's politics of deforestation. Without a useful career, she does not merely lose her bloom: her body desertifies. Her uncle denies the connections between conditions of labor and the flourishing of the organic world, narrowing the botanical vernacular to a reductive symbolism and throwing into greater relief the connections between Caroline's feminism and environmentalism.

Critics beginning with Charlotte's friend Mary Taylor have critiqued *Shirley*'s feminism as an unsatisfactory version available only to "*some* women" who "give up marriage & don't make themselves too disagreeable to the other sex" (*Letters* 2:392). Caroline does fall ill partly because she believes Robert is lost to her—but she survives because climatological conditions change and natural history provides her with meaningful, salubrious occupation. That is not to deny that Caroline desires Robert, but to assert that her health and her human romance are inextricable from her love of natural world. Robert gathers her flowers, tying snowdrops, crocuses, and primroses into a bouquet. They take summer walks "to scent the freshness of the earth," she awaits him in a nook "embowered above with hawthorns and enameled underfoot with daisies," and, going to visit him, she runs "through the branchy garden-shrubs" and "down the green lane sloping to the Hollow, to scent the fragrance of hedge-flowers" (71, 221, 299, 373). She conceives of losing him as being exiled from "Nunnely wood in June" into "her narrow chamber," where she hears only "the rain on her casement," not the "songs of birds" (168). For Caroline, being sexually and domestically fulfilled are preconditions for her continued participation in a multispecies ecosystem. Romance offers her an intensified manner of interacting with the landscape. Shirley is naturally happy—"the free dower of Nature" gifted her with an internal "spring whose bright fresh bubbling in her heart keeps it green" (366–67)—but for Caroline, a life without romance, without the literal and figurative "springs" that keep her heart "green," is a life in a desert.

Jane Eyre similarly links feminism, romance, death, and deserts when Jane ponders the mortal consequences of accepting St. John's demand for a missionary helpmeet. "If I go to India, I go to premature death," she reflects; "mine is not the existence to be long protracted under an Indian sun" (466). Like Caroline, she is snatched from death by an atmospheric disturbance: the electrical transmission of Rochester's cry for Jane from Ferndean to Marsh Glen, and the arrival of the "cooler and fresher ... gale" that flows in answer, which Jane insists are not supernatural but "the work of nature" (516, 482). Just as Jane deems Lowood "pleasant enough" as scenery and a "cradle of fog and fog-bred pestilence" (91), atmosphere in *Jane Eyre* and *Shirley* is not simply decorative. Stressing that atmosphere is a "material property, inhering in the air shared by the world, the text, and the critic," Jesse Oak Taylor argues that "[u]nderstanding the work of art in an age of anthropogenic climate change demands treating cultural artifacts and ecological change not merely as symptoms or representations of one another but as mutual participants in shared processes" (*Sky* 7, 8). In *Shirley*, then, atmosphere is one material medium that transmits Anthropocenic forces back and forth among humans, animals, plants, and landscapes.

Though the desertified "Zaharan" atmosphere departs Caroline's neighborhood, other climatological disturbances pervade *Shirley*. Caroline perceives "something electrical in the air" moments before the Luddite attack—another environmental manifestation of industrialization (317). Recalling Jane's bid for the free exercise of romantic choice, Louis observes, "The night is not calm" on the stormy night when he determines to pursue Shirley (485). In *Jane Eyre*, Rochester is "physically influenced by the atmosphere," when, during a "fiery West Indian night," the kind that "frequently preceded the hurricanes of those climates," the "wind fresh from Europe blew over the ocean and rushed through the open casement: the storm broke, streamed, thundered, blazed, and the air grew pure" (355). Alan Bewell calls this passage "one of the most powerful expressions in Victorian literature of an imperial ecological myth," for "Rochester's quest for health might be said then to be a quest for fresh air" (790). Similar to the quenching of Caroline's desert and the banishment of Rochester's Caribbean airs, St. John's impending premature death in India—*Jane Eyre*'s concluding image—contains the dangers of desertification by projecting them onto the colonies. Danielle Prince has observed this phenomenon in *The Secret Garden*, noting that Anglo-Indian Mary Lennox's garden allows her to "trade her sickliness for health, her yellow skin for white, her Indian nature for an English one," enabling her "inculcation in English ways and values" (4). Like Mary, Caroline takes care of multispecies Yorkshire spaces, re-Anglicizing her half-Belgian beloved, while Jane uses her inheritance to secure and refurbish the decaying "Moor House" and its scathed grounds; all physiologically and psychologically depend on the Yorkshire grounds of which they become stewards.

Though all three novels feature displaced climates, *Shirley*'s industrial context suggests that Yorkshire's putatively temporary assumption of foreign ecologies hints at a future that cannot be exiled to the colonies: England's eventual desertification by over-development. Caroline's natural history, distinct from Mary's horticulture and Jane's Madeiran cash, explicitly associates human mortality with the ecological shifts of industrialization. Because Caroline's health and environment are closely correlated, characters interested in her or in the nonhuman world are brought together, which alleviates the social alienation of capitalism. Wheeled outside by Farren in a "garden-chair," Caroline finds literal and metaphorical common ground with the former mill-hand:

> William and she found plenty to talk about. They had a dozen topics in common—interesting to them, unimportant to the rest of the world. They took a similar interest in animals, birds, insects, and plants; they held similar doctrines about humanity to the lower creation, and had a similar turn for minute observation on points of natural history. The nest and proceedings of some ground-bees, which had burrowed in the turf under an old cherry-tree, was one subject of interest; the haunts of certain hedge-sparrows, and the welfare of certain pearly eggs and callow fledglings, another. (415)

Their shared interest in the natural world around them fosters intimacy while also, in the form of local specificities of "pearly eggs and callow fledglings," contributing multispecies data about regional biodiversity to the narrator's Yorkshire ethnography, recording the flourishing species and spaces that have disappeared by the time the narrator begins telling her tale three decades later. That Caroline insists Mrs. Pryor befriend Farren despite disapproving of associating with "a man of the people" (415) also underscores the social amenities attendant upon the popularization of science in the Victorian era. As Coriale argues, this passage demonstrates Charlotte's knowledge of Robert Chambers's *Vestiges of the Natural History of Creation* (1844) and shows how Caroline creates an "alternative social network organized around natural history's universal appeal" (125, 119). Her interest in natural history therefore unknowingly restores her lost mother, whose happiness also rests on their nature walks, during which "her heart ... shook off a burden ... her spirits too escaped from a restraint" (352).

Caroline's chastisement of her mother reflects the "egalitarian" quality of natural history, which was "open to amateur and professional alike" because of the proliferation of clubs and accessible, affordable texts (Gates, "Natural History" 540). This inclusiveness is also present in Anne's *The Tenant of Wildfell Hall*: Helen Graham, having fled her abusive, genteel husband, takes long walks that dovetail with the agricultural activities of farmer Gilbert Markham. Befriending Helen's traumatized son, Gilbert rehearses his future position as stepfather, becomes a dutiful son to his own mother, and learns that sober, virtuous Helen would be a better mate for him than his customary coquettes. Both *Shirley* and *Tenant* posit that certain forms of interacting with nonhuman organisms repair tears in the social fabric and demonstrate the efficacy of Shotwell's advice for repairing damaged landscapes by "placing oneself in a community of other people who have cared enough to know about species" beyond *Anthropos* (97–98). In this way, it is "the people who are practicing arts of noticing in a damaged world," particularly through amateur natural history, who "manifest the kind of complex care and responsibility" necessary in the Anthropocene (105). Anne's prescient exploration of divorce and abuse locates affection for England's green spaces as integral to domestic healing, similar to the way Charlotte "imagined undeveloped spaces as a common ground on which people divided by social or cultural differences might meet" and thereby "registered a green alternative to progressive reform" (Coriale 130). Although *Shirley*'s portrait of intensifying industrialization does not offer so clear a vision of positive change as *Tenant*—the nature-loving trio form a legally recognized family and rehabilitate the estate—both plumb the ecological and social benefits of popular science.

Shirley's ethnographic project explores these social benefits by providing microcosms of the larger multispecies networks and practices that underpin personal, regional, and national identity formations. Because Shirley and Caroline consistently express (and act upon) an abiding affinity for moors and heaths that is central to their identities and their friendship, this friendship is one such microcosm. Speaking about their natural surroundings during their first outing, the "very first interchange of slight observations sufficed to give each an idea of what the other was," making shared attitudes toward regional landscapes the foundation of friendship:

> "Our England is a bonny island," said Shirley, "and Yorkshire is one of her bonniest nooks."
>
> "You are a Yorkshire girl too?"
>
> "I am—Yorkshire in blood and birth. Five generations of my race sleep under the aisles of Briarfield Church. I drew my first breath in the old black hall behind us."
>
> Hereupon Caroline presented her hand, which was accordingly taken and shaken. "We are compatriots," said she. (199–200)

Whereas Caroline expresses her affinity for Yorkshire by engaging in natural history and by serving Moore's industrial efforts as his ecological advisor, hereditary landowner Shirley expresses it as her birthright, couching her interest as an ancestral responsibility. Shirley, having only recently returned to her family home, assures Caroline of her preference for moorlands when, walking across Nunnely Common, she waxes lyrical about her repatriation.

Shirley's chapter about old maids, the text's most explicit moment of feminist agitation, strengthens these connections among feminism, environmentalism, and regionalism. Addressing "Men of Yorkshire!" it instructs them to care for single women by allowing them employment beyond the "services" for which they are "hardly thanked" but which fill their days with labors for the poor, the ill, and the outcast (177). The narrator then expands her range to the "Men of England!" (371), later narrowing her gaze to "Men of Manchester!" (598), indicating that city, region, and nation are related but distinct, not unified but linked by the need to protect community members who devote their lives to service. Shirley and Caroline's friendship as "Yorkshire girls" who love their "bonny nook" and the "bonny island" in which it is positioned, similarly telescopes consciously between regional ethnography and national politics, indicating that what connects them are the attitudes of appreciation and modes of belonging proper both to a "Yorkshire girl" and to a "Man of Yorkshire." What separates ethnography from politics is an understanding that to *enact* these attitudes—to protect—action must occur on the ecological level of the local and narrative level of the detail.

Such telescoping accompanies (even precipitates) stylistic disjunction. This authorial decision nullifies in advance Stephen's accusation that she conflates the particular and the universal. For example, during a Luddite attack, the narrator describes "a North of England—a Yorkshire—a West-Riding—a West-Riding-clothing-district-of-Yorkshire rioter's yell" (325) to depict the consequences of nonaction. Dashes emphasize how intellectual movements along the scale of the national to the local must be deliberate—by way of, for example, interruptive dashes—even in moments of crisis. Stengerian moments of pause within each dash prevent the particular from becoming the universal too quickly, too unreflectively. Perhaps this fragmentation escapes Stephen because it also demonstrates *Shirley*'s regionalist commitment to detail, which King argues is shared by natural history and realist fiction. King argues that natural histories use "descriptive techniques, detail, and interest in describing the small scale and the local that became essential to the realist novel in Britain" ("Tide Pools" 158). Like natural historians whose passages "of proliferating description [are] made up of inductive details, rather than the architecture of plot or structure," *Shirley* subordinates structural unity in order to "record details in a narrative mode that renders them simultaneously scientific and aesthetic" (156, 155)—a duality evident in the multispecies descriptions whose richness and length create Stengerian moments of slowing down.

Because "natural history teaches the valuable skill of moving adeptly across scale levels ... without deranging them, or collapsing one into the other" (Walls, "Natural History," 196–97), *Shirley* foregrounds this oscillation between the micro level of observation and the macro level of abstraction during scenes of natural history. For example, once the narrator records Caroline and Farren's "pearly eggs and callow fledglings," she leaves the pair alone to search for other observable organisms. The narration drifts too in a passage of complex temporality:

> Had 'Chambers's Journal' existed in those days, it would certainly have formed Miss Helstone's and Farren's favorite periodical. She would have subscribed for it, and to him each number would duly have been lent; both would have put implicit faith and found great savor in its marvelous anecdotes of animal sagacity.
>
> This is a digression, but it suffices to explain why Caroline would have no other hand than William's to guide her chair, and why his society and conversation sufficed to give interest to her garden-airings. (415)

The narrator juxtaposes verbs in the simple present and verbs in the continuous conditional, whose characteristic tone of contingency is partially stabilized by the narrator's repetition ("would have") and interpolation of "certainly." This hypothetical vision of scientific companionship at least twenty years in the future—*Chambers's* was launched in 1832, two decades after *Shirley*'s primary action during the Luddite revolts and over a decade and a half before its narration and publication during the Chartist revival—calls attention to the novel's layered temporalities. This "digression" shows how *Shirley*'s inconsistent structure and tone arise from the complex temporalities that emerge when the narrator's ethnography investigates characters' scientific interests, theories, and endeavors during a period of intense ecological change.

Chambers's "marvelous anecdotes," interpolated among longer articles, model this fragmentation. These brief, vivid stories dramatizing new discoveries about animal behavior, particularly those that displayed animals' intelligence or empathy, proliferated in this popular general-interest weekly, which served as a vehicle for Victorian self-improvement. We know that the

Brontës subscribed to *Chambers's*, that they "read enthusiastically" its lively coverage of nonhuman intelligence, and that their texts were "influenced by—and even perhaps as instances of—such a new Victorian genre of dog or pet narrative" (Kreilkamp 94). Representative anecdotes might include dogs rescuing one another or insects procuring food against improbable odds. Like contemporary multispecies ethnography, they trace the intricate networks binding humans and non-humans by showing how animal intelligence responds to human behaviors. In anecdotes taken from the three-year period before *Shirley*'s publication, "sagacity" is attributed to organisms fifty-four times. Seventeen of these attributions designate nonhumans, including plants, bees, birds, camels, foxes, horses, dogs, and mules. Camels in caravans are lauded for the "picturesque scene" they offer by "keeping their footing with admirable sagacity," while the predatory tamarind tree is noted "to display as much forethought and sagacity as taking up an artery for aneurism, or tying splints round a broken bone" ("Adventures" 269; "Tamarind-Tree" 360).

During this period, depictions of interspecies violence and conflict outnumber the sentimentalized, idealized anecdotes that illustrate pets' unswerving devotion to their human companions. "The Birds of Shetland" deprecates human violence while elaborating "a curious trait in the habits of the herring-gull; namely, the pertinacity and watchfulness with which it takes on itself the guardianship of the seals from their most formidable enemy—man":

> If it is sagacity, it is surely an instance of its exercise quite unique, that one order of animal should expose itself to imminent danger in warning another to escape the same; and, we regret to say, the self-constituted guardian often falls a victim to his philanthropy; for the sportsman, disappointed of his prey, generally discharges his spleen and his ready weapon, so as fatally to revenge the unwarranted interference of the pragmatical gulls. (184)

Gulls' sagacity is taken for granted; what is not is that the animal would willingly use that intelligence altruistically. "Nature at War" catalogues trap-building species, commanding "lovers of natural history" not to be surprised by the violent uses of animal sagacity:

> That the face of nature should be found, on a due examination, to be stained with blood and deformed with civil war; that it should be an ordinance of creation that the life of one should depend upon the death of another creature; that this green world should be the great theatre in which myriads

of bloody dramas are daily enacted—all this ... is sufficiently startling to him who holds narrow views of the system which governs our world. (91)

In *Shirley*, such moments of unsentimental demystification are not reserved to professional scientists. They interrupt even the most flattering descriptions of nature, exemplifying how pastorals, Leo Marx explains, "qualify, or call into question, or bring irony to bear against the illusion of peace and harmony in a green pasture" (25). In instances of the "little event," the pastoral "estranges" its characters by revealing unsavory aspects of nature or signs of civilization in putatively pristine spaces (27). These little events proliferate in *Shirley*'s scenes of ecological degradation and interspecies violence, in addition to descriptions hinging on the tension between Yorkshire's identity as an isolated county of moors and as an early site of industrialization. The narrator describes the onset of spring thusly: "The surface of England began to look pleasant: her fields grew green, her hills fresh, her gardens blooming; but at heart she was no better. Still her poor were wretched, still their employers were harassed" (161). The rhythmic listed examples of the first sentence encourage the reader to build speed, only to be slowed by the semicolon and "but," which introduce a rival set of rhythmic, parallel clauses whose repetition of "still," like the repeated tolling of a bell, slows the reader. In this little event, *Shirley*'s narrator interrupts her own pastoral description, indicating that the effects of industrialization are fully apparent only after the passage of time.

A little event closely related to *Shirley*'s multispecies themes occurs on Whitsuntide when Caroline walks to the school fête, where she perfectly executes the interpersonal labors expected of her. The narrator illustrates her attractive gentility in terms of interspecies relations, observing, "It appeared that neither lamb nor dove need fear her, but would welcome rather, in her look of simplicity and softness, a sympathy with their own natures, or with the natures we ascribe to them" (278). Caroline's animality is complicated by this final aside, which introduces uncertainty with "or" to undermine stereotypes about animals debunked in *Chambers's*. Immediately following this note of doubt, the narrator de-sentimentalizes Caroline by noting, "After all, she was an imperfect, faulty human being" (278), showing that the aside's purpose is less to deny that humans and animals share similarities or sympathies than to reveal that not all similarities and sympathies are flattering. Understanding animals *and* humans requires a more unflinching observation of animal behavior, so the narrator casts doubt on the lambs' and doves' sanctity to cast that same doubt on Caroline. When she reaches Fieldhead to fetch Shirley, and they run "through the fields ... looking very much like a snow-white dove and gem-tinted bird-of-paradise joined in social flight" (279), the narrator questions the homogeneity of the human species-category and its pretensions to a sociability that transcends animals'. These questions perform the "ontological turn" of multispecies ethnography, which troubles the "foundational distinction between nature and culture, humans and nonhumans, as the base of Euro-American epistemology" (Kirksey and Helmreich 148). The upshot for Caroline is a warning that, despite her pretty exterior and sweet demeanor, she is not one of the proverbially vulnerable, peaceful lambs or doves; the upshot for *Shirley* is that human social relations may be repaired by studying the natural world, but only by abandoning the belief that humanity is a stable, homogeneous category perfectly distinct from nonhuman species. What Maggie Berg argues of *Agnes Grey*—that Anne's novel "employs the representation of animals to challenge and denaturalize the 'natural' hierarchy" enforcing "the supposed inferiority of certain human and animal beings" (178)—thus applies to *Shirley*'s multispecies tableaux. It cannot, however, apply to *Jane Eyre*, whose anthropocentrism reflects the attitudes of "most Victorians," who were "not especially sensitive to their own underlying speciesism" (Gates, "Greening" 11). *Shirley* may not wholly transcend *Jane Eyre*'s anthropocentrism, but it does shifts the latter's politics into new ethnographic, economic, and sexual registers—particularly through Shirley Keeldar, who, of all Brontë's human creations, most thoroughly troubles the ontology of species that rigidly separates human from nonhuman.

AN IMPURE COURTSHIP:
THE BIOPOLITICS OF MULTISPECIES CONTAMINATION

Shirley's unorthodox species-identity is most apparent in her relations with Louis Moore, her former tutor and eventual husband. Traditionally disliked by readers, Louis is now interpreted as Charlotte's attempt to complement Shirley's masculinity with Louis's femininity.[4] Though their non-normative courtship does often serve to neutralize Shirley's unfemininities, it also advances the novel's species politics by escalating the multispecies overtones of Caroline's discreet bloom vernacular into a species roleplaying that savors of sadomasochism. After Shirley discloses her unwillingness to become a moral paragon responsible for "improving" her husband, Louis labels her a "sister of the spotted, bright, quick, fiery leopard," and in her acceptance of his classification, she contemptuously dismisses her uncle's plans to "mate [her] with a kid" (581). She prefers instead Louis's classifications of her as "a young lioness or leopardess," in spite of his plan to "manage" her animal instincts, which "must be bent" and "curbed" (491). Louis's performance as a lion tamer succeeds; Caroline smugly observes, "Whatever *I* am, Shirley is a bondswoman. Lioness! She has found her captor" (568). An equally self-satisfied Louis proclaims, "Tame or fierce, wild or subdued, you are *mine*," and Shirley agrees, "I am glad I know my keeper, and am used to him" (586). These exchanges cannot be seen exclusively as antifeminist: they provide Shirley with an erotically satisfying context for negotiating their relationship. If she must marry, she will do it on her own terms. Her *devoirs*—essays written years before as Louis's student—reemerge to reveal that Shirley's past writings, preserved by Louis, have already dictated the terms she will accept. As William A. Cohen writes of *The Professor*, although Brontë's erotics of dominance "could be read as exemplifying patriarchal control, it encodes a more flexible dynamic" of "unstable power relations" and "does not consistently align modes of domination and subjugation with gender" (55, 41). In *Shirley*, Louis's mastery is destabilized by his request to "be treated like Tartar"—her dog of an indeterminate "breed between mastiff and bulldog"—and become "Shirley's pet and favorite" (582, 191, 586). Both desire to control *and* be controlled, their desires all the more intense because they are as mixed as Tartar's origins.

 Brontë's entwining of animal characters and imagery in scenes of amative dominance applies her interspecies explorations to refashioning gender roles. Their flirtations blur scientific classifications that separate man from animal and species from species, foreground the roles of nonhumans in human systems of sexual and economic reproduction, and expose anthropocentric attitudes that normalize man's dominion over nature. Louis frequently refers to himself as Adam, arrogating the first man's right to name and domesticate animals. For him, masculine aggression, so unlike working-class Farren's proclivity for botany, is learned by each succeeding generation of gentlemen. About Shirley's fifteen-year-old cousin, and the boy's infatuation with her, Louis writes, "The young, lame, half-grown lion would growl at me now and then, because I have tamed his lioness and am her keeper. . . . Go, Henry, you must learn to take your share of the bitter of life with all of Adam's race that have gone before, or will come after you" (575). This bitterness animates a scene in which Louis contentedly pets Tartar. When he confides to Shirley, "Around animals I feel like Adam's son; the heir of him to whom dominion was given over 'every living thing,' " her detached diagnosis of his "harsh solitary triumph in drawing pleasure from out of the elements, and the inanimate and lower animate creation" (427) diagnoses the imperious tendencies channeled by his treatment of nature as standing reserve. That Shirley owns the land and animals that lordly Louis surveys, and that she supplies him with the "morsel of sweet cake" that he has forgotten to supply for the birds at his feet, contribute to the irony whereby Louis, "still caressing Tartar, who slobbered with exceeding affection" (427), claims dominion over the very dog he fantasizes about becoming. The tensions produced by Adamic control, its cyclical reinforcement of sexual competition and gender norms, and its monopolization by the gentry are registered in the erotic release the couple achieve by imagining its inversion, redistributing its gendered behaviors, and, ultimately, sharing its social responsibilities through marriage. This is not to say that the couple overcome the struggles for mastery that enliven their courtship. There is a lingering uncertainty in the novel's leonine imagery, one that eroticizes a foundational tenet of multispecies ethnography: humans' inability to classify and control the natural world fully. The ambiguities of scientific classification—Is Shirley "a young lioness or leopardess" or a "pantheress?" Is she "[t]ame or fierce, wild or subdued"? (491, 591, 586)—stimulate arousal because they reveal the ontological and socioeconomic limits of Louis's putative mastery. If, as Harriet Ritvo has established, the Victorians conceived the lion as an "emblem of British might" that is "dangerous and powerful" yet, unlike other big-cat species, is "generous" to its prey and "susceptible to the 'moral dominion' of humankind" (26), then the wandering of Shirley's taxonomic designation calls her domestication into question. Louis's apostrophe, "Pantheress! beautiful forest-born! wily, tameless, peerless nature! She gnaws her chain" (591), fetishizes man's inability to master nature. Brontë's contribution to Victorian leonine politics is that, while revealing how desires to control nature influence human sexual and economic reproduction, Brontë shows how accepting man's inability to master nature can be rendered a pleasurable experience.

Shirley's narrator obsessively classifies and reclassifies organisms. Labeling Shirley "a black swan, or a white crow" conveys how radically she differs from Caroline, who, "still as a garden statue" (368), seems neither human nor animal. Sighting a rare, anomalous black swan or white crow, the narrator crafts one of *Chambers's* animal anecdotes—one of the astonishing events that nevertheless convey truths about nature, seamlessly connecting the part with the whole, the memorable with the representative—to aestheticize the inconsistencies that exist within species designations. *Shirley* extends this instability to the human species, staging a range of conflicting responses to this taxonomic crisis as broad as the range of Yorkshire flora and fauna identified by Mrs. Pryor. Their significance for the feminist threads in Caroline's journey—including her romance with Robert and her natural history—is hinted at when the two women propose a holiday on the Faroe Islands. Visualizing this holiday, Shirley imagines a new kind of hybrid woman: "a human face ... plainly visible—a face in the style of yours," which "looks at us, but not with your eyes" (232). As Shirley imagines a mermaid, she becomes transfixed by the "preternatural lure in its wily glance," becoming so horrified by her own image of alternate species-being for women—"Temptress-terror! Monstrous likeness of ourselves!"—that Mrs. Pryor complains, "We are aware that mermaids do not exist; why speak of them as if they did?" and Caroline protests, "But, Shirley, she is not like us. We are neither temptresses, nor terrors, nor monsters" (232–33). But Shirley confirms the value of her vision, asserting that there are men who believe women are "are all three" and "who ascribe to 'woman,' in general, such attributes" (233). Shirley's fancies reveal that Victorian gender politics treat women as a peculiar kind of *Anthropos* that spans many variants. This mermaid fancy epitomizes how *Shirley* embraces the limitations of anthropocentric individuation and the possibilities of multispecies empathy to a degree that *Jane Eyre* fastidiously eschews. Both Shirley and Jane face death, and in doing so confront their own animality, but Jane rejects it, while Shirley strategically deploys it to transcend class and gender roles and to stoke sexual desire.

Both heroines must overcome a crisis of survival that threatens to overturn their species-being in ways they find profoundly uncomfortable. For Jane, this is her three-day exile on the moors, when she considers briefly becoming a bee, lizard, or bog body; for Shirley, it is when she is bitten by a dog that she believes to be rabid. Bravely cauterizing the wound with a hot iron poker—a scene based on Emily Brontë's own experience—she exhibits the panic that often accompanies disclosures of humanity's physical and taxonomic violability. Ritvo has argued that Charlotte uses "rabies as a convenient *deus ex machina* in the novel *Shirley*, when she needed to soften her prickly and unapproachable heroine.... Once hydrophobia had served its romantic purpose, in a single chapter named after the aggressive dog, it vanished from the plot" (169). Yet the rabies episode explores the ontological and physiological consequences of the interspecies play that titillates Shirley. It also rationalizes her "unfeminine" qualities—her masculine name, her independence, her physical vigor—by constructing her as a steward of nature whose privilege and decisiveness supplement ladylike Caroline's moral leadership to minimize the local costs of unchecked male control over nature. Shirley, attacked by a female pointer owned by one of her unsuccessful suitors, recalls that Phoebe "looked as if bruised and beaten all over" and notes that "Mr. Sam often flogs his pointers cruelly" (476). This story, as Shirley recalls the incident to Louis, indicates her unwillingness to condone animal abuse and her willingness to correct such injustices, even if it exposes her to a dog whose erratic behavior spells potential infection. According to Victorian rabies discourse, "Since the owner had formed the dog's nature ... he or she had in some way participated in the animal's transgression and was also subject to chastisement and special restraint" (Ritvo 175), making Wynne's unrestrained Adamic violence and failed courtship a counterexample to Louis's promise of mutual control and seduction.

The rabies episode advances these negotiations by providing Shirley, who contemplates marriage, with an alternate (but equally corporeal) means of rehearsing her marital duties. As Ritvo documents, one medical theory built on rabies's "powerful association with lust" (181) to hypothesize that dogs who were denied sex contracted it. Other theories similarly drew on the "rhetoric of purity and contamination" that associated rabies "with disorder, dirt, and sin" to conclude that "the afflicted animal had somehow deserved or brought on itself ... a moral as well as medical catastrophe" (174, 175). Shirley's physical vigor and unmarried state suggest that Phoebe's penetrating bite—an interesting instance of same-sex, different-species penetration—is a symptom of and punishment for Shirley's rabid lustfulness. Her subsequent act of self-penetration—she tells Louis, "I took an Italian iron from the fire, and applied the light scarlet glowing tip to my arm: I bored it well in: it cauterized the little wound" (477)—is an oxymoronic attempt to re-seal her body with an additional violent, but volitional, incursion. So too does her demand that Louis administer "such a sure dose of laudanum as shall leave no mistake" if she evinces symptoms of infection (479). By such strategies, she tries to recover both moral self-control and her power over her physical relations with other bodies. Her confession to Louis intensifies their intimacy, accelerating the very wedding night that her fear of rabies (and the paranoid, anti-social behavior she exhibits both after the bite and upon her engagement) indicates a desire to postpone. Rather than full abstention from marriage and sex, Shirley desires full knowledge of (and some control over) the conditions of her little and literal deaths.

Cauterizing the wound may prevent further infection and reassert her threatened bodily integrity, but it also seals in the nonhuman saliva running in her veins. Shirley becomes, beyond metaphor, multispecies. Haraway's "The Camille Stories" also features human/nonhuman hybrids. Camille 1 contains human and butterfly DNA, thus expressing the physical and moral fact that humans intertwine with nonhuman species. For Haraway, writing about hybrids is an attempt to generate the empathic identification necessary for thoroughly reconceiving, without panic, what it means to be human (*Chthulucene* 144–52). However eager Louis and Shirley are to cross species boundaries as foreplay, *Shirley*'s rabies episode registers the fears of multispecies contamination. Fearing death to be the ultimate consequence of Shirley's hybrid intimacies, Louis decrees, "I doubt whether the smallest particle of virus mingled with your blood; and if it did, let me assure you that—young, healthy, faultlessly sound as you are—no harm will ensue.... I shall enquire whether the dog was really mad. I hold she was not mad" (478). Louis's rationalism appears non-anthropocentric, and their courtship emphasizes the overlapping of humanity with animality and allows Shirley to express her wildness through amorous species-play. Yet *Shirley*'s emphasis on the toxicity of multispecies blood regards with horror the prospect of an impure humanity, of humans who are not wholly human. The cultural work of a rabies diagnosis, which "identified suspicious or troublesome kinds of people" and justified the "moral surveillance" over them (Ritvo 176), is thus present in Louis's offer to protect the suspect Shirley by allowing her safe means for embracing her impure hybridity, behind the closed doors of their marital chamber.

Alexis Shotwell identifies such discomfort at impurity as "a feature of classification itself" and argues that we must overcome this "purity politics" if we are to create livable futures in the Anthropocene. Shotwell explains, "The delineation of theoretical purity, purity of classification, is always imbricated with the forever-failing attempt to delineate material purity—of race, ability, sexuality, or, increasingly, illness" (5). If Shirley exemplifies the failure of purity politics, Caroline represents its persistence. As she walks to the fête, an uncontaminated Caroline traverses an uncontaminating world, her purity identical to the landscape's own:

> She glided quickly under the green hedges and across the greener leas. There was no dust, no moisture, to soil the hem of her stainless garment, or to damp her slender sandal. After the late rains all was clean, and under the present glowing sun all was dry. She walked fearlessly, then, on daisy and turf, and through thick plantations; she reached Fieldhead, and penetrated to Miss Keeldar's dressing-room.... Caroline wasted no words ...

and with her own hands commenced the business of disrobing and rerobing her. Shirley, indolent with the heat, and gay with her youth and pleasurable nature, wanted to talk, laugh, and linger; but Caroline, intent on being in time, persevered in dressing her as fast as fingers could fasten strings or insert pins. (278–79)

Caroline's self-control seems to grant her a right to cross clean, thriving green spaces and "penetrate" Shirley's maidenly solitude in order to purify her, serving as Louis's chaste premarital proxy while remaining, herself, "stainless," free of the "dust" and "moisture" that would otherwise "soil" her. Robert's recommendation that his sister consult Caroline when English churchgoers mock the *sabots* she wears "for walking in dirty roads" and warding off "the mud of the Flemish *chaussées*" similarly insists on Caroline's impenetrability (64). But Caroline and the landscape sicken; in this shared illness, both lose their purity, illustrating the interdependence of humans and their biomes. As Shotwell points out, bodies and landscapes in the Anthropocene are always-already polluted; "there is no primordial state we might wish to get back to, no Eden we have desecrated, not pretoxic body we might uncover" (4). Caroline and Shirley's illnesses reveal that no one is immune, just as their contributions to local industrialization (Caroline marries the mill owner, while Shirley lends him capital) show that "it is not possible to avoid complicity.... We are compromised and have made compromises" (5).

In a novel that heroizes women who are loath to compromise—Caroline marshals her chastity and humility to suppress her desires, while Shirley, proud and independent, hides her vulnerabilities—it is unsurprising that they initially engage in what Shotwell calls the "politics of despair." Trying to restore purity, this politics of despair "attempts to meet and control a complex situation that is fundamentally outside our control" and "shuts down precisely the field of possibility that might allow us to take better collective action against the destruction of the world in all its strange, delightful, impure frolic" (8–9). Infected by toxins lurking within animals and landscapes, both respond despairingly. Caroline continues to guard her own sexual continence, becoming increasingly ill with every attempt to suppress her love; when Shirley's "delightful impure frolic" in a multispecies world threatens her with deadly infection, she withdraws from society, believing herself to be uniquely sullied, uniquely contagious. But after this initial despair, both heroines forge ways to engage in the collective action that Shotwell recommends. With Farren and her mother, Caroline resumes the scientific endeavors that heal her; Shirley confesses to

Louis, an act of acceptance allowing her to recuperate and rejoice in a courtship that affords her less toxic ways to experience hybridity. This compromise is also evident in her stoic re-penetration of the wound—an instance of the *pharmakon*, the poison that is also remedy—which re-affirms her decision to be vulnerable to bodily invasion by the sickened world around her. Stacy Alaimo vindicates these risky acts in her analysis of artists' responses to environmental disasters by "performing exposure as an ethical and political act" to

> critique the rational, disembodied Western subject's presumption of mastery or at least objectivity that is, supposedly, granted by detachment from the world. The exposed subject is always already penetrated by substances and forces that can never be properly accounted for. . . . These performances embody the crisis in rationality that feminism has uncovered again and again. But they also intimate that pleasure, desire, sensuality, and eroticism can pulse through the human exposed to place, permeating environmentalist ethics and politics as inspiration, catalyst, and energy. (*Exposed* 5)

By showing Louis her wound and sharing her story, Shirley becomes this "exposed subject" and recruits an ally capable of political action (he tracks down the truth about Phoebe) and ethical conversion (he enthusiastically confirms the desirability of Shirley's permeable body).

Of course, the couple's sadomasochism reflects the tenacity of this belief in mastery even as it reveals mastery to be less a reward bestowed upon sufficiently rational, detached subjects than a fantasy negotiated between desiring, penetrable ones. The question of mastery lingers because their species-crossing courtship cuts across socioeconomic boundaries. By proclaiming, "Tame or fierce, wild or subdued, you are *mine*" (586), the genteelly impoverished tutor equalizes their class discrepancy. As Ritvo explains, rabies discourse "emphasized the social standing of rabies victims, implicitly suggesting that they had been bitten by animals of lower rank" because "stigmatizing infections must have come from elsewhere—imported by an interloper of lesser degree" (179, 183). Consequently, when Louis affirms Shirley's health, then flirts in a far different register of multispecies empathy, she substitutes one bite from an "animal of lower rank" for another. Her uncle's apoplectic opposition to their marriage reinstitutes the politics of despair, causing Shirley to defend her purity—"I am an honest woman"—in response to his expostulation, "Will your principles permit you to marry . . . a man below you?" (520, 519). Uncle Sympson impotently rages against the attenuation of the family's control over hereditary lands. Shirley's appreciation for her responsibilities as a member of the gentry is evident; she directs an extensive campaign of outdoor relief, and after the Luddite attack, she organizes local efforts to dispatch medicine, clean linens, and refreshments. These efforts are compromised—she dispenses charity to underemployed mill hands but owns the millyard tenanted by her eventual brother-in-law—but they do underscore the biopolitical continuities linking Shirley's imagined rabies, her unadvantageous marriage, and her position as local heiress. If biopolitics is a "set of mechanisms through which the basic biological features of the human species became the object of a political strategy, of a general strategy of power" by which "the life of the species is wagered on its own political strategies" (Foucault, *Lectures* 1; *History of Sexuality* 1:143), Shirley's toxic exposures and sadomasochistic performances corporeally register the risks of economic and ecological change as tension mounts between her role as the traditional steward of the local multispecies networks of an agrarian economy and her role supporting an emergent industrialization that sickens her lands and complicates her hereditary position.

Shirley's animal intimacies mediate her two roles. Spending her summers at the contact zone of her kitchen door, she monitors the multispecies spectacle that is her property:

> Through the open kitchen door the court is visible, all sunny and gay, and people with turkeys and their poults, peahens and their chicks, pearl-flecked Guinea-fowls, and a bright variety of pure white, and purple-necked, and blue and cinnamon plumed pigeons. Irresistible spectacle to Shirley! She runs to the pantry for a roll, and she stands on the door step scattering crumbs. Around her throng her eager, plump, happy feathered vassals John is about the stables, and John must be talked to, and her mare looked at. She is still petting and patting it when the cows come in to be milked. This is important; Shirley must stay and take a review of them all. There are perhaps some little calves, some little new-yeaned lambs—it may be twins, whose mothers have rejected them. Miss Keeldar ... must permit herself the treat of feeding them with her own hand. (365)

The "spectacle" of Shirley supervising her "vassals" idealizes a rapidly disappearing agrarian world and renders its feudal leader "irresistible" with a picturesque combination of lordly chivalry and maternal care. Drawn spontaneously from one animal to another, Shirley's activities seem leisurely, but they map her territory as she follows the spatial dispensation of the bodies she owns. This is why she then stalks "over stile and along hedge-row" to inspect the " 'crofts,' 'ings,' and 'holms' under her eye" (365): her multispecies affinities for nonhuman organisms always refer back to her socioeconomic status through the pleasurable powers the latter grants her over the former. Broglio analyzes similar "assemblages of material objects," including Edwin Landseer's *Low Life* and George Morland's *Outside the Alehouse Door*, in which "dogs, beer, and earnest laborers set in a rural environment create a mosaic of a political life that affects the very biological being of the dog and workers, their food, and their rural ecology," to reveal the farm's role as a biopolitical apparatus: a tangle of discourses, practices, and material bodies that exerts power over others' bodies to appropriate their labor power (*Beasts* 4). Broglio, concerned with "the health and well-being of the humans and animals who worked the fields" and with "how these beasts of burden resisted such systems," unpacks moments when multispecies scenes "point to other ways of dwelling," especially those "at odds with the biopolitical regime" (6, 11, 8). Just as the picturesque encode forms of biopower, so does Shirley's "irresistible spectacle" code a nostalgic feudalism—a regime complicated by the novel's Robin Hood imagery, which construes Shirley's marriage as a form of biopolitical resistance and wealth redistribution.

By making Shirley country Robin Hood country, Brontë adopts the theory that he was based in Yorkshire. The novel's Nunnely Park (real-life Kirklees Park) is the site of the old Cistercian nunnery (Kirklees Priory) where Robin Hood's grave is said to be. Louis, in electing to remain at Fieldhead rather than visit the priory, the home of another competing suitor,

> would much sooner have made an appointment with the ghost of the Earl of Huntingdon to meet him, and a shadowy ring of his merry men, under the canopy of the thickest, blackest, oldest oak in Nunnely Forest. Yes, he would rather have appointed a tryst with a phantom abbess, or mist-pale nun, among the wet and weedy relics of that ruined sanctuary of theirs, moldering in the core of the wood. (485)

By accepting the myths that elevate Robin Hood from yeoman into aristocrat (the Earl of Huntington) and emphasizing how Sir Philip Nunnely's family wealth originated from the seizure of a nunnery, Louis's reflection anticipates his own social elevation and highlights the ghostly power of the "weedy relics" of former biopolitical regimes. Louis's preference for traces of the nunnery's wild past over the priory's present tenants suggests his sympathies with the "merry men," lending credence to Uncle Sympson's belief that their marriage steals from the rich and gives to the poor. Not for nothing does Shirley calls Louis a "homeless hunter," "a solitary but watchful, thoughtful archer in a wood" (576). Prowling around Fieldhead as an outlet for romantic frustration, the poacher Louis hunts at Shirley's desk to appropriate somewhat less weedy relics:

> He makes discoveries. A bag—a small satin bag—hangs on the chairback. The desk is open, the keys are in the lock. A pretty seal, a silver pen, a crimson berry or two of ripe fruit on a green leaf, a small, clean, delicate glove—these trifles at once decorate and disarrange the stand they strew. Order forbids details in a picture—she puts them tidily away; but details give charm. (486)

Identifying disarrangement as the mark of a "careless, attractive thing," Louis judges and desires Shirley and her disorderliness: "Whence did she acquire the gift to be heedless, and never offend? There is always something to chide in her" (486–87). Musing that if he could "take her ornaments, her sumptuous dress—all extrinsic advantages—take all grace, but such as the symmetry of her form renders inevitable," then he "should like her," Louis suits the action to the word, locking up her possessions and pocketing "the keys of all her repositories" (489). Planning to force her to "wring them all out ... only by confession, penitence, entreaty" (492–93), Louis playfully rehearses a seizure of assets. Sadomasochism eroticizes their marital redistribution of wealth as much as it does the physical and taxonomic intimacies between animals and humans.

Readers learn of his plan because Louis writes down his reflections on the appeal of disarrangement, suggesting that unincorporated details—parts that might not fit into a whole—stimulate aesthetic production rather than compromise it. His notes contribute to the novel's own disorderliness, and for this reason, they are frequently singled out as *Shirley*'s most egregious digression from formal unification. Because Brontë has "transmitted so much of what the reader is told about Louis Moore through his own musings and his notes, the pointlessness of which was criticized from the start," Thormählen allows that "the imputation of artistic failure seems just" (*Education* 56). Yet the inclusion of Louis's writings and the sudden switch in focalization suit the novel's ethnographic structure, the peculiar realism that collects stories from multiple informants. This very interlude contains a defensive digression on the aesthetic relationship between part and whole: "Order forbids details ... but details give charm" (486). Shirley's desk in disarray provides an ideal stage for an aesthetic battle between order and charm. Louis, the ethnographer describing Shirley's territory, codes the assemblage's incompleteness (there is only one glove), ambiguities (there are one or two berries), and trivialities (there are "trifles") as charming, not merely frustrating. Roland Barthes has argued that such unincorporable details guarantee, not erode, realism's authenticity. If literary criticism tries to

> to encompass the absolute detail, the indivisible unit, the fugitive transition, in order to assign them a place in the structure, it inevitably encounters notations which no function (not even the most indirect) can justify: such notations are scandalous (from the point of view of structure), or, what is even more disturbing, they seem to correspond to a kind of narrative luxury, lavish to the point of offering many "futile" details and thereby increasing the cost of narrative information. (141)

To achieve the reality effect (*l'effet de réel*), the author sacrifices cohesion and lavishes space to the details that are costly, both aesthetically and materially (Louis now controls "her very jewel-casket" [489]). Although other Brontë novels demonstrate this reality effect, *Shirley*'s fragmented structure and mobile focalization elevates this tension between part and whole, this paradoxical reliance on apparently "pointless" and costly details, into a governing principle. Shirley Keeldar, trailing errant objects and allowing her flashes of inspiration to fade, epitomizes the novel's attempt to lend charm to its own waste, disunity, and inconsequence. It also speaks to the novel's value as a record of inspired thought. Shirley possesses genius but does not apply it, wasting "the free dower of Nature to her child":

> If Shirley were not an indolent, a reckless, an ignorant being, she would take a pen at such moments, or at least while the recollection of such moments was yet fresh on her spirit. She would seize, she would fix the apparition, tell the vision revealed ... take a good-sized sheet of paper and write plainly out, in her own queer but clear and legible hand, the story that has been narrated, the song that has been sung to her.... But indolent she is, reckless she is, and most ignorant; for she does not know her dreams are rare, her feelings peculiar. She does not know, has never known, and will die without knowing, the full value of that spring whose bright fresh bubbling in her heart keeps it green. (366–67)

The narrator's dismay clarifies her own project: valuing what Nature offers by assiduously *writing it down*. The proffered inspiration helps to keep Shirley buoyantly alive. But surviving is not enough when the spaces and spirits that inspire her and keep her healthy are under threat.

The narrator's ethnographic project (to register the ecological consequences of human action over a thirty-year period) prevents the novel's moving parts from disaggregating entirely. Louis's entries expose the risks of focalization shifts—in journaling his desire to master Shirley, he commandeers the titular character and the narration itself—but storytelling at the heart of ethnography is not rare. Most characters write letters, Shirley writes essays, Caroline interprets Shakespeare, servant recall folktales, Mrs. Pryor relates her past, and Caroline and Shirley share confidences. During one of their walks, Caroline leads Shirley to a vantage point overlooking ancient forest whose sights and sounds hint at the distant past. Again given powers of "penetration," Caroline contributes a new facet to the novel's Robin Hood imagery:

> "It is like an encampment of forest sons of Anak. The trees are huge and old. When you stand at their roots, the summits seem in another region. The trunks remain still and firm as pillars, while the boughs sway to every breeze. In the deepest calm their leaves are never quite hushed...."
>
> "Was it not one of Robin Hood's haunts?"
>
> "Yes, and there are mementos of him still existing. To penetrate into Nunnwood, Miss Keeldar, is to go far back into the dim days of old. Can you see a break in the forest, about the centre?... That break is a dell—a deep, hollow cup, lined with turf as green and short as the sod of this common. The very oldest of the trees, gnarled mighty oaks, crowd about the brink of this dell. In the bottom lie the ruins of a nunnery." (151)

Caroline's vision supplements *Shirley*'s struggling survivals of (apparently) untouched greenery within an increasingly developed landscape by embedding ruins of human settlements within the lush woods of a majestically re-encroaching nature. Within the forest primeval is the crumbling nunnery. There is no untouched nature left; human history is legible even in this sylvan heterotopia. When Caroline proposes a future visit to the ghost nunnery in the ghost forest, and Shirley stipulates that no men may come, a parallel emerges between the destruction of female communities and of Yorkshire forests. A wistful change in verb tense from future to past—"We were going simply to see the old trees, the old ruins; to pass a day in old times, surrounded by olden silence" (202)—indicates that enriching possibilities have been foreclosed and continues to associate masculinity with the destruction of a past concord between nature and humanity. "The presence of gentlemen dispels the last charm," they lament, making them "forget Nature" and vice versa: "Nature forgets us, covers her vast calm brow with a dim veil, conceals her face, and withdraws the peaceful joy with which, if we had been content to worship her only, she would have filled our hearts" (202). Louis's predilection for property and mastery drives his competition with Sir Philip, but Caroline and Shirley's mystic female communion and love of the locale makes Yorkshire's ghosts a peaceful, instructive conduit to a past made available temporarily through nature walks and, more permanently, through storytelling.

THE LAST FAIRY: CONTINGENCY AND LOSS IN *SHIRLEY*'S COSMOLOGY OF DEEP TIME

In a rapidly industrializing region that bears physical marks of generations of human activity, *Shirley* provides a new sets of stories and revises older ones to construct a collaborative, fragmented vision of Yorkshire's natural and cultural histories. This vision is as eclectic as Chambers's *Vestiges*, as invested in humans' and animals' common inheritance, and as keen on revealing long-distant pasts. As James Secord argues of Chambers, so does too Brontë apply Sir Walter Scott's "methods on a cosmic scale ... to preserve the memory of an older feudal social order that is, on the testimony of the novels themselves, inevitably going to disappear" (*Sensation* 89). But unlike Scott, who associated the novel with "masculine intellectual vigor" (92), Brontë assigns such vigor to women, along with the responsibility of reminding human communities of their material and cultural continuities with nonhuman organisms and landscape formations. Caroline, Shirley, and Mrs. Pryor's storytelling practices align with Anthropocene feminism, which holds that stories can change "*how we conceive of and practice our relation to a world and a self suffused with otherness*" (Shotwell 10). Good stories adopt "the naturalist's art of attention" and "make different agential cuts that allow us to generate ... different modes of attention" and "better narratives, grounded in arts of noticing that open to and allow for noticing in contexts that are already disturbed, already impure" (106). One disturbed space, the ruined priory, is doubly rendered by Louis's and Caroline's differing modes of attention—as both mythological and material, national and local, historical and contemporary—demonstrating how storytelling practices create continuities or discontinuities between human actions and local ecologies, and among the past, present, and future. *Shirley*'s self-referential narrator and eclectic, gap-filled narration creates a storytelling practice to connect, without hiding the differences between, the characters' various modes of attention and ethical orientations toward industrializing Yorkshire. This is how, as Zylinska argues, practices of account-giving establish a constitutive link between ethics and poetics. Indeed, we encounter ethics precisely via stories and images, i.e., through textual and visual narratives—from sacred texts, works of literature and iconic paintings through to various sorts of media stories and images ... [T]he Anthropocene acquires its meanings and values through certain types of artistic, or, more broadly, cultural interventions, both written and visual ones. (107)

Shirley links ethics and poetics by refashioning myths such as Robin Hood—and supplementing them with new ones—to reveal powerful ecological histories of human compromise and model healthier biopolitical alliances. Stories "of different genres and kinds" help us

> make sense of the world and pass on instructions on how to live to younger generations. We need such instructions because we come into the world unformed, lacking the basic capacities to move within it, communicate with others and transform our surroundings. In other words, we lack *sophia*, widely conceived wisdom, which stands for both intelligence and affective-motoric know-how, and without which we are equally inclined to create and destroy ourselves and others, to make love and war. (68)

Shirley allegorizes this dual inclination by documenting how histories of multispecies violence in hypermasculine biopolitical regimes become stories of lost nature. What remains is to show that Shirley's cosmologies offer the alternative *sophia* that Anthropocene feminism requires.

Shirley's stories coalesce around mystical visions of the figure she calls, variously, Eve, Eva, Nature, and Mother Nature. It has long been recognized that Western thought figures nature as a woman and that this figuration secures nature as an easily controlled resource that serves man while establishing woman's role as naturally less perfect than man. Alaimo explains how feminist responses to this entanglement of women and nature have risked falling into two problematic camps: those who accept the binary between nature and culture and merely extend to women the right to control nature, which "forecloses the possibilities for subversive feminist rearticulations of the term" *nature*; and those whose search for a "compelling connection between feminism and environmentalism" leads to "glorifying a female realm that has been produced by the system of gender oppression" (*Undomesticated* 6, 9). Jane Eyre's exile in the moors illustrates both: the latter when she expects Nature to serve her ("I thought she loved me, outcast as I was.... I would be her guest, as I was her child: my mother would lodge me without money and without price" [372]), the former when, disenchanted with her mother's accommodations, she seeks entrance into Moor House and scolds the servant for being willing to offer a dog (but not herself) shelter. Recognizing the difficulty of avoiding these extremes, Alaimo acknowledges that "feminist rearticulations of female natures ... carry with them such overwhelming cultural baggage" but insists that the answer is "shifting the political valence of such formations (rather than simply dismissing them)" via "the discursive construction of natures that are female with a vengeance" (Alaimo, *Undomesticated* 179).

Shirley's cosmological visions offer alternate accounts of the relationship between woman and nature. A new account of the beginning of time overcomes Shirley as she is poised to enter church. Refusing to attend Reverend Helstone's service, she prefers Nature's own:

> she is kneeling before those red hills. I see her prostrate on the great steps of her altar, praying for a fair night for mariners at sea, for travelers in deserts, for lambs on moors, and unfledged birds in woods. Caroline, I see her, and I will tell you what she is like. She is like what Eve was when she and Adam stood alone on earth. (302)

Shirley's identification of nature with the first woman considerably expands the territory of caretaking and thus challenges Caroline's normative vision. When Caroline protests that this vision does not match "Milton's Eve," Shirley responds that women are free to reconfigure Eve:

> No, by the pure Mother of God, she is not! Cary, we are alone; we may speak what we think.... Milton tried to see the first woman; but, Cary, he saw her not.... It was his cook that he saw; or it was Mrs. Gill, as I have seen her, making custards, in the heat of summer, in the cool dairy, with rose-trees and nasturtiums about the latticed window, preparing a cold collation for the rectors.... I would beg to remind him that the first men of the earth were Titans, and that Eve was their mother; from her sprang Saturn, Hyperion, Oceanus; she bore Prometheus. (303)

Shirley's rewriting does not reject that women are natural caretakers per se—she enthuses, "my mother Eve, these days called Nature ... [is] taking me to her bosom, and showing me her heart" (304)—but challenges the banalization of this role into "making custards." Elizabeth Helsinger links Shirley's vision of Mother Nature to Emily Brontë's writing, particularly her late Gondal poems, which feature a "female Earth" (201) that resists the ever-present "danger" for women to be reduced, in textual representations, to "silenced embodiment in and as a rural place" (203). Shirley Keeldar and Emily Brontë, in short, both resist passive feminizations of Mother/Nature and misogynist suspicions of female embodiment. To take one example, in Emily's "Shall Earth no more inspire thee," Mother Nature's mandate is to inspire each "lonely dreamer," to "enchant and soothe" her daughters, even if ministrations inspire "fond idolatry" (*Complete Poems* 130). Shirley's decision not to attend church substantiates this idolatry, as does her alternate homily, which plumbs prehistory to write about the origins of female *Anthropos*:

> The first woman's breast that heaved with life on this world yielded the daring which could contend with Omnipotence, the strength which could bear a thousand years of bondage, the vitality which could feed that vulture death through uncounted ages, the unexhausted life and uncorrupted excellence, sisters to immortality, which, after millenniums of crimes, struggles, and woes, could conceive and bring forth a Messiah. The first woman was heaven-born. Vast was the heart whence gushed the well-spring of the blood of nations, and grand the undegenerate head where rested the consort-crown of creation. (303–4).

Figuring the first woman as a giant, Shirley glories in her strength, accessible to present-day women only if they cultivate impure species identities—becoming, in Shirley's case, a mixture of *Anthropos* and *Panthera*.

This account radically redefines the feminized images of purity that are defended by orthodox Caroline, whose conventional piety repudiates that idea that Eve continues to possess "undegeneracy" after hungrily consuming what fruit she will and consorting with what animals she will. In rewriting the biblical account of a woman, a tree, and a snake, Shirley's multispecies scene reconfigures the atomic unit of cosmic causality prescribed in Genesis. Eve and Mother Nature are exiled from paradise, but neither is defiled or weakened; "Heaven may have faded from her brow ... but all that is glorious on earth shines there still" (304). Like Emily's poem, Shirley's homily conflates aesthetic and spiritual value ("The gray church and grayer tombs look divine with this crimson gleam on them" [302]) and uses painterly terminology, in Shirley's case to describe a "woman-Titan" surrounding Briarfield Church:

> Her robe of blue air spreads to the outskirts of the heath, where yonder flock is grazing; a veil white as an avalanche sweeps from her head to her feet, and arabesques of lightning flame on its borders. Under her breast I

see her zone, purple like that horizon; through its blush shines the star of evening.... Her forehead has the expanse of a cloud, and is paler than the early moon, risen long before dark gathers. She reclines her bosom on the ridge of Stilbro' Moor; her mighty hands are joined beneath it. (304)

Precisely placing her heterodox Eves in local ecologies, Shirley's vision merges prehistory with contemporaneity and grafts fantastic onto naturalistic landscapes. Just the narrator's panoramic view of Nunnwood concludes with an assertion that it "allured the eye as with a remote glimpse of heaven's foundations" (200), *Shirley*'s detailed documentation of landscapes blends cosmological and ecological visions of the past and present.

The centrality of landscape in such passages reveal that Shirley's visions of Eve draw from both from biblical and scientific accounts of the past. Shirley's visions access deep time: the Earth's billion-year history, most of which is only accessible through the geological record. Deep time, first elucidated by eighteenth-century geologist James Hutton and popularized in nineteenth-century scientific texts that "adopted the term ... to mark the incommensurability between geological and historical time scales, between the Earth's gradual changes over hundreds of millions of years and the rapid changes occurring in even a century of human history," has recently come to the forefront of "the intellectual history of the Anthropocene" (Heringman 57, 56). Bronislaw Szerszynski accounts for this trend by pointing out that theories of the Anthropocene and of deep time both posit that the "study of human history was the basis for natural history—not the other way around" (116). Regarding the entanglement of human actions and geological strata as an indication of the Earth's future has only been formally explicated with the onset of Anthropocene theory, but its roots lay in eighteenth- and nineteenth-century science. Szerszynski summarizes,

> geology's roots in the human sciences mean that the notion of the Anthropocene was already in some sense latent in the new science of the Earth. But it also means that the geological concept of "deep" time—in which moving down into the body of the Earth is moving not just from the known to the unknown but from the present to the distant past—itself depends on specific kinds of intellectual, hermeneutic and representational practice. (116)

Martin Rudwick, adapting Steven Shapin and Simon Schaffer's concept of virtual witnessing, explains what these representational practices must achieve:

"Any scene from deep time ... must make visible what is really invisible. It must give us the illusion that we are witnesses to a scene we cannot really see" (*History* 1). Shirley's *devoir* "The First Blue-stocking" generates just such a deep history as it virtually witnesses primeval woman's relationship to nature. Like Jane Eyre, whose admittance into and renovation of Moor House restages the origins of human civilization and the emergence of human history from geological deep time, Shirley Keeldar takes on one of the primary tasks of Victorian anthropologists. They, like Charlotte Brontë, were interested in accessing not only the prehistoric deep time of the origins of *Anthropos*, but also British history through the folk tales and myths that circulate in *Shirley*, including the figure of Robin Hood.

But whereas Robin Hood imagery expands the content and temporality of the novel's multispecies ethnography by including medieval folklore, *Shirley*'s tale of orphan girl Eva's intellectual awakening penetrates further, into "the dawn of time":

> This was in the dawn of time, before the morning stars were set, and while they yet sang together. The epoch is so remote, the mists and dewy gray of matin twilight veil it with so vague an obscurity, that all distinct feature of custom, all clear line of locality, evade perception and baffle research. It must suffice to know that the world then existed; that men peopled it; that man's nature, with its passions, sympathies, pains, and pleasures, informed the planet and gave it soul. (452–53)

Envisioning a scene of such deep time that human cultures "baffle" traditional ethnography, Shirley, like other Victorian science writers, "gropes for the appropriate language" to articulate her "epiphanies" about deep history (O'Connor 4). She forges a feminist cosmology to rewrite the biblical account of humankind's banishment from pristine nature, thus disrupting pre-Darwinian biblical anthropology and contributing to the proliferation of speculative accounts of deep time in the wake of Charles Lyell's *Principles of Geography* (1830–33). At the same time, in terms of the tale's position as an interpolated narrative disrupting *Shirley*'s chronology, this *devoir* suggests what kinds of texts a more motivated Shirley would have written: glimpses into prehistory— both Earth's prehistory and her own, the extradiegetic tale of her girlhood. In this multispecies account of deep time, the orphan Eva is both Shirley's idea of the first woman and her own self-conception. The timeless present of the essay suggests that, unlike Jane Eyre, Shirley never renounces her material enmeshments with the nonhuman world. Thus Eva lives more with the wild beast and bird than with her own kind. . . . Unheeded and unvalued, she should die; but she both lives and grows. The green wilderness nurses her, and becomes to her a mother; feeds her on juicy berry, on saccharine root and nut.

There is something in the air of this clime which fosters life kindly. There must be something, too, in its dews which heals with sovereign balm. Its gentle seasons exaggerate no passion, no sense; its temperature tends to harmony; its breezes, you would say, bring down from heaven the germ of pure thought and purer feeling. (453–54)

Eva enjoys an equilibrium with the forest that "nurses her . . . before the Flood," when nature is "unaltered by the shocks of disease. No fierce dry blast has dealt rudely with her frame; no burning sun has crisped or withered her tresses . . . her eyes not dazzled by vertical fires" (454). By glorifying a time before anthropogenic crises and desertification, the beginning of Shirley's essay grants a wish central to purity politics: the desire to "access or recover a time and state before or without pollution, without impurity, before the fall from innocence, when the world at large *is truly beautiful*" (Shotwell 3). Yet its self-reflexive ending acknowledges its refusal to narrate the fall of man—or rather, of woman, as the feminist politics of the essay lead Shirley to turn away from images of impure femininity or female bodies. As fastidiously as Jane covets her cleaned clothing and purifies her body of peat and mud when she enters Moor House, Shirley refuses to provide a written account of how Satan "refined the polluted cup" and concludes with the question, "Who shall, of these things, write the chronicle?" (457). The essay's position as an intercalated narrative marked with her tutor's annotations allows further commentary on the essay's uneasy purity politics. Whereas Jane's love for Rochester causes her to compromise her nascent identification with nature and to cease fashioning a new species-being for herself, Louis's for Shirley forces them to explore her impurities. Shirley confesses to him, "I never could correct that composition. . . . Your censor-pencil scored it with condemnatory lines, whose signification I strove vainly to fathom" (457), indicating how deep-time narratives are vulnerable to critique, revision, and interpretation, which allows generations of audiences to rewrite them in ways not authorized by the original writer. Scarred by Louis's corrective pencil, "The First Blue-stocking" registers the shorter-term challenges that Shirley's natural cosmology of strong womanhood will encounter in her strife-filled negotiations with the men around her for power (particularly her other suitors and her uncle). By setting Shirley's *devoir* among alternate narratives with conflicting messages about the survival of pure biomes and the efficacy of imaginatively accessing them after the real ones are destroyed, *Shirley* reveals that gender politics structure Victorian conversations about deep time and environmental degradation.

Ecosystemic vulnerability is central to *Shirley*'s importance in the Anthropocene as a moment of cosmopolitical pause, which Stengers explains revels in the "the unknown constituted by ... multiple, divergent worlds, and to the articulations of which they could eventually be capable, as opposed to a temptation of a peace intended to be final, ecumenical" (995). Shirley and Caroline's opposites-attract intimacy indicates that divergent approaches (like natural history and deep-time cosmology) are at *Shirley*'s core. Just as Walls argues of Henry David Thoreau—he combines "the local intensity of White and the planetary extensivity of Humboldt"—*Shirley* combines "White's felt and loving descriptions of local nature" through Caroline, and, through Shirley, Humboldt's ability to visualize "spatial patterns of distribution and change pointing back in an unbroken continuum through human history to the deep geological, and even deeper astronomical, past" (*Passage* 194). *Shirley*'s ethnographic structure combines multispecies empathy and deep-time cosmology to challenge orthodox accounts of man's animality and impact on nature. Doing so "implode[s] the Cartesian dualism separating spirit from body, mind from matter, humans from nature—and history from 'natural' history—by weaving mind and material nature together, showing how humans and nature together create the Cosmos" (194). Furthermore, echoing Humboldt's interest in "the history of *mind*, as an integral part of the history of the planet and of all life upon it" (195), *Shirley*'s "First Blue-stocking" narrates the marriage of "Genius and Humanity." Personifying the air and the moon, Shirley recounts strange atmospheric conditions in which both Air and Moon "pant" in the process of gifting Eva with intellect, her "glorious Bridegroom." "My arid heart revives," Eva gratefully exclaims, and "the wood, the hill, the moon, the wide sky—all change!" (456). Just as Caroline experiences romantic love as an intensification of her aesthetic and ethical awareness of nonhuman life, Shirley's deep-time cosmologies impact her wooing of Louis, her essay's original audience. When Shirley in "laughing satire" calls him "a material philosopher," she identifies the limits of Louis's radicality. By answering that, as "glorious as Nature is, and deeply as I worship her ... I would rather behold her through the soft human eyes of a loved and lovely wife" (578), Louis proves unable to cathect to multispecies worlds through scientific abstraction. He needs heterosexual romance to maintain his bonds with the natural world, again showing how, because "the personal is geological" (Colebrook, "Counterfactual" 2), investigations of anthropocentrism must investigate how gender and sexuality encourage or discourage responsible ecological action. Accordingly, it is the rabies panic—a threat to Shirley's beloved body—that awakens Louis's sensitivity to the toxicity of the organisms and landscapes around them. Through their non-normative, corporeal courtship, Shirley materializes urgent yet abstract ecological lessons of deep time through spoken and written narratives, and, when those fail, her own exposed body. As Chris Washington writes of John Clare's poetry, through Shirley's literal and corporeal writings, Brontë finds a way to use stylistic experimentation and fragmentation to raise "awareness of the fragility and precariousness of all creatures, both human and animal" without becoming "negatively thanatopolitical"—that is, unhelpfully fixated on death in ways that biopolitical approaches to nineteenth-century literature often are (679). In this light, Brontë's decision to rescue her four characters from their brushes with death is less a sentimental desire to fashion a happy ending (the ending is, as we shall see, not strictly happy) than a course correction that balances the novel's thanatopolitical tendencies.

While Shirley's leonine erotics of mastery is racier than Caroline's sweet multispecies empathy, both show how gendered practices impact the Anthropocene. Both expose the ecological consequences of human activities related to courtship, marriage, and household management. While Shirley and Louis's amorous species-play forges new gender roles, Caroline's unobjectionable, sweet multispecies empathy bolsters her beloved's credibility as a mill owner through hers as a steward of nature. This bolstering is achieved because her presence underscores the factory's multispecies setting; Robert gathers her flowers that flourish "under the hot wall of the factory," and they court in the green spaces in which the factory sits (71). Like *Wuthering Heights*'s Heathcliff, who "embodies both the natural world and the potentially industrial products embedded in its rocky depths," Robert "is both nature and industry" (Buckland 151). This duality emphasizes the persistence of nonhuman organisms and spaces after the onset of industrialization. Robert's factory intrudes on the naturalness of the valley—polluting its streams, uprooting its trees—but Brontë imagines its disruptions in far less stark terms than she does the complete destruction of Thornfield Hall in *Jane Eyre*, which requires its romantic leads to flee it in order to marry. This persistence is embodied in the scene when Robert stands at the threshold of his counting-house on a beautiful day, wishing to be out in the fields enjoying it. The breeze and sunshine entered freely; but the first visitant brought no spring perfume on its wings, only an occasional sulphur-puff from the soot-thick column of smoke rushing sable from the gaunt mill-chimney. A dark-blue apparition (that of Joe Scott, fresh from a dyeing vat) appeared momentarily at the open door, uttered the words "He's comed, sir," and vanished. (121–22)

Joe Scott's strangely colored, smoky figure recalls the genii of the Brontës' juvenilia, in which the Brontës explicitly fashioned their authorial personae as genii, conceiving of authorship as a supernatural power of world creation. This appearance of Joe Scott as a mature genius suggests that industrialization, even as it destroys local biomes, also provokes creation. It too can inspire new narrative tropes. In this passage, Joe Scott's apparition dramatically interrupts Robert's enjoyment of pastoral beauties of the Hollow, his suddenness and alien appearance jolting Robert into a temporary awareness of the ecological consequences of his industrial operations.

For Charlotte Brontë, the undimmed dramatic potential of an industrializing Yorkshire should disrupt the metropolitan prejudices of critics like Lewes and Stephen. *Shirley* theorizes the inextricability of natural and industrial spaces and sediments new myths on top of old ones to narrativize industrialization. This commitment to Yorkshire as a literary setting makes sense of strange or arbitrary pronouncements made by *Shirley*'s narrator and heroines—as when Shirley Keeldar begins to theorize another unusual variety of *Anthropos* sexuality. When Caroline worries that Luddite unrest will endanger Robert and desires to be "at his side," Shirley's retort replaces her leonine erotics with an industrial one: "As queen of his heart? His mill is his lady-love, Cary! Backed by his factory and his frames, he has all the encouragement he wants or can know. It is not for love or beauty, but for ledger and broadcloth, he is going to break a spear. Don't be sentimental; Robert is not so" (323). But after Shirley spends time around the mill, she begins to perceive romance in industrialization, admitting to Caroline,

> "I like that romantic Hollow with all my heart."
> "Romantic, with a mill in it?"
> "Romantic with a mill in it. The old mill and the white cottage are each admirable in its way."
> "And the counting-house, Mr. Keeldar?"
> "The counting-house is better than my bloom-colored drawing-room."
> "And the trade? The cloth, the greasy wool, the polluting dyeing-vats?"

"The trade is to be thoroughly respected."
"And the tradesman is a hero? Good!"
"I am glad to hear you say so. I thought the tradesman looked heroic." (195–96)

Romance thrives not in a curated domestic environment, stripped of all but what is considered pretty and natural; it thrives among Robert's "grim metal darlings" (363). New heroes are found as Shirley transvalues Napoleon's criticisms about England as a nation of shopkeepers.

A Luddite attack tests this mill romance. Though the novel's double marriages seem to secure the comfortable reproduction of Victorian values and infrastructures into the next generation, the future they project is fragile, polluted, and uncertain. Shirley and Caroline learn this lesson firsthand that their setting, "romantic with a mill in it," temporally and spatially at the beginning of the Anthropocene, is crisis-ridden when they witness the attack on Robert's factory. In another scene of exposure, the women elect to leave their relatively secure position in the vicarage to creep closer and closer to the battle site, bringing them into contact with a landscape undergoing violent anthropogenic change. Charlotte based this incident on the real-life attack on Rawfolds Mill near Hartshead Church, where Patrick was the incumbent, in April 1812. Over a hundred armed men planned to destroy the new frames being moved along Hartshead Moor to the mill, which was defended by fewer than a dozen employees and soldiers. Charlotte learned about the twenty-minute altercation, which killed two Luddites and damaged the factory, from the personal recollections of her father, her teacher Miss Wooler, family members of Ellen Nussey, and newspapers Charlotte consulted while researching the conflict. Lewes rejects *Shirley*'s contribution to the history of industrialization because Brontë's framing of it is intimate, domestic, and gendered: "The attack on the Mill, too, instead of being described in the natural course of the narrative, is told us in snatches of dialogue between the two girls; who, in utter defiance of all *vraisemblance*, are calm spectators of that which they could not have seen" (169). But if Caroline and Shirley's relationship to the attack is (like Brontë's to early-nineteenth-century Yorkshire) a form of virtual witnessing and deliberate exposure, this is not because the heroines are unreliable but because *Shirley* revels in partial, positioned, situated knowledges.

As a crisis—a short period of time defined by a dramatic event—the Luddite attack supplements the novel's allegorical tales of deep time and its accurate descriptions of lingering Anthropocenic conditions with a more violent account of sudden historical change. Although Fieldhead, based on a real-life fortified Elizabethan manor, might seem the more logical setting, the vicarage, perched at the rim of the hollow at whose bottom the factory sits, serves as a spatial buffer between the factory and the valley's undeveloped spaces. Like the meadow that becomes a mock battlefield between children from rival Sunday schools on Whitsuntide, the parsonage is a nature/culture contact zone that reveals green spaces to be the site of conflict in the Anthropocene. During the battle, the parsonage thus becomes a contact zone between the Holocene and Anthropocene epochs, as well as between bourgeoisie and proletariat. This liminality is at its most intense at the "leafy screen" (318) that barely protects Shirley and Caroline from being discovered on the scene by passing Luddites while still allowing them to view the battle. Like the bushes Jane Eyre must cross to approach Moor House, this hedge provides safety because it is a property marker symbolically and physically enabling exclusion. Although such barriers are reversible (Shirley despairs that Caroline is "afraid of hedges, and the beck which we shall be forced to cross" [321]), it is part of the many nonhuman forces engaging in battle. A "glass of flowers" soothes Caroline and a "glass of new milk" bolsters Shirley as much as the gun with which she has been entrusted, while a barking dog dissuades the Luddites from entering the parsonage (316, 320). This protection seems to indicate the stability of the biopolitical regime represented by the parsonage as a triple contact zone. Yet the air pulses with "something electrical," the narrator compares the sound of the attack to "the felling of great trees," and the two women to "the straight stems of two trees" (317, 324, 325), emphasizing the entanglement of humans and nonhumans and foreshadowing the attack's environmental costs.

These costs are made explicit when morning dawns. No romance infuses the narrator's description of the battle site. There is certainly a mill in it, but it is "no cheering spectacle":

> These premises were now a mere blot of desolation on the fresh front of the summer dawn. All the copse up the Hollow was shady and dewy, the hill at its head was green; but just here, in the center of the sweet glen, Discord, broken loose in the night from control, had beaten the ground with his stamping hoofs, and left it waste and pulverized. The mill yawned all ruinous with unglazed frames; the yard was thickly bestrewn with stones and brickbats; and close under the mill, with the glittering fragments of the shattered windows, muskets and other weapons lay here and there. More than one deep crimson

stain was visible on the gravel, a human body lay quiet on its face near the gates, and five or six wounded men writhed and moaned in the bloody dust. (327–28)

Geological imagery abounds in this passage, where the "pulverized" millyard "yawned all ruinous" and is "thickly bestrewn" with discarded weapons and glass shards, in addition to "stones and brickbats," a layer of "bloody dust," and a dead body. In other words, the battle literally sediments Fieldhead Hollow with a thick vein of man-made and man-altered materials. The scene conforms to a 2011 paper by Zalasiewicz et al. that identifies the "lithographic signals" necessary for the Anthropocene to be admitted as a formal geological designation. Like the mining, urbanization, deforestation, damming, and coastal reclamation cited by geologists, Brontë's battle forms "novel strata" from a mixture of "modified geological materials" and "artificial deposits" from the built environment (1039). Over the last two centuries, these deposits have been "producing a significant 'event layer' . . . [that] may become geologically significant over centennial/millennial time scales" (1036–37)—precisely the scales over which *Shirley* claims knowledge. Local histories are deposited in the landscape, and the battle becomes both story and geology. Effectively, Brontë's ethnographic method mines anthropogenic strata, interpreting each one alongside other stories of class, romance, and ecology. A similar description of war-forged anthropogenic strata occurs in Emily Brontë's "Why ask to know the date—the clime?" In this poem, the speaker is a soldier who repents his unethical actions in the heat of battle. Describing the aftermath of one bloody battle, where a single combatant survived (himself), he notes the same chaotic dispensation of bodies, rocks, and building materials:

> A line of fires, and deep below
>   Another dusker, drearier glow—
> Charred beams, and lime, and blackened stones
> Self-piled in cairns o'er burning bones,
> And lurid flames that licked the wood,
> That quenched their glare in pools of blood (*Complete Poems* 184–85)

Both sisters understand war as an ecological force that, though it occurs as a momentary crisis, entails geological consequences at the scale of deep time.

But whereas Emily's very title—"Why ask to know the date—the clime?"— consciously refuses to historicize this event, attempting to generalize a lesson about the unchangingly violent nature of *Anthropos*, *Shirley*'s attempt to tell in the Anthropocene a story about the Holocene depicts ecological changes so far-flung and systemic that it must bridge gaps in time that appear as extensive as that between recorded history and deep time. Even the distance between the narrator and the time of the narrated events becomes an integral part of *Shirley*'s representation of the Anthropocene as an object of knowledge through acts of storytelling as diverse as the composition of a novel, the publication of a newspaper article, the recollection of a startling personal experience to a close friend, or the telling of a fairy tale or local myth by a servant to the children under her charge. While Barker calls Brontë's decision to depict Luddism, instead of her personal experiences of Chartist agitation near Haworth during her lifetime, "a missed opportunity" (656), the novel's deliberate framing of 1811–12 from the perspective of 1848–49 allows her to thematize how cultural histories gradually emerge out of multiple acts of storytelling that may be inconclusive or contested, layering chaotic strata of stories alongside the material strata coalescing out of man-made materials and processed rocks. Because discursive and lithic layers alike provide historical evidence of human-caused environmental changes, it is appropriate that *Shirley*'s narrator blends discursive and lithic imagery to depict human actions as fundamentally geological. Long before the narrator can describe the bone- and rock-strewn millyard, another such sifting of deposits comprises the novel's opening: "Of late years an abundant shower of curates has fallen on the north of England," the narrator begins, yet "we are going back to the beginning of this century: late years—present years are dusty, sun-burnt, hot, arid; we will evade the noon, forget it in siesta, pass the mid-day in slumber, and dream of dawn" (5). The onset of the narrative's chronological terrain is thus defined by curates being an endangered species ("in those days of scarcity ... the precious plant was rare"), its termination as an era defined by desertification. The narrator's pointed repetitions in this passage makes it the first of the three dozen or so direct addresses to the reader, passages of meta-narrative negotiation that advance justifications of novel's complex temporality. In this case, it serves to temper the reader's expectation of an "unromantic" narrative, which she characterizes a meal of "unleavened bread with bitter herbs, and no roast lamb" (5)—suggesting that, in narrator's present, humans must be abstemious, as oligotrophic as the plants that manage to flourish on the acidic, windy moors. The bitter herbs suggest that the novel is produced during an exodus or to honor a past exodus, and it refuses (or cannot afford) animal sacrifice.

This language of species endangerment, desertification, atonement, and memory is a language of loss. It is a language capable of expressing the

Anthropocene. *Shirley*'s depiction of the extinction of the fairies, while more fanciful than the bitter herbs, explicitly associates this language with industrialization and links to folk practices of storytelling that permeate the novel. When Robert misguidedly courts Shirley to secure capital for his failing business, her autobiographical response to his tale of a hard-working, self-made man indicates that factory-owners and disgruntled mill hands have superseded the fairies:

> "Three nights in the week I sleep in the mill—but I require little rest—and when it is moonlight and mild I often haunt the Hollow till daybreak."
>
> "When I was a very little girl, Mr. Moore, my nurse used to tell me tales of fairies being seen in that Hollow. That was before my father built the mill, when it was a perfectly solitary ravine. You will be falling under enchantment."
>
> "I fear it is done," said Moore, in a low voice.
>
> "But there are worse things than fairies to be guarded against.... For instance, how would you like to meet Michael Hartley, that mad Calvinist and Jacobin weaver? They say he is addicted to poaching, and often goes abroad at night with his gun." (224)

Shirley's warning invokes the biopolitical network that connects them—Hartley poaches (the signature crime against agricultural property owners like Shirley) and protests (against capitalist property owners like Robert)—but it is Louis, not the industrialist who drives out the fairies, with whom Shirley carves a world of enchantment. As Louis and Shirley's species-crossing explores the benefits of hybridity and the effects of toxicity, steward Caroline is entrusted to reign in Robert's industrialist excesses and, in protecting the nonhuman world, protecting Robert himself. He needs it: he ignores Shirley and inflexibly retains his spellbound single-mindedness. Hartley does, in fact, shoot Robert, allegorizing the vulnerability of those who heedlessly accelerate environmental degradation into moments of crisis characteristic of the Anthropocene.

Shirley suggests that periods of ecological change are seductively dangerous—they offer enchantment and destruction, and their atmosphere of contingency and extinction unsettles—and that sharing stories and refashioning old ones are effective coping strategies. Buzard argues that *Shirley*'s ethnographic multivocality allows Brontë to theorize "a redeemed Englishness as something definitively plural," not homogeneous and pure, but hosting "the multiplication of vantage points and vocabularies" (223, 222). This rejection of homogeneity does not only characterize the novel's social and ethnographic philosophies: it infuses its ecological ethics and structures the novel. In *Shirley*, patterns of telling and retelling result in a folk topography that layers myths from different generations, allowing Brontë to acknowledge the onset of the Anthropocene while providing imaginative access to the Holocene. As the narration winds down, an extinction story told initially to the narrator by her servant is retold:

> I can tell, one summer evening, fifty years syne, my mother coming running in just at the edge of dark, almost fleyed out of her wits, saying she had seen a fairish in Fieldhead Hollow; and that was the last fairish that ever was seen on this countryside (though they've been heard within these forty years). A lonesome spot it was, and a bonny spot, full of oak trees and nut trees. It is altered now. (607)

The narrator's servant's mother has witnessed an extinction event. Extinction is the moment when a real organism becomes mythical, when creatures assumed real in previous eras become, for the first time, unreal, sighted only when the viewer suspends disbelief. Such folktales are necessary because it is difficult to pinpoint extinctions; not all species have been classified, and biologists and paleontologists employ different methods. Consequently, the loss of biodiversity requires more myths for the purposes of remembrance, memorialization, and scientific research. And while this particular story is not *endorsed* by the narrator but simply *recorded* as amateur ethnographic data in the form of a regional mythology, extinct species need only be imaginable, not believable. With its complex temporality and framing, *Shirley*'s deep history is not simply myth or fact; it needs both, and it layers both from different generations and intelligences, including *Chambers's* animal, plant, and human sagacities, to craft a folk topography in which ecological change is painfully visible. With an empathetic skepticism, *Shirley* thus dramatizes how nostalgic myths arise from the difficulty of knowing our ecological past and present.

Uncertainty and contingency even animate Robert's final prophesy to Caroline of further anthropogenic change. In it, he judges environmental degradation an acceptable cost for increasing local standards of living for all economic classes:

> "I can double the value of their mill property. I can line yonder barren Hollow with lines of cottages and rows of cottage-gardens—"
>
> "Robert! And root up the copse?"

"The copse shall be firewood ere five years elapse. The beautiful wild ravine shall be a smooth descent; the green natural terrace shall be a paved street. There shall be cottages in the dark ravine, and cottages on the lonely slopes. The rough pebbled track shall be an even, firm, broad, black, sooty road, bedded with the cinders from my mill; and my mill, Caroline—my mill shall fill its present yard."

"Horrible! You will change our blue hill-country air into the Stilbro' smoke atmosphere." (605–6)

Critics have argued that this exchange concludes *Shirley* on an note of overwhelming loss and have linked this loss to Brontë's use of natural history and ethnography to argue that *Shirley* demonstrates Brontë's "yearning to recover and to preserve what was irrevocably lost" (Frawley 176). Coriale argues that *Shirley* "poses social responsibility against natural preservation" because "readers are encouraged to welcome this moment of peace and prosperity regardless of the environmental losses" (130). Yet *Shirley* recognizes that human activities have long ago transformed the area; the epoch of pristine nature has already passed. Moreover, Caroline's protests indeed emphasize these losses, but their exchange is as much flirtation as Shirley and Louis's species-play. The factory must, after all, finance their household. But as a steward, she is comfortable in her knowledge that, paradoxically, the Yorkshire uplands' prior degradation will preserve them from further destruction: "Stilbro' Moor, however, defies you, thank Heaven! What can you grow in Bilberry Moss! What will flourish on Rushedge?" (606) Nor does the narrator depict the valley's transformation as a foregone conclusion. She hedges, "I suppose Robert Moore's prophecies were, partially at least, fulfilled," and then concludes, "The story is told. I think I now see the judicious reader putting on his spectacles to look for the moral. It would be an insult to his sagacity to offer directions. I only say, God speed him in the quest!" (607). Brontë's narrative thus foregrounds the "unpredictable contingency" that Rudwick associates with Victorian science—the sense that "the Earth had not been programmed ... in such a way that its past and future course was fully determined"—along with his assertion that deep history can be recovered "only by piecing together the historical evidence 'bottom up' " (6).

Shirley records human-caused ecological change at the dawn of the Anthropocene, along with the difficulty of crafting a complete, entirely objective account of it. The novel is a moment of pause whose ethnographic method demonstrates how, as Stengers asserts, an "etho-ecological" politics of the Anthropocene may become "disentangled from any reference to some universal human truth it would make manifest" (1001). Brontë's narrative layering acknowledges that "there is no position outside, no straight path, no belief in transparent global systems of knowledge, only modest protests and precarious pleasures, from within compromised locations shadowed by futures that will surely need repair" (Alaimo, *Exposed* 188). In Caroline Helstone, Brontë fashions a character who causes others to slow down (in Stengers's sense) and "notice" (in Tsing's and Shotwell's senses), while Shirley Keeldar's toxic, hybrid body models new ways of being human in the Anthropocene, revealing how *Shirley*'s narrative economy leverages ecosystemic change as a source of temporal and perspectival complexity. Brontë's ethnography of loss also cathects the banal; just as Shirley gathers "single flowers—the last of their race" to make "a hueless and scentless nosegay" in the autumn (450), the novel associates nature with austerity, discomfort, and danger in addition to fecundity, beauty, and nostalgia. In its thirty-year timespan, *Shirley* identifies a potential "golden spike" (the moment of the Anthropocene's emergence from the Holocene epoch) without downplaying the specter of ecological loss, and without expunging the interpretive interventions, historical conjectures, and narrative labors that make such an identification possible. By embedding ecological change in lush word-paintings, Brontë constructs a multispecies ethnography that renders the Yorkshire moors as magical as fairies, as mythical as Robin Hood, and yet as "unromantic as Monday morning."

FOUR

Provisional Survivors in Postnatural *Villette*

LEARNING TO LOVE THE STORM

The austerity of *Shirley*'s autumnal bouquet, its "hueless and scentless nosegay" composed of "single flowers—the last of their race" (450), is echoed in Brontë's final novel, *Villette* (1853), by way of the protagonist's fête dress. When Lucy Snowe seeks a frock formal enough for gala occasions at the *pensionnat* where she works, she selects an unusual fabric. Unlike her pupils, each wrapped in a "clear white muslin dress, a blue sash (the Virgin's colors), a pair of white, or straw-color kid gloves," Lucy wears more subtle apparel. Her choice is motivated not by indifference but by her conviction that only in a "gown of shadow" can she feel "at home and at ease" (144, 145). With "the weather and rooms being too hot to give substantial fabrics sufferance," she "sought through a dozen shops" until she "found a crape-like material of purple-gray—the color, in short, of dun mist, lying on a moor in bloom." Her employer, Madame Beck, wears a dress "almost as quiet" but glitters with a "large brooch bright with gold and fine stones," contrasting with Lucy, who has "no flower, no jewel . . . no natural rose of complexion" (145). Set incongruously among white muslins, Lucy distances herself from what she cannot claim to possess: neither her students' joy, freshness, and simplicity nor Madame Beck's prosperity, authority, and stateliness. This sartorial peculiarity furthers her quest to feel "at home" by implanting misty English moors into sparkling Continental gardens. It also gestures at a temporal exile, in addition to a spatial one, because it celebrates the shadowy beauties of a denuded Earth. Madame Beck similarly tailors a sober holiday wardrobe; both deem it "absurd" to "dress themselves like girls of fifteen" (145). Certainly, the two women incarnate their personal ideals of beauty, but unlike their students, they employ the colors and textures of postnatural spaces, rather than appropriating the visual language of purity. Theirs is a clouded, darker aesthetic authentic to the Anthropocene. Madame Beck's manifests unsustainable human behaviors: her heavy metals, adorning the comfortable silhouette contrasting with Lucy's austere slimness, figuratively and literally cost the Earth. But Lucy's restrained style will not cost the Earth. She foregoes the copious blooms that her pupils pluck for their coiffures, and even her skin refuses the metaphorical theft of a "natural rose." Like Shirley's hueless, durable bouquet, Lucy's fête toilette is a sustainable option.

This austerity comes at great personal cost. Brittle, hungry, reticent, and depressive, Lucy Snowe suffers to create a melancholy aesthetic that registers environmental degradation. In *Villette*—set climatologically after *Shirley*'s position at the end of the Holocene—access to nature is infrequent, privatized, and highly stylized. In urban, polluted Villette, every plant, animal, and rock bears signs of human intervention. Wildness is represented by extradiegetic references to the past. Exiled from the landscapes of her youth and assailed by dangerous extremes of weather, Lucy accesses flora, fauna, and ecosystemic tableaux indirectly. They are attenuated and mediated as commodities (shops are searched for moorland crape), hallucinations (only through them are Villette's fertile ecological unities perceived), or compromises (the gardens that console her are miniscule and marked by death). This atmosphere of crisis, constraint, and artificiality differs from *Shirley*'s resilient landscape, which absorbs crises without collapsing entirely. Still less can Lucy return to *Jane Eyre*'s Holocene. *Villette* is positioned after the moment Jane resumes her anthropocentrism and enjoys the gradual return of all the moral, corporeal, and financial rewards threatened by her ecologically costly romance with Rochester. In *Shirley*, Jane's willfulness no longer answers; the call to minimize human destructiveness, which she hears and rejects, is no longer a choice but a given. Shirley and Caroline cannot opt out of the fragile multispecies network whose fate they are compelled to share and steward. In *Villette*'s Gothic ecology, such suspensions are even more fragile. *Villette*, like *Shirley*, ends in uncertainty and delegates the cognitive and ethical tasks of concluding to the reader. Both disclose how ambiguities plague the identification of a universally agreed-upon "golden spike": a single geographical and temporal site of the Anthropocene's emergence, along with the processes causing it and the evidence proving it. *Shirley* undercuts its own teleology of industrial and romantic development with fairy tales, extinction stories, and allegories of stewardship—an uncanny persistence of obsolete Holocene narratives that relies on multiple modes of interpreting ecological data. But whereas *Shirley*'s lacuna develops around the contested intersection between morality and literary realism—What is the moral of a novel that ends in a double wedding and ecological destruction?—*Villette* withholds not only conclusions, but essential facts as well.

This chapter inspects the blueprint *Villette* offers for surviving ecological crises when basic facts are under dispute and for ameliorating them when the arena for productive human action is constrained. Villette emerges as a postnatural space that embeds highly managed remnants of nature within an overwhelmingly artificial space dominated by polluted skies and pulsing with storms and electricity. Lucy's disenfranchisement as an exile from Holocene England emerges as an early portrait of Anthropocene subjectivity. I identify a formal strategy of "delayed identification," showing how Brontë uses it to link Villette's modernity to Lucy's alienation and arguing that it prefigures tropes in contemporary science writing. I identify other aesthetic tropes of Brontë's Anthropocene, including the performance of resilience by welcoming the stormy weather so common in unstable ecosystems, and the reinterpretation of phenomena experienced as supernatural into potent evidence of the inextricability of human and geological histories. Lucy's narrative demonstrates how to withstand stormy weather, mourn what has been lost, and leave as light a mark as possible on the Earth. By tending what remains without losing herself in grief, Lucy's most powerful instruction for readers is how to keep your head at the end of the world.

NO SECOND EDEN: THE DESANCTIFIED, MUDDY EXILES OF THE CAPITALOCENE

Lucy Snowe is the archetypal mourner of the Anthropocene because she survives so many deaths. *Villette* may open with warm domestic scenes as Lucy enjoys the Bretton family's hospitality, but Brontë disorientingly switches to visions of sickness and catastrophe. A shipwreck conceit reveals that she lost her entire family—"I must somehow have fallen overboard," or "there must have been a wreck at last" because "the ship was lost, the crew perished" (38)—but offers no concrete information. Readers are left with a sense of inarticulable, untraceable loss particular to Lucy but universal in its ambiguity. The silence surrounding this period typifies the narrative pattern by which, in *Jane Eyre* and *Villette*, relocation follows cataclysm. When her employer, Miss

Marchmont, dies unexpectedly, Lucy must leave England; when the mother of her friend Paulina dies, Paulina is summarily—and repeatedly—expelled from houses and inserted into others in response to her father's protracted grieving process; and when Lucy rehearses death with fainting spells and hallucinations, they destabilize her hold on identity as surely as they do her spatial position in the world. Unable to stabilize her own movements, Lucy experiences grief, exile, and homelessness as inextricably connected. Home is lost—and not solely by Lucy, though her position of narrator focalizes her mourning. These lost homes are intimate and national, as when the death of the overdeterministically named "Mrs. Home" costs Pauline mother, motherland, and name. When she reappears, she is "Miss de Bassompierre," the aristocratic *de* efficiently eliding her true birthplace. And when the Brettons' financial collapse necessitates the ancestral manse's sale, the ensuing expatriation ends the family known as "Bretton of Bretton" (7).

This vertiginous dissolution of selfsame relations between person, family, and home shows that in *Villette*, mourning is a practice of responding to the end of the world. Jacques Derrida addresses this double rupture by arguing that an individuals's death "does not announce an absence, a disappearance, the end of *this* or *that* life" but "declares each time the end of the world, in totality, the end of every possible world, and *each time the end of the world as unique totality, therefore irreplaceable and therefore infinite*" (9). Lucy develops her shipwreck conceit to envision the total disappearance of ship and crew into the briny deep, underscoring the shock of loss that arises from the irreplaceability of each world's unique combination of human and nonhuman organisms set in local habitations and bearing corresponding names. *Villette*'s incessant cataclysms support Derrida's argument that in grief, "the repetition of the end of an infinite whole [is] once more possible: the end of the world itself, of the only world that exists each time" (9). This coexistence of infinite possibility and absolute destruction is at the heart of Lucy's will to survive. As "the provisional survivor who endures this impossible experience" (9), Lucy remains as worlds ceaselessly fall and rise. These experiences strengthen her for the next collapse, but melancholy remains because she does not possess the power to conjure a new world. This becomes clear when Protestant Lucy faints at the entrance of a Catholic church visited out of sheer desperation during a lonely summer. She awakes in an unfamiliar mansion into which objects from her childhood have reappeared. There, she falls in love with her rescuer: her estranged childhood friend Graham Bretton. In the apparent return of a superseded world, Lucy believes she has found an exit from this recursive loop of apocalypse. Her "Imagination," "descend[ing] with a quiet flight to the waste—bringing all round her a sphere of air borrowed of eternal sunshine; bringing perfume of flowers which cannot fade—fragrance of trees whose fruit is life; bringing breezes pure from a world whose day needs no sun to lighten it" (256), parlays Graham's reappearance into a new world of love. But "Reason" rises ascendant to forbid

> all weak retrospect of happiness past; commanding a patient journeying through the wilderness of the present, enjoining a reliance on faith—a watching of the cloud and pillar which subdue while they guide, and awe while they illumine—hushing the impulse to fond idolatry, checking the longing out-look for a far-off promised land whose rivers are, perhaps, never to be, reached save in dying dreams, whose sweet pastures are to be viewed but from the desolate and sepulchral summit of a Nebo. (257–58).

As barred from her Promised Land as Moses is from his, Lucy copes with apocalypse by treating her troublesome desire for a better world as a spur to "Reason," not fantasy. Considering that her desire is attached to human subjects who have proven so fragile, it seems a wise course of action.

Such a stoic response is fit for Derrida's provisional survivors, who interminably wake in new worlds, but never in a perfect one. Lucy's migrations show the difficulty of acclimating to new worlds. A perpetual exile, she is always reminded of her homelessness. When Lucy visits Bretton before her family dies, Polly coldly observes, "*your* home is not here" (38). When they die, Lucy admits, "I had no home," and a disembodied voice tells Lucy, "Leave this wilderness . . . and go out hence" (55, 49). Later, she observes to her eventual fiancé, M. Paul, "To be home-sick, one must have a home, which I have not" (402). As Lucy faces her exiles, her resolve differs from other Brontëan figures facing the loss of home. One of the most famous, Emily Brontë's "No Coward Soul Is Mine," is a spiritual statement about resisting imminent death despite believing in the afterlife. Like Lucy, this poem interprets individual losses on a planetary scale:

> Though Earth and moon were gone
> And suns and universes ceased to be
> And thou were left alone
> Every Existence would exist in thee
> There is not room for Death
> Nor atom that his might could render void (*Complete Poems* 182)

The staunch theism of Emily's "no coward soul" interprets the death of an individual or a world as earthly illusions trivial in the face of spiritual immortality. But Lucy responds to a different challenge: survival, not death. She must face the reappearance of a polluted Earth, not its disappearance.

Villette's origins from the ashes of Charlotte's first mature novel also recapitulate this iterative logic of depleted reappearances. In *The Professor*, Brontë clings to a utopian geography whereby the protagonist's painful exile to an urban, industrial space is fully compensated by his return to a pristine English village. For his half-English wife, repatriation "realized the dream of her lifetime" (280), but this dream is unrealizable for Lucy. *Villette* reduces the mobile spatial footprint mapped by *The Professor*, confining her to artificial, enclosed spaces. Lacking resources to hire transit, her mobility dependent on irregular favors from the affluent, Lucy is trapped to the restricted territory traversable by foot. Vulnerable to weather conditions that jeopardize her health and intensify her claustrophobia, Lucy suffers a growing panic that serves as a barometer of the accruing human costs of the Anthropocene. While Lucy's claustrophobia is well-known,[1] I emphasize that it is not merely psychological: *Villette*'s intensifying spatial constriction completes a broader ecological trajectory traced in Brontë's full oeuvre. In *Jane Eyre*, Bertha Mason destroys Thornfield Hall, but Rochester possess another retreat, Ferndean Manor. Disaster seems negotiable; if an ecosystem is compromised, another pure one is always available. In *Shirley*, Brontë first considers that we ought to continue living in the places we pollute. Ecological degradation is traceable, an effect of economic and political decisions. The narrator figures the golden spike as a temporal break that is definite, singular, and remembered but tricky to represent. *Villette* pushes this principle further: unlike the "no coward soul" focused on the moment when loss approaches, unlike *Shirley*'s single moment of planetary rebirth, *Villette*'s peculiar alienation arises from the fact that an unspoiled natural world is no longer remembered. In *Shirley*, Edenic memories (always imagined or secondhand) provide poignance, but in *Villette*, loss is paramount and recurrent. Lucy must adjust to new worlds by actively rebuilding her life. For Lucy, there is no Ferndean Manor—no second Eden to escape to and recuperate in.

Villette contains no liminal spaces poised between village and moor (*Jane Eyre*'s Moor House, *Tenant*'s Wildfell Hall, *Agnes Grey*'s parsonage) or forest (*Jane Eyre*'s Ferndean, *The Professor*'s Hunsden Wood) to restore the equilibrium between man and nature. Lucy lacks *Shirley*'s Robert Moore, whose industrial activities can be influenced; she lacks Gilbert Markham of *Tenant*, whose farm nourishes a family with interspecies harmony, wholesome foods, healthy exercise, and spiritual contemplation. Lucy must remain in an ever-shrinking, urbanizing Villette, and she responds to these confinements and reappearances by leveraging her powers of observation into anthropological fieldwork. As James Buzard argues, Lucy inserts herself into a foreign culture as a participant-observer writing an ethnography (245–73). Whereas Buzard reveals the novel's autoethnographic qualities (Lucy's foreign experiences yield fresh insights about her native culture), I stress that the differences under observation are ecological as well as social, cross-epochal as well as cross-cultural. Reporting from a space where the effects of the emergent Anthropocene are painfully visible, Lucy subjects this new geological epoch to the same investigation as she does Labassecourian culture. Brontë's fictionalization of the Brussels she knew into a subject for postnatural fieldwork means that *Villette* is a speculative ethnography of ecological change. Villette is Brussels rendered *as* an Anthropocenic city.

Thrust unexpectedly from her native ecosystem by a series of catastrophes, attempting to rebuild her life in an alien, postnatural space, Lucy is an exemplary subject of the Anthropocene. Her account of her journey from the country's northern port—Ostend, renamed Boumarine ("Sea Mud")—to its capital city of Villette ("Little Town") describes a wasteland of ecological collapse. Peering out of her diligence, Lucy reports a litany of "deadening influences," including "a thick fog and small, dense rain" and "slimy canals, like half-torpid green snakes" (67). This life-suppressing landscape maintains boundaries neither between earth and water nor between fertile land and dangerous morass. A few degrees more "bare" and "treeless" than Brontë's own moors (67), it is a bog writ large, stripped of its fuel-rich peat and rare birds, a realization of nineteenth-century fears in the scientific community that denuded patches of land bearing the consequences of modern and ancient human activity were rapidly enlarging. In a twist of visual perspective, Lucy perceives the landscape's remaining trees, which are "formal pollard willows" (plantations rather than natural formations), as if from the wrong end of binoculars: the marshy lands are "tilled like kitchen-garden beds," surreally undersized despite the citizens' unflagging attempts to tend them (67). Charlotte's sarcastic name for Belgium—rechristened "Labassecour" ("The Farmyard")—does not only mock non-English societies but also, in its ecological register, uncomfortably highlights the ineffectuality of human stewardship. Despite the relative rapidity of her means of transport, Lucy internalizes the despair of this mismanaged wasteland, making her perceive her destination as precisely as small, confined, and insignificant as Brontë's coinage suggests. As Lucy describes Villette's gates and walls, she sketches a barely adequate defensive outpost, shutting itself ineffectively against the devastation beyond. The sights unsurprisingly activate her "anxiety," which is "lying in wait ... for sun-down to bound ravenous from his ambush" (67). Her eventual admittance, through the "miry Chaussée," to the salvation of the walled *pensionnat*, provides a qualified security, but its position on the Rue Fossette—the "Little Ditch," another muddy, liminal, uninspiring space—indicates that nothing can shut out Labassecour's murky, unsightly wastelands. Education cannot shut them out: Brontë's wryly comic name for the university town is Bouquin-Moisi, "Moldy Old Book." Even the instruments of knowledge are bemired.

Villette's muddiness befits the ambiguities and impurities of post-Holocene Earth. Its banal filth may not seem as powerful an image of a compromised Earth as the romantically grotesque destruction of Thornfield in *Jane Eyre*, nor can it inspire the ardent, erotic stewardship summoned by *Shirley*'s ancient forests, rare botanicals, and charismatic canines. But what *Villette* does do is provide alternatives to the "extinction porn" of contemporary artistic production representing the Anthropocene. As Joanna Zylinska has argued, such works aestheticize ecological destruction, making it beautiful in ways that privilege the sheer perception of the sublimity of man-made space, using aesthetic responses to suppress an ethical attention to human responsibilities. Zylinska unpacks how the exclusion of human beings from sweeping scenes of barren decay heroizes humans' toxic powers. This use of the sublime to represent a postapocalyptic Earth distances its viewers from the grim realities of the ground and

> holds the Anthropocene at bay, foreclosing on the exploration of any ethico-political issues it potentially brings up. In the last instance, the series only restores and strengthens the anthropos, who gave the name to this geological period—the same way gory horror movies do. Narcissism, self-interest and self-comfort thus overshadow any possibility of the emergence of an ethical response and ethical responsibility. (109)

Unlike these unhelpful representations, ethically powerful art must "reimagine life, death and extinction beyond the narrow fatalism and also beyond what we might term the 'rescuism' of the dominant Anthropocene story" (108). Swampy Villette offers no obvious sublime temptation, and Lucy's exemplary but unglamorous survival mechanisms reject "narrow fatalism" and "rescuism" alike. Rather than gift Lucy with the improbable ownership of a portion of unspoiled earth, Brontë forces her to live on in ditchy Villette, whose compromised landscapes Lucy refuses to romanticize—even while she tends assiduously to the straggling fragments under her care. Despite claiming in her conclusion that she remains "naturally no florist," throughout the novel she trains herself to care for local flora, becoming a "gardener of some tintless flowers that grew between its closely-ranked shrubs" and "clear[ing]the relics of past autumns, choking up a rustic seat at the far end" (545, 119). More resilient than careless Shirley, who deigns to gather hueless flowers when no others are available, diligent Lucy "made this seat clean" with "a pail of water and a scrubbing-brush" (119). Like Brontë herself, her relationship to gardens is thus not a matter of *likeness* or *liking*, but a causal web within the material world that links Lucy's health and ecosystemic stability.

Salted with a patience alternately begrudging and amused, Lucy's clear-sighted affection for the inexorably oozing spaces of Villette is a salutary approach to a world in which, as Claire Colebrook argues, "there are no lines of difference that would allow us to clean up and mitigate the past" (Colebrook, "Counterfactual" 18). Lucy depicts murky Villette as mysterious, threatening, and stimulating because its impure urban ecology is physically layered with perplexing remnants of the town's ancient, medieval, and modern iterations. Amid these remnants whose boundaries cannot be definitively established, chance and fate are difficult to distinguish. So are the past and present. Does a chance meeting with a young woman on a steamer determine Lucy's entire future? Is the school's ghost a sinning nun from centuries ago, a lovelorn fiancée who pined away decades ago, or a foppish count very much alive? With many possible explanations for the past, but only one denuded present, Lucy suspects everyone—seconding Colebrook's advice to abandon knee-jerk protests of innocence whereby we insist that, if given a chance to travel back in time and prevent the Anthropocene, "we would or could have acted in a way that was essentially different or noncontaminating" (18). Villette's indeterminate grunginess also supports Colebrook's recommendation to jettison "a notion of stabilized nature, a nature that is ideally there for us and cyclically compatible with production" (18). This is why images of rocks and jewels, of digging and mining, striate soggy *Villette*: the town serves as a microcosm of industrial urbanization. By day it is a grid of right angles "where all is stone around, blank wall and hot pavement," by night a maze of "oil-twinkling streets" (117, 517). Processed natural resources fill its shops, while its enervated plants and animals—herded into parks, stuffed into vases, pinned into corsages, plunged into fishbowls—cannot survive without unceasing human intervention. Brontë conjures a complete (and unsustainable) economic cycle uniting the extraction of resources from the ground, the cultivation of nonhuman organisms, their insertion into circulating systems of value, and their fashioning into cityscapes.

For Brontë, living at a contact zone between moors and mills (as well as visiting London, Manchester, and Brussels) helped her imagine such a space. Her vantage point witnessing ecosystemic shifts inspired a moral unease tantamount to shame, as if also believing herself culpable. In a June 1848 letter to her publisher, in the process of expressing her pleasure at contemplating William Smith Williams's holiday in a "pretty South-of-England village," she explains that she indulged in a daydream about it because it is "so different from our northern congregations of smoke-dark houses clustered round their soot-vomiting Mills" (*Letters* 2:72). This deprecation suggests a fear of being aesthetically compromised by her precociously denuded surroundings. Mary Poovey's application of "uneven development" to intersections of gender and class in the Victorian period is useful for understanding this precocity.[2] Because accounts of the Anthropocene's onset are inescapably inconsistent (as I show in the introduction), Colebrook is right that there are no "lines of difference," no lines in the sand after which we can claim our actions are harmless or too late to matter. In *The Professor*, Crimsworth behaves as if these interdicted lines not only exist, but also provide useful, flattering data. As Heather Glen argues, *The Professor* is Brontë's contribution to the early Victorian self-made man novel (35), and I would argue that this self-making rests upon his accurate diagnosis of environmental conditions. Consider how ecosystemic shifts inform his decision to work at his brother's factory: "Steam, trade, machinery had long banished from it all romance and seclusion. At a distance of five miles, a valley, opening between the low hills, held in its cups the great town of X———. A dense, permanent vapour brooded over this locality—there lay Edward's 'Concern'" (48). Where Lucy perceives continuous flux in Villette, Crimsworth's Yorkshire mill town seems irrevocably changed. No less than "all romance and seclusion" have been "long banished." The valley marks a finite boundary from below, while "dense, permanent" clouds of industrial pollution seal it from above. The double meaning of "Concern" equates his brother's interests wholly with the footprint of his factory complex, perpetuating the Holocenic tautology drawing identity, homes, and names into a watertight, selfsame relation. This assumption drives Crimsworth's decision:

> I forced my eye to scrutinize this prospect, I forced my mind to dwell on it for a time, and when I found that it communicated no pleasurable emotion to my heart—that it stirred in me none of the hopes a man ought to feel, when he sees laid before him the scene of his life's career—I said to myself, "William, you are a rebel against circumstances; you are a fool, and know not what you want; you have chosen trade and you shall be a tradesman. Look!" I continued mentally—"Look at the sooty smoke in that hollow, and know that there is your post! There you cannot dream, you cannot speculate and theorize—there you shall out and work!" (48)

Despite the determinism of his description preceding this decision, Crimsworth believes his relations to the changing Yorkshire landscape are voluntary. He believes he can freely opt out of them. The end of this passage enacts a Jane Eyre-like victory of self-discipline, which seems to purchase control over nearby organisms and spaces. Chiding himself, "Thus self-schooled, I returned to the house" (48), his bootstrapping retains older models of the human as an independent agent who determines the future of the Earth at the same time he decides his own.

Also like Jane Eyre, who privileges human relations while making environmentally impactful decisions, Crimsworth's exit from his industrial vocation is determined by intraspecies struggles of power. His assertion of independence relies on lines of difference he erects between industrial and non-industrial spaces, as when he first encounters the mill:

> we left the clean streets where there were dwelling-houses and shops, churches, and public buildings; we left all these, and turned down to a region of mills and warehouses; thence we passed through two massive gates into a great paved yard, and we were in Bigben Close, and the mill was before us, vomiting soot from its long chimney, and quivering through its thick brick walls with the commotion of its iron bowels. Workpeople were passing to and fro; a wagon was being laden with pieces. (50)

Brontë's semicolons visually reproduce the clear boundary markers between "clean streets" of public buildings and the factory district, whose ceremonial entryway through "two massive gates" and "thick brick walls" underscores the logic that one *elects* to be involved with industrialization. The drama of sudden disclosure—of workers under "vomiting soot" passing "iron bowels"—contrasts the frenetic mobility of human bodies to the mills' walls and gates, which are stolidly *there*, as if the entire industrial quarter (like its arteries) is "paved" into the earth. Were it truly so, were the boundaries between factory and town clear, the convenience of such an arrangement is evident in the ease with which he deserts them for a Brussels school. With the same self-willed speed, he moves to a surviving pastoral corner of England:

> My heart yearned towards my native county of ——— shire; and it is in ——— shire I now live; it is in the library of my own home I am now writing. That home lies amid a sequestered and rather hilly region, thirty miles removed from X———; a region whose verdure the smoke of mills has not yet sullied, whose waters still run pure, whose swells of moorland preserve in some ferny glens that lie between them the very primal wildness of nature, her moss, her bracken, her blue-bells, her scents of reed and heather. (281)

Thirty miles prove a sufficient distance for Crimsworth to escape smoky skies and "sullied" verdure to live in a "primal wilderness" with "pure" waters and "fresh" breezes.

Analyzing this rhetoric of choice, in which characters may escape the Anthropocene, can contribute to other accounts of eighteenth- and nineteenth-century literary ecologies. In Jayne Elizabeth Lewis's *Air's Appearance* (2012), an invisible atmosphere fills with electricity and smoke to become a presence registered by naturalists and writers alike. Its appearance is dangerous but full of scientific and narrative possibility. The metropolitan "artificial climates" of Jessie Oak Taylor's *The Sky of Our Manufacture* (2016) and the petrochemically fueled "unsustainable fictions" of Alan MacDuffie's *Victorian Literature, Energy, and the Ecological Imagination* (2014) are experienced by characters as obstacles to be borne patiently or portents ignored at one's peril. The Brussels of Brontë's *The Professor* and *Villette* pulses with the same energies. They are full of the same pollution, smoke, and fog, the same poverty, disease, and dirt, similarly shaped by railways and suburbs and denuded of pristine natural spaces. In these literary cities, the conversion of "natural" spaces into economically productive spaces and modern cities is novel but inexorable: characters experience the effects of these shifts as unpredictable, yet narrators know them to be otherwise and therefore seed references to concrete historical causes. Consequently, the rate of ecosystemic changes outpaces characters' abilities to respond effectively and to attribute these results to their causes. This leads to bizarre episodes such as Krook's spontaneous combustion in Charles Dickens's *Bleak House* (which began serialization just months before *Villette*'s publication). As Karen Chase and Michael Levenson argue, "Krook's body ... is a figure for the spoilage of the environment," a sign that

Bleak House "is a novel of climate change ... marking the start of Dickens's full absorption in the emergencies of the environment" (213, 201). London is a "dangerously damaged ecology," a "universe of fluids and gases" circulating "a fatally oozy world, where disease can seep through the locked doors of high buildings" (213, 214). Villette is also an oozing space, and Lucy's positions as gardener and teacher resemble the domestic work of Esther Summerson, also "a tireless laborer within a deteriorated ecology" (214–15). Chase and Levenson note that Esther's reward for her stewardship—escape to a second Bleak House in an unspoiled Yorkshire setting—parallels George Rouncewell's departure of London for Chesney Wold. This projected distance between green spaces and urban centers constructs a bifurcated ecology, one epitomized by the title of Gaskell's *North and South*, which sunders polluted north from verdant south. In these novels, new transportation technologies allow characters to move purposefully between natural and man-made environments. But by the time Lucy arrives at the Rue Fossette, this inviolable boundary between north and south has eroded, along with the ability to move fluidly from a denuded space to an uncorrupted one.

The complex blueprint of the *pensionnat* alone dramatizes Villette's differences from Dickens's London and the *The Professor*'s Brussels. Its exterior walls and intricate divisions create a warren of doors, hallways, paths, and fences and divide the garden into smaller spaces, each one enabling different kinds of human-ecosystem interaction. Lucy's first description of the *pensionnat* garden seems to reproduce these internal divisions and bifurcations:

> Behind the house at the Rue Fossette there was a garden—large, considering that it lay in the heart of a city, and to my recollection at this day it seems pleasant: but time, like distance, lends to certain scenes an influence so softening; and where all is stone around, blank wall and hot pavement, how precious seems one shrub, how lovely an enclosed and planted spot of ground! (117)

A note of doubt builds as Lucy realizes that nostalgia and forgetfulness underwrite the garden's attractiveness as an alternative to the barren, paved city beyond. Ultimately, Anthropocene scarcity is what renders the single shrub "precious," the sliver of garden "lovely," and the poetic power generated by the repetitions of "how" and the comma driving wistfully to an exclamation point. Traversing this scarcity when she stalks the garden, "the externes ... gone home, and the boarders quiet at their studies," Lucy sees in it her own sense of lonely self-worth:

> On summer mornings I used to rise early, to enjoy them alone; on summer evenings, to linger solitary, to keep tryste with the rising moon, or taste one kiss of the evening breeze.... The turf was verdant, the gravelled walks were white; sun-bright nasturtiums clustered beautiful about the roots of the doddered orchard giants. There was a large berceau, above which spread the shade of an acacia; there was a smaller, more sequestered bower, nestled in the vines which ran all along a high and grey wall, and gathered their tendrils in a knot of beauty, and hung their clusters in loving profusion about the favoured spot where jasmine and ivy met and married them. (118)

Solitary as the moon whose promised tryst must remain unconsummated, Lucy walks among "doddering" trees and profuse vines capable of interspecies marriage. Such imagery mixes the fertile with the impotent and conglomerations with unities to emphasize Lucy's position as a rare survivor of hard times, like the "orchard giants." The garden visualizes the Anthropocene's unequal development, its internal admixtures of the flourishing spouses and weakened survivors a rebuttal to the stark bifurcations shaping other Victorian novels at the end of the Holocene.

For Lucy Snowe, this straggling green space relieves melancholia because it does not activate misanthropy. Choosing a space to relax in, she selects not the berceau, the turf, or the bower, or the walks, but the "gloomy" *allée défendue* for its "deep and leafy seclusion":

> any girl setting foot there would have rendered herself liable to as severe a penalty as the mild rules of Madame Beck's establishment permitted.... [A]s the walk was narrow, and the neglected shrubs were grown very thick and close on each side, weaving overhead a roof of branch and leaf which the sun's rays penetrated but in rare chequers, this alley was seldom entered even during day, and after dusk was carefully shunned. (117–18)

Doubly insulated through the perceptual consequences of unrestrained botanical fecundity and through the moral force of Madame Beck's interdiction (intended to enforce social hierarchy and sexual purity), this space seems as protected as sphinx-like Lucy's inner states:

> the seclusion, the very gloom of the walk attracted me. For a long time the fear of seeming singular scared me away; but by degrees, as people became accustomed to me and my habits, and to such shades of peculiarity as were

engrained in my nature—shades ... born in and with me, and no more to be parted with than my identity—by slow degrees I became a frequenter of this strait and narrow path. (118)

This passage positions Lucy and the *allée défendue* as exceptional, as worthy of protection. This ability to banish certain people—to render a space *défendue*—underwrites the literary logic of the pastoral retreat, which requires cordoning off places deemed pure. Maintaining this illusion of separation requires, in turn, a good deal of human labor; conscientious Lucy tends her tiny piece of garden to her own taste. As Barbara Gates writes, Brontë's gardens are always "marked by human dimensions and dictated by human taste, and a space in some way attached to human dwellings" ("Garden Paths" 40). Even in private gardens, no inviolable boundaries separate Edenic from fallen spaces.

Hence Lucy's skewering of the *pensionnat*'s sexual geography, which maintains the purity of the school campus to guard the schoolgirls' own (though neither in truth follows Lucy's "strait and narrow" path). *Villette*'s allusions to the property's former function as a nunnery—a retreat for women desiring even fuller seclusion than Lucy—emphasizes the *pensionnat*'s claim to exceptionalism and sexual and ecological purity, but this privacy and purity are illusory. "Finely accomplished ... in the art of surveillance," Madame Beck offers sanctuary to girls of watchful wealthy families until they enter a competitive marriage market (127). But sound marketing practices, Lucy learns, do not accurately describe reality. In the *allée défendue*, "sitting on the hidden seat reclaimed from fungi and mold, listening to what seemed the far-off sounds of the city," she self-corrects: "Far-off, in truth, they were not: this school was in the city's center." A mere "ten-minute walk" leads to "wide streets brightly lit, teeming with life" (120). Seclusion is an effect of expert management, signs of which fill the campus. Loitering in the *allée défendue* soon after Lucy completes her first extensive gardening project, a love letter suddenly drops down from above. Examining the ivory box containing a *billet-doux* resting on a bed of violets, she laments that her "alley, and, indeed, all the walks and shrubs in the garden, had acquired a new, but not a pleasant interest; their seclusion was now become precarious; their calm—insecure. That casement which rained billets, had vulgarized the once dear nook it overlooked" (128). Her dismay shades into horror when Dr. John arrives to investigate. "It was a sacrilege—the intrusion of a man into that spot" (125), Lucy explains, her reflexive adoption of the *pensionnat*'s sexual politics indicating her profound disgust at the impure permeability of its green spaces.

Despite Lucy's attraction to Dr. John, she is repulsed by his intrusion and spends "a moment's leisure to efface [his footprints] very early in the morning" (128). These violations of green spaces—including the amative missile whose trajectory violates a sacred landscape—show how processes that hasten the Holocene's end become visible in urban institutions like the *pensionnat*. Its population density and modern amenities place greater pressures on the land they encompass, including putatively green spaces. These spaces are not pastoral reversions to the Holocene, but vulnerable, contested, and rigorously tended spaces that arrange humans and nonhumans into fragile constellations of organic matter. Small, comforting, and compromised, *Villette*'s gardens complicate the gritty, smoky landscapes in other urban novels of the early Anthropocene. City gardens may alleviate experiences of urban dislocation—functioning, like Dickens's second Bleak House, as reminders of the human desire to escape artifice and alienation—but they are not solely provocations for fantasy: their compromised forms call attention to real possibilities for semi-natural experiences during periods of intensified ecosystemic degradation. As Richard Grove observes, in late-eighteenth- and nineteenth-century literature, the garden served "as an environmental text and metaphor of mind" for "[a]nxieties about environmental change, climatic change and extinctions." "At the core of environmental concern lay anxiety about society and its discontents," Grove continues, such that literary ecosystems encode fears about both "the effect of man on the environment" and "the integrity and physical survival of people themselves" (*Green Imperialism* 14). *Villette*'s gardens invoke these multiple registers, tracking Lucy's tenuous hold on health, her struggles to cultivate a sliver of green space, and her discomfort with Villette's atmosphere of surveillance, sexual intrigue, and sensuous materialism.

Gates and William A. Cohen also interpret Brontë's Brussels as a network of multiple species that exerts evolutionary pressure. For Cohen, Brontë presents the "human subject" as one "actively engaged in palpable, reciprocal exchange with the world, including other embodied subjects," which becomes a problem for her Brussels protagonists because "the climate is such as to induce degeneracy" (64). For Gates, "Brontë's own green settings function more as proving grounds than as objective correlatives for character[s]," who "are made to test out and in turn are tested by a variety of human-made landscapes" (39). To combine these insights with those of Lewis, MacDuffie, and Taylor, *Villette* explores how Anthropocene airs influence intra- and interspecies politics.

Lucy's gardens epitomize them because they posit urbanization as a biopolitical phenomenon in which interspecies entanglements are intensified. For Lucy, anxiety results from being plunged into a bewilderingly modern world in which species relations are weaponized for interpersonal conflicts, especially through Madame Beck's thorough distribution of surveillance apparatuses to frustrate Lucy's romance with M. Paul.

Unbeknownst to Lucy, M. Paul has been watching her from his window since the *billet-doux* episode, which illustrates Anthropocenic frustrations of stable spatial and temporal boundaries. But in the garden, she, too, is a sentry whose presence is contested. In the love letter, the lover refers to Lucy as a "dragon" due to her teaching post:

> How tremblingly I approached the window and glanced into your Eden—an Eden for me, though a desert for you!—how I feared to behold vacancy, or the dragon aforesaid! How my heart palpitated with delight when, through apertures in the envious boughs, I at once caught the gleam of your graceful straw-hat, and the waving of your grey dress—dress that I should recognize amongst a thousand. (123)

This uncertainty over the garden's status as an "Eden" or "desert" translates scientific fears about ecosystemic health during the Victorian era into romantic struggles.[3] The personification of "envious boughs" screening beloved from lover appears hyperbolic only if one ignores how human agency is physically distributed within nonhuman actants throughout contact zones like gardens.[4] Madame Beck's conscious cultivation of trees to screen her pupils materializes the suspicions of their families and suitors, including Dr. John, who investigates the *billet-doux* out of jealousy over Ginevra Fanshawe, Lucy's student. The lover's flight of fancy hyperbolically destabilizes definitions of *Anthropos* by classifying Lucy as a dragon. His misidentification telegraphs his foppish unreliability, but his actions have real consequences—they disabuse Lucy of the illusion that the garden is an exceptional space—and his reference to her power is corroborated in the teaching scenes that display her talent for disciplining recalcitrant Labassecouriennes. Let us reconsider Lucy as a dragon, a being that hoards and protects valuables. When Dr. John takes her to the theatre, she covets what glitters: the fruits of urbanization along

> some of the best streets of Villette, streets brightly lit, and far more lively now than at high noon. How brilliant seemed the shops! How glad, gay, and abundant flowed the tide of life along the broad pavement! . . . By this

time we had got into a current of carriages all tending in one direction, and soon the front of a great illuminated building blazed before us. Of what I should see within this building, I had, as before intimated, but an imperfect idea; for no place of public entertainment had it ever been my lot to enter yet. (233)

En route, Lucy learns why those who have access to rarefied cultural spaces embrace urban development. Through the hyperreal lighting, "far more lively now than at high noon," man's powers literally outshine nature's, while the marine imagery of the "tide of life" and "current of carriages" presents city streets as man-made waterways worthy of aesthetic contemplation. Far from desiring the privacy punctured by the *billet-doux*, she exults in ecologically costly luxuries. Colebrook's question of culpability resurfaces when Lucy describes the theatre's grand entrance,

> whose sweeping circular walls, and domed hollow ceiling, seemed to me all dead gold (thus with nice art was it stained), relieved by cornicing, fluting, and garlandry, either bright, like gold burnished, or snow-white, like alabaster, or white and gold mingled in wreaths of gilded leaves and spotless lilies.... Pendent from the dome, flamed a mass that dazzled me—a mass, I thought, of rock-crystal, sparkling with facets, streaming with drops, ablaze with stars, and gorgeously tinged with dews of gems dissolved, or fragments of rainbows shivered. It was only the chandelier, reader, but for me it seemed the work of eastern genii: I almost looked to see if a huge, dark, cloudy hand—that of the Slave of the Lamp—were not hovering in the lustrous and perfumed atmosphere of the cupola, guarding its wondrous treasure. (233–34)

The theatre assembles a dragon's hoard of precious metals and stones, ominously figured as an alternation between "dead" and "bright" gold, between these golds and the white of "alabaster" and "lilies," and between images of "spotless" purity and "cloudy" darkness, capped violently by "gems dissolved, or fragments of rainbows shivered" by the interventions of "eastern genii," to whom Lucy attributes the labor of all of this mining. She transfers the moral responsibility of plundering the earth and breaking rainbows to conveniently non-European forces, showing how beauty can motivate even sober Lucy to obscure links between human efforts—particularly those of European cultures that led fossil-fuel-based industrial production—and environmental shifts.

The rock-crystal chandelier is especially instructive: its construction required humans to penetrate hundreds of feet down an opaque, resistant earth to mine opaque, resistant rocks before tumbling and faceting them until they become perfectly clear, constructed, it seems, only of light itself. Transforming solid earth to bright light for illuminating the night seems miraculous—but in her orientalizing rapture, Lucy demystifies the chandelier's ominous sublimity too soon. In such ways artistic representations reproduce the disappearance of earth, through the relentless extraction of its resources, into air by way of plumes of smoke far less dazzling than an array of gaslit prisms. Lucy Snowe's culpability partly stems from her attraction to the visually pure and radiant, rooted in her survivor's need to remain as cool as her surname. Only later will she fully realize the promise of her name—"my hair, which, till a late period, withstood the frosts of time, lies now, at last white, under a white cap, like snow beneath snow" (51)—but her Holocenic desire to be frostily pure pulses throughout *Villette*. Polly's picture-book, in which both delight, depicts "a land of ice and snow, without green fields, woods, or gardens," where "they found some mammoth bones: there are no mammoths now" (34). Snow preserves relics, leaving awe-inspiring clues about the past while ensuring that the extinct remain safe memories. If serenity requires extinctions, Lucy seems satisfied with the exchange. In fact, her hard-won equanimity requires such catastrophes for performing and refining this frostiness. She always expects them; the novel's first event is the delivery of a letter that leaves Lucy "expecting I know not what disastrous communication," though "no reference was made, and the cloud passed" (8). While critics have long discussed the contrast between Lucy's outer frosts and inner fires,[5] what is remarkable for the Anthropocene is that Promethean fire imagery, contrasted with snow's living death, refers to its ambivalent power to create or destroy. As chapter 1 shows, this tension between world-creation and apocalypse (the book of Genesis and the book of Revelation) was exploited by Patrick Brontë in an argument that God designed the Crow Hill bog burst as a sample of apocalyptic destruction for inspiring righteousness. But in *Villette*, Lucy's wary negotiations between her snow and fire eventually engender the resignation contained in Colebrook's reflection that "just as there is no pure earth [that] might be claimed, so there is no thought that is not already contaminated and made possible by the very logic of man that ecology might seek to overcome" ("Symbiosis" 198–99).

Polly's picture-book perpetuates this "logic of man" with its paradoxical treatment of mammoths as extinct and vital, objects for scientific inquiry and supernatural speculation. Calling the mammoth "a mighty goblin creature,"

Polly scrupulously specifies that it "would not kill me unless I came quite in its way; where it would trample me down amongst the bushes, as I might tread on a grasshopper in a hay-field without knowing it" (34). A nascent ecological ethics shapes Polly's prattle, which glorifies morphological diversity, models interspecies harmony without glossing over interspecies violence, and recognizes that the ways humans harm nonhumans may not be readily apparent. She echoes the Brontë children's enthusiasm poring over ethnographic accounts of exotic, flora, and fauna in periodicals, the morbid vignettes of *Bewick's Birds*, and scientific allusions to environmental change in their father's library. But in contrast to Patrick Brontë's Providential explanations for violence, Polly is satisfied by the empirical logic that the mammoth does not see the human, who does not see the grasshopper. Her fascination with interspecies violence reflects an amoral justice that rationalizes destruction as a natural consequence of biologically determined morphological variation. Fixated on the catastrophes that threaten them, Polly and Lucy consume the form of extinction porn tailored to their proclivities. While seeking ways to cope with disaster, they covet it. Are mammoths extinct or alive? When will the disaster foreshadowed by the letter occur? Colebrook's assertion that there is no pristinely innocent subject at the end of the Holocene is again instructive: *Villette*'s stream of individual and ecosystemic deaths makes it as difficult to assign blame for the rising toll of damage. The novel's aesthetic responses to signs of large-scale climatalogical shifts exemplify Colebrook's argument that Western feminism is compromised when women pursuing equality ally themselves with ecologically devastating movements in industry, philosophy, and the sciences.

Brontë's oeuvre is sensitive to these alliances. Jane Eyre's determination to pursue domestic happiness is underwritten by anthropocentrism, and *Shirley* exposes the calculus that deems the fairies' extinction an acceptable cost for its heroines to secure family and hearth. In such ways Brontë answers Colebrook's central question of how ecosystemic degradation is bound up with gender roles and with feminist desires to reinvent them. Shirley Keeldar, ecologically closer in age to Lucy, cannily manipulates her impure species identity to drive erotic play with her romantic partner. But for Lucy, whose partner sails across the globe immediately after proposing, there are few compensatory pleasures in transvaluing the cruel optimism by which humans ruin their own ecosystems.[6] She is hyperaware that human immoderation created an appalling present. It is evident in *Villette*'s disgust at Labassecour's "nervous, melancholy" royals, whose inbreeding causes hypochondria and homeliness (238), in her horrified fascination with the passionate actress Vashti (286), and in her critique of Labassecour's galleries, which include landscapes "not a whit like nature" (222). Édouard De Bièfve's *Une Almée* elicits the most severe criticism. To slim Lucy, its well-nourished dancer epitomizes unregulated human appetites. The reclining woman's allure is troubling because—to Lucy—she consumes too much, her "commodity of bulk," estimated at "fourteen to sixteen stone" and fortified expensively by "very much butcher's meat" (223). To be sure, Lucy's fat shaming is more grotesque than the figure of a healthy dancer and reflects her emotional morbidity, not the dancer's corporeal state. The specter of human complicity in overusing resources overwhelms her, and she turns to inhuman beauty: "I soon tired, and betook myself for refreshment to the contemplation of some exquisite little pictures of still life," she recalls, especially "wild-flowers, wild-fruit, mossy woodnests, casketing eggs that looked like pearls seen through clear green sea-water; all hung modestly beneath that coarse and preposterous canvas" (224). This pastoral relieves the "wretched untidiness" of the interior setting around the dancer (223), whose human imperfections contaminate the space around her. Because the "preposterous" canvas is so much larger than the surrounding pictures, the dispensation of paintings along the gallery walls reiterates this image of humans growing too large for habitats they have sullied. Like the chandelier, the gallery reproduces the Anthropocenic instrumentalization of nature by dislodging and preserving fragments of nature for human physical and aesthetic consumption rather than for ecosystemic balance. *Une Almée* is, in short, extinction porn.

LUCY SNOWE, OLIGOTROPH: ASYMMETRIES OF ECOLOGICAL RISK

Though Lucy's Orientalism frames genii and Egyptian dancers for *Anthropos*'s greed, she also associates it with the Catholic church, which inculcates habits of "large sensual indulgence" (140) to keep believers "feeble in soul, fat, ruddy, hale, joyous, ignorant, thinking, unquestioning" (141). Madame Beck typifies this incurious materialism. When she offers Lucy a sedative, Lucy accuses, "you are a sensualist. Under all your serenity, your peace, and your decorum, you are an undenied sensualist. Make your own bed warm and soft; take sedatives and meats, and drinks spiced and sweet.... Leave me, however. *Leave me*, I say!" (493–94). This uncharacteristic vehemence reveals that Lucy's abstemiousness, anti-Catholicism, and fat phobia are linked: those incapable of moderation fall victim to Lucy's considerable powers of sarcasm, whether by face-to-face or pen-and-paper communication. The depth of her horror signals that she suspects these desires are in every human, including herself, making the novel a first-person account of the emotional struggle to moderate one's resource consumption. Foible-filled Ginevra is perceptive in calling her Timon, the famous misanthrope of Athens (260), over teatime, when Lucy customarily cedes half of her rations. Despite her awareness of Ginevra's flaws, Lucy "always contrived that she would be my convive," and "liked to let her take the lion's share, whether of the white beer, the sweet wine, or the new milk" (261). In this way Lucy balances her abstemiousness and misanthropy with a desire to tend others and share slender resources. Always "upon the verge of famine," "on the very extremity of want" (297), Lucy inhabits a world filled by many kinds of hunger. Her oligotrophic sacrifices stave off despair and anger, ever-present though they are to Brontë's severe heroine, and show how to take care of loved ones without arrogating too many resources. The modest expense of the watch-guard she makes M. Paul—"a slight matter of fancy" (364), a "bright little chainlet of silk and gold" (370), whose clasp she dismantles from "the fastening of my sole necklace" (373)—isolates a sustainable scale of value: the slight, the little, the sole. The distance between rock-crystal chandelier and watch-guard, like the distance between the dancer's pounds of meat and Lucy's half of a roll, is crucial. Population pressures and disasters increase resource scarcity—a principle well-known by young Jane Eyre, who struggles against stronger students to "reserve a moiety" of Lowood's hebdomadal "double ration of bread" and "thin scrape of butter" (72). Beleaguered like Jane but more patient, Lucy responds to scarcity by trying to overcome her own intolerant misanthropy and treat her fellow humans generously.

Lucy's desire to tend other beings matters because not all subjects suffer the same under Anthropocene skies. Socioeconomic and racial privilege determines much of these asymmetries. Frivolous, wasteful Ginevra, who manipulates others to acquire the expensive objects of her desire, wards off the pangs of resource scarcity until she achieves her final goal—marriage with a dashing aristocrat—although the deteriorating condition of the Labassecourian royal family hints that her costly choices will damage the bodies of her descendants. Paulina is another privileged white woman for whom the fruits of the earth are gathered. She always "seemed to have got what she wanted . . . and to be in a trance of content" due to her talent for "invit[ing] affection by her beauty and her vivacious life" (17, 460). Paulina's strength and instinct for self-preservation are a rare gift, "a priceless privilege of nature," for, as Lucy observes, "there is no excellent beauty, no accomplished grace, no reliable refinement, without strength as excellent" (417, 347). Graham is similarly buoyed by inborn fortunes, both biological and financial. He inherits his mother's "health without flaw, and her spirits of that tone and equality which are better than a fortune to the possessor," giving him "a fund of deep and healthy strength which, without any exhausting effort, bore down Disappointment" (8, 248). These animal spirits explain Lucy's attraction: she desires to possess his physical and psychological hardiness. But experience teaches Lucy that like attracts like, joining other "human beings so born, so reared, so guided from a soft cradle to a calm and late grave, that ... no tempestuous blackness overcasts their journey" (482). Vulnerable, Lucy attests to the fact that uneven development in the Anthropocene is not solely a temporal and spatial phenomenon, but a social phenomenon that affects some bodies more than others. She never receives her just bequest from Miss Marchmont, which exiles her to postnatural Villette, where Madame Beck expects her to work without love. Unlike indestructible Jane Eyre or vital Shirley Keeldar (powerful enough to expunge her sickly co-heroine Caroline from the novel's title), Lucy cannot be the eponymous heroine of her own story. Decentered by her postnatural residence, which activates her melancholic tendencies, she blames herself: "I suppose it was all the fault of what you call my 'nervous system' " that "a feeling that would make its way, rush out, or kill me—like ... the current which passes through the heart, and which, if aneurism or any other morbid cause obstructs its natural channels, seeks abnormal outlet" (206). The conflicting axioms of scientific, capitalist rationality—that dangerous forces cannot be stopped, but individual afflictions arise from personal flaws—infect even the stories that seek to express the vulnerabilities of mental illness during periods of ecosystemic stress.

In doing so, Lucy's depictions of mental illness can sensitize readers to the asymmetries of Anthropocene suffering. This passage, for example, expands normative conceptions of resource scarcity to include psychological distress:

> The world can understand well enough the process of perishing for want of food: perhaps few persons can enter into or follow out that of going mad from solitary confinement.... [H]ow his nerves, first inflamed, underwent nameless agony, and then sunk to palsy—is a subject too intricate for examination, too abstract for popular comprehension. (303)

Affectionate companionship is a resource crucial for survival in competitive postnatural worlds. Recognizing that not everyone can marry to neutralize these stresses, Lucy reflects that the happiness enjoyed by Paulina and Graham "is not so for all." Apostrophizing the "sufferer," the "tired wayfarer," and "pilgrims and brother mourners," she invites them to join her and cross "the wilderness of this world" and "endure the hardness as good soldiers" together (484). This stirring rhetoric addresses apocalyptic refugees, whose lives are shaped by brutal upheavals each time they must "leave an encampment where food and forage failed" and to prepare a safe space for preparing for the time when "another pitched battle must be fought" (329). This martial imagery differs both aesthetically and ethically from her capitulation to the splendors of unrelenting resource extraction modeled by the theatre's entrance hall. Though certain aesthetic responses are unsustainable, *Villette* employs a host of sustainable ones, such as when adaptable Lucy, during her miry journey through Labassecour, "enjoyed that day": "my fancy budded fresh and my heart basked in sunshine," showing that she "possessed something of the artist's faculty of making the most of pleasant pleasure" (67). As Lucy discovers while looking out at the mucky wasteland, it is the prerogative of artists to uncover the residual beauties of denuded landscapes.

The theme of spatial instability resounds long after Lucy's acceptance into the school's provisional security. The terrain she is allowed to occupy is unrelentingly reduced, creating a pattern of intensifying constriction that surfaces when Lucy nurses her reclusive employer:

> Two hot, close rooms thus became my world; and a crippled old woman, my mistress, my friend, my all. Her service was my duty—her pain, my suffering—her relief, my hope—her anger, my punishment—her regard, my reward. I forgot that there were fields, woods, rivers, seas, an ever-changing sky outside the steam-dimmed lattice of this sick chamber; I was almost content to forget it. All within me became narrowed to my lot. (42)

Trapped in these "hot," "close," and "narrowed" rooms, her view of the outside world obstructed by layers of lattice and steam, Lucy forgets the natural world beyond. The medical logic of the sick room, whose every feature must be carefully controlled, reflects an antagonistic relationship between man and the environment, in which survival requires artificial enclosures to check natural forces. Like Jane Eyre, Lucy does not succumb to communicable disease; unlike her, tarrying in streams as infected children deteriorate indoors, Lucy's immobility reduces her very self as "all within [her]" shrinks to fit the sick room. This pathological shrinkage recurs when M. Paul locks her in the garret—a stifling, gloomy room, decentralized and therefore perfect for temporary exile—to force her to rehearse for the school's theatricals. "The attic," Lucy understates, "was no pleasant place" (148). A Gothic space of climate change, it withstands extreme weather and temperature variability, and it is haunted by stratified layers of long-discarded objects:

> In this summer weather, it was hot as Africa; as in winter, it was always cold as Greenland. Boxes and lumber filled it; old dresses draped its unstained wall—cobwebs its unswept ceiling. Well was it known to be tenanted by rats, by black beetles, and by cockroaches—nay, rumor affirmed that the ghostly Nun of the garden had once been seen here. A partial darkness obscured one end, across which, as for deeper mystery, an old russet curtain was drawn, by way of screen to a somber band of winter cloaks, pendent each from its pin, like a malefactor from his gibbet. (148)

Only later will the ghost nun haunting Lucy be unmasked as Ginevra's beau, yet in the garret, set among less spectral markers of the school's history, the nun is already unmasked as a figure of ever-present yet rarely seen pasts. The nun's "deeper mystery" lay in the piles of untended things, the waste products of human history piling up gradually, in deep time, as new geological strata as they combine with the integuments of dust and cobwebs.

Though the hanged figure imagines ecosystemic subsidence as a fundamentally human drama, Lucy's penchant for privileging the human costs of ecological destruction is challenged by the garret's multispecies scene of deep time. A series of rats, beetles, cockroaches, and spiders compel Lucy to observe (and record) the behavior of non-charismatic species that she, like many ecologists, would rather avoid. Uncomfortable interactions with abject creatures who consume unbeautiful foods and live among waste prompt her claustrophobia. With its hanged figure, the curtained area is a focal point for the ways in which the *pensionnat*—a putatively healthy space full of fresh air—oozes with the decay and pollution saturating Villette:

> I saw a very dark and large rat, with a long tail, come gliding out from that squalid alcove; and, moreover, my eye fell on many a black-beetle, dotting the floor. These objects discomposed me more, perhaps, than it would be wise to say, as also did the dust, lumber, and stifling heat of the place....
> [I] found means to open and prop up the skylight, thus admitting some freshness. Underneath this aperture I pushed a large empty chest, and having mounted upon it a smaller box ... ascended this species of extempore throne, and being seated, commenced the acquisition of my task; while I

learned, not forgetting to keep a sharp look-out on the black-beetles and cockroaches, of which, more even, I believe, than of the rats, I sat in mortal dread. (148)

The "mortal dread" causing Lucy to exercise her wit to exit the airless, cramped space arises at least as much from these animals as from ghostly nun or hanged figure. Encoded in her survival instincts are reactions to the creaturely adaptations to denuded spaces, allowing rats to swell to remarkable sizes and beetles to proliferate. Lucy must wrest control over this postapocalyptic ecosystem to secure her physical safety and finish her work. Literally rising above the garret by erecting an "extempore throne," she asserts sovereignty to transcend the degraded environment, ironically recalling her critique of Labassecourian aristocracy at the theatre (a scene also invoked because Lucy is becoming an actor). In one scene, degenerate rulers to a real throne, watching a drama unfold below their box, suppress the personal griefs torturing them; in another, a pretender to an improvised throne rules a fallen world, perched upon her own box above her own subjects, to train herself in such acting. The task underscores her ironic sovereignty: to assume temporarily the freedoms of male subject, but only of a fictional character whose weak attractions will not satisfy the rigors of sexual selection. These scenes, marked by acting, artifice, and degeneration, display humans responding ineffectively to spectacles of fallenness, their leadership marred by pretense and selfishness.

The hypochondria that she and the king both endure projects a dismal future for the Earth. But Lucy is desperately hot and hungry. Rather than suffering from the genetics of inbreeding, she suffers from environmental conditions that provoke discomfort, alienation, and claustrophobia:

I thought of the collation, which doubtless they were just then devouring in the garden far below.... A *pâté*, or a square of cake, it seemed to me would come very *àpropos;* and as my relish for those dainties increased, it began to appear somewhat hard that I should pass my holiday, fasting and in prison.... I knew that the house and garden were thronged, and that all was gay and glad below; here it began to grow dusk: the beetles were fading from my sight; I trembled lest they should steal on me a march, mount my throne unseen, and, unsuspected, invade my skirts. (148–49)

Lucy suffers from a paradigmatically Anthropocenic uneven distribution of resources. A laborer playing potentate over a tiny wasteland, she is powerless to penetrate the sociable, resource-rich spaces below. The distressingly fertile beetles, which Lucy imagines mounting a sexual invasion in addition to a political coup, are Villette's proverbial postapocalyptic cockroaches, revealing the fragility, even impotence, of human bodies in unstable ecologies. Lucy's acting models two strategies for surviving resource scarcity and its destabilization of *Anthropos*'s dominion: work and aesthetic sublimation. M. Paul imprisons her in the garret until she demonstrates her willingness to work for the common good and perform the role of a person born luckier than herself. When she does, M. Paul delivers the longed-for *pâtés à la crème*. This scene demonstrates the rationale for the novel's many images of migration and claustrophobia: surviving precarious times means negotiating ecosystemic constriction. Unfortunately, Lucy's performance forces her to pretend to possess what she does not (money, mobility, masculinity, the power to pursue her romantic interests) while devaluing what she does possess (the scraps of wasteland no one else desires, with its neglected historical strata). But Lucy does not remain powerless. Halfway through the play, she rebels. Naturally reluctant to assert herself but forced to by crises, she elects to woo the fair maiden whom her character was scripted to alienate. Loss had triggered her latent assertiveness before, but her theatrical performance reflects her adaptability to adverse conditions. It also foreshadows Ginevra's poor mate selection of the fop de Hamal, revealing Lucy's superior fitness.

Later, M. Paul, as a part of his proposal, will gift Lucy with a less moribund fiefdom: a school for her to run and reside in. If the marriage plot symbolizes the continued global domination of Britain, so too are romances in Anthropocene fictions concerned with survival, albeit on a smaller scale. These sites of romantic choice are precisely where Colebrook's dictum for Anthropocene feminism—"the personal is geological," along with its return to "the classically feminist question of the *scale of the personal*"—is dramatized ("Counterfactual" 2, 1). As chapter 2 argues, Jane Eyre chooses between an anthropocentric neglect of ecological degradation, represented by her flight to Ferndean, and a green imperialism putatively justified by religion, represented by her offer to become a missionary. To point this out is less to castigate a fictional character for what is nevertheless collusion (rejecting overwork and premature death is relatable) than to point out how the sexual dimensions of characters' lives profoundly affect the non-human world. In *Shirley*, Robert Moore's credibility while he develops a rural valley into an industrial center is bolstered by his wife's position as a horticulturalist. Caroline's moral guidance as a mother is prefigured by her mentorship of boys, "little ruffians, who take an unnatural delight in killing and tormenting birds" (431). Women commonly teach boys and men to care for animals in the Brontës' works, from Catherine's plea that Heathcliff not shoot lapwings to Agnes Grey's tutelage of a vicious charge to Shirley's stipulation that she will only marry one who is "kind to animals" (206, 205). Brontë heroines habitually wield sexual selection to improve interspecies relations and broader patterns of land management. If castigations of wanton violence are the most blatant examples of the Brontës' multispecies ethics, the image of the garden best spatializes its gendered dimensions. Gendered behaviors in gardens are synecdoches for the sexes' roles in tending ecosystems. Gates diagnoses Crimsworth's "proprietary attitude toward growing things," which is restricted by his female boss, who "does what she likes in her own garden," such as selecting a rival (34). M. Paul, Gates continues, is "least compromised of Brontë's protagonists" because he is "allied with both the natural and the female.... In contrast to the Moores in *Shirley*, he can help insure the authenticity of his beloved's adult survival" (39).

Building on Gates, I argue that M. Paul's dedication to gardening is a clue that he offers Lucy a romantic partner with a non-toxic masculinity different from what Stacy Alaimo has defined as "carbon-heavy" masculinity. The carbon-heavy man destructively, carelessly relies on unlimited fossil-fuel combustion and resource extraction, like mill-owner Robert Moore in *Shirley*. Though his wife urges him to curb his most excessive ecological devastations, domestic bliss requires her complicity in this destruction. The tempestuously sensitive M. Paul, by contrast, exemplifies Alaimo's call for a "vulnerability that refuses to disavow our immersion within a material world" (*Exposed* 102). This is why he lavishes his non-toxic habits of tending on nonhuman species—often to the extent of decentering fellow humans. Lucy writes detailed reports of his gardening. She notes that on one occasion, he speaks "no more to the pupils, nor to the mistresses," but to a "spanieless," who receives "many an endearing word" and responds with many a "glad bark and whine" (455). Angry that he pays her no mind, Lucy recalls,

> M. Emanuel had a taste for gardening; he liked to tend and foster plants. I used to think that working amongst shrubs with a spade or a watering-pot soothed his nerves; it was a recreation to which he often had recourse; and now he looked to the orange-trees, the geraniums, the gorgeous cactuses, and revived them all with the refreshment their drought needed.... There were many plants, and as the amateur gardener fetched all the water from the well in the court, with his own active hands, his work spun on to some

length. The great school-clock ticked on. Another hour struck.... [T]he orange-trees, the cacti, the camellias were all served now. (455)

With a leisurely absorption that resists the regimented discipline of the "great school-clock," M. Paul indulges his "taste" for caretaking by fighting Villette's "drought." The multiple connotations of "taste" suggest that his aesthetic values spring from his moral ones, for which he is willing to labor. This taste that fosters rather than controls is at the heart of his non-toxic masculinity.

His care enfolds native species (pears and roses) as well as non-native ones. Cactuses, camellias, geraniums, and citrus trees arrive from Asia and the Mediterranean and through Columbian exchanges with the New World—precisely the kind of Atlantic migrations that climate scientists identify as one cause of the Anthropocene.[7] Displaced and vulnerable, like Lucy Snowe, they have been transplanted to an unfamiliar climate for which they have not evolved. The orange trees—planted in tubs that must be moved seasonally—epitomize the garden's precarity. No surviving piece of Eden, this garden is an artificed composite of precarious organisms whose mobility is compelled by imperial forces. The timing of M. Paul's exile to a Guadeloupe plantation just as he and Lucy become engaged provides another example of the environmental costs of heteronormative romance. His non-toxic masculinity is fatally compromised by the plantation economy that enslaves human populations, kills native species, and transforms swathes of land into machines for agricultural mass production. M. Paul accepts an active role in this economy to make way for marrying Lucy by clearing his perceived debts to the family of his first love, one of the novel's many mysterious nuns. In doing so, he substitutes for his tender habits of amateur gardening a set of agricultural practices that demanded unparalleled brutality toward humans and non-humans. Brontë's sudden insertion of a Caribbean investment (along with its deferral of marriage) echoes Anglo-Caribbean Richard Mason's outburst at Jane's aborted wedding and Jane's inheritance of a Madeiran fortune. This is one of Brontë's most powerful tropes for the Anthropocene: the sudden disclosure of past human actions that erupt, causing sudden catastrophes. Past decisions that negatively influenced ecosystems suddenly reappear to harm those who made the decisions or profited from them. Some of the characters who suffer from these catastrophes may seem unrelated to these past actions (Jane, Caroline, Shirley, Lucy), but either they rapidly become compromised, or intricate webs of causality exposed by catastrophes reveal, belatedly, that they were compromised all along.

DELAYED IDENTIFICATION:
BELATED REVELATION AS ANTHROPOCENE EPISTEMOLOGY

I call this figure of belated disclosure "delayed identification" to emphasize *Villette*'s parallels with Anthropocene theory, where, I argue, it is an unacknowledged but indispensable narrative construct. Recognizing this trope is not only crucial for measuring the toxicity of M. Paul's love and the efficacy of Lucy's tending; it is crucial for understanding when the Anthropocene thesis developed, why some may be predisposed to reject an idea that emerged so belatedly, and how many different origins of the Anthropocene continue to be posited. Indeed, scientists continue to grapple with determining retrospectively when and where the Holocene ended. Climatologists hope to enact the ultimate delayed identification by attempting to pinpoint a golden spike definitively, yet their disagreements push it back and forth around the Industrial Revolution. Perhaps it occurs at Columbus's 1692? After World War II, with the spread of industrial fertilizer? At a future time when geological samples yield embedded strata of man-made rock? When, in short, was the beginning of the end of the world?

Finding a single answer that satisfies all parties is likely impossible due to the difficulty of integrating data from different scientific and humanistic fields. I argue that it is also inadvisable. It is inadvisable because the proliferation of golden spikes signals the concept's value for framing important data, memories, and emotions about human-caused environmental degradation. Narrative analyses and close readings of literature offer powerful models for such framings. In Brontë's *Villette*, Lucy Snowe's style forces readers to confront the untimeliness of knowledge. She withholds facts, ones she knows at the time *and* ones she learns later (by the time she begins narrating her story), and she is conscious of her choices. Regarding one delayed identification, Lucy confesses, "The discovery was not of to-day, its dawn had penetrated my perceptions long since" (195). So, too, should we should acknowledge that the phenomenon may only become *provable* to the scientific community and the public long after its onset.

Villette's Gothic reconstruction of a mysterious past buried behind an indeterminate break prefigures the narrative structure of Anthropocene theory. Which actions have led to our present, and can we use this deferred but imperative knowledge to predict the future? *Villette*'s first lesson is to recognize that trauma motivates witnesses to forget or conceal evidence. For example, Lucy disguises Graham Bretton's reappearance in her life by referring to him as a new acquaintance, Dr. John. Two traumas motivate Lucy's collusion in the repression of knowledge needed for the reader to reconstruct the past: the grief related to the loss of the English life she most enjoyed at Bretton and the pain of unrequited love. The latter trauma suggests that the former is final: she will never recover her home, even through the incomplete recovery that marriage with Dr. John would represent. Lucy delays her identification until he brings her, unconscious, to his home after her collapse. Waking, she identifies objects from the past that "appeared to grow familiar," including a "round centre-table, with a blue covering, bordered with autumn-tinted foliage" and footstools "worked with groups of brilliant flowers on a dark ground" (186). Like the *pensionnat*'s oranges and cactuses, they migrated, but they are not living species from a new world: they are inanimate surrogates for a lost old world. She wonders, "Am I in England? Am I at Bretton?" but knows that the "heart of Old England ... went out long ago, and the household gods had been carried elsewhere" (190, 188). For the first time, she attempts to confront the loss of her homeland. "Still more I marveled what those scenes and days could now have to do with me," she reflects, the pain of lingering grief melting into the intellectual work of estrangement (187). Not only is the past irrecuperable beyond the break that wrenched Lucy from it; even memories of the past are difficult to recover. When they are, they come in the mediated, subjective form of her own past representations—needlework wrought by her own hand. Wanting to believe she has recovered what she lost, Lucy finally discloses the deferred truth of his identity to readers. But only when she comes to terms with his failure to reciprocate her love will she fully confront her losses.

The first hint that the past remains lost is the imperfection of the surviving objects from Bretton. Casting her eyes over them, she muses, "Of all these things I could have told the peculiarities, numbered the flaws or cracks, like any *clairvoyante*" (187). Memories may not recover that past, but they can indicate the future if one looks closely. Lucy's power to do so fills her with melancholy. Admiring the theatre's rock-crystal chandelier, she has visions of her pedagogical labors, and a "shadow of the future stole with timely sobriety across the radiant present" (233). Embattled by memories and presentiments, the "radiant present" is full of events and signs clustering so thickly that most characters cannot keep up. Quick responses are needed in *Villette*'s postapocalyptic world: it solicits swift action but precludes the leisurely observation and analysis needed for sound decisions. Alexis Shotwell usefully characterizes this compression of temporal layers when she observes, "It is hard for us to examine our connection with *unbearable pasts* with which we might reckon better, our implication in *impossible complex presents* through which we might craft different modes of response, and our aspirations for *different futures* toward which we might shape different worlds-yet-to-come" (8). Characters' responses to the continuous stimuli thrown at them is to place their trust in Lucy, who does observe, analyze, and remember. Miss Marchmont secures Lucy's services before her trial is over; her other employer, Madame Beck, decides to hire her before references can be sought. Ginevra decides instantly upon meeting Lucy to confide in her, and her lover throws his *billet-doux* before he discerns that Lucy waits below. The novel's couples frequently prompt Lucy's strategies of narrative deferral: she does not report immediately that the man at whom Ginevra leers during the amateur theatricals is Dr. John. Only days after seeing a handkerchief fluttering from a carriage will Lucy learn that it marked Ginevra's elopement. And when Dr. John rescues a lady in distress during the chaotic evacuation of a burning building, only later is she revealed as Ginevra's cousin. Later still is this cousin identified as Paulina, the erstwhile Polly Home, when Dr. John and the Count de Bassompierre recognize in each another Graham and Mr. Home.

Both the conflagration and the *billet-doux* associate delayed identification with trauma, sexual violence, and the destruction of beautiful spaces. Delayed identification threatens to awaken fear along with past traumas. When M. Paul arranges a surprise examination of Lucy to prove to his colleagues that he has not forged her work, she realizes they are the men who "half frightened me to death on the night of my desolate arrival in Villette" (445). Recurring sexual violence, which associates street harassment with hostility toward equal education, reveals the high cost of remembering, levied when one plants a golden spike: the cost of an immobile boundary separating *now* from *then*. Lucy's delayed identifications plant multiple spikes, waiting for future revelations as she discovers hidden pasts (or the hidden causes behind known pasts). These explanatory reconstructions help Lucy evade the "the old rack of suspense" (528)—which threatens her when she waits to say farewell before M. Paul sails to the Caribbean. Believing she will never see him again, she agonizes, "must I again assay that corroding pain of long attent—that rude agony of rupture at the close, that mute, mortal wrench, which, in at once uprooting hope and doubt, shakes life; while the hand that does the violence cannot be caressed to pity, because absence interposes her barrier!" (528). Delayed identification mitigates Lucy's suffering by stage-managing actual and anticipated losses. Withholding knowledge from readers whisks characters in and out anonymously, mystifying the causes of her emotions. Readers learn belatedly that the treats secreted into her desk are from M. Paul, that the speaker delivering the Prince's birthday address is him, that the garden "ouvrier" is him, that the man celebrating Villette's fête is his brother, that the young lady there is his ward, and that the priest she confessed to is his old friend. In this way, delayed identification naturalizes M. Paul's presence, making their love a preexisting condition despite Dr. John's apparent precedence in the novel's first half. She has been observing M. Paul all along. He has been there, all along, in scenes from which he seemed absent. But there is no golden spike pinpointing the moment they fall in love.

The novel's nuns serve a predictive function because Lucy is already haunted by M. Paul's first love, who became a nun (and pined away) after her family rejected the match. The nuns demonstrate how delayed identification responds to an epistemological crisis—related to knowledge's incompleteness and belatedness—and an ontological one, created by the presence of the past. Lucy dimly perceives that the past influences the present, but she has incomplete knowledge of these past events. These ontological and epistemological crises link Lucy's personal narrative and Villette's historical transformations. One nun, buried alive in *pensionnat* grounds, stokes her sensitivity to ecosystemic shifts:

> There went a tradition that Madame Beck's house had in old days been a convent. That in years gone by—how long gone by I cannot tell, but I think some centuries—before the city had over-spread this quarter, and when it was tilled ground and avenue, and such deep and leafy seclusion as ought to embosom a religious house—that something had happened on this site which, rousing fear and inflicting horror, had left to the place the inheritance of a ghost-story. (117)

The murky genesis of the tale results from urbanization's threats to the unbroken transmission of local histories and to the spaces of "deep and leafy seclusion" available to vulnerable women. Villette's relentless growth causes "fear" and "horror," penetrates the nunnery, and alters the oral histories that adhere to these altered spaces. In this way, Anthropocene development desanctifies space—but the supernatural fills these vacuums of knowledge and sanctity. *Shirley*'s titular heroine writes deep-time cosmologies, while Lucy frames the ghost as an incomplete story:

> A vague tale went of a black and white nun.... The ghost must have been built out some ages ago, for there were houses all round now; but certain

convent-relics, in the shape of old and huge fruit-trees, yet consecrated the spot; and, at the foot of one—a Methuselah of a pear-tree, dead, all but a few boughs which still faithfully renewed their perfumed snow in spring, and their honey-sweet pendants in autumn—you saw, in scraping away the mossy earth between the half-bared roots, a glimpse of slab, smooth, hard, and black. The legend went, unconfirmed and unaccredited, but still propagated, that this was the portal of a vault, imprisoning deep beneath that ground, on whose surface grass grew and flowers bloomed, the bones of a girl whom a monkish conclave of the drear middle ages had here buried alive for some sin against her vow. (117–18)

Stalwart Lucy depicts the ghost, "built out some ages ago," as yet another farm building replaced by shops. Yet the equivocation in "convent-relics" and "faithfully renewed" boughs imbues her insouciance with respect. Roots, mosses, bones, and stones chafe against the desanctification of space, eroding Lucy's anti-Catholicism through her aesthetic delight in what has survived urbanization. Fear and jealousy construct this gnomic ambivalence: fear of her susceptibility to Catholicism and of her own virginal entombment; jealousy of M. Paul's first love. Because Lucy fears this martyr, forever pure yet sexually powerful, the shamed postulant under "Methusaleh" provides a comforting counterexample. The "sin against her vow" of chastity ironizes the "relics" that suggest sainthood and discredits Justine Marie's vaunted purity. Referring to M. Paul's financial support of her family, Lucy chastises herself, "Was I, then, to be frightened by Justine Marie? Was the picture of a pale dead nun to rise, an eternal barrier? And what of the charities which absorbed his worldly goods? What of his heart sworn to virginity?" Lucy's solution is to redirect this purity from the dead to the living: "If she wore angels' wings, I knew whose poet-fancy conferred them," she concludes, calling him her "Christian hero" (441).

While this generic label conveniently blurs the religious line between her and M. Paul, it binds him more tightly to the medieval past from whose (to her) superstitious clutches she wishes to save him. But she knows the bonds are tight, and seeing him converse intimately with his young female ward, Lucy believes that this ward has eclipsed M. Paul's first love and confirms her "presentiment" that she would lose him (492). She concludes that

the blooming and charming Present prevailed over the Past; and, at length, his nun was indeed buried. Thus it must be. The revelation was indeed come. Presentiment had not been mistaken in her impulse: there is a kind of presentiment which never *is* mistaken; it was I who had for a moment miscalculated; not seeing the true bearing of the oracle, I had thought she muttered of vision when, in truth, her prediction touched reality. (515)

This presentiment reveals that Lucy's acceptance of hard truths does not immunize her from the supernatural—from non-scientific explanations. Lucy stresses her preference for scientific methods over mystical visions: her first mention of the ghost nun ends with a brusque transition ("Independently of romantic rubbish, however"), and after sighting it, she believes "a perfectly natural solution of this seeming mystery will one day be arrived at" (118, 452). Others see Lucy as a rationalist; de Hamal praises Lucy as a "capital ghost-seer" with "such nerves!—real iron and bend-leather!" (524). Yet Lucy *is* suggestible, and she believes this tendency to perceive the supernatural is typical of the human imagination: "What winter tree so bare and branchless—what wayside, hedge-munching animal so humble, that Fancy, a passing cloud, and a struggling moonbeam, will not clothe it in spirituality, and make of it a phantom?" (512). Stylistic variations transfer this sensitivity to readers. Consider the distance between her ghost sighting in a suspenseful passage concluded melodramatically by the capitalized and dashed announcement, "—the NUN!" and the delayed identification that M. Paul's companion is not the ghost of Justine Marie, but an ordinary Labassecourienne (519). There, Lucy observes, "It is over. The moment and the nun are come. The crisis and the revelation are passed by" (512). These apathetic, simply punctuated, unusually short sentences in passive voice eschew the sleight-of-hand drama of delayed identification. This aberrant anticlimax suggests that she has been supernaturally as well as romantically disappointed. If Lucy is "real iron and bend-leather," why do presentiments strike her, and why do specters provoke stylistic flourishes?

Diane Long Hoeveler has suggested that the figure of the nun allows Brontë to disown her indebtedness to the most sensational iterations of the Gothic tradition. The presence of Gothic tropes—such as dream-induced prophecies, grave desecrations, surreal crises, encounters with evil (often in the form of anti-heroines), and textual resurrections via rediscovered letters—makes *Villette*, Hoeveler maintains, "an example of a late female Gothic written in a literary culture that had moved into an embrace of the codes of realism" (41). In the "self-parodying" nun figure, "we can actually see the death of the genre" (42, 43). In the stylistic anticlimaxes, Hoeveler sees Brontë's disavowing the Gothic's cheap narrative tricks. In Lucy's buried letters, meanwhile, we find a "literally buried residue of a forsaken passion, a necessary renunciation if the woman author is to move on to a higher form of creativity and composition"

(Hoeveler 42). As my interpretation of these buried letters in the introduction shows, another level of irony infects this passage because Lucy suspects, rightly, that this burial cannot effectively make the past stay in the past. Her past actions—and those of past generations of *Anthropos* transforming the landscape beneath her—continue to manifest as Gothic apparitions. Just as Brontë's authorial crisis prompts her, paradoxically, to continue deploying the very tropes she wishes to parody, Lucy Snowe's unwillingness to disclose truths (which she hides through delayed identification) allows her to claim rationality and stoke supernatural fears in the reader. The deferral of "a perfectly natural solution" encourages speculation, tempting readers to draw unwarranted conclusions instead of carefully tracing the material, historical causes that denuded and destabilized the lands of Labassecour. Because Lucy withholds information, observed phenomena lack connections between past and present, between identified and unidentified entities, conjuring a mysterious world powered by malevolent agencies. With no empirical method for fully tracing networks of causation, intuition and mythology supplement scientific investigation. Ghosts and monsters, placeholders for future delayed identifications, signal confusing presences that will be explained later.

In *Jane Eyre*, the first meeting between Jane and Rochester takes this form. Jane perceives in his dog a mythical "Gytrash" with "strange pretercanine eyes," while Rochester discloses, "I thought unaccountably of fairy tales, and had half a mind to demand whether you had bewitched my horse: I am not sure yet" (132, 143). In *Shirley*, Caroline's tutelage of fanciful Martin Yorke also recalls fairy tales. Waiting to rendezvous, he dips into his satchel to fetch "not the Latin grammar, but a contraband volume of fairy tales," reading until she emerges out of the snow just like his book's "green-robed lady, on a snow-white palfrey," whom he "must follow ... into fairyland" (531). Before Jane Eyre conjures a Gytrash, she too meditates in and on a cold landscape, personifying the moon:

> pale yet as a cloud, but brightening momentarily, she looked over Hay, which, half lost in trees, sent up a blue smoke from its few chimneys: it was yet a mile distant, but in the absolute hush I could hear plainly its thin murmurs of life. My ear, too, felt the flow of currents; in what dales and depths I could not tell: but there were many hills beyond Hay, and doubtless many becks threading their passes. That evening calm betrayed alike the tinkle of the nearest streams, the sough of the most remote. (132)

Jane remains still while the moon gains ascendance and nonhuman agents become perceptible, revealing the limits of human perception ("I could not tell"). Like Martin's fairy tales, her senses decenter the human they serve, the "most remote" signals reminding her of "nearest" and "remote" streams. Both scenes link romance with a mode of perception whose exhibition of unknown natural phenomena seems like a supernatural channel opening, poised on the cusp of revelation. Jeffrey Jerome Cohen calls this mode of relating to the world "enchantment," an "estrangement and secular enmeshment, sudden sighting of the world's dynamism and autonomy, the advent of queered relation" (9). On Martin's snowy woods are superimposed fairy tales, while Jane's Gytrash opens her to "queered relations" she typically acknowledges through her morbid yet charming paintings, which allegorically depict human encounters with dangerous natural forces. Ecological possibility inheres in these enchantments because they challenge anthropocentric "fantasies of sovereign relation to environment, a domination that renders nature 'out there,' a resource for recreation, consumption, and exploitation" (9). The eponymous, gone-to-seed estate in Anne Brontë's *The Tenant of Wildfell Hall* punctures such fantasies, decades of neglect lending it "a goblinish appearance, that harmonized well with the ghostly legions and dark traditions our old nurse had told us respecting the haunted hall" (23). Other scenes show that inhuman spookiness results from improper stewardship. This juxtaposition of queered enchantment and disenchanting human fallibility is in the Gytrash's dissolution when Jane sees "a rider": "The man, the human being, broke the spell at once," an identification that defamiliarizes *Anthropos* before devaluing it ("goblins ... could scarce covet shelter in "the commonplace human form" [133]). *Shirley*'s namesake does the same when she warns Robert not to propose (to acquire her land and capital) by saying he is "falling under enchantment" (224). Announcing that local fairies went extinct, she hints that marriage would intensify the ecological destruction that caused their extinction.

Though both Shirley and Lucy use scientific reasoning, they use nonscientific language when it better expresses the profundity of glimpsed links between past human actions and the present denuded world. Lucy's delayed identifications provide perfectly natural solutions for unsolved apparitions, but she is still susceptible to the paranormal when connections among organisms, times, and spaces are difficult to reconstruct. Defying ghosts from the past (Justine Marie) can open up new futures (marrying M. Paul), yet these challenges to empiricism are not neutralized automatically once scientific explanations emerge. The Anthropocene is a state of interdependence among humans, nonhumans, and spaces so complex that their existences as discrete phenomena are obsolete as explanatory mechanisms for historical shifts. The importance of this obsolescence is indicated by the ecological undead, like *Shirley*'s extinct fairies and the goblinish Wildfell Hall, which embody humans' failures to fulfill their responsibilities to the nonhuman. Brontë's romantic enchantments highlight the consequences of this dereliction. For Martin, the fairyland Caroline beckons him into will disappoint him—she desires a conduit to Robert Moore, not merely a rival, but a decidedly unromantic personage to boot—and challenge Martin's ability trust future enchantments. Rochester retains his own susceptibility to enchantment by stoking romance, but like Robert Moore's mills, this love endangers the lands left to his responsibility.

Villette's Lucy and *The Professor*'s Crimsworth challenge the anthropocentrism of Jane, Robert, and Rochester by showing that humans behave like flora, fauna, and rocks. Both use a range of scientific imagery, from the emergent discourse of galvanism in their talk of "magnetism" to the parapsychological concept of "animal spirits," to explain love between humans. But in moments of crisis, sudden perceptions of queered relations show Crimsworth and Lucy the centrality of nonhumans to human romance. Like the beetles whose violation Lucy imagines when rehearsing her role as a frustrated suitor, sexual anxieties are embedded in the spaces and organisms she encounters. When Lucy's *allée* is invaded, she has an unwelcome epiphany that the "casement which rained billets, had vulgarized the once dear nook it overlooked; and elsewhere, the eyes of the flowers had gained vision, and the knots in the tree-boles listened like secret ears" (128). This is not a conceit, but a literal observation. Lurkers like Madame Beck, M. Paul, and the beau instrumentalize the garden for personal benefit. Madame Beck, Dr. John, and M. Paul *are* looking and listening, using their privileges to recruit human and nonhuman agents for intelligence gathering: Madame Beck's privileges to shape the garden, Dr. John's to penetrate any space at any time, and M. Paul's to look out his secret window. Multispecies ethnography (which I discuss in chapter 3) illuminates how human recruitments of flora, fauna, and rocks erode the boundaries between human and nonhuman. The more humans interfere with nonhumans, the more "nature" quite literally manifests human intentions. Consequently, if rational Dr. John treats the ghostly nun as a problem of taxonomical identification—"You only spoke of 'something,' not defining *what*. Was it a man? Was it an animal?" (276)—the question is inadequate: in the ontologically unstable *Villette*, these identifications blur. Questions about what individuals did in the past and how they shape present ecosystems very much matter, but the enmeshment of human and nonhuman species means that any singular identification of a single villain or single cause will always be incomplete.

No matter whether Lucy learns surveillance from Madame Beck, no amount of data gathered in the present can overcome her lack of historical knowledge. This is evident when, unwittingly drugged by a "strong opiate," she wanders Villette's annual fête. Lucy correctly intuits the possessive motives of the "secret junta" gathered around M. Paul, but her inclination to anticipate the worst clouds her ability to predict the future (496, 508). Her preference "to penetrate to the real truth" persists in the face of "untold terror" because she believes she will have "swallowed strength" (514). But the ward does not, in fact, wed her guardian. Though nostalgically christened Justine Marie, the ward's "blooming and charming Present" cannot fully vanquish the "Past" (515). The facts Lucy intends to find are not accessible through opiates, but as she wanders "guileless and reckless, urged and drugged to the brink of frenzy" through a "strange vision of Villette at midnight" (504, 497), she accesses a reality described by Richard Doyle, whose ethnobotany plumbs the relationship between psychotropic drugs and human evolution. Drugs, Doyle argues, shatter the illusion that humans are separated from their ecosystems. Those under the influence face the "ecodelic insight" that humans are imbricated in a multispecies web that does not separate human from nonhuman. No longer under the sway of the ego that separates self from cosmos, econauts—people experiencing ecodelic insights—explore the noosphere, the "aware and conscious layer of the earth's ecosystem" (20, 21, 11). In *Villette*, Lucy, "alive to new thought," becomes an econaut: the opiate works "with the suddenness of magic" as she is "plunged amidst a gay, living, joyous crowd" (496–97, 499). Imbued "with the passionate thirst of unconscious fever," she wanders from the isolated, enclosed *pensionnat* into the open noosphere (501). Wandering, Lucy experiences her individuation as entangled in nature by way of her altered state, which mirrors the web of people, trees, stars, animals, buildings, and watercourses around her: "On this whole scene was impressed a dream-like character; every shape was wavering, every movement floating, every voice echo-like" in the "elastic night-air," whose ever-expanding capaciousness unfolds as, one by one, she discovers *all* her acquaintances dispersed around the festival (501).

Lucy's outfit indicates her active entanglement with nature: not her dun-mist crepe but her "garden-costume." Complete with a "large hat" and "shawl," it is not suitable for public (498). But it is suitable for an econaut: outwardly signaling her intimacy with the ground, it also signals the inward interactions between humans and plants she experiences through the drug coursing her veins. As Doyle notes, in the nineteenth century, pharmaceutical companies wrested control over the "global botanical commons" by extracting chemical agents from plants, making "the meshed relations of ecology into a thing available for ownership and control" (15). This shift is represented by Madame Beck's control over the garden and her ability to manipulate Lucy into taking opiates, which reproduce the industrial privatization of the global botanical commons on the scale of the small business (the profitable private school). Lucy, who wishes to improve the health of her environment and enjoy plants *in situ* rather than harvest them, also engages in small-scale practices of horticulture. While wandering Villette in this altered state, rather than seeing the transcendent supernatural—she immediately recants her observation that Madame Walraven looks "more witch-like than ever," clarifying that "she was indeed no corpse or ghost, but a harsh and hardy old woman" (508)—she experiences the immanence of enmeshment instead. Cohen, as we have seen, defines such enmeshment as a "sudden sighting of the world's dynamism and autonomy" (*Stone* 9). *Villette* stages one sighting when the city park becomes "a land of enchantment, a garden most gorgeous, a plain sprinkled with colored meteors, a forest with sparks of purple and golden fire gemming the foliage; a region, not of trees and shadow, but of strangest architectural wealth" (500). Artificial lighting apes natural phenomena, while the erection of temporary festal edifices instantaneously effects urbanization. Both ontogenetically recapitulate in a single space on a single evening the urban development of green spaces. The legacy of intraspecies violence for control over this territory is mapped onto the festival, which commemorates the country's war for independence, along with its "patriots" and "martyrs," who engaged in "a kind of struggling in the streets" (500). Lacking historical knowledge, Lucy tries to evade these histories by fleeing to the park's least disturbed spaces.

But the drug ensures that her ecodelic vision rambles further than she intends. While "navigating an all encompassing complexity not usually available to perception," she perceives generations of long- and short-term environmental change (Doyle 41). Unlike Lucy's supernatural visitations, these visions draw power not from the unnatural overlapping of past and present but from Brontë's depiction of the noosphere as a natural, terrestrial space. Involution—a mutual operation whereby unfolding ecosystems will enfold the unfolder—penetrates Lucy's habitual loneliness as, dressed as a gardener, she deliberately skirts glamorous groups of "assembled ladies" and "guardian gentlemen" to join the "outer ranks . . . of citizens, plebeians and police" (502). Pulling her wide-brimmed hat low, she tries to elude notice, but her bookseller recognizes her and observes, "Mademoiselle is not well placed." Angry, she silently asks, "Who dared accost me, a being in a mood so little social?" but allows him to steer her to a prestigious seat (502). She resists this because her conscious choice to be alienated positions her exile and grief as self-selected. Thus, when she feels the knowing gaze of her erstwhile love Dr. John ("[W]hy did he turn on his chair ... and study me leisurely? ... my identity would have been grasped by his"), it pains her with the recognition of two losses (504). His appearance alongside Paulina, clad in "drapery ... all white and light and bridal," affirms Lucy's loss of him and of Holocene England (499).

Ecodelic experiences cannot, however, entirely eliminate romantic competition. Doyle's discussion of sexual selection is useful for relating Lucy's jealousies, her altered consciousness, and the song- and dance-filled festival. Explaining that each econaut faces a "palpable encounter with Darwin's 'tangled bank' of evolution," Doyle discusses Darwin's *Descent of Man* to position seduction as particularly responsive to ecodelic experience (20). If sexual selection is a "competition for attention" driving evolution, then unsurprisingly, it "excels in the production of aphrodesia" through "the induction and management of ecstatic states through rhythm, song, gesture, and feature" (37). Circulating the park in gardening clothes, energized by poppy extract, Lucy shows how the nonhuman world is "a nontrivial vector in the evolution of Homo sapiens" (15). As Shirley Keeldar uses multispecies experiments to understand her non-normative *Anthropos* species-being and enhance her courtship of Louis Moore, Lucy uses plants to understand her role as a human in the Anthropocene and to negotiate her romantic relationships. Appropriately, Lucy hides behind foliage to gather intelligence on her rival. Watching her beloved and his ward, she stews:

> This was not like enduring the endearments of Dr. John and Paulina.... [M]y sense of harmony still acknowledged in it a charm. This was an outrage. The love born of beauty was not mine; I had nothing in common with it: I could not dare to meddle with it, but another love, venturing diffidently into life after long acquaintance, furnace-tried by pain, stamped by constancy, consolidated by affection's pure and durable alloy, submitted by intellect to intellect's own tests, and finally wrought up, by his own process, to his own unflawed completeness, this Love that laughed at Passion, his fast frenzies and his hot and hurried extinction, in *this* Love I had a vested interest; and whatever tended either to its culture or its destruction, I could not view impassibly. (517)

Born in the Holocene, the "love born of beauty" suffers "hurried extinction" under the pressures of Anthropocenic dislocation. Lucy's love for M. Paul begins when she accepts the permanence of her exile, and their "furnace-tried" love flourishes amid the crises endemic to the Anthropocene—stirring her to action. Countering her "usual base habit of cowardice," which seeks any "pretext to escape action," she cannot "view impassibly" this threat of history repeating itself (84, 514). M. Paul, too, resists Madame Beck's desire to match him with the second Justine Marie, whose overstated potency is necessary because it prompts Lucy to overcome her passivity and prevent the future from being overdetermined by the past's unfurling effects. It also defines healthy romance as that which adapts to the uncertainties of unstable ecosystems. The decline of her love for Dr. John and the ascendance of M. Paul shows that love, action, and vulnerability go hand in hand in the Anthropocene. Nowhere is this danger more evident than *Villette*'s storms.

CITY OF TEMPESTS: BAD WEATHER AND THE UNCERTAIN SINKING OF M. PAUL

Lucy and M. Paul steward an ecosystem wracked by climatological instability. The day after her garden was profaned by *billet-doux* and footprints, Lucy explains, "Villette owns a climate as variable, though not so humid, as that of any English town. A night of high wind followed upon that soft sunset, and all the next day was one of dry storm—dark, beclouded, yet rainless,— the streets were dim with sand and dust, whirled from the boulevards" (128). This unexpected reversal typifies Villette's variability. "Storm" occurs 46 times in the novel. Related words frequently appear, including "wind" (103), "rain" (29), "thunder" (19), "lightning" (9), "tempest" (9), "blast" (6), "snow" (6), and "deluge" (2), with its biblical reference to Earth's first bout of apocalyptically bad weather. The weather systems in this capricious climate particularly endanger its vulnerable members—including Lucy. During a blizzard, she laments that women's "hearts and imaginations are doomed ... to dare stress of weather, to contend with the snow-blast, to wait at lonely gates and stiles in wildest storms, watching listening to see and hear the father, the son, the husband coming home" (310). Exiled from the Holocene, Lucy must adapt to the "stress of weather," which exacerbates her personal traumas. For example, after her Reason trumps her Imagination's desire for union with Dr. John, she seeks a warm nook secure against "the nipping severity of a continental winter: though now but the beginning of November, a north wind had thus early brought a wintry blight over Europe: I remember the black stoves pleased me little when I first came" (257). Though Lucy now appreciates the stoves, she is surprised by the bitter spell. Similar surprises occur, revealing how humans do not understand how intimately related their fates are to bad weather. Thus it is that fine weather breaks just after de Hamal and Dr. John profane the *allée défendue*. To suggest that they *caused* it seems a post hoc fallacy, yet sexual misconduct *does* destroy green spaces in *Jane Eyre*, *Shirley*, and *Wuthering Heights*, linking their heroes to damaged Edens.[8] *Villette* acknowledges the difficulty of understanding how humans affect the Earth and how to express this as a scientific theory, ethnography, or personal narrative; Lucy intuits these relations but cannot analyze their mechanics to her own satisfaction.

Because of this vacuum of knowledge, she often interprets "meteorological phenomena," whether "storm, flood, or whirlwind," as "signs in heavens above, or portents on the earth beneath" (531), with the conjunction "or" serving as a temporizing buffer delaying her final interpretation. Uneasy with equivocation, she seeks "natural solutions" that can correlate her life with Villette's geography. Speculating about her frustrated pursuit of correlations, she recalls,

> Three weeks of that vacation were hot, fair, and dry, but the fourth and fifth were tempestuous and wet. I do not know why that change in the atmosphere made a cruel impression on me, why the raging storm and beating rain crushed me with a deadlier paralysis than I had experienced while the air had remained serene; but so it was. (172–73)

Lucy plumbs these relations in the novel's first major storm, which hastens the death of her employer, Miss Marchmont. When the wind "took a new tone—an accent keen, almost articulate to the ear," a "subtle, searching cry" (42), Lucy's personification anticipates her horror at the *Anthropos*-like consciousness of the *allée défendue*'s surveiling flora. This intermixing of species dramatizes human/nonhuman enmeshments, and her fear of the anthropoid cry registers the threat of an Earth and sky transformed by humans. Another mixture blends literary, scientific, and supernatural explanations to forge an Anthropocenic discourse of stormy weather: such cries

> denote a coming state of the atmosphere unpropitious to life. Epidemic diseases, I believed, were often heralded by a gasping, sobbing, tormented, long-lamenting east wind. Hence, I inferred, arose the legend of the Banshee. I fancied, too, I had noticed—but was not philosopher enough to know whether there was any connection between the circumstances—

that we often at the same time hear of disturbed volcanic action in distant parts of the world; of rivers suddenly rushing above their banks; and of strange high tides flowing furiously in on low sea-coasts. "Our globe," I had said to myself, "seems at such periods torn and disordered; the feeble amongst us wither in her distempered breath, rushing hot from steaming volcanoes." (43)

This "atmosphere unpropitious to life" may be associated with folktales about forces of divine judgment, but long-range forces bind the Earth into a single space of apocalyptically bad weather as winds and currents draw it from one region to another, contextualizing local storms within global phenomena. Perceiving patterns in the bad weather that she cannot accurately interpret, Lucy combines spiritual and scientific speculation to respond to ecological crises that resist explanation but require appropriate responses, nevertheless, if she is to minimize their destructive consequences.

The difficulties of arranging such responses are particularly evident in scenes when the weather seems to improve. Miss Marchmont, for instance, mistakenly interprets it as a sign she will recover because the alteration summons memories she had "thought decayed, dissolved, mixed with grave-mold." So strongly do they return, she insists they are "realities—not mere empty ideas" (44). This struggle to establish the empirical reality of one's interpretations of environmental crises shows that survival requires responding adequately to their intellectual pressures, in addition their physiological and emotional pressures. Her insistence recalls Patrick Brontë's struggle to prove that the 1824 Crow Hill bog burst resulted from an earthquake sent by God to admonish his parishioners, as well as Jane Eyre's argument that her impossible message from Rochester was a natural phenomenon facilitated by God specifically to reunite them. But Lucy, provisional survivor of incessant storms, suspects that such arguments no longer serve. This suspicion is evident in the gap between Miss Marchmont's nostalgic optimism and Lucy's presentist melancholy:

"Is it a fine night?" she asked.

I replied in the affirmative.

"I thought so," she said; "for I feel so strong, so well. Raise me. I feel young to-night," she continued: "young, light-hearted, and happy. What if my complaint be about to take a turn, and I am yet destined to enjoy health? It would be a miracle!"

"And these are not the days of miracles," I thought to myself. (43)

Placing herself beyond the "days of miracles," Lucy's silent rejoinder sunders her from Miss Marchmont along the same temporal split by which Paulina and Dr. John's love is climatologically sundered from her love for M. Paul. Even if Lucy believes the past *is* present to Miss Marchmont, it does not restore her health. Rather, the presence of the past is dangerous for the humans who inherit its ecological consequences. Lucy suspects that bad weather is a portent, but as a climatological migrant living in a highly developed urban space that changes rapidly, she cannot access all the relevant historical and scientific data. As a result, though the character Lucy conscientiously pursues verifiable truths, narrator Lucy does not scruple to represent the unexplained as the inexplicable. Doing so not only constitutes its own psychological realism—character Lucy cannot know what narrator Lucy will eventually know—but also allows Brontë to convey the attraction of supernatural explanations while gently ironizing them.

Along with this irony, *Villette*'s apparitions, delayed identifications, and self-deprecations respond to Alaimo's call for human agency to be "rethought in terms of interconnected entanglements rather than as a unilateral 'authoring' of actions" ("Shell" 102). Unlike Jane Eyre's autobiography, which affirms her agency, Lucy Snowe's narratorial style reflects more complex distributions of power. As Alaimo argues, "Modes of thinking, being, and acting may arise from a political recognition of being immersed in the material world . . . and traversing geocapitalist expanses where one's own small domain of activity is inextricably bound up with networks of harm, risk, survival, injustice, and exploitation" (103). Lucy acknowledges these connections. Poor, lonely, depressed, and often sick, Lucy is subject to risks divided along lines of race, class, gender, sexuality, religion, and able-bodiedness. This division shapes Lucy's remark that the difference between herself and the oblivious, prosperous Mrs. Bretton is that

> between the stately ship cruising safe on smooth seas, with its full complement of crew, a captain gay and brave, and venturous and provident; and the life-boat, which most days of the year lies dry and solitary in an old, dark boat-house, only putting to sea when the billows run high in rough weather, when cloud encounters water, when danger and death divide between them the rule of the great deep. (202)

Lucy reacts to their personality difference by interpreting obstacles as spurs to self-improvement. She pathologizes her drive "to be without heavy anxiety" as an "infatuated resignation" (85). The novel's first minor storm occurs as Polly Home travels to Bretton. Lucy has not been informed she is coming, but she witnesses signs that something will change. "Of what things are these signs and tokens?" she asks herself, reflecting with dismay, "I liked peace so well, and sought stimulus so little, that when the latter came I... wished rather it had still held aloof" (8). Storms invigorate her temperament: during one, Lucy recalls, "I studiously held the quick of my nature":

> [C]ertain accidents of the weather, for instance, were almost dreaded by me, because they woke the being I was always lulling, and stirred up a craving cry I could not satisfy. One night a thunder-storm broke; a sort of hurricane shook us in our beds: the Catholics rose in panic and prayed to their saints. As for me, the tempest took hold of me with tyranny: I was roughly roused and obliged to live. I got up and dressed myself, and creeping outside the casement close by my bed, sat on its ledge, with my feet on the roof of a lower adjoining building. It was wet, it was wild, it was pitch-dark.... I could not go in: too resistless was the delight of staying with the wild hour, black and full of thunder, pealing out such an ode as language never delivered to man. (121)

Sitting on the window-ledge, Lucy does not pray for salvation but courts maximum propinquity to the storm that "obliges" her to live. Alaimo calls this behavior "exposure": ecological activism performed by feminist artists who stage "performances that are critical, strategic, or even intentionally revolting" to contest "carbon-heavy masculinities of impenetrability and aggressive consumption, and... the universalizing modes of detached, scientific vision" (*Exposed* 93, 94). Lucy's exposure to the storm is an intimate, intentionally dangerous act of witnessing climate change. The storm elicits a discourse of extremity—"accident," "never," "terribly"—that counters scientific values of objectivity, probability, and data collection at scale. In Villette, storms are ubiquitous, but never trivial. Each exposure presents unique dangers. Once, Lucy recalls, a storm "gathered immediately above Villette; it seemed to have burst at the zenith; it rushed down prone; the forked, slant bolts pierced athwart vertical torrents; red zigzags interlaced a descent blanched as white metal: and all broke from a sky heavily black in its swollen abundance" (432). With commas, semicolons, and colons, Lucy combines immediacy (crashing, bursting, rushing, piercing, and swelling occur simultaneously) and fragmentation (as lighting divides the sky, punctuation breaks up a chain of booming trochees into nine parts). This effect of sudden chaos shows that each storm is urgent.

Storms keep coming, but Lucy cannot resolve them into a single causal system—making it harder, and more urgent, to adapt to them.

Villette embraces bad weather as an opportunity to cultivate energy and equanimity in spite of corporeal and psychological dangers of the Anthropocene. But accepting the obligation to live does not equalize the asymmetries that render Lucy particularly vulnerable to bad weather. Walking through a storm, she is determined to withstand it—but almost immediately faints:

> horizontal thundered the current of the wind from north-west to southeast; it brought rain like spray, and sometimes a sharp hail, like shot: it was cold and pierced me to the vitals. I bent my head to meet it, but it beat me back. My heart did not fail at all in this conflict; I only wished that I had wings and could ascend the gale, spread and repose my pinions on its strength, career in its course, sweep where it swept. While wishing this, I suddenly felt colder where before I was cold, and more powerless where before I was weak. (181)

All too human, Lucy cannot, like Jane, benefit from the birdlike traits that draw Rochester's protection; nor can she, like Shirley, arrogate the powers of lions and panthers. This passage abruptly ends a chapter with Lucy unconscious in front of the church where she sought sanctuary, underlining how difficult it is to bootstrap one's survival once traditional support systems have collapsed.

Her sociopolitical situation exposes her to further climatological threats. Madame Beck's robust network of surveillance yields intelligence that she applies to decoy Lucy from M. Paul's imminent proposal. Tasked with delivering a gift under "the threatening aspect of a cloudy and sultry day" (428), Lucy describes her affection for this "dark rush of rain":

> I rather liked the prospect of a long walk, deep into the old and grim Basse-Ville; and I liked it no worse because the evening sky, over the city, was settling into a mass of black-blue metal, heated at the rim, and inflaming slowly to a heavy red.... [Such storms] ask only resignation—the quiet abandonment of garments and person to be, drenched. In return, it sweeps a great capital clean before you; it makes you a quiet path through broad, grand streets; it petrifies a living city as if by eastern enchantment; it transforms a Villette into a Tadmor. Let, then, the rains fall, and the floods descend. (429)

Echoing the Orientalist misattributions of the Egyptian dancer and the rock-crystal chandelier, Lucy prophesies a storm that hits Villette with its own apocalypse. An industrial city of "blue-black metal" glowing, as if created artificially by smelting, it becomes the biblical Tadmor, the ruins of the city Solomon established in the wilderness. But Villette is already stratified by ruins. The old quarter, "Basse-Ville," which she is traversing, means "lower town," and the *pensionnat* is located down at the lower level of medieval Villette, buried by urban development. The storm that "sweeps a great capital clean" reveals that the first apocalypse already occurred. It is yet another delayed identification. This storm erases the lightest, newest stratum of accreting human waste, "petrifies" what remains, and layers it atop the remains of the last apocalypse. Resignation seems to be the only course of action left to the humans still traversing the storm-rent territory.

Lucy's resignation is a hard-won product of her survival of bad weather during the school's vacation. "About this time the Indian summer closed," she recalls, "and for nine dark and wet days, of which the hours rushed on all turbulent, deaf, disheveled—bewildered with sounding hurricane—I lay in a strange fever of the nerves and blood" (176). At the apex of her suffering, she sees a vision that represents the annual absence of students as another world-destroying apocalypse:

> One evening—and I was not delirious: I was in my sane mind, I got up—I dressed myself, weak and shaking. The solitude and the stillness of the long dormitory could not be borne any longer; the ghastly white beds were turning into spectres—the coronal of each became a death's-head, huge and sun-bleached—dead dreams of an elder world and mightier race lay frozen in their wide gaping eyeholes.... [A]t this hour there was affection and sorrow in Heaven above for all pain suffered on earth beneath. (177)

Lucy bookends this vision of the "dead . . . elder world and mightier race," whose bodies remain in the dormitory and whose material effects comprise the garret's dusty strata, by acknowledging that loneliness exacerbates her vulnerability to bad weather. Ezra Dan Feldman postulates that *Villette*'s storms are "interruptions that generate and propagate Snowe's independence from familiar institutions, from personal history, and from plot itself" (98). Yet these periodic eruptions of systemic bad weather are more than symbols of Lucy's psyche, and they emphasize Lucy's imbrication in the world around her, not her independence from it. Alaimo's concept of trans-corporeality is useful here: Alaimo stipulates that this imbrication is "always generated through and entangled in differing scales and sorts of biological, technological, economic, social, political, and other systems." Analyzing the obscure, consequential entanglements of Lucy's trans-corporeality beyond her own character development is therefore an act of "social justice and environmental praxis" ("Shell" 101). Lucy's stormy meditations are one of *Villette*'s primary contributions to these goals—but because of her vulnerabilities, her first task is to survive.

Repeatedly facing storms that oblige her to live, Lucy becomes what the contributors of Richard Grusin's 2017 collection would call an Anthropocene feminist. Though she lacks precise information about Villette's past, she cultivates multiple tools of survival. Explaining the feminist dimensions of choosing to act before complete data can be found, Grusin writes, "Counter to the technoscientific desire for specificity, definition, and fact, we coined the term *anthropocene feminism* as an experiment of provocation, expressing a survivalist ethos in regard to the masculinist and patriarchal urge to proclaim mankind an agent of major change" (xi). Unlike heiress Shirley Keeldar, who generates totalizing origin stories about the Holocene's end, exile Lucy learns how to adjust to constant illness and ecological uncertainty. Consequently, when Grusin argues that "the concept of the Anthropocene has arguably been implicit in feminism and queer theory for decades, a genealogy that is largely ignored, or, worse, erased, by the masculine authority of an institutional scientific discourse that now seeks to name our current historical moment the Anthropocene" (vii), I place *Villette* in this forgotten tradition. Compare Lucy's bravery to Shirley's, for instance. After Shirley is bitten by a potentially rabid dog, she collapses under the pressure of facing her mortality and realizing that human mismanagement has sickened animals around her. Shirley's mystical stories may be feminist in their content, but they are compromised by masculinist approaches to deep history and public health. That Shirley sickens until a suitor assures her she is disease-free—and that his reassurance shifts their gendered balance of power and legitimizes his marriage proposal—emphasizes why Anthropocene feminism must resist masculinist accounts of climate change.

Just as Lucy's survival is intimately related to bad weather, so is her sexual selection. As Lucy and Dr. John are repelled at the theatre by an actress who possesses "power like a deep, swollen winter river, thundering in cataract, and bearing the soul, like a leaf, on the steep and steely sweep of its descent," Lucy realizes that the alluring Dr. John, born with "sanguine health" and "hair with a sunny sheen," aligns with good weather (288, 190). He literally seeks a fair-weather friend for a mate:

> to bright, soft, sweet influences his eyes and lips gave bright, soft, sweet welcome ... for what belonged to storm, what was wild and intense, dangerous, sudden, and flaming, he had no sympathy, and held with it no communion.... Cool young Briton! The pale cliffs of his own England do not look down on the tides of the Channel more calmly than he watched the Pythian inspiration of that night. (288)

More privileged than Lucy, capable of rebuffing Anthropocene dangers by way of inherited traits and socioeconomic benefits, Dr. John can afford to dismiss the "Pythian" actress, along with the oracular powers associated with a high priestess of Apollo. His insouciance is a remnant of Holocene England—a calmness put to use when a cry of "Fire!" prompts a stampede and galvanizes him into action to save Paulina, whom he later marries. Certainly, Paulina's and Dr. John's Holocenic approach to life does not make them invulnerable; Lucy discloses that they suffer miscarriages. But beyond the question of survival lies that of desire. Many of Brontë's characters prefer the fiery. *Shirley*'s Martin braves blizzard conditions to see Caroline, expecting her to do the same; he frets, "tempest or tornado, hail or ice, she *ought* to come; and if she has a mind worthy of her eyes and features, she *will* come; she will be here for the chance of seeing me" (552). In *Jane Eyre*, Rochester's warning, "To live, for me, Jane, is to stand on a crater-crust which may crack and spue fire any day," excites her (250). Kate Flint interprets this desirable fire as a vivid example of how "Brontë's language both internalizes the characteristics of the sublime, making the very business of living one of almost pleasurable terror, and disperses it where it might break out unpredictably" (153). Lucy's desire for storms updates this coupling of fear with pleasure for the Anthropocene by internalizing bad weather as both a permanent feature of Villette's climate *and* an unpredictable force in terms of its discrete manifestations. She is coached into loving storms by her fellow teacher M. Paul. For to love him is to love the storm.

Lucy is attracted to M. Paul not in spite of, but *because* he is a "fiery and grasping little man [who] kept down when he could," but "when he could not, he fumed like a bottled storm" (170). Dr. John and de Hamal sully the garden, but not M. Paul in "his paletôt ... hung dark and menacing" with "the tassel of his bonnet grec sternly shadowed his left temple; his black whiskers curled like those of a wrathful cat; his blue eye had a cloud in its glitter" (170). When the portress calls him "a coup-de-vent" (134), she intends to criticize, yet Lucy finds it endearing each time that, "[as] usual," in entering the classroom, "he broke upon us like a clap of thunder" (265). We are accustomed to interpret parallels between character and environment as information about characters; Shlomith Rimmon-Kenan acknowledges that one popular method for conveying character is to set up a "relation of contiguity" with the character's environment (66). In close reading, typically, the state of the environment is the vehicle for which the character is the tenor. But diegetic storms are not exclusively symbols of Brontëan heroes. Let us reverse vehicle and tenor: M. Paul becomes a symbol of bad weather, and sexuality a platform for enhancing the reader's sense of the reality of postapocalyptic ecosystems. Love for M. Paul *as* a storm allows Lucy to come to terms with living in a chaotic, denuded postnatural world. His threat galvanizes her. For example, when he locks her in the garret, she not only extemporizes new lines but also refuses to wear the costume he selects: "M. Paul might storm, might rage: I would keep my own dress. I said so, with a voice as resolute in intent, as it was low, and perhaps unsteady in utterance" (153). Literal and figurative storms demand she improvise her survival, improvisations that involve stormy demonstrations by both parties. Jealousy, integral to the process of sexual selection made evident in the midnight fête, is one of the trials that their love endures. Storms become a mode of courtship. When M. Paul tempestuously commands Madame Beck to leave him and Lucy alone, she recalls, "I loved him in his wrath with a passion beyond what I had yet felt" (531). Before his new passion, on the day he "fumed like a bottled storm," she confesses, "I liked, for instance, to see M. Emanuel jealous; it lit up his nature, and woke his spirit; it threw all sorts of queer lights and shadows over his dun face, and into his violet-azure eyes (he used to say that his black hair and blue eyes were 'une de ses beautés'). There was a relish in his anger" (170, 171). By desiring his tempests and perceiving them as "beautés," Lucy accepts his challenge to love the storm-wracked world, allowing her to delight in her growing fortitude by rehearsing future blasts. He perceives her intimacy with storminess when he ends his tantrum by claiming she too is tempestuous, hiding "passionate ardour" and looking at him with "fire shot into the glance! Not mere light, but flame: *je me tins pour averti* [I took it as a warning]" (171). Each lets the other enjoy stormy weather in the form of the romantic sublime, stoking desires that increase their chances of surviving and propagating a new generation.

Such a future seems possible in moments such as the country picnic M. Paul organizes for the school. With the May day "calm as summer" (419), he is the scene's only bad weather:

> Well might we like him, with all his passions and hurricanes, when he could be so benignant and docile at times, as he was just now. Indeed, at the worst, it was only his nerves that were irritable, not his temper that was radically bad; soothe, comprehend, comfort him, and he was a lamb; he would not harm a fly. Only to the very stupid, perverse, or unsympathizing, was he in the slightest degree dangerous. (424)

Lucy's distinction between "nerves" and "temper" alleges that he is, like Lucy, threatened by external forces though he produces storms. As Lucy's confidence builds, she softens his spiky personality, which blurs his moral responsibility for Villette's tempestuousness. Rimmon-Kenan observes that indirect representations of character through environmental traits are common in modern literature because it has lost the "medieval belief in the cause and effect relations between disorder in the human world and upheaval in nature." Links between character and environment are "grasped as purely analogous" because "the causal connection is no longer strongly operative" (67–68). In depicting M. Paul, anxious Lucy attempts to convert potential causal links that connect human actions to the destabilization of nature into analogies. She does so for self-protection, as when she occupies a safe position during one of his pedagogical storms:

> my ears regaled themselves with listening to the crescendos and cadences of a voice haranguing in the neighboring classe, in tones that waxed momentarily more unquiet, more ominously varied. There was a good strong partition-wall between me and the gathering storm, as well as a facile means of flight through the glass-door to the court, in case it swept this way; so I am afraid I derived more amusement than alarm from these thickening symptoms. (359)

For a vulnerable immigrant, Lucy's invulnerability to storms is vital. For his students, his storms may not be merely a figure of speech. But just as Lucy-the-narrator downplays mortal webs of causality by dissolving M. Paul's storms into analogies, Lucy-the-character learns practical strategies for preventing his storms. Comfortable as a teacher, she is no longer a homesick nursery maid who "looked a poor creature, and in many respects actually was so" (88). Flaunting her newfound strength, Lucy deliberately antagonizes him by wearing a bright pink dress to the country picnic. Comparing her actions "to travers[ing] a meadow where pastured a bull" while "clad in a shawl with a red border," she gloats that he "went off . . . as mildly as the menace of a storm sometimes passes on a summer day," with "one flash of sheet lightning in the shape of a single bantering smile from his eyes" (420, 421). Jubilant at her ability to ward off storms, Lucy narrates them as analogical character traits rather than causal webs, insulating herself and M. Paul morally and physically from the tempests to which they are so intimately connected.

Ultimately, Lucy's attempts to minimize these webs of causal relations fail. If flirtation converts Anthropocenic threats into evolutionary exercises, it can strengthen one's resolve to survive them, but it does not allow one to opt out of them. They continue to surface, manifesting as storms, apparitions, and ecodelic visions. The greatest challenge to Lucy's sporting affection for the storms bringing ecosystemic chaos occurs in the conclusion, when she recounts M. Paul's presumed death at the hands of one final tempest. Sailing to Europe after three years in the Caribbean, M. Paul faces a "wild south-west storm," which blows familiar "Banshee" winds back to Lucy "till the Atlantic was strewn with wrecks," among which, it is rumored, is his own ship (546). This seven-day storm apocalyptically reverses the seven-day creation of the new world. It seems that, as Gates argues of Brontë's gardens, another "Eden preparing for a fall" has fallen (40). Fittingly, the last time Lucy sees M. Paul, they walk through "such moonlight as fell on Eden—shining through the shades of the Great Garden" (541). But Brontë gives Lucy no second Eden. In recounting M. Paul's experiences, Lucy reshapes her life story from one of mourning a single Eden (Holocene England) to one about a series of losses. His uncertain death sets Bretton and Villette in uneasy relation to global weather systems and ecologies. His lifelong passion for amateur horticulture transforms into a bleak managerial role overseeing slave labor. Exiled to a "climate hazardous" by friends who "wished that in the mean time he might die" (510), he escapes the climatological dangers enumerated in *Jane Eyre*'s concluding scene of St. John Rivers's death in India—only to die returning home. Finally, Brontë subverts the imperialist logic that lets the English abandon their exhausted ecosystems to appropriate fresh territories elsewhere. M. Paul's fortunes were already linked to imperialist economies, but as his ship sinks, the ecological repressed surfaces: far from new, the New World is fully incorporated into long-established systems of old-world ecological destruction.

Villette's Edens were fallen all along. Crises multiply, creating the illusion of ever more Edens that seem just now to have fallen, or to be just on the cusp of falling. By the end of *Villette*, Lucy is not mourning the loss of a pre-fall homeland but instead is absorbed by withstanding the crises that occur locally, whether they emerge out of local or global phenomena. Banal and sublime crises proliferate, absorbed into the narrative tropes of stormy weather, delayed identifications, and submerged histories. Just as the fire in the crowded theatre during Vashti's performance turns out to have been but a "spark ... which had blazed up and been quenched in a moment," this apparently definitive seven-day apocalypse is not (294). No longer can a tale of a single, pristine homeland explain Lucy's losses. Golden spikes promising to pinpoint the end of the world are abundant—too abundant. This helps explain why *Villette* concludes with a final temporization. Suspending, rather than resolving, the novel's concluding action, Lucy leaves M. Paul's fate ambiguous: "Here pause: pause at once. There is enough said. Trouble no quiet, kind heart; leave sunny imaginations hope. Let it be theirs to conceive the delight of joy born again fresh out of great terror, the rapture of rescue from peril, the wondrous reprieve from dread, the fruition of return" (546). This ambiguity beautifully recapitulates the lack of knowledge that continually frustrates Lucy (and scientific consensus about the Anthropocene). Just as Lucy improvises, refusing to play the scripted role of a fop whose courtship *must* fail, this suspension works against a fixed sense of plot development, introducing Anthropocenic contingency into the novel's realist plot. Sometimes, an unfortunate contingency appears as a crisis—as a total collapse, like the deaths that remove Lucy from England. At other times, it is a condition, like the urbanization and surveillance that pervade Villette but that Lucy rarely observes directly. The uncertain sinking of M. Paul perfectly captures this duality: he is dying and living, returning imminently and lost forever. Like Catherine Earnshaw's peat-preserved corpse, he is dead and not-dead. *Villette*'s final delayed identification will never surface, showing why it is Brontë's most powerful technique for staging the Anthropocene. Such a proliferation of golden spikes may itself be the most reliable indication that the Holocene has ended. We live after the beginning of the end of the world, but our knowledge of it has been deferred. Those who wish to ignore it—to believe that M. Paul still lives—may choose to do so.

A PEDAGOGY OF TENDING: HOW TO THRIVE IN A WORLD OF CRISIS

A living M. Paul may tempt readers because his forcefulness makes a last-minute shipwreck seem surprising. Yet no individual can control a world so uncertain. At his first appearance, when his assessment of Lucy's physiognomy convinces Madame Beck to hire her, she acknowledges that the "resolute compression of the lips, and a gathering of the brow, seemed to say that he meant to see through me"—but by naming him "this vague arbiter of my destiny," she sounds underneath this language of fate the note of contingency characteristic of the Anthropocene (73, 74). An ironic reversal awaits in the penultimate chapter. There, a newly affianced Lucy consciously recalls this language of destiny: "He deemed me born under his star: he seemed to have spread me over its beam like a banner." She contrasts her prospects exultingly with her former precarity, exclaiming "How different the look—how far otherwise the fate!" (542). But the chapter's news of the shipwreck punctures this optimism. Lucy writes succinctly, as if exhausted, "Men cannot prophesy. Love is no oracle" (543). Her unsentimental refusal to gratify readers' morbid curiosity with particulars about M. Paul's fate or her own transports of grief deftly avoids the extinction porn castigated by Zylinska. It cannot affirm the power of a non-toxic romantic love to neutralize the devastations of the Anthropocene. M. Paul's caring efforts to secure a future for her are as compromised as Robert Moore's mill and Jane Eyre's Madeiran inheritance. Brontë's refusal to grant Lucy a conventionally happy ending reveals that no lovers can escape the vicissitudes of the Anthropocene. But Lucy Snowe, born under the star of the stormy Anthropocene, determines to thrive. Obliged by bad weather to withstand conditions "unpropitious to life" (43), she cultivates a number of adaptive practices. One is not overinvesting in grief or dwelling on lost hopes: always declining the "Barmecide's loaf" that cannot "nourish" but makes her "thin as a shadow" (297). She shares more active strategies, as well.

The first strategy is working. "Listen," she instructs the reader in her conclusion: "I commenced my school; I worked—I worked hard. I deemed myself the steward of his property, and determined, God willing, to render a good account" (543). This work cure is inspired by M. Paul, whose gift of a school she accepts as his "faithful steward" who will "work hard and willingly" (537). Just as she grows to appreciate storms, she transforms her understanding of teaching from a confrontation with "a row of eyes and brows that threatened stormy weather," giving "difficult lessons ... on the edge of a moral volcano that rumbled under my feet and sent sparks and hot fumes into my eyes," to a practice of tending (87, 91). As a teacher, she pursues "the nobler charge of laboring and living for others" (401). The comforting products of her sewing for Mrs. Bretton enrich the family's exile, and she always shares her resources, just as M. Paul shares the stewed fruit that she fetched him (394), one example of the mutual care that animates their courtship and culminates in his provision of the modest establishment where she continues tending humans, nonhumans, and scarce resources. "My school flourishes," she reports, its plants "in bloom" and its "little library" full (545). Her school is oligotrophic—a jewel box of small proportions that uses few resources, contrasting with the copiotrophic *pensionnat*. Madame Beck, one of Alaimo's carbon-heavy men because of her large campus and her luxuries, runs a school very different from Lucy's establishment, which takes just enough spaces, materials, and energy to support her tending. Lucy increases the chances that oligotrophic tending will be adopted by others through her pedagogy and her practices of writing, book-buying, and storytelling. That her landlord is the same bookshop owner who secures her a better place at Villette's town fête suggests that reading and writing are given safe homes at the Faubourg Clothilde. She tends M. Paul's records and writes chronicles to reduce the kinds of historical knowledge gaps that frustrated her own efforts to understand Villette's past, present, and future. Her oligotrophic desire not to waste precious resources extends to the written word, evident in her desire to write down M. Paul's inspired speeches to "gather and store up those handfuls of gold-dust, so recklessly flung to heaven's reckless winds" (422). Before his presumed death, he does write to her as a form of care. "A generous provider supplied bounteous fuel" for Lucy's hope, for "he wrote as he gave and as he loved, in full-handed, full-hearted plenitude" (544).

Though material resources may be scarce, information need not be. Lucy's practices of storytelling, book collecting, and letter writing put Doyle's ecodelic practices into practice. If writing is the mind's "external symbolic storage," Lucy's autobiography attempts to alter the "brain-culture chemistry" of readers through the production of stories, which are "efficacious pharmacopiea to be selected for" and inherited by future generations through oral and textual persuasion (Doyle 27, 31). From her positively received outburst of jealousy—M. Paul responds to "the whole history" of her jealousy with "indulgence," not "strong reproof"—Lucy learns that storytelling, even if it is "ardent" and "bitter," is an effective response (541). *Villette* therefore contributes to Anthropocene feminism's aims: securing "the continued flourishing of speculation and imagination as forms of queer and feminist knowledge production," engaging with "the question of where and when the Anthropocene should be said to begin," and "assembling ... small-scale systems" working "toward a goal of mutual thriving" (Grusin xi). As Lucy Snowe narrates her life, transmitting to her readers how to cope productively in an ecological and moral climate of loss, competition, and uncertainty, she maintains a delicate balance between forging concrete, causal links between the past and present and speculating about the uncertain future. In doing so, Lucy becomes one of Donna Haraway's "chthonic ones," those figures who "offer an alternative, feminist device for imagining more manageable futures for what comes next" (*Chthulucene* 2).

Conclusion

CLIMATES FOR MOURNING,
EDITING, AND SCHOLARSHIP

Living temporally and geographically at the onset of the Anthropocene, the Brontë family created a body of literature that grapples with changes in the built and natural environments—changes that we retroactively identify as characteristic of the Holocene's cessation. Seeking this new geological epoch in their texts has shown the Brontës to have engaged extensively with this shift. They leveraged personal experiences, scientific discourses, and narrative conventions to generate insightful correlations between human actions and putatively natural phenomena. Hardly naïve rhapsodists of a timeless, bucolic landscape, they encode signs of environmental degradation and development even in the midst of enchanting word-paintings. Hardly instrumentalizing taxidermists or miners of a nature treated as a convenient repository of symbols used to describe humans, they emplot the material entanglements that bind humans to the nonhuman organisms and inorganic materials surrounding them. As their speakers and characters navigate dangerous landscapes with varying degrees of success, they construct a suite of adaptive responses to ecological instability. First, they emphasize the need to witness: they observe bravely and report accurately the eruptions of this new epoch, whether through crises (such as bog bursts and storms) or sudden disclosures of ongoing decay or morbidity (such as bog bodies and extinctions). Careful attention to local conditions is paramount for reconstructing past ecological states and for linking them to past and present human actions. *Jane Eyre*, in addition to dramatizing the witness's tasks of observation and reportage, assigns to Anthropocene citizens the necessity to rethink definitions of the human as the novel's shifting settings chart ecological degradation to stage conflicts that test the limits and consequences of human control over the natural order. *Shirley* stipulates that witnessing and redefining be integrated into complexly framed ethnographies drawn eclectically from spiritual, scientific, and folkloric discourses. Only by constructing compelling narratives, *Shirley* alleges, will readers perceive how deeply the Earth has been transformed, how difficult it is to agree on when and how this has happened, and how necessary it is to engage in stewardship. *Villette*'s protagonist can neither remember a pastoral past nor access a pristine natural space, yet is assailed by crises; the practical needs of tending the environment she lives in—and of maintaining the physical strength and psychological equanimity it requires—take precedence.

Uncovering such a trajectory is why I focus on Charlotte Brontë to study the early literary ecology of the Anthropocene. Her settings, whether Yorkshire, Derbyshire, London, Brussels, or imperial colonies (Jamaica, Madeira, an imagined east African coast), occupy varying positions along a spectrum of naturalness and artificiality. What Charlotte's total body of work offers is a halting but inexorable transition into a postnatural world. While moving from *The Professor*'s pastoral nostalgia to *Jane Eyre*'s anthropocentric *Bildung*, from *Shirley*'s multispecies ethnography to *Villette*'s urban green spaces, Charlotte explores, then rejects, the reactionary urge to use art to reconstruct pure, pastoral environments. A profound sense of loss animates the trajectory by which her characters recognize the dawn of the Anthropocene and begin to craft compelling stories about it and design efficacious—or inefficacious—adaptations to it. Underneath the clarion calls of crisis demanding that we attend to the urgent tasks of witnessing, redefining, storytelling, and tending, quietly sounding is the need to mourn. The right way to mourn is, however, unfixed for the Brontës. The family's narratives of witnessing death and destruction draw intensity by making painfully explicit the value of individual organisms and biomes. Witness Patrick Brontë's fear for the children's safety in the 1824 Crow Hill bog burst. Helen Burns, though, less than a year from her own death, warns Jane Eyre against thinking "too much of the love of human beings" (82). *Shirley* jealously draws its two heroines back from the brink of death, but the death of young Jessie Yorke, abruptly inserted as a long digression, casts a shadow over the novel's teleology of embattled survival. And Charlotte does not revise out of *Shirley* the stylistic break that separates the section she wrote before the deaths of Emily and Anne from the section written afterward. *Villette*, which opens with the deaths of its protagonist's entire family, seems to interdict mourning, but once its exiled heroine successfully masters her grief for her lost homeland, and all supernatural apparitions have been debunked, the pointedly unconfirmed loss of her fiancé suspends this grieving process indefinitely. In the Anthropocene, grief always calls: losses must be recognized, but without derailing the other operations necessary for survival.

Mourning is an essential act for the Anthropocene because it affirms the dignity of life, but Charlotte's letters and novels admit how difficult it is to grieve well, to chart a path that respects the dead without neglecting the living beings and landscapes that remain. Surviving the losses of her mother, aunt, and siblings makes mourning one of the legacies Brontë's family left Charlotte—along with their literary effects. This is why, though mourning can be clearly related to the tasks of witnessing (observing destruction directly), redefining (diagnosing *Anthropos*'s morbidity while resisting misanthropy), and tending (taking care of ill bodies and fragile spaces), for Charlotte, most crucial is the task of storytelling—of crafting literary legacies that preserve the ephemeral experiences and thoughts of fragile individuals. In May 1850, after Emily and Anne died, she wrote to her publisher to express the difficulty of editing her sisters' poems for publication when she must walk the moors "alone" (*Letters* 2:403). Memories of her sisters physically inhere in each bush and hillock, altering the moors' aesthetic:

> I am free to walk on the moors; but when I go out there alone, everything reminds me of a time when others were with me, and then the moors seem a wilderness, featureless, solitary, saddening. My sister Emily had a peculiar love for them, and there is not a knoll of heather, not a branch of fern, not a young bilberry leaf, not a fluttering lark or linnet, but reminds me of her. The distant prospects were Anne's delight, and when I look round she is in the blue tints, the pale mists, the waves and shadows of the horizon. (403)

The moors are already a space of loss, prefiguring the tourists who stalk Brontë Country for signs of the siblings. In the summer of 1850, this loss is a living problem for Charlotte—the problem of editing her sisters' works for republication. The letter confesses that her moorland rambles involuntarily cause her to recite her sisters' poetry. She laments, "Once I loved it—now I dare not read it—and am driven often to wish I could taste one draught of oblivion and forget much that, while mind remains, I never shall forget" (403). To remember is to exacerbate grief, but remembering their poetry, and making readers remember, was precisely the task she set herself. As she resisted the temptation to forget, her editorial tasks processed not only the loss of her sisters, but the loss of the landscapes they traversed together and wrote about. In doing so, she bequeathed to us one final strategy for surviving the Anthropocene: how to mourn.

A GOOD GRIEF:
MOURNING THE LANDSCAPE OF HOME

To explore (but not resolve) the contradictions in Brontë's approach to mourning, I now examine the use of bluebells in the three sisters' works and their relationship to Charlotte's 1850 editorial labors. Bluebells flourish in the moorland ecosystems in which the Brontës lived. *Hyacinthoides non-scripta* flourish, too, in their poetry and prose, from Emily's "To the Bluebell" of May 1839 and her more famous untitled poem of December 1838 (named "The Bluebell" by Charlotte in her 1850 edition) to Anne's poem "The Bluebell" of August 1840. In their poems, bluebells function serially as reminders of the cyclical rebirth of spring and as subjects for the poetic repetitions of rhyme, refrain, and alliteration. In their novels, particularly Charlotte's *Shirley*, Emily's *Wuthering Heights*, and Anne's *Agnes Grey*, bluebells function as inspiration for mourning. They are botanical agents whose annual bloomings precipitate characters' negotiations of grief and homesickness. Figured oxymoronically as fragile survivors, as ghostly ambassadors of ancient forests and anticipatory symbols of spring rebirths, the Brontës' bluebells inhabit a temporality of loss that chafes against the rhythms of seasonality, thereby modeling an aesthetically powerful response to environmental insecurity. Only now, while scholars look backward to propose that we have always *been* in the Anthropocene, can we read backward into the Brontës' works the dawn of an era characterized by human-caused ecological destruction. Analyzing their bluebells as witnesses to biome loss, with particular attention to Emily's 1838 bluebell poem alongside Charlotte's 1850 revision of it, calls attention to the ecological dimensions of her grief at her siblings' deaths. The Brontës' literary bluebells offer synecdoches of human and ecosystemic loss and rebirth—synecdoches, not metonyms, because of the inherent materiality of the interactions linking characters to their ecosystems and to the bluebells dotting them—whose digressive temporal and spatial repetitions of literary mourning redirect readers' attention from mourning to rebirth, memory, and stewardship.

The Brontës' flower imagery does so by reconstructing microcosmic stories of grief that are emphatically emplaced in particular ecosystems. Precisely rendered representations of bluebells just as they blossom, poised between winter and spring as colorful harbingers of warmer weather, populate these stories of loss. Flourishing on roadsides as signs of "ghost forests" long cut down, yet blooming annually *en masse* as "bluebell woods" in remnants of ancient woods, *Hyacinthoides non-scripta* bear witness to ecosystems long upset by human actions. But as signs of anthropogenic environmental destruction, the flowers are ambiguous. Their presence on the side of a road may indicate a forest vanished long ago, but when they riotously bloom into the "bluebell wood" of early spring, creating a lush carpet of vibrant bluish-purple, they signal that the canopy poised to unfurl above is an undisturbed remnant of a prehistoric or medieval wood. The bluebells of *Shirley* and *The Tenant of Wildfell Hall* are unspecified, while those of *Agnes Grey* and *Wuthering Heights* are stipulated as roadside blossoms, as are those of Anne's "The Bluebell" and Emily's "The Bluebell." The Brontës' bluebells ambiguously indicate survival or loss, signaling that the natural world is at once vulnerable and resilient. This ambiguity makes it difficult to determine once and for all if a particular local population or ecosystem is thriving or dying, but it does encourage practices of empathy (including poetic practices) that seek out or care for fragile organisms and landscapes.

Bluebells therefore offer a locus for guiding stewardship. Compared to the pampered hothouse flowers deprecated by characters like Agnes Grey, these wild, humble blossoms are oligotrophs: species that can flourish under difficult conditions and without copious nutrients. These are examples of the "surprisingly tenacious" species that "survive in safe havens" created during periods of deforestation "where conditions, even if not ideal, were enough for a plant or its propagules to remain viable," thus providing a "refugia for the plants during times of unfavorable conditions" (Rotherham, "Ghosts" 44). In the Brontës' Anthropocene ethics, even hardy flowers require some aid, though it may be from indifferent gardeners, as in *Villette*, whose Lucy Snowe is "naturally no florist" (545). Bluebells are thus for the Brontës what toads are for Alexis Shotwell's narratives of climate change, what bees are for Jake Kosek's ethnographies of insect-human interaction, and what matsutake mushrooms are for Anna Tsing: a flashpoint for thinking through efficacious responses to climate change. Tsing explores how the prized matsutake mushroom, which flourishes in regions destabilized by deforestation, signifies "possibilities of coexistence within environmental disturbance" through its ability to coax reforestation and provide foragers, who are mostly "displaced and disenfranchised cultural minorities," with stable employment (*Mushroom* 4). Tsing shares her fieldwork to persuade readers to take up the "arts of noticing," a mode of patient attention to the minutiae of recuperating ecosystems (25). These arts of noticing reward nature-walkers with visions of a "mosaic of open-ended assemblages of entangled ways of life," as well as a means of "exploring indeterminacy and the conditions of precarity, that is, life without the promise of stability" (4, 9). These are just some of the "arts of living on a damaged planet"—to quote the title of Tsing et al.'s 2017 collection—which include the ability to identify, observe, and appreciate "tenacious" species, like the Brontës' bluebells.

The fragility of their characters' bodies and the narrators' emphases on the contingency of life underscore this fundamental instability, while their many walks and descriptions of nature teach readers these arts of noticing. In *Shirley*, Caroline's offer to show Shirley local trees, mosses, berries, and flowers—many of them rare or ancient, some both—embodies this art of noticing. Many of the Brontës' word-paintings are reminders to *look*. Emily's Cathy Linton spends the summer hours from "dinner to tea" on one of the spaces that Emma Marris points to as the Anthropocene's signature space: the unexpected patch of nature that survives within developed spaces, such as "the highway median," the "bees whizzing down Fifth Avenue in Manhattan," or "the old field overgrown with weeds and shrubs" (2). "On one side of the road," *Wuthering Heights*'s Nelly Dean recalls, "rose a high, rough bank, where hazels and stunted oaks, with their roots half exposed, held uncertain tenure: the soil was too loose for the latter; and strong winds had blown some nearly horizontal" (230). In this eroding patch of ghost forest, Nelly deploys her own considerable arts of noticing on a single surviving bluebell:

> "Look, Miss!" I exclaimed, pointing to a nook under the roots of one twisted tree. "Winter is not here yet. There's a little flower up yonder, the last bud from the multitude of bluebells that clouded those turf steps in July with a lilac mist. Will you clamber up, and pluck it to show to papa?"
>
> Cathy stared a long time at the lonely blossom trembling in its earthy shelter, and replied, at length—
>
> "No, I'll not touch it: but it looks melancholy, does it not, Ellen?" (230)

Cathy's refusal to pluck the last bluebell identifies her as a steward of nature whose own health is intimately tied to that of her environment. Nelly's response that it looks "about as starved and sackless as you" intensifies this parallel between Cathy and this patch of struggling yet tenacious ground. Both are survivors surrounded by death; she may bravely "sit in the branches, swinging twenty feet above the ground," but she is also weakened by grief for her dying father. She muses, "How life will be changed, how dreary the world will be, when papa and you are dead." Though Nelly chides her, calling it "foolish to mourn a calamity above twenty years beforehand" (230), this proleptic aside invokes the complex temporality of mourning in the Brontës' texts, by which the copresence of sickly bodies and ecosystems embeds death as a palpable presence in life.

Just as materially as the ecosystems that bear traces of human activities generations ago, the Brontës' sick bodies and corpses—from the grave imagery of the Angrian and Gondal sagas to the illnesses of Caroline Helstone, St. John Rivers, and Helen Burns, to Catherine Earnshaw's body, preserved in the churchyard's peaty soil—physically connect the present to the past and the future. Pastoral episodes featuring bluebells, for example, hint at past and future destruction. *The Tenant of Wildfell Hall*'s Helen Huntingdon recalls, after picking bluebells for her son, "I was kneeling before him ... enjoying the heavenly beauty of the flowers, through the medium of his smiling eyes," and thus "forgetting, for the moment, all my cares, laughing at his gleeful laughter" (250). During this rare moment of lighthearted hope, Helen's recollection emphasizes the lingering presence of past traumas and impending future ones. A literal shadow is then cast on the scene with the arrival of a friend who alerts her to her husband's treacherous refusal, despite promising to return home, to relinquish his London libertinism. Naming this action a "premeditated transgression," Helen recognizes that she was *already* bound by a trauma not yet perceived (251). The theme of picking bluebells, which unites Cathy Linton's rambles and Helen's moment of compromised pastoral pleasure, signals another shared attention to complex webs of causality that blur the boundaries between past and present and between life and death.

With their cyclical deaths and rebirths, their ability to bear evidence of past ecological states, and their significance for the Brontës' fictional courtships, flowers are powerful links between large-scale historical processes of ecological change with the more intimate processes visible at the scale of individual lives. At the end of *Shirley*, the narrator reflects on the Hollow's industrial development and ironizes Caroline Helstone's attempts to curtail the industrial expansion led by her fiancé. She strives to steward local ecosystems, yet she too treats nature as standing reserve available for her personal needs. Grieving for Robert during a strained period in their relationship, Caroline nostalgically recalls "scenes where he and she had been together":

> divine vignettes of mild spring or mellow autumn moments, when she had sat at his side in Hollow's Copse, listening to the call of the May cuckoo,

> or sharing the September treasure of nuts and ripe blackberries—a wild dessert which it was her morning's pleasure to collect in a little basket, and cover with green leaves and fresh blossoms, and her afternoon's delight to administer to Moore, berry by berry, and nut by nut, like a bird feeding its fledgling. (167–68)

Flowers and berries are not only a metaphor for romance: they are a physical medium through which it advances. These multispecies exchanges do not require a pure nature but instead thrive in the factory's own green spaces. Robert gathers her flowers that "bloomed in the sunshine under the hot wall of the factory"; nearby, Caroline is "glad to run down the green lane sloping to the Hollow, to scent the fragrance of hedge-flowers sweeter than the perfume of moss-rose or lily" (71, 373). Simultaneously natural and man-made, Hollow's Mill is a space whose hybridity makes it difficult to perceive and evaluate the ecological costs of human action. But because industrial expansion is a major agent of anthropogenic change to the environment and because supporting a family requires Robert to expand his mill, Caroline's desire to care for local flora and fauna will always exist in tension with her desire to care for her family.

For the Brontës, ecological stewardship is a complex matter, a goal as elusive as it is worthy. Emily plumbs the limits to human stewardship in two *devoirs* from 1842. "The Cat" defines *Felis catus* as "an animal who has more human feelings than almost any other being," destabilizing species distinctions to critique humans' "hypocrisy, cruelty, and ingratitude" (*Belgian Essays* 56). Anticipating the objections of her presumed reader, a "delicate lady," Emily alleges that she has "murdered a half-dozen lapdogs through pure affection" and that her husband "snatche[d the fox] from the jaws of the hounds and saves it to suffer the same infliction two or three more times" to enjoy the pleasures of hunting more frequently (56, 58). The *devoir* blames feline violence on the humans who domesticated them: cats "remember always that they owe all their misery and all their evil qualities to the great ancestor of humankind" (58). "The Butterfly" extends this cynicism by declaring that nature "exists on a principle of destruction. Every being must be the tireless instrument of death to others" (176). This epiphany is generated by a flower

> fair and freshly opened, but an ugly caterpillar had hidden itself among the petals and already they were shriveling and fading. 'Sad image of the earth and its inhabitants!' I exclaim. 'This worm lives only to injure the

plant that protects it. Why was it created, and why was man created? He torments, he kills, he devours; he suffers, dies, is devoured—there you have his whole story." (176–78)

But this is *not* man's whole story: immediately after the narrator throws down the flower to trample the caterpillar, "like a censoring angel sent from heaven, there came fluttering through the trees a butterfly with large wings of lustrous gold and purple." She realizes that the flower-destroying caterpillar is to the lustrous butterfly what "this globe is [to] the embryo of a new heaven and a new earth whose poorest beauty will infinitely exceed your mortal imagination" (178). Original sin not only compromised humanity, but also triggered a cycle of natural violence disrupted only by God's forgiveness, which produces both earthly beauty and the immortal grace for which beauty serves as surety. Yet this guaranteed "new earth" does not divert Emily from tracking human responsibility for the toxic condition of terrestrial ecologies, nor from plumbing the complex Anthropocenic temporalities that make the "whole story" so difficult to write.

This inability of a promised heaven to absolve humans of ecological responsibility shapes *Wuthering Heights*, which, like *Shirley*, plumbs the degree to which feminine stewardship can counterbalance masculine transgression. While dying, Catherine Earnshaw is still intent on protecting vulnerable species while ripping up her pillowcase and "pulling the feathers from the rents she had just made, and ranging them on the sheet according to their different species":

> this—I should know it among a thousand—it's a lapwing's. Bonny bird; wheeling over our heads in the middle of the moor. It wanted to get to its nest, for the clouds had touched the swells, and it felt rain coming. This feather was picked up from the heath, the bird was not shot: we saw its nest in the winter, full of little skeletons. Heathcliff set a trap over it, and the old ones dared not come. I made him promise he'd never shoot a lapwing after that, and he didn't. Yes, here are more! Did he shoot my lapwings, Nelly? Are they red, any of them? Let me look. (122–23)

In the midst of delirium, Catherine activates her taxonomical knowledge to plumb the extent to which masculine violence has decimated local wildlife. Yet she will not live long enough to know whether her efforts to curtail Heathcliff's violence will succeed. Like *Shirley*, which recognizes that Caroline's eagerness to "save" the Hollow will only partially succeed, *Wuthering Heights* insists on active stewardship though it may fail. And just as Caroline's recuperation from long illness is indicated by her renewed interest in tending her garden, Catherine's illness also reveals connections between human and animal health when she exclaims that she "couldn't die" due to the "pigeons' feathers in the pillows" (122). Because, as Beth Newman explains, "Pigeons' feathers in the pillow or mattress of a dying person were believed to interfere with an easy death" (137), Catherine intends to remove them. But before she does, she prophesies further ecological destruction: "I see in you, Nelly, an aged woman: you have grey hair and bent shoulders. This bed is the fairy cave under Penistone crags, and you are gathering elf-bolts to hurt our heifers; pretending, while I am near, that they are only locks of wool. That's what you'll come to fifty years hence" (123). Catherine's allegations of environmental destruction require counterfactual disturbances of linear time, underscoring how the difficult task of tracing Anthropocenic responsibilities requires combining scientific and non-scientific knowledges.

The causal connections linking past, present, and future of sick landscapes and bodies can often be traced when the narrative structures of realism are applied. The Lowood epidemic of *Jane Eyre* is one example; it results from a combination of the school's insalubrious situation and the students' weakened states. Still, the appearance of death and disease in these texts are figured as ruptures, allowing the Brontës to emphasize the consequences of environmental destruction. The etiology of the Anthropocene becomes clear when evidence from the past and present can be correlated to predict the future, but for those without full datasets—characters, as opposed to narrators—these consequences will be unforeseen, making suffering difficult to ameliorate. Two of *Shirley*'s prominent deviations from chronological narration, for instance, revolve around Jessie Yorke's premature death. The narrator proleptically holds up a "magic mirror" to disclose her death "twenty years from this night" and shifts the scene temporarily to her foreign gravesite (144). In another chapter, the narrator interrupts an autumn scene to evoke analeptically "an evening some years ago—a howling, rainy autumn evening too—when certain who had that day performed a pilgrimage to a grave new-made" (385). In these digressions, *Shirley* depicts mourning as a state of temporal multiplicity and spatial dislocation, which the Brontës associate with bluebells and homesickness: the mourning for the loss of home.

In the Brontës' texts, this loss of home is sometimes effected by a beloved landscape's transformation into a more developed one (as in *Shirley*), but sometimes by exile (as in the Gondal and Angria poems). *Agnes Grey*'s tenure as a governess is troubled not only by her charges' animal cruelty but by this grief for the moorland home she has left. Walking along a green path, weighed down by "sad thoughts of early childhood," she recalls,

> I presently fell back, and began to botanize and entomologize along the green banks and budding hedges.... As my eyes wandered over the steep banks covered with young grass and green-leaved plants, and surmounted by budding hedges, I longed intensely for some familiar flower that might recall the woody dales or green hill-sides of home: the brown moorlands, of course, were out of the question. (106–7)

Though the moorlands themselves are "out of the question," certain flowers that serve as botanical ambassadors of them are not. Spying "between the twisted roots of an oak, three lovely primroses" that "grew so high above" she cannot retrieve them, Agnes tears up until her love interest, Mr. Weston, volunteers to fetch them (107). For repayment, he requests information: her favorite species. He seconds her preference for the "wild flowers" that most "young ladies" dislike, but her more specific answer—"Primroses, blue-bells, and heath-blossoms"—provokes a surprised demurral, "Not violets?", until she confesses her homesickness: "No ... there are no sweet violets among the hills and valleys round my home" (108). One of the novel's few scenes centered on their growing intimacy, this exchange compares two types of homesickness. Whereas Weston is heartened by the "great consolation" given to Agnes because she does "have a home ... however remote or however seldom visited," she is pained that "he had *no home*" (109). The comfortingly wide range of certain blossoms, which have adapted to thrive in many ecosystems, militates against the lonely, stubborn singularity of "home" for which both Agnes and Weston pine. The blossoms' lesson is that home *can* be recreated—albeit in an altered form—if a certain latitude is given. Perfectly recreating the moors' particular dispensation of primroses, bluebells, and heath-blossoms may not be possible, but with the help of someone who shares one's preferences in the arts of noticing, enough may be found to maintain a connection to a lost home and redirect the affectionate attentions of stewardship toward one's new ecosystem.

BLUEBELL TEMPORALITY IN THE BRONTËS' POETRY

Unfortunately, not all mourners are as adaptable as Agnes Grey. Those without the rosy prospects of a loving and fruitful marriage and the ability to roam a moorland substitute in search of the flowers of home—like the speakers of Anne's and Emily's Gondal poems—accordingly fixate on their melancholic grief for their lost home. Memories of lost ecosystems haunt the utterances of exiled speakers. Whether the force parting speaker from home is imprisonment, travel, winter, illness, or death, the speakers are all united by an all-pervasive sense of loss that lends the Gondal poems a post-Holocene feel. In them, the repetitions of anaphora, epizeuxis, and internal- and end-rhyme perform loss as an eternally recurring cycle, giving a sense that though mourning is perceived as a momentary crisis, it is also an enduring condition that transcends any particular outbreak of grief. Like Agnes Grey, who "longed intensely for some familiar flower that might recall the woody dales or green hill-sides of home" (95), the speaker of Anne's "The Bluebell" recalls a sudden onset of homesickness. She regards a "single sweet bluebell" clinging to a roadside bank, its liminal position at the side of a road recapitulating both the speaker's spatial distance from home and her mental leap past the temporal border of the present into a blissful domestic past (*Poems of AB* 74). After recalling, "O, that lone flower recalled to me / My happy childhood's hours / When bluebells seemed like fairy gifts / A prize among the flowers," the narrator concludes, the "lovely floweret . . . made me mourn" for the times "dwelt with kindred hearts / That loved and cared for me" (74). Despite the fragility of the "little trembling flower," the speaker asserts, "There is a silent eloquence / In every wild bluebell" (74, 73). The unexpected, anthropomorphic attribution of "eloquence" to a "wild" flower refers to its testimony about lost ecosystems, making its "eloquence" a fundamentally Anthropocenic awareness that living organisms and landscapes are physically embedded with past and future deaths. The task of the artist of damaged landscapes is thus not only to trace ecological responsibilities, but also to articulate the beauty and pain of this interpenetration.

In Emily's "To the Blue Bell," the flower itself—not only the speaker—becomes a "sacred watcher." Here, the bluebell's eloquence intensifies that of Anne's flowers: "Blue bell, even as wan and frail / I have seen my darling fail / Thou hast found a voice for me / And soothing words are breathed by thee" (*Complete Poems* 99). Emily's bluebell thus inverts Anne's: from being simply a sign interpreted by walkers who possess the arts of noticing, the bluebell and speaker watch and speak to each other. To document this complementary eloquence, the speaker quotes the flower's dialogue—"Mourner, mourner, dry thy tears" (99)—as it consoles the grieving speaker. Emphasizing that what is fragile may still speak, the speaker and the flower she apostrophizes speak through one another, making the enunciation of consolation and poetry an exchange across species boundaries. As Gezari demonstrates, what all of these species possess is the breath that enables life, speech, and poetry: in Emily's poems, "not only humans but trees, violets, and bluebells have breath," which "pervades all living beings and broods over them" (131). Paradoxically, the breath that enables life also enables the expression of grief. Emily's bluebells, poised on the margins between road and field, provide a powerful image of the interpenetration of life and loss in the Anthropocene. They also provide a model for understanding why there has been considerable resistance to arguments, like those of Emma Marris, that "[t]here is no going back" to a pristine environment and that we instead live in "a global, half-wild rambunctious garden, tended by us" (2). Emily's speaking, breathing bluebells demonstrate the continued pull of what has been lost by a postnatural world. They also demonstrate how this resistance may be linked to the difficulties of differentiating between the flourishing and the damaged, the natural and the anthropogenic, the temporarily lost and the permanently lost.

Emily's second poem about *Hyacinthoides non-scripta*, known as "The Bluebell" but left untitled in her manuscript, continues to celebrate bluebells as a melancholy reminder of a lost home. It demonstrates the persistence of this affective pull of mourning and the power of literature to intensify or to clarify the ambiguities that make it tricky to parse Anthropocene landscapes. Emily's speaker witnesses the changing of the seasons from a foreign prison cell, "the dank and darkened wall" recalling the language of other Gondal prisoner poems written around this time (*Complete Poems* 92). The poem opens with a summer scene, opining with pastoral simplicity and contentedness, "The blue bell is the sweetest flower / That waves in summer air," only to switch abruptly to an icy scene in which the "heavens have lost their zone of gold" and the "earth its robe of green" (91). The cyclical mourning of wintertime is a figure for the speaker's seasonless need to "mourn the fields of home" (92). This conflation of the permanent and impermanent recurs in a verse describing the bluebell's appeal: "The slight and stately stem / The blossom's silvery blue / The buds hid like a sapphire gem / In sheaths of emerald hue" (91). This speaker replaces the imagery of breath in "To the Bluebell" with that of precious gems and metals. Apparently less hopeful than the speaker whose grief is assuaged by the speaking bluebells, this speaker ironizes the perennial blooms' fragility and transiency. The agony of exile causes her to conflate the annual cycle of death and rebirth with the inorganic permanence of sapphires and emeralds, showing how deeply loss shapes our perceptions of plant and animal life. Through the inviolable memory of exile, inaccessible, mutable landscapes persist impossibly. But in its ironic conflations, this backward glance is unflinching as well as nostalgic. Emily's paradoxical bluebells—they are, essentially, breathing rocks—thus recapitulate the moral that J. Hillis Miller reads in the caterpillar *devoir*: that life "does not grow out of life, as butterfly from caterpillar, but only from death, as the butterfly rises from the crushed caterpillar" (202). Death makes eternal life possible, while grief makes earthly beauty possible. Because the bluebells will die, they pulse with a gem-like beauty.

Emily's bluebells do what the caterpillar *devoir* does in its critique of aesthetic disgust at parasitic, easily quashed caterpillars: to question why we consider certain natural spaces and organisms beautiful. Emily's bluebells embody the thesis uniting Jeffrey Jerome Cohen's collection *Prismatic Ecology*: the insistence that ecocriticism should not study only what is green, but also organisms and spaces in a range of colors, including the intensely vibrant tones of Emily's flowers and the more muted grays, browns, and purples of the Brontës' fictional and poetic moorlands. As Charlotte claims of Emily, "Flowers brighter than the rose bloomed in the blackest of the heath for her; out of a sullen hollow in a livid hill-side her mind could make an Eden" (Preface to "Selections" 401). Shirley Keeldar's inheritance of Emily's love for moorlands commemorates this preference for spaces eschewing the greenly bucolic. In "The Bluebell," Emily's Gondal speaker, prompted by grief, describes such a non-normative space, with its purple heath "[t]oo wildly, sadly drear," its violets whose "fragrance will not cheer," and its wood flowers that she will not "moan" (91). Her exiled prisoner echoes those Anthropocene denizens who insist on setting "baselines": "reference states, typically a time in the past or a set of conditions, a zero point before all negative changes." Once set, these assumptions of what is "ideal" for each particular landscape are "woven into the culture of ecology and conversation" (Marris 3). As Emily's prisoner mourns a lost Eden, her notion of home frozen at a particular moment in time and corresponding to a fixed notion of natural beauty, so do ecologists often insist on our duty to restore landscapes to baseline states and contemporary documentaries "edit out any trace of the modern world" (150). For Marris, the solution is to become a "rambunctious gardener" working joyously to tend an imperfect world. Some spaces can and should, indeed, be brought back to earlier states "for historical restoration, for species preservation, for self-willed wildness, for ecosystem services, for food and fiber and fish and flame trees and frogs. We've forever altered the Earth, and so now we cannot abandon it to a random fate. It is our duty to manage it" (171). Caroline Helstone, M. Paul, and Lucy Snowe all embrace this challenge. Even the fragile landscape of *Shirley* maps a space of diverse ecological states and human purposes, with its the "ancient forest" for preservation and cultural value, its mills and grazing fields for human economic needs, and its green spaces and farms for spiritual needs and horticulture.

But for some, before Marris's rambunctious gardening can be celebrated, the lingering pain of grief can continue to pull mourners toward the opposite pole: toward restoring a superseded, perfect world or reviving a beloved, extinct organism or eroded landscape feature. Charlotte's edits to the poem for her 1850 edition of Emily's poetry dramatize this desire to restore a pure state. Many have argued that Charlotte's editorial labors, including the critical notices and prefaces written after her sisters' deaths, functioned as coping mechanisms to "bear the burden of Charlotte's agony of bereavement" (Harman 300). In the process, Charlotte crafted "an irresistible narrative" in which Emily's figure looms "proud, uncompromising, distant, stoical" (312). Similarly well known is Charlotte's impulse to sanitize her sisters' posthumous reputations and control the reception of their works. Lucasta Miller elaborates how Charlotte subordinated "Emily's original intentions" to her own "overwhelming feeling of loss" (*Myth* 201). Feeling "uncomfortable about the nature of her sister's rebellious imagination," Charlotte crafts an acceptable public image by "stifling Emily's originality" through regularizing her punctuation, scansion, diction, and tone (195, 201). Into this image Charlotte deposits her own, more orthodox religious and political leanings, as well as her belief in the "purifying force of divine genius," to purge the "disturbing" elements of Emily's imagination (196, 197). What is missing from this account, I argue, is an understanding of how Charlotte's purgative editing serves as a site for negotiating two types of death: the loss of a sister and the loss of a biome.

Charlotte's editing erases the ambiguities of the Anthropocene. To fit Emily's 1838 bluebell poem for publication, Charlotte regularizes the punctuation and bestows a title upon it, "The Bluebell." This focuses the reader's attention on the single flower, despite the original manuscript's detailed catalog of the moorland species lost to he: the violet, the heather-bell, the purple heath, the wood flower. Similarly, in Emily's original line, "But though I mourn the heather-bell," Charlotte substitutes "sweet blue bell," or *Erica cinerea*, also known as bell heather, which boasts similarly bell-shaped and colorful blooms (E. Brontë, *Complete Poems* 91, 212). Cutting the forty-eight-line poem down to thirty-two further reduces the poem's biodiversity, omitting a verse dedicated to a sweet-smelling "wood flower that hides so shy" (91). Charlotte's radical simplifications replace the ambiguous "if" to the unequivocal "when" in the line, "If chilly then the light should fall" (41, 92). She also replaces Emily's ambivalent, unexpected "drear" in the poem's opening lines, "There is a spell in purple heath / Too wildly, sadly drear," with the more positive and conventional "dear" (91, 211). Yet, as Stevie Davies observes, "dreary" is the "favorite word" that recurs in all the Brontë sister's poetry, such that Charlotte's substitution enacts the "Angrian solution," by which "a brighter and more magical reality could be substituted for the dreariness of everyday life" ("Introduction" 10, 13). In another move to render the poem legible as a pastoral, Charlotte genders the Earth, lending it an anthropomorphic approachability by revising Emily's alienatingly neutral reference to "its robe of green" to "her robe of green" (212). The deletion of Emily's tenth verse removes another instance of "dreary," as well as the speaker's tendency to "In longing weep—but most when guided / On withered banks to stray" (92). The original poem's deep sorrow is lightened; its ambiguities are resolved and its multiplicities diminished. In an act of editorial mourning, Charlotte dutifully tidies the poem so that both the poem and the landscape it delineates more closely resemble a conventional pastoral.

The editing of Emily's poem recapitulates Anthropocenic losses suffered by flora and fauna, both in terms of individual organisms and the extinction of entire species, just as her father's poems about of the bog burst craft four epic lists of moorland species, each one less biodiverse and less flourishing than the last. And just as Patrick instrumentalizes nonhuman sacrifices to emphasize the deaths of humans and their ultimate salvation in the Second Coming, so does Charlotte reiterate the loss of her sisters in the poetic extinction of heather-bells and wood flowers. Clarity is achieved and a straightforward pastoral produced, one more appropriate for the Holocene. But there is a heavy cost: the historically and biotically richer landscape of Emily's manuscript seems to begin on its own path to depopulation and desertification. The landscape of Emily's unedited poem is far closer to Marris's "rambunctious garden" of the Anthropocene, far closer to what ecologists term "grubby landscapes" (Rotherham and Wright). Grubby landscapes are spaces bearing traces of incomplete clearance, particularly forests leveled in the medieval period for agricultural or grazing usage, but which were either left with some trees or bushes or allowed to revert to forest. If, as J. Hillis Miller argues, Charlotte crafted her preface to *Wuthering Heights* to purify the novel (198), so does this editorial work purify post-Holocene Yorkshire by emphasizing its allegedly untouched remoteness. In this preface, Charlotte meditates, "Whether it is right or advisable to create things like Heathcliff, I do not know; I scarcely think it is. But this I know; the writer who possesses the creative gift owns something of which he is not always master" ("Editor's Preface" liii)—the implication being that if Emily cannot "master" the impurities of her genius, Charlotte can and will. This may seem a harsh interpretation. And indeed, as Harman argues sympathetically, the biographical preface possesses "somber power and beauty" that arises from a profound "depth of personal pain" (312, 313). Nevertheless, I would add that Charlotte's efforts to create aesthetic beauty from her pain provide an instructive model for why ecologically maladaptive responses to the Anthropocene—ones that nostalgically assume that restoring "pure" nature is possible and desirable—proliferate.

Reconstructing this transformation of Emily's grubby, prismatic, rambunctious landscapes shows that complete mastery over loss is not possible. In some ways, Charlotte's efforts reproduce Emily's own desire to freeze the fragile bluebells into immortal jewels, revealing how tempting it is to respond to Anthropocene vulnerabilities by substituting an aesthetics of purity and immortality for one of death and fragility. Alexis Shotwell calls this pervasive preference a "purity politics" that must be resisted in order to create livable futures in the Anthropocene. Shotwell explains, "The delineation of theoretical purity, purity of classification, is always imbricated with the forever-failing attempt to delineate material purity—of race, ability, sexuality, or, increasingly, illness" (5). It is useful to examine these historical traces of purity politics to account for its persistence in a world characterized by overwhelming grief. While pure ecosystems cannot be restored, nor sisters brought back from the grave, it is necessary to recognize how an appreciative attention to "grubby" ecosystems frequently coexists with other responses that are less effective but feel equally compelling. Ultimately, Charlotte's grief, channeled through writing and editing, reveals a family of oligotrophs, who, like bluebells, survived on very little but used writing to process grief. The Brontë's bluebells provide evidence that paying attention to the editorial and emotional labors of mourning in the early Anthropocene can work actively to prevent an ahistorical forgetfulness that would otherwise erase both the losses of the past and the uncertainties of the future. Without exploring the contradictory and complex responses to this early period, we risk reifying the present state of fragile ecosystems, making it more difficult to link past human actions with our climatological present and futures.

Affirming the need to mourn while exploring the ways in which it can distract from necessary acts of witnessing, redefining, storytelling, and tending will help to address the practical realities of addressing climate change, mass extinction, ocean acidification, erosion, and other ecological problems of the Anthropocene. Calling attention to the ecological dimensions of the Brontës' works can help to galvanize their readers who are likely to care about moorland preservation because of the family's iconic portraits of this ecosystem; indeed, the family is already a touchstone for ecological activists (Natural England, "Peatlands"). The family's power to entice readers into pilgrimages to this bureaucratically identified South Pennines Special Area of Conservation could certainly be used for good, as threats to the health of moorland landscapes are many and ongoing. In the Brontës' time as in our own, these landscapes are threatened by drainage, mining, burning, grazing, grouse hunting, and air pollution. Pressures to construct wind farms and to accommodate a rising population—as well as busloads of tourists—pose imminent threats. The cumulative effects include reduced biodiversity and peat degradation, which pollutes local drinking water and destabilizes the greenhouse gases sequestered in the peat. Because England's moors constitute a substantial carbon sink, moorland destruction is a catastrophe of international concern. The disastrous flooding in winter 2015–16 in Yorkshire underscored the significance of the moors for water management and prompted conversations about reviving traditional moorland management techniques to mitigate climate change. Attending to such environmental crises is a timely and relevant way to enrich our understanding of the impact of the Brontë family on local, national, and international perspectives on Yorkshire and moorlands.

It is also important not to flatten the fraught complexity of the family's relationship with Yorkshire and its landscapes. Rhapsodic poetry about bluebells, bucolic walks featuring rare plants and animals, and nostalgic memories of the moorlands are common themes in the Brontës' works, but so too are deprecatory descriptions of Haworth and breathless admiration for modern metropolises. This ambivalence, as I argue in chapter 1, reflects tensions in the cultural roles of the moors as beautiful wastelands, barren yet biodiverse, deprecated yet valuable. They inspire powerful aesthetic responses partly *because* of the sublime inhospitalities of their bogs, winds, soils, torrents, and extreme temperatures. They are worthy of preservation, despite being one of England's first anthropogenic landscapes, formed from rich forests into acidic scrublands by centuries of human mismanagement. As James D. Proctor reminds us, among "the Anthropocene's challenges to naturalness" is its challenge to a half-century of ecological thought that has relied on a "perennial nature refrain" even though "nature is no longer as natural as it once was (or seemed)" (83). For the Brontës, "nature" was in flux—already fragile, hybrid, and compromised—and one goal for this project has been to challenge conceptions of the Brontës' moors as timeless idealizations unrelated to the fragile landscapes of the twenty-first century. Consequently, attempts at preserving or recreating a specific vision of the Brontës' moors savor slightly of irony; what they value is not a pristine, wholly natural landscape but an instantiation of Anthropocenic degradation and instability—an instance from a particularly valued historical moment. Such attitudes reflect a quandary about which conservationists typically remain silent. After what cut-off date is human intervention intolerable? Respect and affection for the compromised landscapes that we *do* and *can* have after the Holocene is one of the Brontës' most important ecological legacies. But we must recognize that they are unstable. And like Heathcliff's recovery of Catherine's peat-preserved body—which cannot resurrect her but disrupts the natural process by which the acidic peat modulates her decomposition—idealizing the Haworth moors at, say, the time the Brontës lived reproduces attitudes that deem some anthropogenic landscapes worthy of protection, but others undesirable and therefore ripe for extreme interventions.

If the legacy of the Brontë family offers a powerful cathexis for attracting ecological awareness and stewardship, readers and critics should leverage this and similar opportunities to call attention to the complexities of these ecological issues and to the affordances of literature for thinking through them. As Bruno Latour argues, we compose the common world—constructing how the world appears and what appears in it to be valuable—through the arts as well as through politics ("Waiting for Gaia"). And as Donna Haraway argues, the processes of sympoiesis ("making with"), which provide ways out of political stalemates around climate change, are not solely the realm of scientists but are "the gifts for needed thinking offered by theorists and storytellers" (*Chthulucene* 5). These include the Brontës and readers willing to use literature as a lens for discerning the Anthropocene's emergence, telling stories about it, valuing the resources it leaves us, and withstanding its pressures. Clear answers may not emerge, but the contradictions within Brontë's oeuvre are productive for furthering complex conversations about ecological change because they are the kind of "situated knowledges" of Haraway's essay of the same title that challenge scientific claims to neutrality, objectivity, and universality.

Shirley's narrator appropriately disavows the clarity of such imagined omniscience by concluding, "The story is told. I think I now see the judicious reader putting on his spectacles to look for the moral. It would be an insult to his sagacity to offer directions. I only say, God speed him in the quest!" (607). The gentle sarcasm casting doubt on the sagacious reader's ability to find a single, correct "moral" acknowledges the power of readers' desire to do so as much as its impossibility. Brontë's own desire in writing the novel was, as Elizabeth Gaskell recounts, to paint a portrait of Emily: "to depict her character in Shirley Keeldar, as what Emily Brontë would have been, had she been placed in health and prosperity" (300). Imagining Emily born in a better world, destined for a better future, displays the same longing—for compensatory forms of richness, for being able to create a world we desire more than the one that we have—that some preservationists and Brontë pilgrims might have for returning to Emily's own world. Charlotte's nostalgic act of gifting Emily a better world and future does recognize something that Emily did possess, in the imperfect Anthropocene, that the pilgrims themselves appreciate: her power of storytelling. Even Shirley Keeldar does not possess this ability, though, the narrator laments, she does possess Emily Brontë's raw imagination and force:

> If Shirley were not an indolent, a reckless, an ignorant being, she would take a pen at such moments, or at least while the recollection of such moments was yet fresh on her spirit. She would seize, she would fix the apparition ... she would take a good-sized sheet of paper and write plainly out, in her own queer but clear and legible hand, the story that has been narrated, the song that has been sung to her, and thus possess what she was enabled to create. But indolent she is, reckless she is, and most ignorant; for she does not know her dreams are rare, her feelings peculiar. She does not know, has never known, and will die without knowing, the full value of that spring whose bright fresh bubbling in her heart keeps it green. (367)

The narrator's regret is that this inward spring, which stays "green" even while the landscape around it over time shows signs of its age as it shades into various tints of gray, brown, black, and purple, is not shared with others. The Brontës themselves, however, as vulnerable to the asymmetries of health in the Anthropocene as Lucy Snowe in *Villette*, did assemble stories of ecological change. For Charlotte Brontë, the solution is not to lament the passing of a world, but to tell—and to pay attention to—more stories about worlds of the past and present.

Because of the centrality of storytelling for understanding the Anthropocene, scholars and teachers of literature interested in ecocriticism, climate change, or the environmental humanities have important roles to play. Julia Adeney Thomas writes eloquently about the need for humanists to intervene in scientific conversations about climate. In making this call, she allows, "We are not junior biologists, nor should we wish to be," but persuasively argues that it is humanists who are the thinkers needed in these conversations

> to articulate the value of what is endangered and produce the wisdom, grace, and humor, the cultural, political, and social resources available in our records to help address the problem. In the end, what is most endangered is not our fragile bodies but the even frailer edifices of decency, justice, playfulness, and beauty.... Engaging with [the sciences] reveals a multiplicity of human figures and delimits the possible answers to humanistic questions of value—but cannot decide them. Ultimately, defining what is most endangered by climate change is the role of the humanists. (1606)

Beyond analyzing value of life and the spaces that support it, humanists also have the power of analyzing the role that language plays in making these evaluations and articulating it to others. When James Proctor argues that the "science and politics of living well in this enduring age of the Anthropocene may require attention less to generalities of nature than the interwoven details that constitute our environment" (83), I interpret this attention to details as specifically the purview of literary criticism, linguistics, and cultural studies, which are well positioned to understand how these details emerge and how precisely they are interwoven. Lynne Huffer's call to resist nostalgic "fantasies of resuscitation" and to "skirt the danger of universalizing the historically contingent frames of our present world as a new metaphysics of life" (84) similarly requires literary and language analysis to puncture idealizations of past ecosystems and counter universalism by making present-day readers aware of past and imagined worlds.

Like the Brontës, Victorian literary criticism is uniquely positioned to further these goals as it focuses on the transitional moment between the Holocene and the Anthropocene. I hope I have sketched one model of doing so by reinterpreting Charlotte Brontë's oeuvre as a lifelong engagement with ecological change and by suggesting further avenues for interpreting the other Brontës' works in a similar vein. It will take more literary criticism to show why nineteenth-century literature should be understood as equally as foundational for understanding the literature of anthropogenic ecosystemic change as contemporary climate fiction (the "cli-fi" of J. G. Ballard, Margaret Atwood, Kim Stanley Robinson, Ian McEwan, and others). As analyses of literary landscape, animals, plants, or science in literary texts consider how environmental change shapes these representations, more work should be done to understand climate change and other forms of ecological devastation as *narrative devices*—as a structuring agents and stylistic tropes—rather than solely as themes, images, or passive historical contexts. How does the realist plot depend on the historical processes that degrade our environment? To what extent are the temporal and causal teleologies that manifest realist fiction's assumptions about probability, normativity, and subjectivity reliant on ecological shifts?

My arguments about Charlotte Brontë's particular insights about the Anthropocene are my attempts to make some headway toward posing and answering these questions. I have found three recurring themes of her novels particularly compelling: her attention to the melancholy and misanthropy experienced by those who are particularly vulnerable to its pressures, her dual representation of the Anthropocene's temporal condition as a series of momentary crises *and* an abiding condition, and her respectful treatment of the difficulties of overcoming destructive definitions of the human and curtailing ecologically maladaptive behaviors. Above all, Brontë offers us a series of portraits of our responsibilities: to witness the conditions and crises of the Anthropocene, to redefine the human in light of our species' role in creating the conditions and crises, to craft and communicate stories about our experiences encountering these conditions and crises, to tend the spaces and organisms who remain, and to mourn those who have been lost.

NOTES

INTRODUCTION

1. See Ellis.
2. I discuss moors as anthromes in chapter 1. See also Atkins.
3. See Small.
4. See Tyrrell; Colbert; Heise; Allen; and Cornwall.
5. See Gowdy and Krall; Crumley et al.; Barnosky; and Zalasiewicz et al., "When did the Anthropocene begin?"
6. See William F. Ruddiman, "Anthropogenic Greenhouse Era" and "Early Anthropogenic Hypothesis."
7. See Lewis and Maslin.
8. See Steffen et al., "Trajectory."
9. See Secord, *Visions*; and Lightman.
10. See R. Davis; Fressoz.

CHAPTER ONE

1. See Foley.
2. See Bower; Dimbleby; Simmons.
3. For more on blanket bogs and prehistoric deforestation, see P. Moore.
4. See also Imeson; Marine et al.
5. See Warburton; Warburton, Holden, and Mills.
6. Richard Lindsay and Olivia Bragg document the painful irony by which wind-farm erections on peatlands can release more carbon dioxide than they can contain. For more on moors as carbon sinks, see Natural England, "Peatlands."
7. For examples, see Hewitt; Wood and Brears.
8. For more on literary tourism to Brontë country as ghostly encounters, see Pouliot.

9   Shawna Ross, "Remembering the 1824 Crow Hill Bog Burst," under review at *Brontë Studies*.

CHAPTER TWO

1   For more on Thornfield as a deceptive Garden of Eden, see Poteet. While this essay does not consider the ecological implications of Rochester and Jane's Edenic preoccupations, its analysis of the novel's religious themes helps illuminate the instrumentalism of their attitudes towards Rochester's estates.

CHAPTER THREE

1   For exceptions to these readings, see Shuttleworth (84); Glen (147).
2   See Buzard; Frawley.
3   See D. Davis.
4   For accounts skeptical of Louis, see Lawson; Morris. For accounts of gender balance, see Nestor; Gezari.

CHAPTER FOUR

1   See Bertrandias; A. Lewis.
2   Poovey's *Uneven Developments* draws from Louis Althusser's *For Marx*.
3   Chapter 1 interprets key Victorian science texts as forerunners of Anthropocene theory.
4   See Latour, *Reassembling the Social*.
5   See Johnson.
6   See Berlant.
7   See Lewis and Maslin.
8   See Chard.

WORKS CITED

Abel, Elizabeth, Marianne Hirsch, and Elizabeth Langland, editors. *The Voyage In: Fictions of Female Development*. Dartmouth, 1983.
"Adventures in the Libyan Desert." *Chambers's Edinburgh Journal*, vol. 278, Apr. 1849, pp. 267–70.
Alaimo, Stacy. *Bodily Natures: Science, Environment, and the Material Self*. Indiana UP, 2010.
———. *Exposed: Environmental Politics and Pleasures in Posthuman Times*. Minnesota UP, 2016.
———. "Trans-Corporeal Feminisms and the Ethical Space of Nature." *Material Feminisms*, edited by Stacy Alaimo and Susan J. Hekman, Indiana UP, 2008, pp. 237–64.
———. *Undomesticated Ground: Recasting Nature as a Feminist Space*. Cornell UP, 2000.
———. "Your Shell on Acid: Material Immersion, Anthropocene Dissolve." Grusin, pp. 89–120.
Alexander, Christine. *The Art of the Brontës*. Cambridge UP, 1995.
———. "Educating 'The Artist's Eye': Charlotte Bronte and the Pictorial Image." *The Brontës in the World of the Arts*, edited by Sandra Hagan and Juliette Wells, Ashgate, 2008, pp. 11–29.
Allen, Myles. "Liability for Climate Change," *Nature*, vol. 421, 2003, pp. 891–92.
Althusser, Louis. *For Marx*. Vintage, 1969.
Armstrong, Nancy. *Desire and Domestic Fiction*. Oxford UP, 1989.
Atkins, William. *The Moor: A Journey into the English Wilderness*. Faber & Faber, 2014.
Autin, Whitney J., and John M. Holbrook. "Is the Anthropocene an Issue of Stratigraphy or Pop Culture?" *GSA Today*, vol. 22, no. 7, 2012, pp. 60–61.
Barker, Juliet. *The Brontës: Wild Genius on the Moors*. Pegasus, 2012.

Barnard, Robert, and Louise Barnard. *A Brontë Encyclopedia*. Blackwell, 2007.
Barnosky, Anthony. "Palaeontological Evidence for Defining the Anthropocene." *Geological Society, London, Special Publications*, vol. 395, no. 1, 2014, pp. 149–65.
Barthes, Roland. *The Rustle of Language*. Hill and Wang, 1975.
Berg, Maggie. " 'Hapless Dependents': Women and Animals in Anne Brontë's 'Agnes Grey.' " *Studies in the Novel*, vol. 34, no. 2, 2002, pp. 177–97.
Berlant, Lauren. *Cruel Optimism*. Duke UP, 2011.
Berman, Ronald. "Charlotte Brontë's Natural History." *Brontë Society Transactions*, vol. 18, no. 4, 1984, pp. 271–278.
Bertrandias, Bernadette. "*Villette* and the Poetics of the Haunted Self." *Brontë Society Transactions*, vol. 26, no. 2, 2001, pp. 129–38.
Bewell, Alan. "*Jane Eyre* and Victorian Medical Geography." *ELH*, vol. 63, no. 3, 1996, pp. 773–808.
Bibby, Andrew. *The Backbone of England*. Frances Lincoln, 2008.
"The Birds of Shetland." *Chambers's Edinburgh Magazine*, vol. 298, Sep. 1849, pp. 182–95.
Bower, M. M. "The Cause of Erosion in Blanket Peat Bogs." *Scottish Geographical Magazine*, vol. 78, 1962, pp. 33–43.
Braje, Todd J and Jon M. Erlandson. "Looking Forward, Looking Back: Humans, Anthropogenic Change, and the Anthropocene." *Anthropocene*, vol. 4, 2013, pp. 116–121.
Brewington, Seth, et al. "Islands of Change vs. Islands of Disaster: Managing Pigs and Birds in the Anthropocene of the North Atlantic." *Holocene*, vol. 25, no. 10, 2015, pp. 1676–84.
Brewster, David. "Notice of the Rarer Atmospheric Phenomena in 1824." *Edinburgh Journal of Science*, vol. 3, no. 1, 1825, pp. 49–58.
Brierley, Harwood. "The Swamp of *Wuthering Heights*." *Leeds Mercury*, 6 Aug. 1928.
Broglio, Ron. *Beasts of Burden: Biopolitics, Labor, and Animal Life in British Romanticism*. State U of New York P, 2017.
———. *Technologies of the Picturesque*. Bucknell UP, 2010.
Brontë, Anne. *Agnes Grey*. Oxford UP, 1998.
———. *The Poems of Anne Brontë*. Edited by Edward Chitham, Macmillan, 1979.
———. *The Tenant of Wildfell Hall*. Penguin, 1996.
Brontë, Charlotte. *Jane Eyre*. Penguin, 2006.
———. *The Letters of Charlotte Brontë*. Edited by Margaret Smith, Oxford UP, 1995–2000. 3 vols.
———. Preface to "Selections from Poems by Ellis Bell." *The Professor*, Smith, Elder, 1850, pp. 401–3.
———. *The Professor*. Penguin, 1989.
———. *Shirley*. Penguin, 2006.
———. *Villette*. Penguin, 2004.
Brontë, Charlotte and Emily. *The Belgian Essays*. Edited by Sue Lonoff, Yale UP, 1996.

Brontë, Emily. *The Complete Poems.* Edited by Janet Gezari, Penguin, 1992.
———. *Wuthering Heights.* Penguin, 2003.
Brontë, Patrick. *Brontëana: The Rev. Patrick Brontë, A. B., His Collected Works and Life. The Works; and the Brontës of Ireland.* Edited by J. Horsfall Turner, AMS Press, 1978.
———. *The Letters of the Reverend Patrick Brontë.* Edited by Dudley Green, Nonsuch, 2005.
Buck, Holly Jean. "On the Possibilities of a Charming Anthropocene." *Annals of the Association of American Geographers,* vol. 105, no. 2, 2015, pp. 369–77.
Buckland, Adelene. *Novel Science.* U of Chicago P, 2013.
Butzer, Karl. "Anthropocene as an Evolving Paradigm." *Holocene,* vol. 25, no. 10, 2015, pp. 1539–41.
Buzard, James. *Disorienting Fiction.* Princeton UP, 2005.
Caldwell, Janis McLarren. *Literature and Medicine in Nineteenth-Century Britain.* Cambridge UP, 2004.
"The Cooper of Thorsund and His Family." *Blackwood's Edinburgh Magazine,* vol. 22, Dec 1827, pp. 692–721.
Carroll, Joseph. "The Cuckoo's History: Human Nature in *Wuthering Heights.*" *Philosophy and Literature,* vol. 32, no. 2, 2008, pp. 241–57.
Chakrabarty, Dipesh. "Brute Force." *Eurozine,* 7 Oct. 2010, www.eurozine.com/brute-force/.
———. "The Climate of History: Four Theses." *Critical Inquiry,* vol. 35, no. 2, 2009, pp. 197–222.
———. "Postcolonial Studies and the Challenge of Climate Change." *New Literary History,* vol. 43, 2012, pp. 1–18.
Chard, M. Joan. "'Apple of Discord': Centrality of the Eden Myth in Charlotte Brontë's Novels," *Brontë Society Transactions,* vol. 19, no. 5, 1988, pp. 197–205.
Chase, Karen, and Michael Levenson. "Bleak House, Liquid City: Climate to Climax in Dickens." *A Global History of Literature and the Environment,* edited by John Parham and Louise Westling, Cambridge UP, 2017, pp. 201–17.
Chen, Mel Y. *Animacies: Biopolitics, Racial Mattering, and Queer Affect.* Duke UP, 2012.
Chitham, Edward. *A Life of Emily Brontë.* Blackwell, 1987.
———. *Western Winds: The Brontë Irish Heritage.* History Press, 2015.
Cohen, Jeffrey Jerome. *Stone: An Ecology of the Inhuman.* Minnesota UP, 2015.
———, editor. *Prismatic Ecology.* U of Minnesota P, 2013.
Cohen, William A. *Embodied: Victorian Literature and the Senses.* U of Minnesota P, 2009.
Colbert, Elizabeth. *The Sixth Extinction: An Unnatural History.* Henry Holt, 2014.
Colebrook, Claire. *Death of the PostHuman: Essays on Extinction,* vol. 1. Open Humanities, 2014.
———. "Not Symbiosis, Not Now: Why Anthropogenic Change Is Not Really Human." *Oxford Literary Review,* vol. 34, no. 2, 2012, pp. 185–209.

———. "We Have Always Been Post-Anthropocene: The Anthropocene Counterfactual." Grusin, pp. 1–20.

Coriale, Danielle. "Charlotte Brontë's *Shirley* and the Consolations of Natural History," *Victorian Review*, vol. 26, no. 3, 2010, 118–32.

Cornwall, Warren. "Efforts to Link Climate Change to Severe Weather Gain Ground." *Science*, vol. 351, 18 Mar. 2016, pp. 1249–50.

Cowper, William. *The Task and Selected Other Poems*. Edited by James Sambrook, Routledge, 1994.

Crist, Eileen. "On the Poverty of Our Nomenclature." J. W. Moore, pp. 14–33.

Crumley, Carole, et al. "Concluding Remarks on the 'The Anthropocene in the Longue Durée.'" *Holocene*, vol. 25, no. 10, 2015, pp. 1721–23.

Crutzen, Paul. "Geology of Mankind." *Nature*, vol. 415, 3 Jan. 2002, 23.

Crutzen, Paul, and Eugene Stoermer. "The 'Anthropocene.'" *IGBP Global Change Newsletter*, vol. 41, 2000, pp. 17–18.

Crutzen, Paul, and Will Steffen. "Editorial Comment: How Long Have We Been in the Anthropocene Era?" *Climatic Change*, vol. 61, no. 3, 2003, pp. 251–57.

Darwin, Charles. *On the Origin of Species*. Edited by Gillian Beer, Oxford UP, 2008.

Davies, Stevie. *Emily Brontë*. Northcote House, 1998.

———. *Emily Brontë: The Artist as a Free Woman*. Carcanet Press, 1983.

———. "Introduction: The Brontës as Poets." *The Brontë Sisters: Selected Poetry*, edited by Stevie Davies, Routledge, 2002, pp. 9–28.

Davis, Diana K. "Deserts and Drylands Before the Age of Desertification." *The End of Desertification?* edited by Roy H. Behnke and Michael Mortimore, Springer, 2016, pp. 203–24.

Davis, Robert V. "Inventing the Present: Historical Roots of the Anthropocene," *Earth Science History*, vol. 30, no. 1, 2011, pp. 63–84.

Davison, Carol Margaret. "Emily Brontë's *Ars Moriendi*." *Victorians*, vol. 134, Winter 2018, pp. 151–65.

Davy, Sir Humphry. *Consolations in Travel; Or, The Last Days of a Philosopher*. John Grigg, 1830.

———. *Elements of Agricultural Chemistry*. Eastburn, Kirk & Co., 1815.

Defant, Ivonne. "Inhabiting Nature in Emily Brontë's *Wuthering Heights*." *Brontë Studies*, vol. 42, no. 1, 2017, pp. 37–47.

Derrida, Jacques. *Chaque fois unique, la fin du monde*. Edited by Pascale-Anne Brault and Michael Naas, Galilée, 2003.

Dewhirst, Ian. *Gleanings from Victorian Yorkshire*. Ridings, 1972.

Dimbleby, G. W. "Soil Regeneration on the North-East Yorkshire Moors." *Journal of Ecology*, vol. 40, no. 2, 1952, pp. 331–41.

Dolin, Tim. "Fictional Territory and a Woman's Place: Regional and Sexual Difference in *Shirley*." *ELH*, vol. 62, no. 1, 1995, pp. 197–215.

Doyle, Richard. *Darwin's Pharmacy*. U of Washington P, 2011.

Duckett, Bob. "Patrick Brontë as a Local Author." *Brontë Studies* vol. 37, no. 3, 2012, pp. 238–49.
Dykes, A. P., and J. Warburton. "Mass Movements in Peat: A Formal Classification Scheme," *Geomorphology*, vol. 86, 2007, pp. 73–93.
Dykes, A. P., and K. J. Kirk. "Slope Instability and Mass Movements in Peat Deposits." Martini, Martínez Cortizas, and Chesworth, pp. 377–405.
Eagleton, Terry. *Myths of Power: A Marxist Study of the Brontës*. Palgrave Macmillan, 2005.
Ellis, Erle C. "Anthropogenic transformation of the terrestrial biosphere." *Philosophical Transactions of the Royal Society A*, vol. 369, 2011, pp. 1010–35.
Ellis, Michael A., and Zev Trachtenberg. "Which Anthropocene Is It to Be? Beyond Geology to a Moral and Public Discourse." *Earth's Future*, vol. 2, no. 2, 2014, pp. 122–25.
Ellsworth, Elizabeth, and Jamie Kruse. "Introduction." *Making the Geologic Now*, edited by Ellsworth and Kruse, Punctum, 2013, pp. 1–26.
Erlandson, Jon M., and Todd J. Braje. "Archeology and the Anthropocene." *Anthropocene*, vol. 4, Dec. 2013, pp. 1–7.
Ewen, Frederick. *A Half-Century of Greatness*. New York UP, 2007.
Feldman, Ezra Dan. "Weird Weather: Nonhuman Narration and Unmoored Feelings in Charlotte Brontë's *Villette*." *Victorians*, vol. 130, 2016, pp. 78–99.
Felski, Rita. *The Limits of Critique*. U of Chicago P, 2015.
Flaherty, Clare. "A Recently Rediscovered Unpublished Manuscript: The Influence of Sir Humphry Davy on Anne Brontë." *Brontë Studies*, vol. 38, no. 1, 2013, pp. 30–41.
Flint, Kate. *The Victorians and the Visual Imagination*. Cambridge UP, 2008.
Foley, June. "'The Life of Charlotte Brontë' and Some Letters of Elizabeth Gaskell." *Modern Language Studies*, vol. 27, no. 3–4, 1997, pp. 27–46.
Ford, Thomas H. "Punctuating History Circa 1800: The Air of Jane Eyre." Menely and Taylor, pp. 78–95.
Foucault, Michel. *The History of Sexuality*. Vol. 1, Pantheon, 1978.
———. *Security, Territory, Population: Lectures at the Collège de France 1977–1978*. Edited by Michel Senellart, Palgrave Macmillan, 2007.
Frawley, Maria H. "Elizabeth Gaskell's Ethnographic Imagination in *The Life of Charlotte Brontë*." *Biography*, vol. 21, no. 2, 1998, pp. 175–94.
Frank, Katherine. *A Chainless Soul: A Life of Emily Brontë*. Ballantine, 1992.
Fressoz, Jean-Baptiste. "Losing the Earth Knowingly: Six Environmental Grammars Around 1800." *The Anthropocene and the Global Environmental Crisis*, edited by Clive Hamilton, François Gemenne, and Christophe Bonneuil, Routledge, 2015.
Gallagher, Catherine. *The Industrial Reformation of English Fiction*. U of Chicago P, 1985.
Gaskell, Elizabeth. *The Life of Charlotte Brontë*. Everyman, 1997.

Gates, Barbara T. "Down Garden Paths: Charlotte Brontë's Haunts of Self and Other." *Victorian Newsletter*, vol. 83, Spring 1993, pp. 35–43.
———. "Greening Victorian Studies." *Victorian Review*, vol. 36, no. 2, 2010, pp. 11–14.
———. *Kindred Nature*. U of Chicago P, 1998.
———. "Introduction: Why Victorian Natural History?" *Victorian Literature and Culture*, vol. 35, no. 2, 2007, pp. 539–49.
Gérin, Winifred. *Emily Brontë: A Biography*. Clarendon, 1971.
Gezari, Janet. *Last Things: Emily Brontë's Poems*. Oxford UP, 2007.
Gilbert, Sandra, and Suban Gubar. *The Madwoman in the Attic*. 1979. Yale UP, 2000.
Gladwin, Derek. *Contentious Terrains: Boglands, Ireland, Postcolonial Gothic*. Cork UP, 2016.
Glen, Heather. *Charlotte Brontë: The Imagination in History*. Oxford UP, 2002.
Goff, Barbara. "Between Natural Theology and Natural Selection: Breeding the Human Animal in *Wuthering Heights*." *Victorian Studies*, vol. 27, no. 4, 1984, pp. 477–508.
Gordon, Lyndall. *Charlotte Brontë: A Passionate Life*. Verso, 1995.
Goudie, Andrew. *The Human Impact on the Natural Environment*. 6th edition, Blackwell, 2006.
Gowdy, John, and Lisi Krall. "The Ultrasocial Origin of the Anthropocene." *Ecological Economics*, vol. 95, Nov. 2013, pp.137–47.
Green, Dudley. *Patrick Brontë: Father of Genius*. History Press, 2009.
Grove, Richard. *Green Imperialism*. Cambridge UP, 1995.
Grusin, Richard, editor. *Anthropocene Feminism*. U of Minnesota P, 2017.
Haraway, Donna. *Primate Visions*. Routledge, 1989.
———. "Situated Knowledges: The Science Question in Feminism and the Privilege of Partial Perspective." *Feminist Studies*, vol. 14, no. 3, 1988, pp. 575–99.
———. *Staying with the Trouble: Making Kin in the Chthulucene*. Duke UP, 2016.
Harman, Claire, *Charlotte Brontë: A Fiery Heart*. Vintage, 2017.
Heise, Ursula K. *Imagining Extinction*. U of Chicago P, 2016.
Helsinger, Elizabeth K. *Rural Scenes and National Representation*. Princeton UP, 1997.
Hennelly, Mark M. "Jane Eyre's Reading Lesson." *ELH*, vol. 51, no. 4, 1984, pp. 693–717.
Henson, Eithne. *Landscape and Gender in the Novels of Charlotte Brontë, George Eliot, and Thomas Hardy*. Ashgate, 2013.
Heringman, Noah. "Deep Time at the Dawn of the Anthropocene." *Representations*, vol. 129, no. 1, 2015, pp. 56–85.
Hewitt, Peggy. *Brontë Country: Lives & Landscapes*. History Press, 2004.
Heymann, Matthias "The Evolution of Climate Ideas and Knowledge." *Climate Change*, vol. 4, no. 1, 2010, pp. 581–97.
Higgins, David. *British Romanticism, Climate Change, and the Anthropocene: Writing Tambora*. Palgrave Macmillan, 2017.

Hill, Kerrow. *The Brontë Sisters and Sir Humphry Davy*. Jamieson Library, 1994.
Hoeveler, Diane Long. "The Brontës and the Gothic Tradition." *A Companion to the Brontës*, edited by Diane Long Hoeveler and Deborah Deneholz Morse, Wiley & Sons, 2016, pp. 31–48.
Hoeveler, Diane Long, and Deborah Denenholz Morse, editors. *Time, Space, and Place in Charlotte Brontë*. Routledge, 2017.
Hogg, James. "A Scots Mummy." *Blackwood's Edinburgh Magazine*, vol. 14, no. 79, pp. 188–90.
Holland, Nick. *In Search of Anne Brontë*. History Press, 2016.
The Holy Bible: King James Version. Hendrickson, 2011.
Huffer, Lynne. "Foucault's Fossils: Life Itself and the Return to Nature in Feminist Philosophy." Grusin, pp. 64–88.
von Humboldt, Alexander. *Aspects of Nature, in Different Lands and Different Climates*. Lea and Blanchard, 1849.
Imeson, Anton. "Heather Burning and Soil Erosion on the North Yorkshire Moors." *Journal of Applied Ecology*, vol. 8, 1971, pp. 537–44.
Jakob, Matthias, and Oldrich Hungr. *Debris-flow Hazards and Related Phenomena*. Springer-Verlag, 2005.
Johnson, Patricia E. "'This Heretic Narrative': The Strategy of the Split Narrative in Charlotte Brontë's *Villette*." *Studies in English Literature*, vol. 30, no. 4, 1990, pp. 617–31.
Joosten, Hans, and Donal Clarke. *Wise Use of Mires and Peatlands*. International Mire Conservation Group and International Peat Society, 2002.
Kaplan, Carla. "Girl Talk: *Jane Eyre* and the Romance of Women's Narration." *NOVEL: A Forum on Fiction*, vol. 30, no. 1, 1996, pp. 5–31.
Keighley, William. *Keighley, Past and Present, or an Historical, Topographical and Statistical Sketch of Keighley*. A. Hey, 1879.
Kier, Bailey. "Interdependent Ecological Transsex: Notes on Re/production, 'Transgender' Fish, and the Management of Populations, Species, and Resources." *Women & Performance: A Journal of Feminist Theory*, vol. 20, no. 3, 2010, pp. 299–319.
King, Amy M. *Bloom: The Botanical Vernacular in the English Novel*. Oxford UP, 2003.
———. "Reorienting the Scientific Frontier: Victorian Tide Pools and Literary Realism." *Victorian Studies*, vol. 47, no. 2, 2005, pp. 153–63.
Kirksey, S. Eben, and Stefan Helmreich, "The Emergence of Multispecies Ethnography." *Cultural Anthropology*, vol. 25, no. 4, 2010, pp. 545–76.
Knight, John. *Animals in Person: Cultural Perspectives on Human-Animal Intimacy*. Berg, 2005.
Kosek, Jake. "Ecologies of Empire: On the New Uses of the Honeybees." *Cultural Anthropology*, vol. 25, no. 4, 2010, pp. 650–78.
Kreilkamp, Ivan. "Petted Things: *Wuthering Heights* and the Animal." *The Yale Journal of Criticism*, vol. 18, no. 1, 2005, pp. 87–110.

Latour, Bruno. "An Attempt at a 'Compositionist Manifesto.'" *New Literary History*, vol. 41, 2010, pp. 471-90.

———. *Reassembling the Social: An Introduction to Actor-Network-Theory*. Oxford UP, 2007.

———. "Waiting for Gaia: Composing the Common World Through Arts and Politics." Lecture at the French Institute, London, Nov. 2011, www.bruno-latour.fr/sites/default/files/124-GAIA-LONDON-SPEAP_0.pdf.

———. "Why Has Critique Run Out of Steam? From Matters of Fact to Matters of Concern." *Critical Inquiry*, vol. 30, no. 2, 2004, pp. 225-48.

Lawson, Kate. "The Dissenting Voice: *Shirley*'s Vision of Women and Christianity." *Studies in English Literature*, vol. 29, 1989, pp. 729-43.

Lemon, Charles. *The Brontë Society: A Centenary History of the Brontë Society, 1893-1993*. The Brontë Society, 1993.

Le Roux, G., and W. Shotyke. "Weathering of Inorganic Matter in Bogs." Martini, Martínez Cortizas, and Chesworth, pp. 197-216.

Lewes, George Henry. Review of *Shirley*, by Charlotte Brontë. 1850. *The Brontës: The Critical Heritage*, edited by Miriam Farris Allott, Routledge, 2003, pp. 160-70.

Lewis, Alexandra. "Stagnation of Air and Mind: Picturing Trauma and Miasma in Charlotte Brontë's *Villette*." *Picturing Women's Health*, edited by Francesca Scott, Kate Scarth, and Ji Won Chung, Routledge, 2014, pp. 59-76.

Lewis, Jayne Elizabeth. *Air's Appearance*. U of Chicago P, 2012.

Lewis, Simon L., and Mark A. Maslin. "Defining the Anthropocene." *Nature*, vol. 519, 12 Mar. 2015, pp. 171-80.

Lindsay, Richard, and Olivia Bragg. "Wind Farms and Blanket Peat: A Report on the Derrybrien Bog Slide." 2nd ed., V. P. Shields & Son, 2005.

Lightman, Bernard. *Victorian Popularizers of Science*. U of Chicago P, 2007.

Lock, John, and W. T. Dixon. *Man of Sorrow*. Hodgkins & Co, 1979.

Locy, Sharon. "Travel and Space in Charlotte Brontë's 'Jane Eyre.'" *Pacific Coast Philology*, vol. 37, 2002, pp. 105-21.

Lorimer, Jamie. "Multinatural Geographies for the Anthropocene." *Progress in Human Geography*, vol. 36, no. 5, Oct. 2012, pp. 593-612.

Luciano, Dana. "The Inhuman Anthropocene." *Los Angeles Review of Books*, 22 Mar. 2015, avidly.lareviewofbooks.org/2015/03/22/the-inhuman-anthropocene/.

Lutz, Deborah. *The Brontë Cabinet: Three Lives in Nine Objects*. Norton, 2016.

MacDuffie, Allen. *Victorian Literature, Energy, and the Ecological Imagination*. Cambridge UP, 2014.

MacEwan, Helen. *The Brontës in Brussels*. Peter Owen, 2014.

Malm, Andreas. *Fossil Capital*. Verso, 2016.

Mangum, Teresa. "Animal Age." *Victorian Review*, vol. 40, no. 1, 2014, pp. 24-27.

Marine, D., et al. "Impact of moorland grazing and stocking rates." *Natural England Evidence Review*, vol. 6, 2013.

Marris, Emma. *Rambunctious Garden: Saving Nature in a Post-Wild World*. Bloomsbury, 2011.

Marsden, Simon. *Emily Brontë and the Religious Imagination*. Bloomsbury, 2014.
Marsh, George Perkins. *Life and Letters of George Perkins Marsh*. Edited by Caroline Crane Marsh, vol. 1, Scribner's, 1888.
———. *Man and Nature: or Physical Geography as Modified by Human Action*. Scribner's, 1864.
Martini, I. P., A. Martínez Cortizas, and W. Chesworth, editors. *Peatlands: Evolution and Records of Environmental and Climate Change*. Elsevier, 2006.
Marx, Leo. *The Machine in the Garden*. Oxford UP, 1964.
McDonagh, Josephine. "Rethinking Provincialism in Mid-Nineteenth-Century Fiction: *Our Village* to *Villette*." *Victorian Studies*, vol. 55, no. 3, 2013, pp. 399–425.
McGurl, Mark. "The New Cultural Geology." *Twentieth-Century Literature*, vol. 57, no. 3–4, Fall/Winter 2011, pp. 380–90.
McKusick, James C. *Green Writing: Romanticism and Ecology*. St. Martin's, 2000.
Menely, Tobias, and Jesse Oak Taylor, editors. *Anthropocene Reading*. Penn State UP, 2017.
Meredith, Dianne. "Hazards in the Bog: Real and Imagined." *Geographical Review*, vol. 92, no. 3, July 2002, pp. 319–32.
Miall, Louis Compton. *The Geology, Natural History, and Pre-Historic Antiquities of Craven in Yorkshire*. J. Dodgson, 1878.
———. "On a Yorkshire Moor." *Proceedings of the Royal Institute of Great Britain*, vol. 15, no. 92, 1898, pp. 621–40.
Miller, J. Hillis. *The Disappearance of God*. U of Illinois P, 2000.
Miller, Lucasta. *The Brontë Myth*. Vintage, 2002.
———. "Introduction." *Shirley*. Penguin, 2006, pp. xi–xxxii.
Mitchell, James. *Dendrologia: Or, A Treatise of Forest Trees*. R. Aked, 1827.
Montgomery, Katherine. "'I Never Liked Long Walks: Gender, Nature and Jane Eyre's Rural Wandering." *Gender and Space in Rural Britain, 1840–1920*, edited by Gemma Goodman and Charlotte Mathieson, Pickering & Chatto, 2014, pp. 103–16.
Moon, Michael. *Darger's Resources*. Duke UP, 2012.
Moore, Jason W., editor. *Anthropocene or Capitalocene?* Kairos/PM Press, 2016.
Moore, P. D. "The influence of prehistoric cultures upon the initiation and spread of blanket bog in upland Wales." *Nature*, vol. 241, 1973, pp. 350–53.
Morris, Pam. "Heroes and Hero-worship in Charlotte Brontë's *Shirley*." *Nineteenth-Century Literature*, vol. 54, no. 3, 1999, pp. 285–307.
Morrison, Blake. *We Are Three Sisters*. Nick Hern Books, 2011.
Morrison, Nancy Brysson. *Haworth Harvest*. Vanguard, 1969.
Morse, Deborah Denenholz. "The Forest Dell, the Attic, and the Moorland: Animal Places in Charlotte Brontë's *Jane Eyre*." Hoeveler and Morse, pp. 157–68.
Morse, Deborah Denenholz, and Martin Danahay, "Introduction." *Victorian Animal Dreams*, edited by Morse and Danahay, Ashgate, 2007, pp. 1–12.
Morton, Timothy. "Ecologocentrism: Unworking Animals." *SubStance*, vol. 37, no. 3, 2008, pp. 73–96.

———. *Hyperobjects: Philosophy and Ecology after the End of the World*. U of Minnesota P, 2013.
Natural England. "England's Peatlands: Carbon Storage and Greenhouse Gases." Natural England, 17 Mar. 2010, publications.naturalengland.org.uk/publication/30021.
———. "National Character Area Profile: 36 Southern Pennines." Natural England, 2 July 2012, publications.naturalengland.org.uk/publication/511867.
"Nature at War." *Chambers's Edinburgh Journal*. Reprinted in *The Living Age*, vol. 13, no. 161, Apr. 1847, pp. 182–85.
Nestor, Pauline. *Charlotte Brontë*. Palgrave, 1987.
Nicholson, John. "The Phenomenon," *The Bradford Antiquary*, vol. 9, no. 45, 1971, p. 42.
O'Connor, Ralph. *The Earth on Show*. U of Chicago P, 2007.
Orel, Harold, editor. *The Brontës: Interviews and Recollections*. Macmillan, 1997.
Parsons, Edward. *The Civil, Ecclesiastical, Literary, Commercial, and Miscellaneous History of Leeds, Halifax, Huddersfield, Bradford, Wakefield, Dewsbury, Otley, and the Manufacturing District of Yorkshire*, vol. 2. Hobson, 1894.
Penman, Chloe, dir. "The Crow Hill Bog Burst." *Being the Brontës*, 1 Sep. 2017, vimeo.com/232007259.
Perkins, David. "Compassion for Animals and Radical Politics: Coleridge's 'To a Young Ass.'" *ELH*, vol. 65, no. 4, 1998, pp. 929–44.
Pike, Judith. "*Agnes Grey*." *A Companion to the Brontës*, edited by Diane Long Hoeveler and Deborah Denenholz Morse, Wiley & Sons, 2016, pp. 135–50.
Polhemus, Robert. *Lot's Daughters*. Stanford UP, 2005.
Poovey, Mary. *Uneven Developments*. U of Chicago P, 1988.
Poteet, Clara. "Restored by God, Restored as God: An Exploration of the Genesis Myth in Wuthering Heights and Jane Eyre." *Victorians*, vol. 134, Winter 2018, pp. 250–64.
Povinelli, Elizabeth A. "The Three Figures of Geontology." Grusin, pp. 49–64.
Pouliot, Amber. "Reading the Revenant in Charlotte Brontë's Literary Afterlives: Charting the Path from the 'Silent Country' to the Séance." *Charlotte Brontë: Legacies and Afterlives*, edited by Amber K. Regis and Deborah Wynne, Manchester UP, 2017, pp. 96–115.
Prince, Danielle E. "Cultivating Mary: The Victorian *Secret Garden*." *Children's Literature Association Quarterly*, vol. 26, no. 1, 2001, pp. 4–14.
Proctor, James D. "Saving Nature in the Anthropocene." *Journal of Environmental Studies and Sciences*, vol. 3, no. 1, 2013, pp. 83–92.
Raymond, Ernest. *In the Steps of the Brontës*. Rich and Cowan, 1948.
Richards, Richard A. *The Species Problem: A Philosophical Analysis*. Cambridge UP, 2010.
Rigby, Elizabeth, "Vanity Fair—and Jane Eyre." 1848. *Jane Eyre*, edited by Richard Nemesvari, Broadview, 1999, pp. 588–95.
Rimmon-Kenan, Shlomith. *Narrative Fiction*. Routledge, 2002.

Ritvo, Harriet. *The Animal Estate*. Harvard UP, 1986.
Rose, Deborah Bird. "Introduction." *Australian Humanities Review*, vol. 49, 2009, p. 87.
Rosengarten, Herbert. "Charlotte Brontë and Her Critics: The Case of *Shirley*." Hoeveler and Morse, pp. 30–48.
Ross, Sarah. "*Wuthering Heights* and the Work of Loving One Dead." *Victorians*, vol. 134, Winter 2018, pp. 166–80.
Ross, Shawna. "Remembering the 1824 Crow Hill Bog Burst." Forthcoming, *Brontë Studies*.
Rotherham, Ian D. *Peat and Peat Cutting*. Shire, 2009.
———. "Searching for 'Shadows' and 'Ghosts' in the Landscape." *Arboricultural Journal*, vol. 39, no. 1, Nov. 2016, pp. 39–47.
Rotherham, Ian D., and Barry Wright. "Assessing Woodland History and Management Using Vascular Plant Indicators." *Aspects of Applied Biology*, vol. 108, 2011, pp. 105–12.
Rowe, Karen. "'Fairy-Born and Human-Bred': Jane Eyre's Education in Romance." Abel, Hirsch, and Langland, pp. 69–89.
Rowan, Rory. "Notes on Politics after the Anthropocene." *Progress in Human Geography*, vol. 38, no. 3, 2014, pp. 447–50.
Ruddiman, William. "The Anthropogenic Greenhouse Era Began Thousands of Years Ago." *Climatic Change*, vol. 6, no. 13, 2003, pp. 261–93.
———. "The Early Anthropogenic Hypothesis: Challenges and Responses." *Reviews of Geophysics*, vol. 45, no. 4, 2007, doi:10.1029/2006RG000207.
Ruddiman, William, et al. "Does pre-industrial warming double the anthropogenic total?" *Anthropocene Review*, vol. 1, no. 2, pp. 147–53.
Rudwick, Martin. *Earth's Deep History*. U of Chicago P, 2014.
———. *The Great Devonian Controversy*. U of Chicago P, 1988.
Ruskin, John. *The Stones of Venice*. John B. Alden, 1885.
Sanders, Karin. *Bodies in the Bog and the Archaeological Imagination*. Chicago UP, 2009.
"scathe, v." *OED Online*, Oxford University Press, www.oed.com/view/Entry/172132.
Schneiderman, Jill S. "The Anthropocene Controversy." Grusin, pp. 169–95.
Second Report of the Commissioners Appointed to Enquire into the Nature and Extent of the Several Bogs in Ireland, and the Practicability of Draining and Cultivating Them. The Literary Panorama and National Register, vol. 2, Miltonian Press, 1815, pp. 177–91.
Secord, James. *Victorian Sensation*. U of Chicago P, 2000.
———. *Visions of Science*. U of Chicago P, 2015.
Shotwell, Alexis. *Against Purity*. U of Minnesota P, 2016.
Shuttleworth, Sally. *Charlotte Brontë and Victorian Psychology*. Cambridge UP, 1996.
Silver, Brenda R. "The Reflecting Reader in *Villette*." Abel, Hirsch, and Langland, pp. 90–111.
Simmons, I. G. *The Moorlands of England and Wales*. Edinburgh UP, 2003.

Singer, Kate. "Limpid Waves and Good Vibrations: Charlotte Smith's New Materialist Affect." *Essays in Romanticism*, vol. 23, no. 2, 2016, pp. 175–92.

Small, Ernest. "The New Noah's Ark." *Biodiversity*, vol. 12, no. 4, 2011, pp. 232–47.

Snow, Stephanie J. *Blessed Days of Anaesthesia*. Oxford UP, 2008.

Spencer, James. "A Geological Ramble from Halifax to Haworth." *The Yorkshire Magazine*, vol. 1, Oct. 1871–Sep. 1872, pp. 76–80.

Spivak, Gayatri. "Three Women's Texts and a Critique of Imperialism." *Critical Inquiry*, vol. 12, no. 1, 1985, pp. 243–61.

Steffen, Will, et al. "The Anthropocene: Conceptual and Historical Perspectives." *Philosophical Transactions of the Royal Society*, vol. 369, no. 1938, 2011, pp. 842–67.

Steffen, Will, et al. *Global Change and the Earth System*. Springer, 2005.

Steffen, Will, et al. "The Trajectory of the Anthropocene: The Great Acceleration." *The Anthropocene Review*, vol. 2, no. 1, 2015, pp. 81–98.

Stengers, Isabelle. "The Cosmopolitical Proposal." *Making Things Public*, edited by Bruno Latour and Peter Weibel, MIT Press, 2005, pp. 994–1003.

Stocking, George. *Victorian Anthropology*. Macmillan, 1987.

Stephen, Leslie. "Hours in a Library XVII: Charlotte Brontë." *Cornhill Magazine*, vol. 36, 1877, pp. 723–39.

Strickland, Hugh Edwin. "The Dodo and Its Kindred." *Blackwood's Edinburgh Magazine*, vol. 65, no. 399, Jan. 1848, pp. 81–98.

Stuart, Erskine. *Brontë Country: Its Topography, Antiquities, and History*. Haskell House, 1971.

Struve, Laura. "The Perils of Representation in *Shirley*: Portrayals of Women and Workers in Charlotte Bronte's Industrial Novel." *Victorians*, vol. 130, Fall 2016, pp. 58–77.

Sutherland, John. *Brontësaurus*. Icon, 2016.

Szerszynski, Bronislaw. "The Anthropocene Monument: On Relating Geological and Human Time." *European Journal of Social Theory*, vol. 20, no. 1, 2017, pp. 111–31.

"The Tamarind-Tree." *Chambers's Edinburgh Journal*, vol. 310, Dec. 1849, pp. 359–60.

Taylor, Jesse Oak. *The Sky of Our Manufacture*. U of Virginia P, 2016.

———. "Where Is Victorian Ecocriticism?" *Victorian Literature and Culture*, vol. 43, no. 4, 2015, pp. 877–94.

Taylor, Susan B. "Image and Text in *Jane Eyre*'s Avian Vignettes and Bewick's *History of British Birds*." *Victorian Newsletter*, vol. 101, 2002, pp. 5–11.

Thomas, Julia Adeney. "History and Biology in the Anthropocene: Problems of Scale, Problems of Value." *The American Historical Review*, vol. 119, no. 5, 2014, pp. 1587–1607.

Thormählen, Marianne. "Agriculture and Industry." *The Brontës in Context*, edited by Thormählen, Cambridge UP, 2012, pp. 276–82.

———. *The Brontës and Education*. Cambridge UP, 2011.

Treftz, Jill Marie. "Attention-Deficit/Hyperactivity Disorder and *Jane Eyre*'s Helen

Burns: '[My thoughts] continually rove away.'" *Journal of Literary and Cultural Disability Studies*, vol. 11, no. 4, 2017, pp. 443–59.

Tsing, Anna Lowenhaupt. *The Mushroom at the End of the World*. Princeton UP, 2015.

———. "Unruly Edges: Mushrooms as Companion Species." *Environmental Humanities*, vol. 1, 2012, pp. 141–54.

Tsing, Anna Lowenhaupt, et al. "Introduction." *Arts of Living on a Damaged Planet*. Edited by Tsing et al., U of Minnesota P, 2017, pp. 1–15.

Turner, J. Horsfall. *Haworth: Past and Present*. J. S. Jowett, 1879.

Turner, Whiteley. *A Spring-Time Saunter Round and About Brontë Land*. Halifax Courier, 1913.

Tyrrell, Toby. "Anthropogenic Modification of the Oceans." *Philosophical Transactions of the Royal Society A.*, vol. 369, 2011, doi.org/10.1098/rsta.2010.0334.

van Beek, Rens, et. al. "Hillslope Processes: Mass Wasting, Slope Stability, and Erosion." *Slope Stability and Erosion Control*, edited by Joanne E. Norris et al., Springer, 2008, pp. 17–64.

Walls, Laura Dassow. "Natural History in the Anthropocene." *A Global History of Literature and the Environment*, edited by John Parham and Louise Westling, Cambridge UP, 2017, pp. 187–200.

———. *The Passage to Cosmos*. U of Chicago P, 2009.

Warburton, Jeff. "Peat Landslides." *Landslide Hazards, Risks, and Disasters*, edited by Tim Davies, Elsevier, 2015, pp. 159–88.

Warburton, Jeff, Joseph Holden, and Andrew J. Mills. "Hydrological Controls of Surficial Mass Movements in Peat." *Earth Science Reviews*, vol. 67, no. 1–2, 2004, pp. 139–156.

Washington, Chris. "John Clare and Biopolitics." *European Romantic Review*, vol. 25, no. 6, 2014, pp. 665–82.

White, Gilbert. *The Natural History and Antiquities of Selborne*. St. Martin's, 1981.

Whitehead, Tom. "Bronte heritage put before green energy in key wind turbine ruling." *Telegraph*, 17 Feb. 2013, www.telegraph.co.uk/news/earth/environment/9875900/ Bronte-heritage-put-before-green-energy-in-key-wind-turbine-ruling.html.

Wilkins, John S. Review of *The Species Problem*, by Richard A. Richards. *Systematic Biology*, vol. 61, no. 2, 2012, pp. 362–63.

Wolfe, Cary, editor. *Zoontologies: The Question of the Animal*. U of Minnesota P, 2003.

Wood, Steven, and Peter Brears. *The Real Wuthering Heights*. Amberley Press, 2016.

Wright, William. *The Brontës in Ireland*. Hodder and Stoughton, 1893.

Wrigley, E. A. *Energy and the English Industrial Revolution*. Cambridge UP, 2010.

Wulf, Andrea. *The Invention of Nature: Alexander Von Humboldt's New World*. Vintage, 2016.

Wynter, Sylvia. "1492: A New World View." *Race, Discourse, and the Origins of the*

Americas, edited by Vera Lawrence Hyatt and Rex Nettleford, Smithsonian, 1995, pp. 5–57.

Zalasiewicz, Jan, et al. "Stratigraphy of the Anthropocene." *Philosophical Transactions of the Royal Society A: Mathematical, Physical and Engineering Sciences*, vol. 369, no. 1938, 2011, pp. 1036–55.

Zalasiewicz, Jan, et al. "When did the Anthropocene begin?" *Quaternary International*, vol. 383, no. 5, Oct. 2015, pp. 196–203.

Zalasiewicz, Jan, et al. "The Working Group on the Anthropocene: Summary of evidence and interim recommendations," *Anthropocene*, vol. 19, Sep. 2017, pp. 55–60.

Zylinska, Joanna. *Minimal Ethics for the Anthropocene*. U of Michigan P, 2014.

INDEX

Adam and Eve. *See* Garden of Eden
adaptation (biological). *See* evolution
Agnes Grey, 102, 190, 226, 248, 282–283, 288–290
agriculture: as biopolitical apparatus, 198–199; and capitalism, 26, 42, 49, 146, 148; and environmental degradation, 10, 12, 29, 54–55, 86, 145; impact on biodiversity, 63; moorland, 30–31, 42, 61, 296; pre-industrial growth of, 12–13; scientific farming, 55, 146, 148; in *Shirley*, 198–199, 293; in *The Tenant of Wildfell Hall*, 146–148, 185, 227. *See also* horticulture
Angria (imaginary world). *See* juvenilia
animal abuse, 101–103, 194, 289
animal cruelty. *See* animal abuse
animal rights, 32, 102–103, 106–107, 130, 145. *See also* animal abuse
anthromes: as erotic terrain, 32; instability of, 29; moorlands as, 6, 32, 52, 56; mentioned, 19
Anthropocene: aesthetic tropes of, 73, 111, 164, 222–223, 228, 234, 236, 239, 249; drivers of, 18–19, 23; and gender, 20–22, 93–94, 96, 211; as loss, 76, 178, 281, 295; as narrative, 16–17, 28, 34, 26, 88–89, 94, 165, 172, 216, 250, 299–300; and race, 242–243; relevance for the humanities, 7, 9–16, 250, 299; temporalities of, 15–17, 28, 31, 111, 156, 300; theory of, 5, 9–16, 29–30, 207, 250. *See also* masculinity: carbon-heavy; etho-ecology; feminism: Anthropocene
anthropocentrism: anti-anthropocentrism, 63–164; and Christian doctrine, 79, 81, 83, 154, 175; conflicted, 83–84; 86, 156; gendered, 33, 115, 191, 211, 240; in *Jane Eyre*, 120–123, 134, 137, 141, 190, 222; limits of, 35, 193, 258; in *Wuthering Heights*, 104, 131–132; mentioned, 19
anthropogenic biomes. *See* anthromes
anthropogenic hypothesis, 7, 12–14, 54–55, 301n6a
Anthropos: definitions of, 32, 92–93, 107, 122, 135, 237; embodiment and, 20, 22, 97, 108, 122–123, 139, 141, 160, 241, 247; gender and, 114, 118, 193, 204, 208, 212; hybridity and, 105, 123, 158–159, 206, 257; Jane Eyre's recognition as, 8, 33, 94, 113, 141, 145, 157–158; oppositional models of, 111, 135, 142, 155, 261;

317

interspecies sociality and, 185, 263. *See also* species-being

anthropomorphism: of architecture, 157–158; of the Earth, 20, 294; of flora, 156–157, 181, 290; of natural disasters, 65–66; resistance to, 8

apocalypse: Crow Hill bog burst as, 45, 74, 77, 80, 239; in *Villette*, 159, 224–225, 228, 244, 246–247, 251, 262, 264, 268, 271. *See also* Second Coming

Arctic, the, 98–99

assemblage, 16, 73, 117, 170, 179, 190, 199–200, 284

atmospheric reading (concept), 97–98, 112

Bewick, Thomas, 25, 57, 59, 75, 117. *See also* History of British Birds

biblical references: Lot, 159; Moses, 225; Noah, 76, 78, 208–209; Second Coming, 75, 79, 294. *See also* Garden of Eden

Bildung: anthropocentric, 93–94, 105, 109, 114, 122–124, 126, 160, 280; in *Jane Eyre*, 34, 91, 119, 145, 158; in *Wuthering Heights*, 131, 133

biodiversity: human impact on, 12, 62–63; loss of, 218, 293, 296; moorland, 58–59, 62, 112, 144, 184; taxonomies of, 104

biome: affect toward, 96, 111, 126, 133, 280, 282, 293; destruction of, 5, 8, 28, 35, 64, 88, 210, 212; human dependence on, 196; moorland, 34, 47–48, 58, 178; multispecies, 162, 176–178; preservation of, 58; supernatural, 138. *See also* anthrome; biodiversity

biopolitics, 190, 198–199, 204, 211, 214, 236

birds: blackbird, 77; canary, 106; crow 113, 135, 192; cuckoo, 285; dove 108, 189–190; duck, 78, 100; eagle, 108; falcon, 105, 108; goose, 78, 100; Guinea-fowl, 198; gull, 78, 100, 188; in *Jane Eyre*, 8, 91–92, 101, 105, 107–108, 112–113, 116, 120, 122, 135, 145, 157; lark, 62, 77, 281; linnet, 77, 281; moorcock, 77–78, 127; and moorland ecosystem, 62; of paradise, 189; peahen, 101, 198; pigeon, 101, 288; raven, 135; rook, 77; in *Shirley*, 174–175, 182, 184, 188, 190, 192, 205, 209, 247; sparrow, 105, 117, 184; swan, 192, 147; turkey, 198; in *Villette*, 227, 267; in *Wuthering Heights*, 287. *See also* Bewick, Thomas: *History of British Birds*

Blackwood's Edinburgh Magazine, 24, 27, 56, 100, 110, 126–127, 158

bluebell (*Hyacinthoides non-scripta*): and biome loss, 178, 282–285, 291–294, 296; and grief, 35, 292, 295; and homesickness, 288–290; mentioned, 178. *See also* heathers: heather-bell (*Erica cinerea*)

bogs: anthropogenic origins of, 55–59; biodiversity in, 59, 60, 63–64, 294; as contaminating, 130, 141–142, 173; as liminal spaces, 123; loss of, 61–63, 66, 227; as supernatural phenomenon, 137–139; as "wastes," 49–52

bog bursts: as anthropogenic, 32; Derrybrien bog slide, 61, 68; physical explanation of, 38–40, 69; temporalities of, 86–88, 124–126, 131–134, 172. *See also* bogs; bog bodies; Crow Hill bog burst

bog body, 33, 151, 169, 172, 279; Catherine Earnshaw as a, 128–129, 133–134; Cowanscroft, 127–128, 131, 135; Jane Eyre as a, 126–128, 134, 193; temporalities of, 126, 128, 172; Thornfield Hall as a, 157; Tollund Man, 126. *See also* bogs; bog bursts; Crow Hill bog burst

Brontës, the (family): illnesses and deaths in, 46, 120, 285; interest in science: 23–26, 56, 240; relationship to

the moors: 46–47, 296, as witnesses to the Anthropocene, 279, 296
Brontë, Anne: "The Bluebell," 282, 290; death of 120, 280–281. See also *Agnes Grey*
Brontë, Branwell, 26, 38, 43, 47, 138; death of, 120
Brontë, Charlotte: anti-essentialism of, 105; attitude toward animals, 8; ecological imaginary, 32; as editor, 292–295; gender politics of, 203; mourning of, 120, 161, 280–282, 293–295, 298; and natural history, 24–26; natural theology, 79; relationship to the moors, 280–281; as theorist of ecological change, 5–7, 21, 300
Brontë, Elizabeth, 120
Brontë, Emily, anti-anthropocentrism of, 80–81; attitude to nature, 45, 286; "The Bluebell," 291–294; "To the Bluebell," 282, 290; and Brontë tourism, 67; "The Butterfly," 286–287; "The Cat," 286; death of 120, 161, 280–281; diary of, 50; Gondal poems, 84–85; "High Waving Heather," 45, 80–84, 88, 156; "No Coward Soul is Mine," 81–82, 225–226; "The Outcast Mother," 151; "Shall Earth no more inspire thee," 206; as theorist of humanity, 104–105, 131; "Why ask to know the date—the clime?," 215
Brontë, Maria, 120
Brontë, Patrick: anthropocentrism of, 79–81, 154, 294; approach to ecosystemic change, 32; brother of, 151; *The Cottage in the Wood*, 154; on Crow Hill bog burst, 40–46, 64–89, 91, 125–127, 133, 138, 162, 239, 264; education of, 23–24, 50; efficacy as father, 43–44, 79, 280; "Extraordinary Disruption," 4, 46, 66, 75–77, 82, 86, 153–154, 172; *The Maid of Killarney*, 171–172; on morality of fiction, 172; natural theology of, 30, 32, 79, 133; as popular scientist, 71–75; reception of burst writings, 68–69
Brontë country, 18; conservation of, 62–64; environment, 48–49, 179; history of, 61, 65; Stuart's guide to, 169, 177; tourism and, 65–68, 281, 296, 301n8b
Bronze Age, 54, 181
Brussels: as Anthropocene city, 236, 280; Charlotte's education at, 81, 230; as inspiration for Villette, 2–3, 227; in *The Professor*, 232–233

Calder: River, 48; Valley 178
canine: bulldog, 191; dog (domestic), 199, 286; hyena, 107; in *Jane Eyre*, 92, 101–107, 256; mastiff, 191; *in Shirley*, 179, 188, 191–195, 199, 205, 214, 228, 269
capitalism: and agriculture, 7, 54, 56, 58, 146; and ecological change, 7, 18, 20, 23, 49, 163; and enchantment, 31, 257; and gender, 149; and humanism, 160, 184; and industrialization, 12, 196, 217; rationality, 243, 256
carbon emissions. See greenhouse gases
Caribbean, the, 152–153, 183, 249, 252, 273
cat. See feline
catastrophe. See ecological disaster
Chambers, Robert (publisher), 25, 28, 184, 203
Chambers' Edinburgh Journal, 24, 27, 56, 187–189, 192, 218
Chartism, 162, 165, 169, 187, 216
civilization: and labor, 145; moorlands as in need of, 54, 64, 146, 167; origins of, 207; in the pastoral, 189; shift in meaning of, 112; ruins of, 143
Civil War (British), 152, 170
climate change, anthropogenic explanations of, 10–14, 28–29; causes of, 55, 62, 180–181, 249; consequences of, 61;

Index 319

climate change (cont'd)
in Dickens's *Bleak House*, 233; and gender, 19–21, 115; in *Jane Eyre*, 118, 145; and narrative, 17–18, 73, 89, 283, 299–300; responses to, 296–297; scale of, 15–16; in *Shirley*, 183; in *Villette*, 245, 266; mentioned, 8, 53, 296

colonialism, 13, 157–159, 181, 183–184, 280. *See also* imperialism

Columbian Exchange, the, 13, 249

conservation, 143, 147; of moorlands, 64, 296–297. *See also* Brontë country: tourism

consumerism, 21. *See also* capitalism

contact zones: definition of, 108; gardens as a, 237; in *Jane Eyre*, 109, 114, 116–117, 124, 135, 145, 152; moorlands as a, 126, 230; in *Shirley*, 179, 198, 214, 229; Yorkshire valley as a, 163. *See also* multispecies ethnography

Cowan Bridge, 45–47, 120–121

Crow Hill bog burst: anthropocentric fetishization of, 80–84, 156; and Brontë tourism, 65–67; description of, 38, 40–41, 66–67; effect on surrounding areas, 41–42, 87; literacy legacy of, 73 88–89; as natural disaster, 73–75, 279; physical explanation of, 67–70; as religious event, 73–79, 153–154, 239, 264; significance for the Brontës, 45–47. *See also* Brontë, Patrick, on Crow Hill bog burst

Darwin, Charles, 7, 26, 104, 105, 131, 261. *See also* evolution; adaptation; sexual selection

Davy, Sir Humphry: *Consolations in Travel*, 25, 26, 85–86, 143–144, 147; *Elements of Agricultural Chemistry*, 55–58, 148; theory of moorlands, 59, 61, 75; 147; mentioned, 59, 61

decay: of biomes, 64, 132, 228, 279; of buildings, 143–144, 147–148, 175, 183, 245; of people, 21, 120, 125, 128, 134–135, 142, 157, 169, 297; of plants, 39, 49, 55, 116, 124, 126, 135, 159; of sentiment, 264

decomposition. *See* decay

deep time: allegories of, 155, 213; and bogs, 124–125, 133–134, 172; explanation of, 6, 207–208; and gender, 163, 209–211, 245; and moorlands, 86–88; warfare and, 215–216

deforestation: as anthropogenic change, 7, 12, 86, 98, 215; and bog formation, 54–60, 125–126; Mesolithic, 54–55; of moorlands, 147, 157, 177–178; prehistoric, 6; 97, 180–182, 227, 283, 301n3b; and refugia, 283. *See also* desertification

delayed identification, 223, 250, 252–253, 255–257, 265, 268, 274

desertification, 29, 60, 84, 147, 180–181, 294; in *Shirley*, 180–184, 209, 216. *See also* deforestation

Dewsbury, 169, 177

Dickens, Charles, *Bleak House*, 233, 236

disease: bogs as, 7, 50, 71; environmental change and, 209, 263, 268, 288; and extinction, 179–180; rabies, 179, 193–195, 197–198, 211, 269; scarlet fever, 46; tuberculosis, 120–121; typhus, 115, 118–121, 156, 158, 288; urban spaces as source of, 232–233, 244; whooping cough, 46

dog. *See* canine

ecocriticism, 7, 299

ecologocentrism, 108–110, 157

ecology: ancient, 178; Brontëan, 7–8, 215, 292; capitalism and, 18, 260; of crisis, 34; feminist, 18–23, 157, 240; founding of, 6, 28–29, 176; Gothic, 222; literary, 232, 280, 299–300; moorland, 39, 47–65; multispecies, 199; pure, 99–100, 239, 116; Romantic, 20, 102, 143, 146–147 ecological disasters, 14, 31, 83, 95, 156, 158, 226, 240, 242; anthropogenic, 60; archives of, 84; bog bursts as, 38–39, 43, 47, 62, 71–72, 172; impending, 138, 145, 149; as narrative device, 300; refugees from, 120, 197; as religious sign, 73–80, 153–154; as a result of deforestation, 60

ecological stewardship, 34, 59–60, 148–149, 222, 233, 300; as gendered, 193, 222, 233, 262, 287–288; improper, 227–228, 257, 285; and industrialization, 198, 211, 217–219, 222–223; of the moorlands, 180–181, 183; necessity of, 280, 282–284, 286, 289, 297, 300

ecosystems: in *Jane Eyre*, 95, 98, 113, 122, 131, 135–136, 141, 149, 154–155, 226; liminal, 35, 108, 144; lost, 44, 76, 84, 237, 289–290; literary, 6–8, 31, 236, 299; moorland, 5, 282–285, 296; postapocalyptic, 244, 271; pure, 295; in *Shirley*, 163, 175–180, 182, 210, 220; in *Villette*, 222–223, 227–233, 240–241, 243, 245–249, 253, 258–260, 262, 273

enchantment (concept), 21, 31, 217, 260, 267; definition of, 257–258

Enlightenment, the, 93–94, 107, 154–155, 176

epidemics. *See* disease

ethics: Anthropocene, 95–97, 106, 165, 171–172, 196, 203, 215, 239, 244; of climate science, 22, 32; of ecological stewardship, 59, 174, 222; of human action in the multispecies, 165, 170, 248, 283; natural history as, 176; poetics and, 77, 79, 89, 172, 204, 210, 218, 228. *See also* etho-ecology

ethnography: Brontë's use of, 163, 168, 220; amateur, 218; Anthropogenic, 179; autoethnography, 167, 169, 227; participant-observer, 227; thick description, 165, 200–201; of Yorkshire, 163, 168, 176, 184–186, 215. *See also* ethnography, multispecies

ethnography, multispecies: explanation of, 8, 258; in *Jane Eyre*, 91–93, in *Shirley*, 163–178, 185–192, 201–202, 208–220 passim, 258, 280. *See also* contact zone; ethnography

etho-ecology, 170–172, 174, 218–220, 228, 240

evolution: adaptation, 174, 262, 266, 280, 289; human, 145, 160, 259–261; fitness, 121, 131; sexual selection, 246–248, 261, 269, 271; theory of, 28; mentioned, 7–8, 16, 130, 236, 273. *See also* Darwin, Charles

exile: in Emily's poetry, 84, 151, 291–292; in *Jane Eyre*, 97, 112, 115, 134, 139, 141, 158, 193, 204; from paradise, 76, 153–154, 206; in *Shirley*, 182, 184; in *Villette*, 34, 221–226, 243–245, 249, 261–262, 269, 273, 275, 281

exposure: in *Jane Eyre*, 96–97, 110, 115; in *Shirley*, 197, 213, 266

extinction: human-caused, 29, 63, 155; of humanity, 59, 236; increase in, 7, 10; mass, 5, 11, 64, 77–78, 89, 98, 112, 296; porn, 228, 240–241, 275; in *Shirley*, 179, 217–218, 222, 240, 257; in *Villette*, 239, 261–262; witnesses to, 279, 294

fall of man. *See* Garden of Eden

farming. *See* agriculture

Faroe Islands, 99–101, 110, 193

fauna: ape, 205; camel, 188; cow, 40, 77–78, 198, 288; fish, 57, 77; fox, 143, 188, 286; hare, 77; horse, 84–86, 92, 101, 188, 256; lamb, 108, 189–190, 198, 205, 216, 272; lizard 92, 136–137; mammoth, 239–240; mule, 188; pig, 99, 122, 168; rat, 245–246; sheep, 40, 48–49, 78, 101, 105, 111–112, 146; toad, 105, 283. *See also* feline; canine; insects feline: domestic cats, 57, 77, 105, 270, 286; leopard, 191–192; lion, 105, 147, 191–192; panther, 105, 192; tiger, 107

feminism: Anthropocene, 20–21, 93–94, 98, 115, 136, 203–204, 247, 269, 276; ethics, 283; in *Jane Eyre*, 33, 102, 108, 114, 150, 182, 205; in *Shirley*, 162–163, 165, 181–182, 186, 190–193, 206, 208–209; in *Villette*, 173, 268–269, 276–277; Western, 240

flora: cactus, 248–249, 251; camellia, 249; crocus, 182; daisy, 177, 180, 182, 195; fern, 25, 58, 138, 159, 232, 281; geranium, 248–249; honeysuckle, 178; ivy, 1–2, 115–116, 140, 143, 146, 177, 234; jasmine, 234; lily, 238, 286; moss, 49, 75, 88, 125–126, 147, 173, 177; moss-rose, 286; mushroom, 283; nasturtiums, 205, 234; orchid, 63; pansy, 63; primrose, 63, 182, 289; rose, 115–116, 153, 178–179, 205, 221–222, 249, 292; snowdrop, 182; strawberry, 177; violet, 235, 289, 291–293; wood anemone, 178–179; wood sorrel, 178–179. *See also* tree; shrub; bluebell; heather

fossil fuels, 10–12, 15, 21, 28, 75, 143, 238, 248. *See also* industrialization; climate change; greenhouse gases

fossil record, 10, 13, 22–23, 57

Garden of Eden, 6, 85, 263; as ecological paradise, 153; in *Jane Eyre*, 92, 154, 158–160, 302n1c; loss of, 226, 273–274, 292; in Patrick Brontë's writings, 76–77, 152–154; in *Shirley*, 204–208, 226; in *Villette*, 226, 237, 249, 273–274

Garrs, Sarah and Mary, 38, 42

Gaskell, Elizabeth: on Charlotte, 3, 64, 298; industrial novels of, 161, 170, 233; on the moorlands, 26, 51–54, 120, 168–169; on Patrick, 43–44; on *Shirley*, 168–169

geology: Brontës' knowledge of, 26–27; chronological scale of, 9, 54, 86; cultural, 9, 29; urban, 2; mentioned, 24, 28, 88, 207, 215. *See also* deep time; fossil record

geological time. *See* deep time

ghosts. *See* haunting

ghost forest, 178–179, 202, 283–284

Global Boundary Stratotype Section and Point, 5–6, 11, 15, 17

Global Standard Stratigraphic Age, 5–6, 11, 15, 17

global warming. *See* climate change

golden spike: British Industrial Revolution as, 12, 33; debates over, 13–15, 222, 250; definition of, 5; proliferation of, 31, 76, 274; in *Shirley*, 220, 226; in *Villette*, 252–253. *See also* Global Boundary Stratotype Section and Point; Global Standard Stratigraphic Age

Goldsmith, Oliver, 25, 29, 57

Gondal (imaginary world). *See* juvenilia

Gothic: ecologies, 7, 141, 222, 245, 256; horror, 106, 124; narratives, 3, 123, 125, 250, 255. *See also* novel: Gothic

Great Acceleration, the, 12–13

greenhouse gases: England's contributions to, 17; and genocide, 13; and peatlands, 296, 62, 75; pre-Industrial increase in, 55; as a result of industrialization, 10, 12–13; mentioned, 301n6a. *See also* climate change; Industrial Revolution; fossil fuels.

grief. *See* mourning

homo (species): faber, 145; ludens, 145; sapiens, 163, 261

homoeroticism. *See sexuality*

Hartshead, 169; church in, 213

Hathersage Vicarage, 136, 144

haunting, 67; and Brontë tourism, 67, 301n8b; ecological ghosts, 7, 45, 245, 282, 289; ghost stories, 50, 253–254;

in *Jane Eyre*, 107, 110; in *Shirley*, 199, 201–203; in *Villette*, 3–4, 23, 35, 229, 245–246, 253–258, 260; in *Wuthering Heights*, 133–134. *See also* ghost forest

Haworth Parsonage: Gaskell's writings on, 26, 53–54, 64; insalubriousness of, 120–121; intellectual activity at, 23–24, 32, 67, 74, 167; literary influence on the Brontës, 58, 164, 169, 216, 296–297; moorlands surrounding, 6, 37, 48–52, 55, 66, 84; servants of, 38; weather conditions at, 39, 48; mentioned, 11, 45

heather, 135–136, 147, 177, 232, 281; and bog bodies, 124–125, 129, 132; and bog formation, 38–39, 52–53, 62, 64, 125; burning of, 52, 144; heath-blossom, 37, 289; heather-bell (*Erica cinerea*), 150, 293–294; as oligtrophs, 49. *See also* Brontë, Emily: "High Waving Heather"

History of British Birds: in *Jane Eyre*, 93, 98–99, 101, 109–112, 116–119, 135, 138, 150, 158; read by the Brontës, 25, 57, 59, 75, 116, 240. *See also* Bewick, Thomas (natural historian)

Holocene: coinage of, 28; end of, 5–6, 18, 163, 214, 250, 279; human activity during, 9–10, 12, 61; *Jane Eyre* and, 34; narratives of, 6; *Shirley* and, 34, 63, 215, 218, 220, 222; and Victorian literature, 234, 294, 297, 299; and *Villette*, 223, 228, 236, 261–262, 269–270, 273–274

horticulture, 152, 184, 235, 248–249, 260–261, 273, 293

human exceptionalism. *See* anthropocentrism

ignis fatuus, 137–141

imperialism, 51, 94, 149, 158, 181, 183, 247, 249, 273, 280

India, 180–182, 273

industrialization: and biome loss, 76, 99, 162, 179, 212, 217; as end of Holocene, 6, 18; increase in carbon levels, 10, 12, 15; increase in fossil fuels, 11, 15, 18, 74–75, 238; Industrial Revolution, 6, 15, 55, 250; in *Jane Eyre*, 152; and peat bog loss, 50, 58, 61, 75; and pollution, 121, 198, 211, 230–231; in *Shirley*, 161–163, 165, 175, 178–179, 183–186, 196, 198, 212–213, 217, 222, 285–286; in *Villette*, 260; in *Wuthering Heights*, 211; of Yorkshire, 27, 33, 159, 166, 183–184, 189, 203, 212. *See also* urbanization

urbanization, 7, 11, 58, 215, 234; and pollution, 97, 222; in *The Professor*, 226; in *Shirley*, 247; in *Villette*, 2–3, 34, 222, 226–227, 229, 236–238, 253–254, 260, 264, 267–268, 274, 280; of Yorkshire, 54. *See also* industrialization

Industrial Revolution. *See* industrialization

insects, 64, 79, 143, 152, 173, 184, 188, 283; bee, 78, 92, 136–138, 151, 184, 188, 193, 283; butterfly, 115, 195, 286–287; beetles, 245–247, 258; caterpillar, 286–287, 292; cockroaches, 245–247; cricket, 57, 77; moth, 152

Jane Eyre (novel): animality of Bertha Mason, 92, 106–107, 114; animality of Rochester, 92, 104–108; as *Bildung*, 34, 91, 93, 105, 109, 122, 124, 131, 145, 160, 280; death of Bertha Mason, 152, 157–158; destruction of Thornfield Hall, 91–95, 112–115, 126–127, 136, 143, 146, 149, 152–157, 176; ecosystems in, 95, 98, 113, 122, 131, 135–136, 141, 149, 154–155, 226; gender politics of, 21, 94, 114, 149, 156–159, 204, 240; Helen Burns's anti-anthropocentrism, 92–93, 106, 121, 135; interspecies politics of, 91–95, 99, 101–109, 115, 117, 136, 142, 156, 158; landscapes in, 51, 96–97, 110–112, 113–

Index 323

116, 120, 135, 138–142, 204; narration in, 109, 116, 119; science in, 57–58, 61; species-being in, 20, 33–34, 91–97, 99, 101–107, 111, 138–139, 193, 280; taxonomies in, 101–108, 110, 114; violence in, 107, 157–158; writings about, 62–63

Jane Eyre (character): animality of, 92, 99, 102–108, 110, 144–145, 193; as artist, 98, 117–119, 135, 137, 139–140, 150, 257; body of, 108, 115, 119, 267; health of, 119–120; as supernatural being, 108, 117, 138–139; as plant-like, 159; engagement and marriage to Rochester, 91–92, 96, 108, 143, 150–153, 158. See also *Anthropos*; *Jane Eyre* (novel)

juvenilia, Brontës': Angria, 47, 285, 288, 294; Gondal, 45, 47, 84, 205, 285, 288, 290–292; mentioned, 128, 179, 212

Keighley and Haworth Mechanics' Institutes, 23

Kirklees: Park, 199; Priory, 199

Leeds Intelligencer, 24, 26, 41–44, 65–66, 71, 76

Leeds Mercury, 24, 26, 42–43, 65, 69–72, 76, 79, 88

London, 129, 166–167, 181, 230, 233, 280, 285

Luddism, 103, 165–166, 169, 179, 183, 186–187, 198, 212–216

marsh. *See* moorlands

Marsh, George Perkins: *Man and Nature*, 28, 59–62, 73, 75, 84–85, 114–115, 144, 176, 179; mentioned, 64, 86, 143, 153

masculinity: carbon-heavy, 21–22, 35, 276; toxic, 248–250

mass wasting, 38, 61, 64, 70

melancholy, 83, 290–291, 300; in *Villette*, 1, 222, 224, 234, 240, 243, 251, 264; in *Wuthering Heights*, 284

Miall, Louis Compton (Victorian scientist), 24, 40, 42, 48, 63–64, 75, 85, 88, 143

miasma. *See* disease

migration: of organisms, 136, 248; of people, 97, 173, 247

misanthropy, 80, 234, 242, 281, 300

moorlands: in *Agnes Grey*, 289; as anthromes, 32, 52, 48–65, 70, 75, 301n2; biodiversity in, 62–63, 75, 77–78, 112, 144, 296; deforestation of, 54–60, 80, 124, 178, 181; destruction of, 296; as erotic terrain, 151; in *Jane Eyre*, 122–123; Mesolithic inhabitation, 54–55; temporality of, 86–88, 124, 172; in *Villette*, 221, 227; as wastes, 49–50. *See also bogs*

moss. *See* flora

Mother Nature, 135–136, 141, 145, 158, 204–206

mourning: of Charlotte for her sisters, 35, 37, 280–281, 293–294; for the human past, 22–23, 36; through literature, 282, 291, 294–295; for a lost Eden, 6, 273, 292–293; for lost home ecosystems, 42, 288, 291, 296, 300; temporality of, 285, 288–290; in *Villette*, 2, 223–224, 244

opiates, in *Villette*, 259–260

natural disaster. *See* ecological disaster

natural history: Brontës' study of, 24–26, 57–58, 219; as contact zone, 109; definition of, 174; and human history, 11, 207; in *Jane Eyre*, 135; as new science, 27; in *Shirley*, 34, 162, 168, 173–174, 176, 180, 182, 184–188, 192, 210; mentioned, 8

natural theology: anthropocentrism of, 81; Brontës' interest in, 23–24, 30, 32, 76–77, 79; Charlotte's belief in, 30; scientific departures from, 28

nostalgia, 87, 199, 220, 259, 264, 280, 285;

for lost ecosystems, 76–77, 84, 218, 233, 292, 295–296, 298–299
novel: Gothic, 3, 107, 123, 255; industrial, 161–162, 170; realist, 7, 23, 89, 93, 105, 181, 186, 274, 300; romantic, 161, 173
New World, the: European exploration of, 13, 273; species migrations from, 249
North Atlantic, the, 98–101, 158, 249
Nussey, Ellen, 6, 51, 57, 136, 153, 213

oligotrophism, 35, 48–49, 216, 242, 276, 295
Orientalism, 238–239, 241, 268

pastoral (literature), 57, 77, 189, 235, 241, 294
peat: loss of, 61–62, 64, 70, 227; value of, 49–51. *See also* bogs; bog bodies; bog bursts; moorlands
Pennines, the, 48, 52, 61, 296
Pensionnat Héger-Parent, 2–3
Ponden: Clough, 45, 67; Hall, 38, 40, 46, 50, 66, 78; House, 67; Kirk, 66–67; Valley, 70
polar ice, 11, 13
pollution: as Anthropocene condition, 5, 196, 209, 226; and bog failure, 42, 61–62, 73, 79, 142; human-caused, 5, 7, 179; as metaphor for sin, 76, 84; or moorlands, 296; urban forms of, 34, 61, 97, 211–213, 222–223, 230, 232–233, 245
preservation: of biomes, 58; by bogs, 33, 50, 86, 124–134, 274, 297; of history, 4, 203, 219, 281; of land, 52, 232, 293, 296–298; of objects, 2, 191, 239, 241; of species, 292. *See also* bog bodies; conservation.
Professor, The: and ecological crisis, 34–35; exile in, 226; gender politics in, 21–22, 191; industrialization in, 230–232; interspecies politics in, 101–102, 104, 258; mentioned, 151, 280

queer theory, 18, 269

Rawfolds Mill, 169, 213
realism: Anthropocene, 27; Brontë's, 170, 172, 300; in *Jane Eyre*, 93, 98; literary, 89, 93, 98, 105, 161, 167–168, 186, 201, 223, 255; and science writing, 17, 23, 26–27, 33–34, 181, 288; in *Shirley*, 165–166, 174, 200; speculative, 9; in *Villette*, 265, 274
Robin Hood, 199, 202, 204, 208, 220

sadomasochism. *See* sexuality
sexuality: Anthropocene, 94, 212, 295; ecological consequences of, 21–22, 146, 210–211, 263; homoeroticism, 196; interspecies, 191–194, 247, 258; in *Jane Eyre*, 150–157, 247; plant, 181; sadomasochism, 197–198, 200; in *Shirley*, 34, 163, 182, 190, 195–196; in *Villette*, 4, 35, 234–236, 254, 265; violence, 252. *See also* evolution, sexual selection
Scott, Sir Walter: "The Covenanters Fate," 151, 203
Second Coming. *See* biblical references; apocalypse
settler colonialism. *See* colonialism
Shirley: animality of Caroline Helstone, 189–191, 193–195; class politics, 196–199, 202–203, 212–213, 215, 218–219, 286; gender politics of, 21, 173, 181–182, 190–197, 202, 204–206, 210; interspecies politics in, 162–165, 174, 179–184, 188–194, 197–199, 211, 216–217; landscape in, 163–164, 177–178, 181, 196, 202; marriage and courtship in, 173, 194–195, 197, 211; narration in, 161, 168, 171–172, 180, 186–187, 189, 201, 203, 211, 216–217; natural history in, 25, 162–163, 173–177, 180–188, 218; reception of, 161–162;

Shirley (cont'd)
　　sexuality, 191–197, 200, 206, 210–212, 215, 228, 261; taxonomies in, 192–193, 195
shrub: bilberry, 129, 136, 281; blackberry, 286; bush-holly, 139–140. *See also* flora; tree
speciesism. *See* anthropocentrism
species-being, 36; in *Jane Eyre*, 8, 32, 124, 134–135, 138–142; in *Villette*, 258; in *Shirley*, 190, 192–194, 198, 206, 217, 219, 240, 261; in *Wuthering Heights*, 131. *See also* species concept
species concept, 104–106
species boundaries. *See* multispecies ethnography; species-being

The Tenant of Wildfell Hall, 33, 38, 56, 226–227, 257, 283, 285; gender politics in, 184–185; interspecies politics in, 185; landscapes in, 146–149, 185
toxicity: of bodies, 93, 121, 195–198, 217, 220, 228; crises of, 34–35, 89; of Haworth Parsonage, 120–121; of landscapes, 6, 8, 31, 33, 95–96, 122, 211; of masculinity, 248–249; of romantic love, 250, 275. *See also* pollution; disease
trauma: of ecological disasters, 45; in *Jane Eyre*, 107; in *The Tenant of Wildfell Hall*, 185, 285; in *Villette*, 250–251, 262
tree: acacia, 234; ash, 169–170, 177; beech, 152, 177; birch, 177–178; cherry, 184; chestnut, 95, 97, 125, 152–159; firs, 139, 147, 149; hawthorne, 48, 117, 178, 182; hazel, 178, 284; laurel, 147, 152–153, 156; oak, 154, 170, 175, 177–178, 199, 202, 218, 284, 289; orange, 248–249, 251; pear, 1–5, 22, 249, 254; tamarind, 188; willow, 227. *See also* flora; shrub

ultrasociality, 145–149

Venezuela, 180–181
Villette, class politics in, 246–247, 270; death of M. Paul, 274–276; gender politics in, 224, 240–241, 246–248, 252–253; interspecies politics in, 234, 236–237; Lucy Snowe as supernatural being, 237–238; masculinity of M. Paul, 248–250; marriage and romance in, 223, 235, 243–244, 247, 251, 261, 275; narration in, 265; sexuality, 234–237, 243, 247, 252–254, 261; role of weather in, 262–264, 266–274
violence: animal, 286; anthropogenic, 13, 110, 213–215; ecosystemic, 38–39, 45–46, 66–67, 71–72, 80, 87, 125, 127, 156, 172; gendered and sexual, 107–108, 157, 194, 204, 252, 287; human death, 132, 134–135; imperial, 158; interspecies, 101–102, 162, 188–189, 194, 204, 240, 247–248; intraspecies, 96, 101, 169, 260; poetic, 81–82, 85; warfare, 84–86, 213–215

warfare. *See* violence
White, Gilbert, 56, 58, 62, 179
World War II, 13, 250
Wuthering Heights, 33, 45, 128–134, 169, 211, 282, 287; body of Catherine Earnshaw Linton, 128–134, 169, 248; Charlotte's introduction to, 294–295; Heathcliff, 128–134, 169, 211, 248, 287, 294; interspecies politics of, 130

Yorkshire: as contact zone, 163–164, 174, 176, 183; dialect, 168; environmental degradation of, 60–61, 136, 180–181, 184, 202; cultural perceptions of, 167–168, 185; natural features of, 26–27, 34, 42, 54, 169, 178, 192–193; industrialization of, 27, 33, 55, 159, 166, 189, 203, 212, 231–232; regional identity, 185–186; tourism in, 65; writings about, 54–55. *See also* moorlands

www.ingramcontent.com/pod-product-compliance
Lightning Source LLC
Chambersburg PA
CBHW030128240426
43672CB00005B/62